eTourism Case Studies
Management and Marketing Issue

Edited by
Roman Egger
Dimitrios Buhalis

ELSEVIER

AMSTERDAM · BOSTON · HEIDELBERG · LONDON · NEW YORK · OXFORD
PARIS · SAN DIEGO · SAN FRANCISCO · SINGAPORE · SYDNEY · TOKYO
Butterworth Heinemann is an imprint of Elsevier

Butterworth-Heinemann is an imprint of Elsevier
Linacre House, Jordan Hill, Oxford OX2 8DP, UK
30 Corporate Drive, Suite 400, Burlington, MA 01803, USA

First Edition 2008

British Library Cataloguing in Publication Data
A catalogue record for this book is available from the British Library

Library of Congress Cataloging-in-Publication Data
A catalog record for this book is available from the Library of Congress

ISBN: 978-0-7506-8667-9

For information on all Butterworth-Heinemann publications
visit our web site at books.elsevier.com

Typeset by Charon Tec Ltd., A Macmillan Company.
(www.macmillansolutions.com)

Printed and bound in Hungary

08 09 10 10 9 8 7 6 5 4 3

Working together to grow
libraries in developing countries

www.elsevier.com | www.bookaid.org | www.sabre.org

ELSEVIER   BOOK AID International   Sabre Foundation

Contents

List of figures

List of tables

Editors

Dimitrios Buhalis

Professor Dimitrios Buhalis is Established Chair in Tourism, Deputy Director of the International Centre for Tourism and Hospitality Research and Professional Observer at the University Senate, Bournemouth University. He was previously programme leader, MSc in Tourism Marketing and MSc in eTourism, Leader of eTourism research and Reader in Business Information Management at the School of Management, University of Surrey and elected member of the University Senate (2003–2007). Dimitrios is also adjunct Professor at the MBA in Hospitality Management at the IMHI (Cornell University-Ecole Superieure des Sciences Economiques et Commerciales ESSEC) in Paris and Professor Associado at the University of Aveiro, Portugal. He has been teaching tourism-related subjects in more than 30 universities around the world. He is regarded as an expert in the impacts of ICTs in the tourism industry and eTourism, the management of tourism distribution channels as well as strategic tourism marketing and management. Dimitrios has been involved with a number of European Commission FP5 and FP6 projects and regularly advises the World Tourism Organization, the World Tourism and Travel Council and the European Commission in the field of information technology and tourism. He has written or co-edited a total of 14 books and published more than 80 articles in scholarly journals, books, conference proceedings and consultancy reports. He was Vice President of the International Federation of Information Technology for Travel and Tourism (IFITT) and served as Chairman of the Scientific Committee of the ENTER 1998, 1999 and 2000 conferences on tourism and information technology.

Roman Egger

Professor Roman Egger attended the Tourism and Hospitality Management School in Klessheim from 1989 to 1994. He graduated in Communications Sciences and gained his Doctorate from the University of Salzburg, where he specialized in the fields of Information and Communication Technologies in Tourism. He then worked at the Tourism Board of Salzburg as a marketer. Nowadays Roman is Professor in eTourism at the Salzburg University of Applied Sciences and Head of tourism research at the department of Innovation and Management in Tourism. Roman advises a number of national and international projects in the fields of Information Technologies in Tourism and counsels a number of international eTourism-development activities. He has written and co-edited four books, published a number of articles in books and journals and he is a co-editor of the scientific Journal 'Zeitschrift für Tourismuswissenschaft'. He is a member of the International Federation of Information Technology for Travel and Tourism (IFITT), member of the ANET (the Austrian eTourism Centre), ÖGAF and DGT.

Contributors

Philip Alford
University of Bedfordshire, England
Philip.Alford@beds.ac.uk

Dr Philip Alford is Senior Lecturer at the University of Bedfordshire where his specialist teaching area is eTourism. He also contributes to other courses including research methods and international air transport. Philip is a Certified Trainer for Tiscover – the world's leading supplier of destination marketing solutions. He is a regular contributor to Mintel International having written reports on e-business in the travel industry, destination marketing and the Global Distribution Systems. He is a visiting lecturer at Institut de Management Hôtelier International – ESSEC Business School, Paris and the Center for Tourism Management, CERAM Sophia Antipolis European School of Business, Nice. Prior to working in higher education, Philip worked in the fields of destination marketing and tour operating.

Bill Anckar
Omena Hotels Ltd and IAMSR at Abo Akademi University, Turku, Finland
bill.anckar@omena.com

Dr Bill Anckar is a real estate director at the Abo Akademi Foundation and an Associate Research Fellow at the Institute for Advanced Management Systems Research (IAMSR) at Abo Akademi University, Turku, Finland. He served as CEO of the hotel chain Omena Hotels Ltd from 2003 to 2007. His research focuses on consumer adoption of electronic and mobile commerce; in particular applications and services relating to travel and tourism. His work has appeared in several books and international journals, as well as in proceedings of numerous international conferences.

Sanna Andersson
Finland Travel Bureau Ltd, Finland
sanna.andersson@smt.fi

Sanna Andersson works as a Client General Manager at American Express Business Travel Finland. During the time this article was written she used to work as a freelancer at the same time when she was employed as a district manager by Finland Travel Bureau Ltd, the leading travel management company in Finland. Sanna also contributes to the fields of travel education being a regular lecturer at the Institute of Marketing, Helsinki where her specialist teaching area is Travel Management and Technology and a visiting lecturer at Jyväskylä University of Applied Sciences. She has written reports on how to develop travel management and utilize latest technology. Prior to her present responsibilities, Sanna worked in tour operating, e-business development in the travel industry and with multinational business travel accounts. She also committed herself as a market representative of Finland at the Amadeus Multinational Customer Forum.

Rodolfo Baggio
Master in Economics and Tourism, Bocconi University, Milan, Italy
rodolfo.baggio@unibocconi.it

Rodolfo holds a degree in Physics from the University of Milan, Italy. He is presently a lecturer at the Bocconi University where he teaches courses in Computer Science and coordinates the Information and Communication Technologies area at the Master in Economics and Tourism. After having worked for the IT industry, he is now involved in a number of educational and research projects in the travel and tourism sector. His current research interest centres on the uses of information and communication technologies in tourism and on the analysis of complex networks, on which has completed his PhD at the University of Queensland in Australia. He is a founding member of Società Internet, the Italian chapter of the Internet Society and member of the Società Italiana di Fisica and of the International Federation for Information Technology and Travel and Tourism (IFITT).

François Bédard
Université du Québec à Montréal, Canada
bedard.francois@uqam.ca

Dr. François Bédard has 35 years of experience in tourism as manager, international consultant and academic. Since 1993, Dr. Bédard has been Professor in the Department of Tourism and Urban Studies at the Ecole des Sciences de la Gestion, a business school of the Université du Québec à Montréal (UQAM). He is director of the International Centre for Education and Research in Tourism (CIFORT) and liaison officer between UQAM and the United Nations World Tourism Organization (UNWTO). Since

April 2000, Dr. Bédard has been an adviser on new technologies at UNWTO. In February 2007, he was appointed as Director General of the World Centre of Excellence for Destinations (CED). Dr Bédard was a guest speaker at many international conferences and seminars, and has published articles about the application of information technology to tourism and higher education.

Jose L. Caro
Escuela Universitaria de Turismo, Malaga University, Spain
jlcaro@uma.es

Dr Jose L. Caro is Professor of 'Information Systems applied to Tourism' in the School of Tourism. He is a Researcher in SICUMA (Cooperative Information Systems of Malaga University) computer science research group centred in information systems methodology and development. He is researcher in several projects about information technologies and tourism and is Principle Investigator in a project about the application of workflow technologies in hotel information systems.

Roland Dessovic
elements.at New Media Solutions GmbH, Salzburg, Austria
roland.dessovic@elements.at

Roland Dessovic is a registered manager and associate of the full-service Internet agency elements.at. Beside his tasks as a member of the executive team, he is responsible for key accounting and customer care as well as for project management for accounts like the Vienna Stock Exchange. Roland is also in charge of elements' tourism software 'Digital Tourism Assistant' (www.tourismusassistent.com) and cares about its further development and future trends. Furthermore, he is a lecturer at diverse events and congresses concerning eMarketing and eTourism.

Astrid Ch. Dickinger
New Media Technology, MODUL University Vienna
astrid.dickinger@wu-wien.ac.at

Before joining MODUL University Vienna, Astrid Dickinger was Assistant Professor at the Institute for Tourism and Leisure Studies of Vienna University of Economics and Business Administration. There she completed her dissertation on (un)observed heterogeneity in mobile service usage. Before starting her position at WU-Wien she was a Visiting Scholar at the University of Western Australia, Perth. Her research interests are in the areas of service quality in electronic channels, electronic and mobile service usage, IT and Tourism, and Web 2.0. Results of her research have been published in journals and conference proceedings.

Kathrin Ecker

Krems Research Forschungsgesellschaft mbH, Austria
kathrin.ecker@kremsresearch.at

Kathrin Ecker has been working as a Researcher at TRC since October 2005. She studied Knowledge Management at the University of Applied Sciences in Eisenstadt, Austria and is now studying at the Vienna University of Economics and Business Administration. She is involved in several research projects at TRC. Her research focus is on dynamic packaging and the calculation of value added of several events.

Roland Fleischhacker

LOVO Lifestyle Service GmbH, Austria
roland.fleischhacker@lovo.cc

Roland Fleischhacker studied electrical engineering at the Technical Universities of Vienna and Munich. In the early 1980s, Roland developed individualized software for major enterprises. In 1988 he founded SET-EDV Beratung GmbH, the first SAP consulting company in Austria. In 1992, while still a student, he sold the company to Plaut AG, an international consultancy, but con-tinued to work for the company as a member of the top management. He helped turn Plaut Austria into one of Austria's top consulting firms. In 2001, he left Plaut to realize the idea of LOVO. As CEO he is responsible for technology, strategy and partnerships at LOVO Lifestyle Service GmbH.

Cyril Francis

Tourism Management, University of Pretoria, South Africa
cyril.francis@up.ac.za

Cyril Francis is Senior Lecturer in the Department of Tourism Management at the University of Pretoria in South Africa. He holds an MCom degree from the University of Johannesburg. His field of specialty is hospitality with a specific focus on the gaming industry. He has contributed to various publications and papers in the field of tourism and he is also a member of the board of directors of the Chefs Association of South Africa.

Claudia Freidl
Krems Research Forschungsgesellschaft mbH
claudia.freidl@kremsresearch.at

Claudia Freidl is a Researcher at TRC and is involved in several projects concerning Information and Communication Technologies in tourism. She studied Sociology at the University of Graz. Currently, she is studying for her PhD at the University of Vienna. Her research focus is on trend analysis, multivariate methods and acceptance of new technologies.

Michael Fux
Forschungsgesellschaft mbH
michael.fux@iwi.unibe.ch

Michael Fux holds a Master of Science degree in Business Administration from University Berne in Switzerland. Since 2004, he is working as research and teaching assistant at the Institute of Information Systems at University Bern. Further, he is Managing Director of a research and consulting organization. His primary research interests are online marketing, electronic customer service and website evaluation. Currently he is working on his PhD, focusing on cooperative customer relationship management (CRM) in tourist destinations.

Andrey Glazov
Destimation.com, St. Petersburg, Russia
gman@destimation.com

With his engineering background and passion for computer technologies Andrey Glazov worked as Technical Director and owner of several pre-press, design studios and computer companies in St Petersburg, Russia in the 1990s. Software development, a freelance business for him during those years, led to Destimation project in 2000. His current position is senior developer, general manager and partner of Destimation.

Robert Goecke
University of Applied Sciences, München
robert.goecke@fhm.edu

Dr Robert Goecke was appointed as Professor for 'Wirtschaftsinformatik und Dienstleistungs management' at the

Department of Tourism at Munich University of Applied Sciences. Since 1999 he has been CEO of Segma Service Engineering & Management AG, Munich; 2002–2006 – Head of SIG 'Entrepreneurial Management of IT Organizations' of SICUS e.V. – Siemens IC Users Association; 1999–2005 – Lecturer for Service Management and E-Services TUM (Technische Universität Munich); 1998–1999 – Coordinator of the federal research initiative on Service Engineering for the 21st century of the German Ministry of Education and Research BMBF; 1996–1998 – Director of BPU GmbH; 1996 – Doctor of Business Administration; 1991 – Dipl.-Inform. (TUM) Computer Science Diploma.

Joan Miquel Gomis
Universitat Oberta de Catalunya, Spain
jgomisl@uoc.edu

Dr Joan Miquel Gomis is Lecturer at the Open University of Catalonia (UOC), Director of the Tourism Program and member of the Business and Economy Department. He is a academic director of the master degree in Marketing and Management of Tourism Companies, organized by UOC and UIB. He has a PhD in Business and Economy and a degree in Information Science. He is President of the NGO Fair Tourism (Turisme Just) and has been Director of the professional Tourism Revue EDITUR. His research domain is eTourism, especially focused on intermediation.

Francesc González-Reverté
Universitat Oberta de Catalunya, Spain
fgonzalezre@uoc.edu

Dr Francesc González-Reverté is Lecturer at the Open University of Catalonia (UOC) in the Tourism Program and member of the Business and Economy Department. He has a degree and a PhD in Geography. He is Academic Director of the degree in Culture Tourism and he has written several books on tourism and territorial planning. He is doing research on culture tourism and e-marketing.

Ulrike Gretzel
Texas A&M University, Texas, USA
ugretzel@tamu.edu

Dr Ulrike Gretzel is Assistant Professor in the Department of Recreation, Park & Tourism Sciences at Texas A&M University and Director of the Laboratory for Intelligent Systems in Tourism. She received her doctoral degree in Communication from the University of Illinois at Urbana-Champaign. Her research focuses on persuasion in human-technology interaction, the representation of sensory and emotional aspects of tourism experiences, and issues related to the development and use of intelligent systems in tourism.

Rainer Gruber
Pegasus Solutions GmbH, Germany
Rainer.gruber@pegs.com

Rainer Gruber is VP Sales and Account Management at Pegasus Solutions, which is the leading company for travel technology solutions within the hospitality industry and a global leader when it comes to innovations. Gruber has been working within the hospitality industry for the past 17 years and is regularly contributing outlooks and research findings during hospitality events within Europe.

Antonio Guevara
Escuela Universitaria de Turismo, Malaga University, Spain
guevara@uma.es

Dr Antonio Guevara is Research Director in the School of Tourism at Málaga University. He is Professor of 'Information Systems applied to Tourism' and 'Information Technology in Tourism' in Computer Science Department. He is the Director of SICUMA (Cooperative Information Systems of Malaga University) computer science research group centred in information systems methodology and development. He is the main researcher in several projects related to Information Technologies and Tourism.

Cathy Guthrie
Tourism Management Institute, London, UK
cathy.guthrie@dsl.pipex.com

Dr Cathy Guthrie is Hon. Secretary and Past President of the Tourism Management Institute. After 14 years experience in destination management with English local authorities, her 2002 MSc research studied the impact of ICT on the TIC role in destination marketing. Her PhD research focused on the impact of visitor interactions on destination image. As Tourism Manager for Darlington, she implemented a destination management system, working with Northumbria Tourist Board to develop inter-operability between the Darlington website and the regional data-base. She thanks Andrew Daines, eTourism Partnerships Manager at VisitBritain, for his encouragement and assistance in providing access to information for the development of this case study.

Harald Heichele
Revenue Management Services, Lufthansa Systems, Germany
Harald.Heichele@dlh.de

Since 2005 Dipl.-Kfm. Harald Heichele is Head of Revenue Management Services at Lufthansa Systems, Neu-Isenburg; 2000–2004 – Manager Pricing and Yield Management at Deutsche Lufthansa AG, Frankfurt am Main; 1999–2000 – Manager Decision Support Systems Network Planning at Deutsche Lufthansa AG, Frankfurt am Main; 1999 – Dipl.-Kfm. (Ludwig-Maximilians-Universität Munich) Business Administration Diploma.

Pongsak Hoontrakul
Sasin of Chulalongkorn University, Thailand
pongsak@hoontrakul.com

Dr Pongsak Hoontrakul is known for both scholar and practitioner work. Academically he is a senior research fellow at Sasin of Chulalongkorn University, Thailand. Capital market, derivative products, banking and financial economics are among his recent studies. His current research is in information economics, travel industry and new economy. Internationally, he is a member of the International Advisory Council of Schulich School of Business, York University, Toronto and a past member of the World Economic Forum, Geneva. Commercially, Dr Pongsak served as past Chairman of the Audit Committee and currently is independent Director of the United Overseas Bank (Thai) Plc. In the political area, his past positions include advisor to Deputy Prime Minister (for ICT), advisor to the Parliament Committee for (1) Economic Affair and (2) Human Rights and advisor to the Senate Committee for Fiscal, Banking and Financial Institution.

Florian M. Hummel
ANGELL Business School Freiburg, Germany
f.hummel@angell.de

Mr. Hummel is a member of the Board of Directors of the International Society of Travel and Tourism Educators (ISTTE). Florian M. Hummel holds a BA (Hons) in Travel Management from the University of Brighton and an MSc in Air Transport Management from Cranfield University, United Kingdom. After working with an airport management company and an international rental car company he is presently a Senior Lecturer at the ANGELL Akademie Freiburg, Germany and Director Degree Programmes at the ANGELL Business School Freiburg, Germany.

Axel Jockwer
HolidayCheck AG, Kreuzlingen, Switzerland
ajockwer@holidaycheck.ch

Since 2005 Dr Axel Jockwer is Marketing Director and spokesman of HolidayCheck AG, the largest hotel reviewing platform in the German-speaking area. He holds a doctor's degree in Philosophy from the University of Constance, Germany, where he was also teaching communication sciences (Internet) and history from 1998 to 2004. He has been working in the marketing field of fun sports, trends, Internet and online-commerce since 1999.

Emmanouil Kaldis
Emmantina and Palmyra Beach hotels, Athens, Greece
manoliskaldis@gmail.com

Emmanouil Kaldis obtained his BSc degree in Business Management and Administration with specialization to Management Information Systems from Athens University of Economic and Business in Greece. He obtained his Masters with Distinction in Business Information Technology from the Computation Department of UMIST in Manchester. Currently, he is a PhD candidate at the School of Informatics, University of Manchester. His research is in the area of Cybernetics and Strategic Management.

Konstantina Kaldis
Emmantina and Palmyra Beach hotels, Athens, Greece
kkaldis@emmantina.gr

Konstantina Kaldis is the manager and co-owner of the 'Emmantina' and 'Palmyra Beach' Hotels, in Athens, Greece. Her role includes formation of hotel distribution strategies and sales. She earned her BSc in Business Administration, in Athens at the American College of Greece, Deree College. She pursued her studies in the United Kingdom, at the University of Surrey where she earned her MSc in Tourism Management. She has won the HEDNA Scholarship for attending the relevant event. Before entering the hotel sector she worked on IT projects, including an Enterprise Resource Planning (ERP) implementation project. Her interests include management, tourism, technological applications in tourism and electronic distribution.

Faustin Kamuzora
Mzumbe University, Morogoro, Tanzania
frkamuzora@mzumbe.ac.tz or frkamuzora@yahoo.co.uk

Prof. Kamuzora holds a Master of Science in Agricultural Economics from North Carolina Agricultural and Technical State University, United States and a PhD in Informatics from University of Bradford, United Kingdom. He teaches courses in Economics, Business Information Systems, and Information and Communication Technologies for Development (ICT4D), Research Methodology, and Knowledge Management at Mzumbe University and other institutions in Tanzania. His research interest include using holistic approaches in synthesizing how developing countries can use ICTs in raising their economic development by concentrating on quick win sectors such as tourism as well as education. He has written and edited five books and published several papers on eTourism as well as in other areas of Economic Development.

Karsten Kärcher
Tiscover UK, Luton, England
karsten.karcher@tiscover.com

Karsten Kärcher is Director of Tiscover UK, Europe's leading destination management system provider. Previously, he held the position of Executive Director for Sales/Marketing/Finance at Tiscover AG (Austria) as well as Managing Director of Tiscover's subsidiaries in Germany, Italy and the United Kingdom. Kärcher joined Tiscover in 2001 from United Kingdom media and communications group Telewest, where he was the strategic account and business development director for travel. Prior to Telewest, Kärcher gained strategic management and consultancy skills in a variety of senior roles in Germany, the United Kingdom , Brazil and Switzerland.

Ola Kastensson
Destimation.com, Russia
ola@russkie-prostori.ru

Born in Sweden, Ola Kastensson graduated from the IHM Business School Sweden and the Ecole Hotelière de Lausanne, Switzerland.

His decades of hospitality industry include management positions in Europe and the Middle East. In Russia since 1992, he managed the pre-opening of a 5-star hotel and one of Russia's first International DMC's, with offices in Moscow and St Petersburg. He is a partner of Destimation and member of IFITT, SITE, MPI, HCIMA and leads the only ISO 9001:2000 accredited Russian DMC Russkie Prostori.

Rob Law
The Hong Kong Polytechnic University, Hong Kong
hmroblaw@polyu.edu.hk

Dr Rob Law received his PhD, MSc and BASc in Computer Science from Canadian Universities. He is presently Associate Professor of Information Technology at the Hong Kong Polytechnic University's School of Hotel and Tourism Management. Dr Law actively serves the international academic community. He works for 30 research journals, and he has served on the committees of 50 international conferences.

Rosanna Leung
Hotel Nikko, Hong Kong
Rosanna.Leung@inet.polyu.edu.hk

Rosanna Leung received her Bachelor (Hons) degree in Electronic Commerce and MSc in Hospitality and Tourism Management in Hong Kong. She has been in Hospitality IT for over 20 years and has been involved in various hotels' pre-opening and system migration projects in Hong Kong and Mainland China. Presently, she is the IT Manager at Hotel Nikko Hong Kong and Visiting Lecturer at Hong Kong Polytechnic University. Her expertise includes applications of Information Technology in hospitality and tourism operations, web analysis and e-marketing.

Marie Claire Louillet
University of Sherbrooke, Canada
louillet-mc@ithq.qc.ca

Marie Claire Louillet has been Professor at the Institut de Tourisme et Hôtellerie du Québec (ITHQ) since 2005. She has 20 years of experience in tourism and more particularly as a manager in the hospitality field in Paris, London, Montreal and Rome as well as in Puerto Rico and Cuba. She is currently enrolled in the Doctorate of Business Administration (DBA) at the University of Sherbrooke in Canada. The topic of her thesis is "A balanced scorecard to evaluate the performance of Destination Management Systems".

Berendien Lubbe
Tourism Management, University of Pretoria, South Africa
berendien.lubbe@up.ac.za

Berendien Lubbe is Associate Professor in the Department of Tourism Management at the University of Pretoria in South Africa. Her career spans a number of years in the travel and tourism industry as a travel agent and consultant. She is the leading academic in tourism distribution in South Africa and established the field as an academic discipline in South Africa. She holds a DCom (Communication Management) degree, has authored, edited and contributed to a number of books in the fields of tourism and public relations, among them the first book on tourism distribution in South Africa. She has presented and published papers at international and local academic and industry conferences and also authored articles in international and local scientific journals.

Ian McDonnell
Faculty of Business, University of Technology, Sydney, Australia
Ian.mcdonnell@uts.edu.au

Ian McDonnell lectures in the marketing and management of leisure and tourism services at the University of Technology, Sydney. Prior to becoming an academic he enjoyed a 25-year marketing and managerial career with Qantas Airways. He is best known as the author of *Festival and Special Event Management*, now in its 4th edition.

Esther Pérez Martell
Universidad de Las Palmas, Gran Canaria, Spain
eperezmartell@gmail.com

Esther Pérez Martell is Professor at the Universidad de Las Palmas. She has a degree in Applied Physics: Oceanography and Physic Processes in the coastal environment. She has been Director of the Tourism Program at the UOC (Open University of Catalonia) and Academic Director of the WTO Master degree on Policy and Strategy Management in Tourist Destinations.

Patrick S. Merten
University of Fribourg, Switzerland
patrick.merten@unifr.ch

Patrick S. Merten is research assistant at the international institute of management in technology (iimt) at the University of Fribourg, Switzerland. With a Master degree in Information Management, he conducts research in the field of innovation and technology management. For his PhD studies he focuses on the diffusion, adoption and acceptance of technological innovations in the passenger process of the aviation industry.

Oriol Miralbell
Universitat Oberta de Catalunya, Spain
jmiralbell@uoc.edu

Oriol Miralbell is Lecturer at the Open University of Catalonia (UOC) where he teaches in the Tourism program and is a member of the Information and Communication Science department. He has a degree in Philology, in Tourism Management, in Information Systems and Telecommunications and a Master degree in Information Resources Management. His research focus is on innovation and social networks in tourism.

Michael Mrazek
ncm.at - Net Communication Management, GmbH, Austria
Michael.Mrazek@ncm.at

Michael Mrazek is CEO of the Internet agency ncm.at in Salzburg, Austria. As an expert for web marketing he holds lectures, seminars and workshops for numerous education and further education institutions. He is also involved in internal company training sessions or presentations at professional conferences such as the Austrian Tourism Summit or the Public Trade Fair. Furthermore, he is Chairman of the advertising section of the Salzburg Economic Chamber.

Jamie Murphy
The University of Western Australia Business School, Australia
jmurphy@biz.uwa.edu.au

Jamie Murphy's hospitality background and MBA led to an international marketing career and a PhD studying the Internet. His industry and academic career spans five continents and includes publications in both academic journals and leading newspapers such as *The New York Times* and *Wall Street Journal*. His research focus is effective use of the Internet for citizens, businesses and governments.

Miroslaw Nalazek
Polish Open University & University of Economics, Warsaw, Poland
miroslaw.nalazek@wp.pl

Dr Miroslaw Nalazek is the Head of Tourism and Hospitality Management Department at the Polish Open University in Warsaw. He is also a Senior Lecturer at the University of Economics in Warsaw. He has graduated with an MS from the Faculty of Geography at Nicolaus Copernicus University (UMK) in Toruń, and with an BSc on Foreign Trade from the Warsaw School of Economics (SGH). His PhD research focused on the impacts of Internet distribution channels on the tourism market. His professional career includes management positions in various tourism and IT enterprises, both in Poland and abroad (USA & Switzerland). He is an expert at the Polish Tourism Organization on Internet marketing strategy. He has published widely in scientific and professional publications both in Poland and abroad.

Peter O'Connor
IMHI, Essec Business School, France
oconnor@essec.fr

Dr Peter O'Connor is Professor of Informat3ion Systems at Essec Business School France, and Academic Director of Institute de Management Hotelier International (IMHI); an MBA programme specializing in international hospitality management. His primary research, teaching and consulting interests focus on the use of information technology in hospitality. He has authored two leading textbooks: *Using Computers in Hospitality* (Cassell, UK – now in its third edition) and *Electronic Information Distribution in Hospitality and Tourism Industries* (CABI, UK) as well as numerous articles in the trade and academic press. He regularly teaches seminars on technology management, distribution and electronic marketing for both international hospitality companies and international industry associations.

Alexis Papathanassis

Bremerhaven University of Applied Sciences, Germany
apapathanassis@hs-bremerhaven.de

Alexis Papathanassis was born in Rhodes (Greece). He completed his undergraduate studies in Business Administration at the University of Bath (UK). As a post-graduate he specialized in the area of information systems, gaining a masters degree from the London School of Economics (UK) and subsequently a PhD from Hanover University (Germany). Following a 6-year professional career in TUI, he has been recently appointed as Professor for Tourism and Maritime Tourism at the Bremerhaven University of Applied Sciences (Germany).

Young A Park

Texas A&M University, USA
yapark@tamu.edu

Young A Park is a research associate at the Laboratory for Intelligent Systems in Tourism. She received her PhD in Recreation, Park and Tourism from Texas A&M University and holds a Masters degree in Marketing from the Catholic University of Daegu, Korea. Her research focuses on Internet-based tourism marketing, e-service quality, online travel shopping styles and IT adoption and use by travellers.

Irene Püntener

University of Fribourg, Switzerland
i.puentener@gmx.ch

Irene Püntener finished her Master of Management at the University of Fribourg, Switzerland in March 2006. In her Master thesis at the International Institute of Management in Technology (IIMT), she analysed the airline distribution environment with a focus on Amadeus as a global distribution system provider. She is currently working for a marketing consulting company.

Francesco Ricci

University of Bozen-Bolzano, Bolzano, Italy
fricci@unibz.it

Francesco Ricci is Professor of Computer Science at the University of Bolzano. Francesco Ricci holds a degree in Mathematics from the University of Padova, Italy. From 1986 to 1987 he was with Enichem S.p.A., Milano, Italy, where he was engaged in developing expert system applications. From 1988 to 2006 he was a Researcher at ITC-irst, where he was responsible for internal laboratories (Expert System group, Knowledge Representation, eCommerce and Tourism Laboratory). From 1998 to 2000, he worked with Sodalia S.p.A. as a software architect designing the corporate web application model. His current research interests include recommender systems, constraint satisfaction problems, machine learning, case-based reasoning and information technologies and tourism.

Alexander Rind
Tourismus Research Center Krems GesmbH, Krems, Austria
alexander.rind@kremsresearch.at

Alexander Rind is a researcher at TRC. He is working on several projects relating to Information and Communication Technologies in tourism since December 2004. He received his MSc in Business Information Technology from the Vienna University of Technology in 2004 and is currently pursuing Master programme in Information and Knowledge Management. His research focus is on web engineering and semi-structured information.

Constanze Russ-Mohl
University of Konstanz, Germany
constanze@russ-mohl.de

Constanze Russ-Mohl holds an MA in Politics and Management from the University of Constance in Germany. She further studied tourism at the Universidad de Granada in Spain and Shanghai Jiao Tong University in China. She has been working in the national, regional and private marketing field of the tourism industry and in online-commerce since 2002. Since 2007 she organises the marketing for HolidayCheck's international platforms.

Sunil Sahadev
School of Management, University of Sheffield, UK
s.sahadev@sheffield.ac.uk

Sunil Sahadev is Lecturer in Marketing at the University of Sheffield, United Kingdom. He completed his PhD from the Indian

Institute of Technology, Chennai, India and his Post-Doctoral Fellowship from the Asian Institute of Technology, Bangkok. Before joining the University of Sheffield, he worked as an Assistant Professor at the Indian Institute of Management, Kozhikode, India. He does research in the areas of distribution channel management, high-technology marketing and tourism marketing.

Markus Schröcksnadel
Feratel media technologies AG, Innsbruck, Austria
markus.schroecksnadel@feratel.com

Markus Schröcksnadel was awarded the Doctor of Laws degree by the Innsbruck Leopold-Franzens-University in 1988. Since then he has held a variety of positions, usually several ones at a time, including the position of 'Prokurist' (holder of a general commercial power of attorney), managing director and member of the supervisory boards of companies affiliated to the feratel Group and/or their legal predecessors and companies affiliated to the Sitour Group. He also served as 'Prokurist' (1989–1995) and Managing Director (1995–2000) of feratel international GmbH. 'Prokurist' of Sitour Management GmbH (since 1996), and Managing Director of Vereinigte Bergbahnen GmbH (since 1999). Dr Schröcksnadel is also Chairman of the supervisory board of the Austrian eTourism competence centre ANET and Chairman of the Tyrolean Fishing Association.

Frank Schröder
ISO Software Systeme GmbH, Germany
Frank.Schroeder@isogmbh.de

Frank Schröder holds a Bachelor's degree in Computer Science from Nuremberg University, Germany. Since 1990 he has been working in the IT business and accumulated 15 years experience in designing and developing high quality software architectures. For more than 10 years now Frank Schröder has been sales and project manager for ISO's IT solutions for the tourism and mobile application market. In addition he is a responsible sales manager of ISO's business charter airline solution and customer relationship management solution. Within the Aladdin project ISO was in charge of the project coordination and Frank Schröder was project director and workpackage leader of the Exploitation and Dissemination activities.

Maria Immacolata Simeon
Institute for Service Industry, National Research Council, Italy
m.simeon@irat.cnr.it

Maria Immacolata holds a degree in Sociology from the University 'Federico II' of Naples, Italy. She is presently Senior Researcher and Project Manager at the Institute for Service Industry Research (National Research Council), where she has been working since 1985. After early research experiences in the field of social services organization, she has been involved in research on Tourism and Cultural Heritage. She took part in national and international research projects, promoting sustainable tourism and cultural resources in Southern Italy and Mediterranean countries. She also has experience in training courses and projects design. Her current research interest is focused on integrated management and marketing of cultural resources for sustainable tourism and local development.

Charles Tee
T3E Global, Singapore
charles.tee@t3eglobal.com

Over 21 years of experience in the hospitality and tourism industry in on-line travel, corporate travel, hotels and resorts and destination management, in the areas of sales, marketing, and strategic management covering South East Asia, Hong Kong and Sri Lanka. Charles was Chief Operating Officer – Asia for Wotif.com, an Australian-based accommodation website, prior to starting his own company. He is also a part-time lecturer in both undergraduate and post graduate courses in Singapore. Charles holds a Master of Arts degree in Marketing Management from Macquarie University, Australia and a Diploma in Marketing from the Chartered Institute of Marketing, United Kingdom .

Immacolata Vellecco
Institute for Service Industry, National Research Council, Italy
i.vellecco@irat.cnr.it

Immacolata holds a degree in Economics from the University 'Federico II' of Naples, Italy. She has been working at the Institute for Service Industry Research (National Research Council) since 1983 and she is, presently, Senior Researcher. She took part in many national and international research projects, conducting research on small business strategies and management through multiple case studies. Early experiences focused on entrepreneurial culture in Southern Italy. Further studies focused on the demand for services supporting small business internationalization and on supply chain integration in mature industries. A recent field of interest is information technology in Tourism and Destination Management.

Adriano Venturini
eCTRL Solutions S.r.l, Trento, Italy
venturini@ectrlsolutions.com

Adriano Venturini is Manager and co-founder of eCTRL Solutions, a company specialized in providing and developing recommendation technologies for the eTourism sector. He is the technical director responsible for Trip@dvice development and its integration in next generation tourism portals. He is the author of several papers on tourism recommender systems published in books and proceedings of specialized international conferences. His research interests are in the areas of tourism recommender systems (applying case base reasoning and intelligent query management methodologies), software architectures (component-based development, web and distributed architectures) and data integration techniques (mediator architectures, XML).

Marta Viu
Universitat Oberta de Catalunya, Spain
mviu@uoc.edu

Marta Viu is Lecturer at the Open University of Catalonia (UOC), teaching in the Business and Economy Science Department. She has a degree in Business and Economy (business branch), in Marketing and business strategies applied to distribution, she is alos Associate Professor at the School of Business and Economy of the Universitat de Barcelona. She is teaching and researching on management of production, business organizations and management informatics.

Klemens Waldhör
Krems Researh Forschungsgesellschaft mbH, Austria
klemens.waldhoer@kremsresearch.at

Klemens Waldhör holds a doctoral degree in Computer Science from the University of Linz, Austria. He is Director and Scientific Manager of the TRC, a research organization which is part of ANET, the Austrian network for eTourism. He also is active as a lecturer at the University of Applied Science in Krems where he teaches a course on 'Product development and New technologies' for tourism students. Besides overseeing and guiding the research work of the TRC, his main interests are applying ambient intelligence technologies in the hotel room of the future, using natural language technologies in the touristic field as well as modelling touristic behaviour with various statistical modelling approaches.

Paul Weeks
Southern Cross University – The Hotel School, Sydney, Australia
pweeks@scu.edu.au

Paul Weeks is Academic Director at the Hotel School (a partnership between Southern Cross University and Mulpha Australia). He has 17 years experience in hotel, motel and food service management, and has been lecturing in management, services management and information technology with Southern Cross University since 1991. Paul has published widely in academic and industry journals, and has co-authored two Australian industry texts: club management and managing convention businesses. Research interests include IT in hospitality, education, history, convention services and club management.

Hannes Werthner
Technical University of Vienna and EC3, Vienna
hannes.werthner@ec.tuwien.ac.at

Hannes Werthner is Professor for e-commerce at the Technical University of Vienna; and Founder and President of the eCommerce Competence Center (EC3) in Vienna. He was also Professor for Computer Science and e-commerce at the Vienna University of Economics and the University of Trento, Italy. He holds a Master and PhD from the Technical University, Vienna. He was visiting professor at several universities, published over 100 papers and books, and was a fellow from the Austrian Schrödinger foundation. His research activities cover e-commerce, Internet-based information systems, decision support systems, simulation and artificial intelligence.

Dieter Westermann
Airline Management Solutions Lufthansa Systems, Germany
dieter.westermann@lhsystems.com

Since 2006 Dieter Westermann is Head of Portfolio Management and Innovations at Airline Management Solutions, Lufthansa Systems; 2004–2005 – General Manager Strategic Projects, Lufthansa

Systems; 2002–2004 – Vice President Business Solutions & Services, Swiss International Air Lines, Zurich, Switzerland; 1998–2001 – General Manager Global Distribution, Swiss Air Transport Ltd., Zurich, Switzerland; 1989–1998 – Manager Revenue Management Systems Development, Deutsche Lufthansa AG, Frankfurt am Main; 1989 – Bachelor of Science Degree in Business Administration and Computer Science, FH Dortmund, Germany.

Leonhard Wörndl
University of Applied Sciences, Salzburg, Austria
leonhard.woerndl@fh-salzburg.ac.at

Leonhard Wörndl is Dean of the School of 'Innovation and Management in Tourism' of the Salzburg University of Applied Sciences as well as of the Institute of Tourism and Hotel Management of the Tourism Schools Salzburg. After having developed awareness campaigns and special training programmes for Austrian tourism SMEs, he joined the Salzburg University of Applied Sciences to develop the programme and to teach eMarketing on an academic level. At the moment he is involved in national and international eTourism training programmes. His main research interest is focused on the effect of eTourism on Austrian SMEs, but also on SMEs of developing countries.

Senem Yazici-Malkoclar
School of Management, University of Surrey, England, UK
msp1sy@surrey.ac.uk

Senem Yazici is a PhD candidate Entrepreneurship and Tourism at the University of Surrey in the United Kingdom. Her research aim is to find out what are the factors the influence growth of the hotels in Cyprus. She has completed a master's degree in Tourism Management at the University of Surrey. She has started her academic career as Lecturer in Tourism and Hospitality Management at the University of Yeditepe in Istanbul, Turkey. In the past, Senem has worked in the field of tourism and travel in managerial positions.

Andreas H. Zins
Vienna University of Economics & Business Administration, Austria
andreas.zins@wu-wien.ac.at

Andreas H. Zins is Associate Professor at the Institute for Tourism and Leisure Studies at the Vienna University of Economics and Business Administration. He lectures in international marketing, business administration, tourism marketing planning, consumer and travel behaviour models. Dr Zins is active in research in the fields of tourist information behaviour, marketing research, cost-benefit analyses, social impacts, computer-assisted and web-based interviewing, theme parks and related leisure attractions.

Marianna Zoge
Bournemouth University, UK
mariannazoge@yahoo.gr

Marianna is a tourism marketing professional with a specialization in technology applications. After having obtained an undergraduate degree on International and European Studies at the Panteion University of Athens (Greece), she graduated from the MSc in Tourism Marketing at the University of Surrey (Guildford, UK) with a specialization on the impacts of eTourism on the tourism industry structure. Since then she worked in a Marketing Consultancy company and at youtravel.com, an online accommodation provider, where she contributed to the launch and marketing of the company. She is interested in strategic destination marketing and utilization of ICTs and emerging technologies in the tourism industry.

Preface

Information Technology has changed our economy, our society and our daily life. The Web, the related e-commerce phenomenon, and systems supporting enterprises and guiding users are just the 'latest' examples of this development. And this change is accelerating. The next technological wave, where (nearly) invisible system will accompany, monitor, guide, understand and maybe also persuade humans is just ahead of us. Systems will be embedded, personalized, adaptive and anticipatory; access will be provided anywhere, at any time and for everybody. The interaction, based on intelligent, non-traditional interfaces, will change from the lean-forward mode of today, being work centric, towards a relaxed laid-back mode.

The second 'background' of the cases presented in this book is the general development in the e-commerce and e-business domain, where one can observe an ongoing deconstruction of value chains, accompanied by selective outsourcing. This leads to value networks (in contrast to chains) and flexible cooperation forms, calling for dynamic service design and engineering. Here one can refer to the concept of smart business networks or to the emerging field of service science.

Both developments, the technological/futuristic as well as the economic/structural one, will have an obvious impact on tourism, on its products and services and on the market structure. This impact will be as important (and maybe even more) as the technological developments in the past. Beginning only slightly more than a decade ago, the Internet/WWW has changed the industry, it has become the primary source for travel information worldwide, enabling access to well over a billion web pages describing hundreds of thousands of tourism enterprises and destinations. And user started to create communities and virtual worlds, to organize the Web along their needs, they increasingly turn around the market.

But not only user interaction and access means have improved. Today there is also evidence from the industry that ICTs contributed to the operational efficiency of organizations and it expanded market coverage. Integrated technological solutions with elaborated data management support internal processes as well as networking with trusted partners. In tourism, as a networked industry, such electronic cooperations seem to be the only way for organizations to address the emerging challenges in the global marketplace. In this context technology empowered interoperability is critical for the effective networking. This enables tourism organizations not only to improve their operations and cost effectiveness but also to expand their geographical and operational scope.

The book *eTourism Case Studies – Management and Marketing Issues* offers a timely and rich resource of best practices and it provides an 'empirical' prove of the mentioned developments. Organized along the structure of the travel and tourism industry it contains a wide range of case studies in domains such as transportation, hospitality, intermediation and destinations. The two final chapters deal with specific technology applications and systems (e.g. mobile applications), somehow orthogonal to the other cases described. As such the book presents a number of great examples where technology is used effectively to maximize operational efficiency and to support the respective core business. A number of special cases demonstrate that technology is fundamental in the ability of these organizations to reorganize themselves in order to address the challenges of the future. In several other examples it is evident that technology is critical for the creation of innovative tourism products and the networking of organizations in either geographical or operational clusters.

The book demonstrates that tourism organization will be required to employ innovative technological solutions – not only in the future – to be able to remain in the global competitive arena, it illustrates the need for understanding, developing and applying technological solutions for obtaining operational and strategic benefits. With its set of cases the book fills a gap in the current eTourism literature, it is a rich source of information for practitioners and academics.

Hannes Werthner
Professor for e-commerce
Vienna University of Technology, Austria

Preamble and acknowledgements

Like all projects there is a great story behind this book too. Back in 2002 a smiling Austrian young person arrived at the University of Surrey to spend a semester attending eTourism classes and using Library facilities to research for his Doctorate. Roman came into Dimitrios office asking whether he could attend classes and reassuring him that he will not cause any problems! This was the start of a fruitful collaboration and a good friendship. Having completed his PhD, Roman joined the Salzburg University of Applied Sciences as Faculty and Researcher and started a great number of projects. A couple of years and many beer later in Salzburg further collaboration was achieved between the two universities. At the ENTER 2005 conference Roman initiated the idea of best practice case studies and invited Dimitrios at the 2006 eTourism Futures Forum to join him as a co-editor to this volume. Several months later, 42 chapters contributed by 65 authors were sourced, developed and edited to create this book.

The book aims to demonstrate that information and communication technologies (ICTs) are an integral part of the strategic management of tourism. Unless tourism organizations appreciate the wide range of opportunities availed by ICTs they will not be able to extend their strategy to achieve their full potential. Equally, unless the ICT strategy is not led by the business strategy and objectives, technology will be unable to fulfil its full potential and provide useful, profitable and innovative solutions that will enable the business to survive, develop and deliver competitive offerings in the marketplace. The case studies demonstrate clearly a number of organizations that have embedded technology in their operations and strategy and have supported their expansion, competitiveness and profitability.

Naturally, many people have been involved in this project. First, we would like to thank our contributors for finding the time to produce excellent quality chapters and Prof Hannes Werthner in particular for offering the preface. Sally North and Francesca Ford from Butterworth Heinemann adopted and managed the project throughout whilst Ismail Khan and Deena Burgess assisted the production phase of the book. Research assistants Jacob Horl and Thomas Hinterholzer in Austria supported the project by preformatting the book whilst Marianna Zoge in Bournemouth supported the editorial process. Finally, we also would like to acknowledge the support of our families and loved ones for the achievement of this project. We hope that students, researchers and professionals will find this book useful and we welcome feedback and suggestions towards a second edition in the near future.

Dimitrios Buhalis
Roman Egger

Introduction

Roman Egger
Dimitrios Buhalis

Tourism is considered to be the world's largest economic activity and is responsible for 10% of the global GDP and 8.7% of all jobs (WTTC, 2006). In our post-industrial society, which is among others characterized by shifts of stress and perception, upheavals and the obsessive liability to new developments, tourism can be seen as a result of ongoing social progression which becomes an integral part of modern life (Egger, 2006). The Internet is the fastest growing medium of all time and is establishing a global communication and transactions infrastructure. Nearly 1 billion people currently use the Internet and, especially in populous regions such as in Asia, high growth rates in usage are being observed. Thus, the merging tourism and Internet developments lead to a subject area marked by exceptional dynamism. In the last four decades, information and communication technologies (ICTs) have become an essential support for tourism. In the beginning, it was important for increasing efficiency in the processing of information. Nowadays, ICT is relevant on all operative, structural and strategic levels.

While the aims set for ICTs by tourism providers are mainly to increase efficiency of business operations, achieve cost savings as well as expand sales, the vast amount of tourism product offers available in the market place lead to increased product and price transparency and improved service quality for tourists. But the rapid advancement and dynamism of eTourism, along with its possibilities, also requires new skills which put providers and consumers in a challenging position. The Internet leads to the restructuring of the industry along the entire tourism supply chain (Buhalis, 2003). A number of conflicting trends such as disintermediation and reintermediation, cooperation and concentration, globalization and customer reorientation indicate the dynamics of the market. A range of new players emerge in the marketplace to provide new tools for both the consumers and the industry, to deal with the volume of information and to process the global tourism offerings efficiently. The system of tourism is therefore constantly redefining itself and requires continual reorientation in marketing and management along the way. Change seems to be the only constant. Hence flexibility and innovativeness are needed to build and maintain competitiveness on the long run.

The last few years have seen an increasing research interest in the relationship between ICTs and tourism. The topic is multifaceted and therefore requires an interdisciplinary approach, which results in a variety of standpoints and approaches. Sheldon (2000) observed

> *the maturation process of tourism information technology research, [...] requires passages through the stages of research such as descriptive, applied, empirical, theoretical and conceptual.*

The majority of the existing literature is from a more descriptive and empirical standpoint than a theoretical and conceptual one. Hence, an argument founded in analytically scrutinized examples of best practice is still missing.

This book attempts to bridge the gap in the contemporary literature on this subject by carefully examining the marketing and management issues of companies that have successfuly implemented eTourism solutions. A total of 42 case studies can be found in six sections, with the intention of exploring the newest developments in this field, introducing and discussing emerging trends, approaches, models and paradigms, providing a vision for the future of eTourism and supporting discussion and elaboration with the help of pedagogic aids.

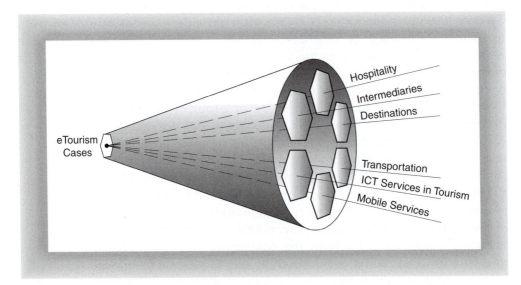

Figure I.1 The case study frame work

This book is unique in giving insights in using ICT best practice at an innovative and successful level in the Tourism industry. It prepares future students and professionals to take advantage of emerging trends, techniques and methodologies to create new products, industry structures and management practices. The book provides a vision that will encourage both final year undergraduate and post-graduate tourism and hospitality students to take a proactive and reactive approach to the fast emerging opportunities and challenges in the industry. It will also be useful for research students who would like to undertake research in the area and will stimulate further investigation in the field.

It is also hoped that this book will provide inspiration to professionals to develop their organizations in a competitive manner and to use ICT tools to shape their future. The book also aspires to supply information and vision to decision makers in public and private sector tourism organizations globally and to empower their pursuit for competitiveness in the emerging challenging global environment. The dynamic nature of this area should not been underestimated and the readers should always be alert to developments and technological innovation that would change techniques, methods and best practice.

References and Further Reading

Buhalis, D. (2003). *eTourism: Information technology for strategic tourism management.* London: Pearson; Financial Times/ Prentice Hall.

Egger, R. (2006). Online Forschung in der Touirsmuswissenschaft. In R. Bachleitner, R. Egger, & T. Herdin (Eds.), *Innovationen in der Tourismusforschung: Methoden und Anwendungen* (pp. 41–62). Münster: LIT.

Sheldon, P. J. (1997). *Tourism information technology.* Wallingford, UK: CAB International.

Sheldon, P. (2000). Introduction to the special issue on tourism information technology. *Journal of Travel Research*, 29 (2), 13–135.

Werthner, H., & Klein, S. (1999). *Information technology and tourism – a challenging relationship.* Vienna: Springer-Verlag

WTTC (2006). The 2006 Travel & Tourism Economic Research. Retrieved from www.wttc.org/2006TSA/pdf/world.pdf.

Part One

Hospitality
Roman Egger
Dimitrios Buhalis

Introduction

In comparison to other tourism sectors, the hospitality industry was relatively late in starting to use information and communication technologies (ICT). The structure of the accommodation sector is extremely heterogeneous, ranging from tiny bed and breakfasts to large 5-star chain hotels. The location of the properties as well as the types of clientele determines the demands and requirements made on ICTs (Buhalis, 2003). A number of the factors set out in Table PI.1 are ultimately decisive for whether, and to what extent, ICTs are used in hotels (Camisón, 2000).

In particular it is the ownership, relationships and size of the business that determine the degree of technology used in hotel properties. Larger tourism

Table PI.1 Variables relevant for the features of the hotel trade

Factors	Examples
Place	Urban/metropolitan/peripheral/alpine/rural
Size	Small/medium/large
Ownership relationships	Family/chain/franchise/state
Price	Exclusive/expensive/affordable/cheap
Activities	Sport/all-inclusive/club
Services	Hotel/bed and breakfast/boarding house
Guests' travel reasons	Leisure/business/conference/incentive
Transport links	Airport/motorway/railway

Source: Buhalis (2003)

enterprises and particularly hotel chains have more complex in-company processes and possibly distances in time and space to overcome, which require the use of advanced ICTs. At the same time, they also have the necessary financial resources in order to employ specialists and to be able to implement the corresponding applications (Egger, 2005). Thus, for instance, city hotels differ fundamentally from holiday hotels, and chain hotels differ decisively from small and medium-sized tourism enterprises (SMTEs).

Strategic Use of ICT for Hotels

Although the accommodation sector was for years regarded as 'the most under-automated segment of the international travel industry' (Buhalis, 2003) the rapid development of the Internet has led to most hospitality businesses, irrespective of their size, to engage actively with ICT. In many occasions computers were primarily introduced to facilitate the distribution function of hotels, as intermediaries would often refuse to collaborate with hotels that had no access to the Internet or were unable to receive emails or update their availability online. This push factor would bring a computer into the hotel environment which would then be used for the entire range of business functions and processes. There are many ways in which accommodation establishments can be supported by ICTs at both product and process level. These technologies promote the efficiency and effectiveness of operative processors, accompany strategic planning and are useful for the question of specialization and differentiation. They can be used within the company and between companies, support communication and coordination with all stakeholders. ICTs, for instance, can facilitate the administration and organization of the inventory, reduce distribution and communication costs, open new markets, permit the provision of up-to-date information and support flexibility in terms of pricing and product structure (O'Connor, 1999). In addition, they allow long-term customer relationships to be developed and support the creation of strategic partnerships. They encourage inter-organizational knowledge and know-how transfer and permit well-founded marketing research. The Carnival City study (Case 5), for instance, investigated the marketing strategy importance of ICT-assisted loyalty programmes and the contribution that the analysis of customer value can bring to an enterprise.

The internal and cross company structures in the hospitality industry are complex, and the requirements made of process-assisting information technology is accordingly varied. Figure PI.1

Business Infrastructure	Expert Systems; Management Information Systems; Yield Management Systems; CRM Systems; Property Management Systems – Back Office		
Human Resource Management	Personnel Information Systems		
Information	Presentation, Consulting and Information Systems; Internet		
Procurement	eProcurement		
	Internet (CRS/GDS) HRS DMS (Interactive TV Mobile Business)	Enterprise Resource Planning	PMS – Front Office Point of Sale Systems; Restaurant Management Systems	Customer Data Base Internet
	Marketing & Distribution	**Logistics**	**Service Production**	**After Sales**

Figure PI.1 ICT in the hospitality industry
Source: Mathies and Weiermair (2003)

by Mathies and Weiermair (2003) uses the value chain analysis to provide an overview of the technologies used in the hospitality industry. The most important are described above.

However, sometimes ICTs support not only individual corporate sectors but also central elements of the entire business model. The example of Omena hotels (Case 4) presents a premium budget-class hotel which challenges the traditional service concept and revenue models by fully exploiting the Internet and other forms of ICT in its operations. The hotel chain takes full advantage of technology to operate its properties with no staff on the premises. Although arguably this is detrimental to the customer service required, there is sufficient evidence from the success of the company to suggest that there is a market segment that would appreciate this type of business proposition.

The fact that today almost every hotel, irrespective of size, has its own website, is an impressive demonstration of the penetration of ICT amongst accommodation establishments. However, the use of this technology must be based on their business's aims and strategies. The fact that there must be a strict coordination of all e-business activities with business operational and strategic management has not yet become sufficiently widespread. This problem is common particularly amongst SMTEs, that have not recognized the need for a coherent marketing strategy or who do not have the know-how required through their existing human resources.

In recent years, the tourism market has increased hugely in complexity, while at the same time the customer has acquired a new and stronger role that requires a change of paradigm in the understanding of the market. Whilst only a few years ago it was possible to speak of a customer-centric market, today a customer-driven market prevails, in which the consumer has the greatest market power. The development of Web 2.0 applications, such as Tripadvisor and HolidayCheck in the German market (Case 15), empower consumers to share reviews and to assess hotels publicly. In a recent article the Hotels magazine explained that consumer reviews on Tripadvisor are becoming more important that the official star ranking that hotels have. Hence if a hospitality company wishes to maintain its market share in the future, it will have to focus on both the distribution channels and also address the community/networking sites used by potential guests.

Distribution

While many SMTEs only upgraded technologically in the last few years, numerous hotel chains first began using ICTs as early as in the 1970s. In the past, the chain hotel industry identified the need to develop international distribution networks that give both customers and the trade the possibility of carrying out price and vacancy enquiries. The development of computer reservation systems (CRS) and global distribution systems (GDS) brought central reservation offices (CRO) of hotel chains to collaborate with Switch companies such as Pegasus to interconnect systems, display availability and rates and to allow reservations on a global scale (Buhalis, 2000; O'Connor, 1999).

Depending on the type of hotel, ICTs have revolutionized the distribution function. A typical business hotel can use a wide range of distribution channels, namely: direct sales ('walk-in'), the hotel chain's own CROs, its own website, marketing via online and offline travel agencies, online intermediaries, destination management systems (DMS), hotel representation and consortium groups or a GDS (O'Connor and Frew, 2000). Depending on the marketing channel selected, numerous intermediaries can be involved, who are ultimately also responsible for the amount of the marketing costs incurred. In order to serve different markets and address relevant target groups, it is necessary to differentiate in the handling of the individual marketing channels. The InterContinental Hotel group case study (Case 2) shows the significance of brand integrity and price parity as well as the need for coordinated channel management at the group level.

Internal Systems: Property Management System (PMS) and CRS

While larger hotels have implemented comprehensive software solutions in order to manage the inventory, hotel chains use group-wide systems that permit the control of the individual business operation and the management across the hotel chain. The InterContinental Hotel group case study (Case 2) shows in this context how the 'Holidex Plus' solution inter alia optimized capacity and inventory management.

Property management systems (PMS) such as Micros Fidelio Opera are in-house applications that support the central electronic structure of the hotel. They contain all the information about the units of a hotel such as number, price, category and status of rooms whilst managing customer reservations and billing processes. PMSs take on both front office and a number of back-office functions. They administer the booking and reservation processes and are used as an aid to decision-making in management functions through the production of comprehensive reports. The back-office applications include stock management, controlling, book-keeping, financial planning and wage payment. Front office applications simplify and enhance customer contact through customer relationship management and thus contribute to increased service quality. This includes reservations, check-in, room management and customer charging. In addition, PMS can also act as a hub between the different systems of a hotel, bringing all functions under one system (Egger, 2005). The case study of the Sino Group of Hotels (Case 3) shows the advantages that result through the joint use of a central PMS by a number of properties.

Buhalis (2003) identifies the most important functions of a hotel CRS and PMS:

- Improving capacity management and operations efficiency.
- Facilitating central room inventory control.
- Providing last room availability information.

- Offering yield management capability.
- Providing better database access for management purposes.
- Supporting extensive marketing, sales and operational reports.
- Facilitating marketing research and planning.
- Providing travel agency tracking and commission payment.
- Tracking frequent flyers and repeat hotel guests.
- Direct marketing and personalized services for repeat hotel guests.
- Enhancing handling of group bookings and frequent individual travellers (FITs).

External Systems

Direct marketing is often the preferred distribution option, because it is the least expensive and at the same time provides loyal clientele that engage directly with the hotel, rather than whoever happens to be on a distribution channel or cheaper than anyone else. In order to reach the markets needed, however, it is necessary to have access to intermediaries who have a much wider reach to the marketplace via a wide range of channels. In the pre-Internet era the developments in the field of GDS, which originally came from the airline sector, finally made the electronic link-up of CRS possible. From then on, chain hotels were able to participate in the global market by means of GDSs. The electronic marketing channel was gradually extended through the integration of PMS, CRS and GDS. The Switch companies described in further detail in Part Four, ICT Systems, were created in order to ensure interconnectivity and interoperability between the CRS and the GDS. The resulting advantages were reflected in increased efficiency and economy, a simplified controlling system and reduced personnel costs and time spent. The distribution of hotel services via GDS is, however, not without its problems. Firstly, the membership fees charged by the GDS and the costs per booking are too high for small enterprises. At the same time the GDS only permit a limited representation of the hotel and room information and they require considerable maintenance efforts. Figure PI.2 demonstrates the representation of the Bristol Hotel in Salzburg on the Amadeus system.

In the USA, roughly one half of all hotels are marketed online via GDS and CRS, however, this figure is only around 10% in Europe. The reason lies in the structure of the market. As already mentioned, the majority of businesses in Europe are SMTEs. GDS and CRS are ideal for marketing standardized products such as flight tickets or hire cars or large hotel chains that have standardized

```
EXP ** ANR ··· LB ·· VB ··· ·· ·    ···················
···· ·
**** SUMMIT HOTELS & RESORTS ****                    ······
AT  329                          FR 100CT03-130CT03      *SGL*····
 XL*BRISTOL HOTEL                   SZGBRI  D  TAXI  EUR   ····
ENJOY THE WORLDS HIGHEST STANDARDS                    ····
-----------------------SELL INFORMATION-------------------····
  1)128.00          CORPORATE RATE                    ····
   C1TCOR   6S                                        ····
              HTL/BC-A08AOD                            ····
----------------------PRICE INFORMATION-------------------····
      128.00 PER NIGHT STARTING 100CT FOR 3 NIGHTS     ····
      384.00 TOTAL RATE STARTING 100CT FOR 3 NIGHTS    ····
TAXES AND SERVICE CHARGES INCLUDED                    ····
STANDARD SINGLE BEDDED ROOM                           ····
EITHER WITH CITY VIEW OR COURTYARD SIDE               ····
-----------------------LOCATION-LOC------------------------····
BRISTOL HOTEL                                         ····
MAKARTPLATZ 4                                         ····
SALZBURG, AT 5020                                     ····
PROPERTY PHONE: 0662-873557 FAX: 0662-8735576         ····
PROPERTY IS 5 MI NORTHWEST OF SZG AIRPORT             ····
MORE·······················································
>_
```

Figure PI.2 GDS listing of a hotel inquiry
Source: Amadeus

processes and procedures. However, if heterogeneous products such as rooms in European SMTEs are to be marketed, the systems very rapidly reach their limits (O'Connor, 1999). Leaving aside the excessive user charges, SMTEs do not have the brand names that could guarantee the quality of the service. Accordingly, the Internet is much more suited for the presentation of services in the hotel trade.

Hotel websites and those that offer hotel representations are able to display all hotel facilities and provide photographs and texts that reduce the intangibility of the tourism products. In particular, hotel third-party distributors such as hotels.com or booking.com are increasingly seen as reliable intermediaries by consumers. This makes them ideal collaborators with smaller independent hotel properties, as they offer the quality assurance that they lack. It is becoming evident therefore that branded hotels such as Hilton and Intercontinental will be increasingly dependent on their branded websites for their representation and distribution whilst independent properties will rely more on third-party distribution.

The developments in the hotel trade are, unlike in the airline industry, not primarily due to the disintermediation tendencies that helped to save commission fees. On the contrary, they are due to the need to meet the demands of the do-it-yourself bookers while at the same time distinguishing each enterprise from the competition (Egger, 2005). In traditional tourism regions in particular, hotel businesses have been successfully run from generation to generation without there being any need for radical changes in the management. It was only with the triumph of the Internet, giving the customer a completely new role and restructuring the market, that rethinking distribution strategies has become unavoidable. These mostly family-owned enterprises have centralized business structures. The hotel owner is often the manager and decision-maker, and thus the strategic decisions depend on him or her. The extent to which ICTs play an operational or strategically relevant role is determined thus by the awareness and ICT affinity of the decision-maker. In addition, limited financial resources, the lack of major advantages, seasonal dependency and an often short-term management perspective constitute obstacles to the successful path into the new economy (Buhalis & Main, 1998). Buhalis (2003, p. 328) comments

> *SMTEs frequently perceive ICTs as a problem and challenge. [...] They feel that ICTs take away some of their independence, as they have to depend on technology experts for their systems.*

Nevertheless, there are numerous opportunities for SMTEs to use ICTs relatively easily and without major investments. The Hotel Sallerhof study (Case 6) examines the strategies for small hotels in detail and describes how technology can provide competitive advantage through direct distribution. However, even SMTEs such as the Emmantina and Palmyra Beach Hotels (Case 7) need to enter into strategic partnerships in order to be able to be present on the various online channels. Channel management and ensuring brand integrity and price parity are of major importance even for small enterprises.

Rogers' innovation theory becomes obvious when considering SMTEs, since there is hardly any other tourism sector that so clearly reveals differentiated ICT penetration rates as tourism. While a number of innovators have already dedicated themselves to the online market entirely and while the broad mass seems to be adopters, there still remains a residue of deniers for whom the Internet will continue to remain a challenge. In the future, therefore, we can expect hotel businesses to fall into three categories:

1. Enterprises that continue to be present independently and autonomously on the Internet. These enterprises will be exposed to aggressive competition and need to develop strategies to reach their prospective clientele effectively.
2. The third group of businesses will be integrated in international networks and third-party sites. While attention will be attracted by integration in large networks, there is still the risk of losing the capability to control one's own distribution

channel. Hence comprehensive distribution strategies are required to manage their online presence across all channels (Egger, 2005).

3. Those businesses will have to withdraw from the Internet through having neglected their online strategy. These properties will effectively be invisible to the emerging online market.

Increasingly hospitality organisations will realise that their ICT strategy will be critical for their competitiveness and long term prosperity.

References

Buhalis, D. (2000). Information technology in tourism: The state of the art. *Tourism Recreation Research*, 25 (1), 41–58.

Buhalis, D. (2003). *eTourism: Information technology for strategic tourism management*. Pearson: Financial Times/Prentice Hall.

Buhalis, D., & Main, H. (1998). Information Technology in small and medium hospitality enterprises: Strategic analysis and critical factors. *International Journal of Contemporary Hospitality Management*, 10 (5), 198–202.

Camisón, C. (2000). Strategic attitudes and information technologies in the hospitality business: An empirical analysis. In: *Hospitality Management*, Vol. 19, pp. 125–143.

Egger, R. (2005). *Grundlagen des eTourism. Informations- und Kom munikationstechnologien im Tourismus*. Aachen: Shaker Verlag.

Mathies, C., & Weiermair, K. (2003). *Technological change in the accommodation industry – enhancing and constraining factors of IT adaptation*. Biennial Conference: Leisure, Change and Diversity, Sydney.

O'Connor, P. (1999). *Using computers in hospitality*, 2nd edn. London: Cassell.

O'Connor, P., & Frew, A. (2000). Evaluating electronic channels of distribution in the hotel sector: A Delphy study. *Information Technology and Tourism*, 3 (3/4), 177–193.

Case

1

InterContinental Hotel Group: dealing with online intermediaries

Peter O'Connor

Learning Objectives

- Appreciate the opportunities that the Internet brought to hotel chains.
- Identify the challenges of the online marketing environment.
- Explain the issues related to distribution and intermediation for hotels.

Introduction

InterContinental Hotel Group (IHG) is the world's largest hotel company, operating more than 3500 hotels and 538,000 guest rooms in nearly 100 countries. It uses primarily a franchise model, with a portfolio of brands that includes InterContinental, Crowne Plaza, Holiday Inn, Holiday Inn Express, Staybridge Suites and Candlewood Suites. IHG has always been a pioneer in hospitality e-commerce – it was the first to have a CRS, the first to offer booking facilities on the Internet and the first to introduce a loyalty programme – Priority Club Rewards – which is now the world's largest with 22 million members.

Business Model

At the beginning of this century, electronic commerce was having a major effect on how hotels were being distributed. As more consumers moved online, travel had become the most commonly sold online product. However, hotel sales lagged behind those of other travel sectors in the online environment. And those that were occurring were not being made directly, but through online travel agencies – intermediaries that provided one-stop-travel-shopping to the consumer, allowing them to book all their travel needs on a single site.

For online intermediaries, selling hotel rooms was increasingly important. Faced with declining airline commissions, most were putting increased emphasis on the sale of non-air travel products, including hotel rooms. At first they utilized the hotels listed on the GDS – the computerized systems traditionally used by travel agents. However these were not ideal as they were mainly business hotels and not a good fit for the more leisure orientated online systems, and the compensation they earned for selling such rooms was not sufficient. After investing in a connection to the GDS, building an online brand to attract customers, successfully merchandising to make the sale, all they received was the 10% commission traditionally paid to offline travel agents. Under stock market pressure to continue their growth and become profitable, they urgently needed to find a more attractive source of hotel rooms.

Their solution lay in the merchant model – an adaptation of how hotels had traditionally worked with tour operators. Hotels would contract a specified number of rooms each night (known as an allocation) to the intermediary at a highly discount commission free rate (known as a net rate). The latter could then offer these rooms for sale at whatever price they wished to earn a margin. When a room was sold, they pay the hotel the agreed net rate. When they could not fill their allocation, they returned the unsold rooms to the hotel, typically 24 hours before the arrival date and did not have to pay anything. In an unstable economic climate – where hotels were scrambling to fill rooms at any cost – such an arrangement seemed like a win-win situation for both parties. Hotels got access to a powerful new channel of distribution that helped fill rooms that would otherwise have remained empty, and the online intermediaries got access to the hotel rooms they needed and could potentially also make higher margins as they, not the supplier, controlled the retail price. Online intermediaries invested heavily in contracting with hotels, focusing in particular on finding properties more suited to the needs of the leisure traveller.

Contracts were generally negotiated with individual hotels, and tended to be biased heavily in favour of the intermediary. One bone of contention quickly became control over inventory and retail price. The online intermediaries had fixed allocations of rooms, large discounts and control over the retail price. Thus they could undercut hotels' direct prices by accepting a lower margin, or could earn profits by selling their allocation at a premium when the hotel itself was sold out. In addition, they had no risk. If they sold their allocation, they collected their margin. If they failed, they could return rooms for no penalty, leaving the hotel with unsold inventory at the last minute. Hotel companies slowly began to realize that although the merchant model brought benefits in the short run, it also meant that they no longer controlled how and at what price their product was being sold. At the 2004 Berlin Hotel Investment Conference, speakers cited the threat to room rates and profitability posed by third-party booking sites as the biggest single challenge facing the hotel industry.

Online intermediaries were indeed becoming increasingly powerful and capturing a larger share of the online market. Partly this was because they were investing heavily in online marketing. They bid on keywords so that whenever the consumer searched on search engines, they would invariably end up on an online intermediary site. They also started using aggressive retail merchandising techniques to convert these visitors. Many felt that some of these techniques were unethical. For example, some sites add hidden booking fees at the last stage of the purchase process to make their prices look cheaper, promote non-existent discounts, inaccurately list properties as sold-out when they had exhausted their allocation and use 'bait and switch' tactics to lure customers towards higher margin products. When a customer encounters a problem during the booking process, they complain not to the online intermediary, but to the hotel when they arrive, according to Jim Young, senior VP of global distribution for IHG.

Technological and Business Innovation

Contracting directly with individual hotels quickly gave rise to an unanticipated problem – hotel owners questioning the role of the hotel chain. As online intermediaries were capturing an increasing share of the expanding online market, they were delivering increasing numbers of much needed reservations to ailing hotels. One reason owners sign up for a franchise is to give access to the hotel chain's distribution network. However the volume of reservations flowing through chains' CRS was squeezed by external events. Owners began to compare the two and question if it still was good value. Could the expensive brand over the door be replaced by business from the new online players?

As a company, IHG was in a better position than most. Over 70% of its online reservations were being booked directly via its own websites, well above the industry average of 50%. Furthermore, bookings from third-party online intermediaries made up less than 2% of room revenue. However it clearly felt threatened by the growth of these new players and its reaction was sudden and dramatic. In April 2004, it publicized a set of third-party intermediary certification criteria, to which intermediaries had to conform if they wished to sell IHG hotels. These stated that IHG would work only with distributors that agreed to allow the hotel to respond to market fluctuations by varying rate and room allocation without penalty; were able to (or would commit to) connect electronically to their CRS to access up-to-date inventory and rates and deliver reservations electronically; respected IHG's trademarks in the online environment; did not engage in confusing and potentially unclear marketing practices; and clearly presented taxes and fees to the customer. 'These are fundamental issues that we believe need to be addressed in order for us to protect our customers, franchisees and brands', said Peter Gowers, Executive Vice President, Global Brand Services, for IHG.

Almost immediately, IHG announced that it would discontinue its relationship with two of the largest online intermediaries – Expedia.com and Hotels.com – saying they would not agree with the new standards. Both lacked an electronic link to the CRS, instead sending reservations and billing paperwork by fax. IHG also claimed that other Expedia practices were misleading. For example, when Expedia sold out of merchant inventory for a given hotel, they listed that hotel as being sold out, while in fact inventory might still be available on other channels. Similarly IHG claimed that Expedia misled the customer as to the price of the room by not clearly separating taxes and service fees. Referring to Expedia, Seddon said 'We just don't want to be on a shelf that doesn't share our core values.'

Expedia refuted IHG's criticisms. On automation, they claimed that they were actively testing technology to connect to hotels' CRS. Experiments with both Hyatt and Outrigger had been smooth and they expected a wider rollout quickly. On the 'sold out' issue, Expedia claimed that alerting consumers that rooms might be available elsewhere was not their responsibility. 'If a Walmart sells out of Tide, they will put up a sign that says "Sold Out" or they will offer the next best thing,' said Jason Reindorp, an Expedia spokesman. 'Walmart would not put up a sign that says, "Please go to Target to buy more Tide."' On taxes and fees, Expedia feels that customers are aware of booking fees and that 'it is not as high a priority as IHG seems to be making it'.

Expedia and Hotels.com downplayed the significance of the IHG move. 'Hotel chain and online distributor relationships are fluid, strengthening during a tough economy and weakening as downturns appear to end', said Reindorp. 'All of the relationships with our supplier partners are important to us; that said, there won't be a noticeable impact to our consumers. If and when IHG disappears from our sites, we will still have one of the strongest hotel offerings in all major markets for our consumers. I don't want to sound arrogant, but part of our strategy is never to depend on one supplier for a part of our business.'

While IHG's Owners' Association publicly supported the certification process, not all franchisees were happy with the requirement to pull their inventory from the two most popular online travel sites. However, taken together Expedia and Hotels.com only generated about 1% of the company's revenue and IHG felt that it could be easily replaced. At the time of the announcement, hundreds of franchise owners had agreements with Expedia/Hotels.com and each of these needed to be cancelled. To ensure compliance, the company established an escalating set of penalties for those who continued to work with non-certified sites. Initially rogue properties would be removed from IHG's own websites, which delivered significantly more revenues to the majority of hotels than third-party distributors. If they continued to defy company policy, they would be removed from the CRS and GDS, potentially losing up to one third of their revenue. IHG also indicated that it was ultimately willing to drop franchisees that refused to comply. However the company did not expect to impose such drastic sanctions frequently. According to IHG SVP of America's brand performance officer, Tom Seddon:

We've had extraordinary consultation with property owners and wouldn't be going down this path if we hadn't spent a lot of time talking to people.

Key Challenges for the Future

Clearly the key issue for IHG was to replace the business (or potential business) lost from not working with the two most successful online intermediaries. Even before the announcement, the company was taking action to ensure that it could replace those bookings with higher margin ones and reinforce the value of its brand to its hotel owners.

Throughout 2003, IHG invested heavily in its direct websites, implementing state of the art technology to ensure that the online customer experience was second to none. This included incorporating multilingual facilities, content management tools and the use of scalable resources so that increased visitor numbers could be handled without deterioration in response speed. Their sites were also redesigned to be more sales orientated, thus helping to increase the look-to-book ratio and drive more reservations directly. These efforts were helped by the introduction of their introduction of a Best Rate Guarantee. This promised that if a consumer found a lower rate within 24 hours of making a reservation, IHG would honour that rate and give an additional 10% discount. This helped reinforce the impression that the best place to purchase Intercontinental products was directly over the web.

However, to get these efforts to work, they first needed to get consumers to visit. To do this, IHG engaged in the most extensive online marketing campaign ever mounted by a hotel company. They invested heavily in search engine marketing, both optimizing their websites to get good placement in organic search listings and engaging in keyword bidding wars with the online intermediaries. They also experimented with the developing meta-search engines and took legal action against anyone infringing their trademarks in the online environment. Their ultimate aim was to ensure that whenever a consumer searched for an Intercontinental brand, they would end up on a direct, rather than an intermediary, site. They also leveraged their relationship with existing customers, particularly members of their extensive loyalty club, using email marketing techniques to reinforce the benefits of doing business directly with the company.

Despite this focus on driving business directly, IHG also realized the value of working with online intermediaries. According to Andrew Rubinacci, VP of business development at IHG, 'Our strategy is to use third-party Internet sites to extend the reach of our brands and get access to customers we wouldn't otherwise', he said. 'We have seen fantastic partnerships that benefit both parties.' IHG quickly certified several online intermediaries, including Expedia's main competitors Travelocity and Lastminute.com:

> *We think that we'll be properly merchandised and fairly displayed on these sites and are more than happy to work with distributors that bring us more business and more bookings on equitable terms. We are continuing negotiations with other online distributors who wish to work through the critical issues and have the best interests of our customers and hotel owners in mind, and we expect to be able to announce certification of other companies shortly.*

Future of the Company

The big question is whether this fight is over. Will IHG's actions be successful or will they have to bow to franchisee pressure to be more flexible? To date no other hotel company has (publicly at least) followed their lead. Will franchisees defect to brands that allow them to distribute in whatever way they want? Or will Expedia make the changes it needs to become more supplier friendly? 'The economy is improving and as demand returns we will see less room inventory available,' said Henry Harteveldt of Forrester Research.

> *The product that gives the lowest margin will be the first to go. The third-party channel needs to realize that hotel companies are getting stronger and will not be bullied anymore.*

But other analysts point out that the industry works in cycles. What will happen next time the industry takes a dive and hotel companies are left with a mass of empty rooms to sell?

Key Conclusions

- Brand integrity and price parity are important for a comprehensive marketing strategy.
- Selecting third-party distributors should contribute to the overall strategy.
- Hotel chains increasingly aim to increase their direct sales.
- It seems that third-party distributors will be primarily used by non-branded hotels.

Review and Discussion Questions

- How can hotel chains select their distribution partners?
- What are the qualities that a hotel chain should look for when selecting distribution partners?
- How can hotel chains increase their direct sales?
- Identify the costs and benefits of direct distribution versus third-party distribution.

Further Reading

Anderson, S. (2003). *Online Hotel Sales and Third Parties: A Review and Analysis*. Retrieved from http://www.hsmai.org/docs/Online_Hotel_Sales_and_3rd_Parties.pdf.

Carroll, B., & Siguaw, J. (2003). The evolution of electronic distribution. *Cornell Hotel and Restaurant Administration Quarterly*, August, 38–47.

Company's website: www.ichotelsgroup.com.

Estis Green, C. (2005). *De-mystifying distribution: Building a distribution strategy one channel at a time*. McLean, VA: Hospitality Sales & Marketing Association International.

Helsel, C., & Cullen, K. (2005). *Hotel distribution nirvana: A multi-channel approach.* HEDNA 2005 White Paper Series, HEDNA, Falls Church, VA.

O'Connor, P., & Piccoli, G. (2003). Marketing using global distribution systems revisited. *Cornell Hotel Administration Quarterly*, 44 (5 & 6), 105–114.

Case

2

InterContinental Hotel Group: managing inventory with HOLIDEX PLUS

Rosanna Leung and Rob Law

Learning Objectives

- Demonstrate technological innovation within the hotel chain environment.
- Appreciate the use of computer reservation systems within hotel chains.
- Explain how interactive property management systems can improve efficiency.

Introduction

Holiday Inn was firstly founded by Kemmons Wilson in Memphis, Tennessee in 1952 with an initial aim to serve the travel needs of US families. In 1988 InterContinental Hotel Group (formerly called Bass Hotels and Resorts) acquired the Holiday Inn chain and since then it has become one of the largest hotel chains in the world (InterContinental Hotels Group Plc, 2005). InterContinental Hotel Group (IHG) has been further developed and it currently has seven brand names, including InterContinental Hotels and Resort, Crowne Plaza Hotel and Resort, Hotel Indigo, Holiday Inn Hotels, Holiday Inn Express, Staybridge Suites and Candlewood Suites. At present, the group has more than 3600 hotels, and over 539,000 guest rooms in more than 100 countries. In 2005, there were more than 27 million Priority Club members over the world. In general, these Club members make high-yield rate reservations (50% higher than the customers through travel agent), and normally generate 30% of the room revenue. IHG assigns highest priority to these members in order to encourage them to visit the group's hotels repeatedly. According to the group's strategic plan, by end of 2008, there should be 588–598 more properties and with 50,000–60,000 additional guest rooms as compared to 2005. In Mainland China alone, there will be about 125 hotels with 30 of them being InterContinental Hotels.

Main Products

With the large growth of the hotel group, a comprehensive reservation network is one of the key factors to the success of the group. To cater for such a need, HOLIDEX, a computer reservation system (CRS) was developed, which was also the first CRS in the hospitality industry. Originally, HOLIDEX was developed as an internal central reservation office (CRO). During the operation, when customers want to make reservations to any Holiday Inn hotels in the world, they can simply make a toll-free phone call to the CRO or to any IHG Hotels for inquiry. Reservation staff can access the IHG Hotels' room inventory to check for the availability of the requested rooms and can also make reservations via the system. After HOLIDEX has been launched, many hotel chains attempted to follow a similar approach by developing their own CRSs. Examples of these CRSs include the SPIRIT of Hyatt and CRS of Marriott. Through the CRSs, management executives can easily get the necessary information to prepare for the inventory and rate strategies.

Originally, HOLIDEX was used as a stand-alone system, and each hotel had its own property management system (PMS). However, there was no communication between the two systems. A dedicated HOLIDEX operator had to manually retrieve and update information inside HOLIDEX and PMS separately. This method was not only time consuming but could also introduce human error. With the rapid development of the Internet, customers and travel agents can now make use this system to make air-ticket and hotel reservations. In order to cater for this demand, HOLIDEX was further developed on its interface, so that GDSs were able to have a direct link. This enhances its marketing channel potential and minimizes human interaction and potential for error.

Business Model

Having been in the hospitality industry for more than 50 years, IHG has played an important role in this industry. Prior to the group's decision to develop the Asian market, the Holiday Inn brand mainly focused on the mid-scale clientele in North America. At that time, hotels were generally small with very limited service provision. In mid-1970s, the group started to expand their business to the Asian market and started changing their focus to the up-scale market. At present, customers can easily find an IHG hotel in most of their destinations, and they generally understand the IHG's service standard. As such, they can have a realistic expectation of the service that they will receive. With the launch of Holiday Express in 1991 and the completed acquisition of InterContinental in 1998, the group has developed a wide range of brand names that offer various choices to meet different customer needs.

IHG has more than 3600 hotels in over 100 countries. Hence, the group needs to have an efficient marketing network and business partners to fill up the hotel rooms. Since travel agencies are the first contact point for customers, it is necessary to provide a convenient way for the agencies to make reservations. To achieve this goal, a data exchange between HOLIDEX and the systems of the travel agencies was built. With the increasing popularity of the Internet, electronic data interchange (EDI) between different systems can now break the geographical barriers. This, in turn, enables customers to easily get in touch with IHG through different channels (e.g. websites, GDS and Hotels) (Figure 2.1). Online travel agents, such as Travelocity and Priceline.com also connect directly their system with HOLIDEX. When customers are accessing these websites, they can obtain the latest room availability and rate information. Besides,

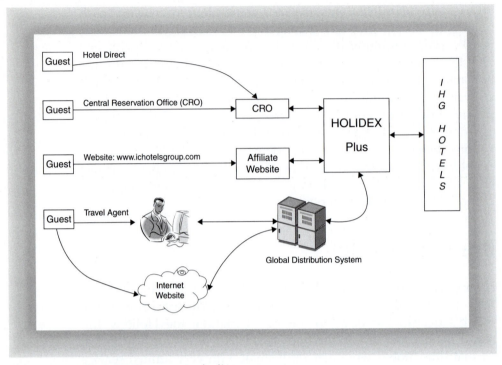

Figure 2.1 HOLIDEX Plus network diagram

all bookings through these online travel agents will be directly sent to HOLIDEX and transferred to individual hotel's PMS without any human interaction.

Technological and Business Innovation

Currently, each IHG property has a communication point that is connected to the head office in Memphis. The connection may go through a dedicated lease line, multiprotocol label switch (MPLS), virtual private network (VPN), or even using satellites for remote properties. In particular, HOLIDEX has three modes of operation, including a stand-alone mode, a one-way interface and a two-way interface. The stand-alone mode is mainly used by small-size hotels that have limited incoming reservations from the CRO and the Internet, and the interface with HOLIDEX to PMS is not available. The one-way interface was launched in late 1980s but it was only limited to one dedicated PMS called ENCORE. In this mode, only the reservations received from HOLIDEX were automatically updated to the PMS, but information from PMS needed to be manually updated to HOLIDEX when necessary.

After years of operation, and with the rapid development of the Internet, a new version of HOLIDEX, called 'HOLIDEX Plus', was launched in 2002. HOLIDEX Plus hosts more than the information of 3200 hotels on a single platform. Additionally, it does not only provide room reservations through the hotel Intranet but also allows external participants such as travel agencies, GDS suppliers, wholesalers and individual customers to make bookings via this system. This latest version of the system provides a two-way interface between HOLIDEX Plus and the selected PMS – Opera, so that reservation information can be directly transferred to the individual hotel's PMS without any human interaction.

The new version of HOLIDEX does not need to be run on any dedicated computers. The system can be operated on any PC inside a hotel that has Internet connection. Each PMS user can now access HOLIDEX through any PC workstation, and there is no need to queue in front of the HOLIDEX terminal. Moreover, HOLIDEX Plus provides more detailed description of IHG properties, room rates and promotions to GDSs and travel websites. In addition, the system enables individual hotels to design their own rates and packages the display sequence in order to target different customers' needs. The new version also integrates with IHC's own yield management system called Holiday Inn Reservation Optimizer (HIRO). HIRO calculates the hurdle rate for different marketing segments based on historical data. Moreover, it enables hotels to set up various levels of privileges to different customers. During the busy trade fair period, for example, high paying customers will not be booked out by low profit clients. This, in turn, can maintain a good relationship with valuable guests and increase a hotel's yield.

Before HOLIDEX was interfaced with GDSs, hotel managers usually needed to stop accepting reservations from websites and GDSs to prevent overbooking during peak seasons. Such a policy, however, may result in having unoccupied rooms. With the interface between HOLIDEX Plus, hotel websites and PMS, hotel managers can easily control the room inventory so that the last available room can be sold through a website or GDS. HIRO also automatically rejects any reservation that is below the hurdle rate booked from GDS and in order to maximize the yield.

Key Challenges for the Future

The design of HOLIDEX is similar to an airline's CRS system. Therefore, most of the system operations were in text commands.

Operators had to memorize numerous system commands, and it required more time and resources on training. In this way, the information provided on screen was often limited, and operators had to interpret technical codes. Besides, HOLIDEX was only available in English, and operators in the non-English speaking countries may have had difficulties when inputting their correspondence. Such a limitation in natural language required further modifications of the system. As an example, double-byte characters like Chinese and Japanese are a natural extension of the ongoing improvement.

Future of the Company

Competition between hotels is vigorous, and the hotels' primary goal is to increase profit. In order to do so, a hotel must maximize each guest room's yield. Since corporate customers can generate higher yield than travel agents, IHG is developing an Extranet for their corporate customers. Each corporate business will have its own user ID and password, and the corporate members can retrieve their own special room rates from a specific website. These members can easily create and amend reservations through the website. Also, hotels can reduce the amount of commissions paid to travel agencies. With the implementation of promotional rates inside the IHG website, customers can be attracted to make reservations directly rather than going through GDSs and travel agencies. For this reason, the commission paid to intermediaries can be saved. To conclude, with the continuous popularity of the Internet, travellers can interact better with hotels generating more business opportunities.

Key Conclusions

- Integrated PMS such as the Micros-Fidelio Opera allow integrated management of properties and better control.
- Integrated systems should be used for customer relationship management (CRM) and improvements in service.
- Interoperability with GDSs and third-party distributors can enhance operational benefits.

Review and Discussion Questions

- Discuss how hotel chains can use technology to integrate their management across properties.
- How can technology enhance the operational efficiency of hotels?
- How can hotel chains improve their third-party distribution using technology?

References and Further Reading

Buhalis, D. (2003). *eTourism: Information technology for strategic tourism management*. NY: Financial Times/Prentice Hall.

InterContinental Hotels Group PLC (2005). *InterContinental Hotels Group PLC – About Us – Our History*. Retrieved 20 December 2005 from http://www.ihgplc.com/aboutus/history.asp.

InterContinental Hotels Group (2006). *InterContinental Hotels Group Hotel Reservations – The Official Web Site*. Retrieved 19 February 2006 from http://www.ichotelsgroup.com/h/d/6c/1/en/home.

O'Connor, P., & Frew, A.J. (2002). The future of hotel electronic distribution: Expert and industry perspectives. *Cornell Hotel and Restaurant Administration Quarterly*, 43 (3), 33–45.

Tesone, D.V. (2006). *Hospitality information systems and e-commerce*. NJ: John Wiley & Sons.

Company's website: http://www.ichotelsgroup.com.

3

Sino Group of Hotels: handling multi-property operations

Rosanna Leung and Rob Law

Learning Objectives

- Demonstrate how the Sino Group of Hotels, one of the largest hotel chains and publicly listed companies in Hong Kong, deals with ICTs.
- Illustrate how the Enterprise Version PMS assists Sino to handle multi-property operations.
- Explain how the implementation of the Micros-Fidelio Opera Enterprise Version allowed all four Hong Kong hotels to share one single database so that all customer and corporate information can be centralized and shared among different properties.

Introduction

As one of the largest hotel chains and publicly listed companies in Hong Kong, the Sino Group of Hotels (hereafter named as Sino Hotels) comprises four hotels, a Yacht & Country club in Hong Kong and one deluxe hotel in Singapore. The chain contains a full-range of hotel categories including a 3-star business hotel – Island Pacific Hotel (IP), a 4-star business hotel – City Garden Hotel (CG), two 5-star business hotels – The Royal Pacific Hotel & Towers (RP) and The Fullerton Hotel in Singapore, and a 5-star Resort Hotel – Gold Coast Hotel (GCH). In total, these hotels have 2370 guest rooms, and 22 restaurants and bars (Table 3.1). The Group's first hotel in Hong Kong was RP, opened in 1988. Sino Hotels are also affiliated with Sino Land Company Limited in Hong Kong and the Far East Organization in Singapore, which owns and operates five other hotels in Singapore and a list of commercial and residential properties (Sino Group of Hotels, 2005).

Table 3.1 List of Sino Group of hotels

	Categories	No. of rooms	No. of outlets
Island Pacific Hotel	3-star business	343	2
City Garden Hotel	4-star business	613	5
The Royal Pacific Hotel & Towers	5-star business	674	2
The Fullerton Hotel	5-star business	400	5
Hong Kong Gold Coast Hotel	Leisure Resort	340	4
Gold Coast Yacht & Country Club	Club	–	4
Total		2370	22

Source: Sino Group of hotels (2005)

Key Product and Business Model

Sino Hotels aim to provide a full range of hotel accommodation to cater for different customer needs. RP is located in the centre of the Hong Kong commercial area that provides a very convenient location for both business and leisure guests. Similarly, CG and IP are located in easy-access regions in Hong Kong Island, where customers can easily reach the city centre within 5–10 minutes by cars.

GCH is the only 5-star resort hotel and convention centre in Hong Kong that provides both sun-and-beach environments, and comprehensive meeting facilities for corporate companies to organize their conferences and meetings. Whether guests are coming for business or vacation, looking for deluxe or budget hotels, planning to stay in hotels that are in the city centre or remote area, Sino Hotels are able to provide a choice to fit their requirements.

In 2003, the Hong Kong government implemented the Individual Visit Scheme to residents living in Guangdong Province and 17 other cities in Mainland China. Since then, residents in these regions can travel to Hong Kong independently without the need to join a group tour. As these travellers can freely travel to Hong Kong, the demand for accommodation has thus significantly increased during weekend. Based on official data (Hong Kong Tourism Board, 2005), the total number of visitors increased from 15.5 million in 2003 to 21.8 million in 2004, representing a 40.4% increase. The corresponding figure in 2005 was 23.3 million, which shows a further 50.3% increase. Among the visitors to Hong Kong, about 53.6% were from China. Based on the financial reports of Sino Hotels, in 2002/2003, their annual turnover and net profit were HK$112 million and HK$34 million respectively (HK$7.8 = US$1). In 2003/2004 and 2004/2005, there was a significant increase of net profit to HK$96 and HK$112 million respectively, representing 182% and 229% increase compared with 2002/2003. Table 3.2 shows the 5-year financial summary performance of Sino Hotels.

Tourists to Mainland China result in a high demand for budget hotels but within Sino Hotels, only IP provides budget accommodation. In the period 2004–2005, only a few new budget hotels were opened (excluding guest houses). The more new hotels open up, the stronger the competition becomes. However, most of Sino Hotels' properties have been in business for more than 10 years. To remain

Table 3.2 5-year financial summary performance of Sino Hotels

Year	Turnover (millions)	%	Net profit (millions)	%
2000/2001	154	0.0	38	0.0
2001/2002	126	+18.8	39	+2.6
2002/2003	112	−11.1	34	−12.8
2003/2004	136	+21.4	96	+182.4
2004/2005	163	+19.8	112	+16.7

Source: Sino Group of Hotels (2005) 5 years consolidated financial summary

competitive, Sino Hotels decided to implement the latest technology to assistant their hotels for better service provision. The group firstly implemented Opera Enterprise Version Property Management System in 2005, which enables staff to handle multi-properties operation. Using this system, hotel managers can retrieve customers' reservation history in order to customize the services for individual guests.

Technological and Business Innovation

Enterprise Version PMS is primarily designed for handling multi-property operations. The system provides general PMS functions, and it also enables staff in each hotel to gain access to other properties. Authorized staff can access each property's room inventory and guest history profile. When an individual hotel is running out of rooms, reservation staff can immediately check sister hotels' room availability and provide recommendations to customers. This can help prevent business leaking to competitors. Moreover, the reservation history of customers in each hotel can be consolidated into one single guest profile so that hotel staff can easily identify repeat guests in the group.

In addition, the Sino Hotels group was the first one in Hong Kong to implement the Micros-Fidelio Opera Enterprise Version as their PMS. This version allows all four Hong Kong hotels sharing one single database so that all customer and corporate information can be centralized and shared among different properties. Before the implementation of the Enterprise Version, hotels had different PMS systems that ran independently. As a result, when one hotel was full, reservation staff could not cross-sell sister hotels' rooms. Moreover, a VIP guest of the RP could only be treated as an ordinary customer when visiting the GCH. This might upset the guest as a VIP level of service is expected. In the new environment, whenever customers call up for hotel reservations, staff can immediately retrieve their profile that was stored inside the system. Their personal preferences and special requirements are automatically copied to new reservations. Such an approach can help the group to keep their repeating customers. Moreover, from the centralized customer database, the Marketing Department can easily identify the top spending customers and corporate accounts, and then sent out promotional materials to these target customers. Staff can also provide selection criteria and the system will retrieve the data that matches with the criteria. The advantage of using a single customer database is to eliminate duplication of promotional messages to customers, and thus to increase the response rate.

Key Challenges for the Future

In Hong Kong, the major network infrastructure for Sino Hotels is mainly located at RP, and other hotels use high-speed dedicated leased-lines to access the server in RP. To prevent communication line failure, each hotel has installed a spare communication line provided by a separate Internet Service Provider so that the communication between RP and other hotels can be up and running without interruption. Currently the whole network consists of three database servers, four application servers, four interface servers and two web servers. Among the three database servers, two of them act as backup servers. Data inside the database server are mirrored to the other two backup servers so that if any of the two servers failed, the remaining one is still available for providing service without interruption. The four application servers are located in different hotels so that if any of the servers are down, there are still three servers functioning. This ensures effective and efficient system performance to all hotels.

Although the Enterprise Version PMS provides comprehensive functions for reservation staff to make multi-property bookings, Sino Hotels' staff sometimes have difficulties when cross-selling. Such difficulties are largely due to the different location and service standard of different hotels. For instance, the hotel staff cannot recommend customers to stay in the 3-star IP if they want to book the 5-star RP. Since the functionality of the reservation department in each hotel is similar, it is recommended that Sino Hotels should form a central reservation office (CRO) to simplify the organizational structure. Customers can then simply call the CRO on one single telephone number and the CRO will be able to make reservations for any properties of the Sino Hotels.

Future of the Company

All four properties of the Sino Hotels have their own websites that provide online booking facilities. The group is currently working on the interface between the web booking engine and PMS. When this function is implemented, individual hotels will have full control on promotional room rates and room inventory in each rate category. Moreover, hotels also work with a series of GDS such as

Expedia, Travelocity and Zuji to promote their rooms. However, GDSs' booking engines does not have any interface with their PMS system. If the GDS is running out of their room inventory (allotments), customers will not be able to make reservations even though rooms are still available. Moreover, all bookings through GDS have to be manually input into the PMS. To reduce laborious effort, hotels should develop an interface with different GDS systems to minimize manual work and maximize room production.

Sino Hotels can also further expand their PMS system so that not only the hotels in Hong Kong are networked together but hotels in Singapore can also be linked up. It would be a good start to build up the company's own hotel reservation network and CRO. Besides, they can also carry out cross-selling in both regions.

The company realises that technology is critical for their operations and strategy.

Key Conclusions

- The Micros-Fidelio Opera Enterprise Version supports cross-selling of sister hotels' rooms and benefits profitability.
- Effective CRM which acknowledges personal preferences and special requirements can support direct marketing and profitability.
- To improve labour efficiency, hotels should develop an interface with different GDS systems so as to minimize manual work and maximize room production.

Review and Discussion Questions

- Who are the key stakeholders for Sino hotels and how are they served by ICTs?
- What are the key success factors for the use of ICTs in Sino hotels?
- How can Sino hotels improve interoperability with partners?

References and Further Reading

Ham, S., Kim, W.G., & Jeong, S. (2005). Effect of information technology on performance in upscale hotels. *International Journal of Hospitality Management*, 24 (3), 281–294.

Hong Kong Tourism Board (2005). *Hong Kong Tourism Board – PartnerNet*. Retrieved 17 January 2006 from http://www.partner-net.hktb.com/pnweb/jsp/comm/index.jsp?pageContent=%2Fjsp%2Frso%2Frso_pub.jsp&charset=en.

Kasavana, M.L., & Brooks, R.M. (2005). *Managing front office operations*. Mich: Educational Institute of the American Hotel & Lodging Association.

O'Connor, P. (2004). *Using computers in hospitality*. London: Thomson.

Sino Group of Hotels (2005). *Sino Group of Hotels: Welcome Page*. Retrieved 19 January 2006 from http://www.sino-hotels.com.

Sino Group. (2005). *Sino Group Investors' Information>Financial Reports>Sino Land Company Limited>2004*. Retrieved 15 January 2006 from http://www.sino-land.com/eng/main.asp?xid=corpinfo_fr_sl_0405#n.

Company's website: http://www.sino-hotels.com.

4

Omena Hotels: technology towards operational efficiency

Bill Anckar

Learning Objectives

- Demonstrate how technology can reduce operational costs and prices.
- Illustrate and challenge all operational practices in hotels.
- Explain how ICT and e-commerce can be instrumental in developing new business models.

Introduction and Company Background

While the hotel sector has reached a stage of development in which a few major chains have come to dominate the international market, the Internet has in many ways fulfilled its early promise of bringing unprecedented opportunities for small and medium-sized hospitality organizations to improve their competitive position and global visibility (Sheldon, 1997; Buhalis & Main, 1998; Werthner & Klein, 1999).

From a historical perspective, many players in the travel industry have been forerunners in the field of information communication Technology (ICT). In spite of that, the information systems and technologies used in the hospitality industry have, as a rule, been constructed merely to support or extend – but never to replace – the existing, conventional business models. The traditional services and functions continue to exist abreast with the new technological solutions, and the business models tend to remain relatively unchanged after the implementation of new technologies and systems. The Internet is thus typically seen by suppliers as merely an alternative marketing channel, and e-commerce is used primarily to broaden the market share (by making the products available to more people), to enhance the efficiency of a particular business process, and/or to cut distribution costs and reduce the over-dependency upon intermediaries for promoting and distributing the products. However, with continuing technological advances, the progress to the next generation of online services, and increasingly positive attitudes among consumers towards e-commerce, companies have learned to embrace ICT and the Internet in search of new business opportunities and competitive advantages. As a result, even the rather conservative accommodation sector has witnessed the emergence of new and innovative business models.

This case portrays the unique and novel accommodation concept and business model launched by Omena Hotels (Omena = Finnish for 'apple'), a new Finnish premium budget class hotel chain which challenges the traditional service concept and revenue models used by most other players in the field by fully exploiting the Internet and other forms of information and communication technologies (ICT) in its operations. The innovative, ICT-based concept allows the hotels to be operated without on-site reception desks and reception personnel.

Originally a joint effort by the current owner, Ab R. Grönblom International Ltd (RGI), and a major Finnish hotel chain, Omena Hotels Ltd was founded already in the early 1990s, but all plans and projects were terminated at the onset of the recession only a few years later. In 1999, the Omena project was reactivated by RGI, spurred by (i) recent market studies indicating an increasing demand for budget accommodation and (ii) the proliferation of the Internet and e-commerce, which offered entirely new opportunities for cost savings.

The first authentic Omena Hotel was opened in October 2003 in Tampere, Finland. Now, 3 years later, the company operates four hotels, with three more units to be opened in the next few months, and contracts for several new hotels currently being finalized. The company's aim is to expand into the 20 largest cities in Finland by the year 2012 (with a market share of 3–4%), and to start an international expansion (initially into selected Scandinavian, Russian and Baltic cities) from the year 2008 onwards.

The Offering

The basic idea in Omena's business concept and the main promise of the company is to offer travellers high standard hotel accommodation at prime locations – in city centres – at a truly affordable rate. High class yet inexpensive prices seems like an impossible equation, but Omena's unconventional business model excels in cost-efficiency by concentrating fully on the core product of hotel operations – a room for the night – without expensive built-in auxiliary services. The hotels are always situated in the absolute city centre, within the vicinity of shops, services, activities and good transport connections, meaning that the services the hotel does not offer can be found right outside the hotel.

The business concept builds on the comprehension that the traveller's motives and interests can be found outside the hotel. The appeal of travelling and staying in hotels has decreased significantly, and most guests come to city centre hotels just to sleep and shower. The typical city hotel guest – who travels frequently and with tight schedules – doesn't need sauna/pool departments, hotel restaurants, conference facilities, etc., but the guest rooms need to be well equipped and high-class.

At the Omena hotels, all guest rooms are similar in terms of size, amenities and interior design. The rooms are equipped with a toilet, shower, large TV, wireless keyboard, refrigerator, microwave oven, tea/coffee maker, double bed, bed sofa, a dinner table for four and high-speed Internet connection. Maximum occupancy per room is four persons, and the room rate is the same irrespective of the number of guests staying in the room.

The entire booking/payment/cancellation process is handled by the customer himself on the Internet. Having made a valid advance payment (using secure online banking/credit card payment solutions), the customer receives an electronic booking confirmation which shows the room number and the key to the room – a 5-digit numerical personal door code that is valid throughout the stay. Since all reservations have been paid for and the keys delivered electronically in advance, there is no need for check-in or check-out procedures such as handing over keys or charging the customer. Consequently, all the Omena hotels operate without on-site reception desks and reception personnel. The entrance and the hallways are monitored by recording surveillance cameras, and only guests with a valid door code can enter the premises. In problem situations, the hotel guests can contact the hotel chain's remote reception (open 24 hours) through the TV or by phone. The entrances are equipped with booking kiosks for walk-in customers.

The new hotel concept by Omena has turned out to be appealing to travellers within almost all customer segments, except for elderly people and travellers that look for extravagance or a high service level. The Omena hotels represent a natural – and very inexpensive – choice especially for (leisure) travellers that are willing to share the room with friends or relatives; young people, sports clubs/teams and other non-profit associations, and families with children. According to a number of studies, the Finns spend 3–4 nights in the homes of friends and relatives (for free) for each night spent in a registered accommodation facility. Accordingly, Omena wants to attract new customer segments to the convenience of hotel accommodation by offering the huge untapped market of leisure travellers a high quality, yet affordable alternative to the guest bed at their friends' or relatives' place.

In spite of the apparent suitability of Omena's concept for the leisure travel segment, the business travellers represent, interestingly, a surprisingly high percentage of all guests, and a rapidly growing number of companies are signing key customer agreements with the hotel chain.

The Business Model

Omena represents not only a new and innovative accommodation concept, but also an entirely new hotel category as it combines low budget lodging with high standard hotel rooms and first class (expensive) locations in the absolute city centre. The company has been a forerunner in terms of ICT and e-commerce by introducing an entirely new – and unique – business model: the inexpensive rates are largely a result of the radical cost cutting achieved by truly maximizing the use of ICT and the Internet in the operations. Most traditional/routine work tasks have been arranged according to self-service principles or fully automated using ICT, and hence the company is, to a certain extent, managed by its customers and by computerized systems.

The business model of Omena Hotels marks originality also when observing the company's organizational structure: Omena has only one full-time employee – the managing director. Instead, the company draws on a rather extreme outsourcing strategy, relying on a large network of partners to handle – rather independently – key tasks such as housekeeping (cleaning and maintenance), customer service, security, system monitoring, server hosting, marketing, project management relating to opening new hotels (architect and engineering firms), etc.

The key value proposition of Omena Hotels relates to:

- The provision of real-time information on availability and rates to all online customers at all times.
- Instant gratification: bookings can be made, paid, modified and cancelled online at all times.
- High quality of technological solutions, including content and applications online and in the hotels.
- Simplicity of lodging: no check-in/check-out procedures and no physical keys.
- Unbundled products and transparent pricing: the customers do not have to pay for any auxiliary services that they do not use.
- A superior price/quality ratio.
- Excellent locations in the absolute centre of major cities.

The novel business model of Omena Hotels offers numerous advantages and efficiencies in comparison to the highly traditional business model used by most conventional hotel chains, which often have relatively complex, non-standardized concepts that are hard and expensive to manage and change. The outcome is an extremely cost-efficient hotel chain with the major strengths and competitive advantages listed below. Omena Hotels may, in part, be doing to the hotel industry what Swatch and Ikea did to their industries: i.e. introducing entirely new business models, and in doing this, changing or redefining established industry standards.

- *Easily expandable*: Almost any vacant facilities in city centre can be transformed into Omena hotels as there is no need for infrastructures relating to supplementary hotel services (restaurants, lobbies, reception desks, saunas, etc.). The hotels can, for instance, be operated in multi-function/-user buildings.

- Very small units are seen as fully acceptable and equally profitable due to low fixed costs, meaning that (i) suitable premises are easier to find and (ii) profitable hotels can be established even in small cities.
- *Uniformity*: A standardized and uncompromising concept and a rigid business model: All functions have been tailor-made to support the automation and the far-taken standardization; all units are vigorously managed to follow the same theme, producing cost-efficiency, speed, predictability, and consistent standards of quality and finish.
- Low planning and investment costs per unit due to highly standardized solutions.
- *Rapid expansion and fast launch of hotel operations*: Almost any existing building can be converted into an Omena hotel in a short time period as a result of the high level of standardization.
- *Easily adjustable concept and policies*: Omena's automated business concept allows for chain-wide simultaneous changes (system updates) to be made with minimum effort, delays and costs.
- *Light organization and automated solutions*: Low administration costs, no human resource problems.
- *Inexpensive distribution strategy*: No parallel systems, but instead full focus on electronic distribution channels. No commissions to intermediaries (or middlemen's commissions paid by the customer).
- Tailor-made, modern (proprietary) information systems and a convenient booking process.
- The concept is attractive for the untapped market segments.
- *It is 'recession-proof'*: Budget hotels are typically not affected by economic downswings to the same extent as more expensive alternatives.

In spite of the rapidly expanding use of computers and ICT in hotel operations in general, no other hotel businesses can be found – even on a global scale – in which new technologies would be utilized to the extent that the business model itself could be considered to be essentially based on ICT. When seen as an entirety, Omena's business model is unique. No identical concepts can be found in Finland or even the international marketplace, although some international chains operate hotels using business models sharing some similarities. Yet, these hotels tend not to utilize ICT to nearly the same extent as Omena Hotels.

Technological and Business Innovation

ICT and e-commerce were seen as the corner stone in the business model of Omena Hotels from day one onwards. The main driving factor in Omena's chosen strategy and business model was that a company is unable to exploit, in full, the many potential benefits electronic channels and ICT can offer both sellers and buyers by using new technologies just to support, or as an extension of, existing processes and operations.

Although many big players in the traditional marketplace have been able to attain a dominant position in the electronic marketplace as well – thanks to their established reputation and sufficient financial resources – such a phenomenon reflects the insecurity and lack of trust among online customers in the early phases of e-commerce rather than superiority in terms of online value creation.

Optimizing the special advantages offered by ICT and e-commerce requires, as a rule, pure e-business models and a lack of restraints set by existing bricks-and-mortar operations. For Omena Hotels, this meant focusing almost exclusively on electronic sales channels, thus not actively promoting alternative (traditional) channels such as out-sourced call centres. This strategic decision displays a conviction that a new wave of technological adoption has started, and that the steady growth that has been seen across all segments of the online travel market in the recent years will continue, and even increase. Especially when booking low-complexity travel products such as hotel rooms, the Internet – fixed or mobile – is seen as a convenient and useful tool by an increasing number of business and leisure travellers.

The core product offered by Omena Hotels is not, as such, new or innovative. The hotel rooms are fully comparable to any traditional hotel room, and the limited supplementary services offered are rather conventional. Instead, Omena represents a good example of a company that has pursued and achieved value innovation, which is characterized by making the competition irrelevant by creating uncontested market space, not by beating the competition within the confines of the existing industry (Kim & Mauborgne, 2005). Accordingly, Omena Hotels aims at creating 'blue oceans' of uncontested market space by (i) eliminating factors that the industry has taken for granted, but that adds no perceived value to customers; (ii) by creating new sources of value that the industry has never offered; (iii) by breaking the value-cost tradeoff (seeking greater value to customers and low cost simultaneously) and (iv) creating and capturing new demand rather than exploiting existing demand (Kim & Mauborgne, 2005). All functions – even minor details in Omena's business concept – are vigorously managed towards this end.

Omena has also successfully capitalized on modern technology to accomplish its goals in terms of automation. With a business model which fundamentally draws on ICT, the issues relating to system selection, design and integration are of crucial importance for the company, especially since the technological requirements of Omena Hotels are very different from those of traditional hotels, and since the company has ambitious growth plans. Consequently, Omena uses a proprietary reservation and hotel management system which the company has designed and built from scratch in order to generate a solution that is tailor-made for its exceptional business model, taking into consideration, among other things, the following special demands:

- Automated communication with (i) the interactive TV (info, communication and entertainment) system, (ii) a large number of online payment systems (banks, credit card institutions) and (iii) the passage control system.
- A user-friendly online booking interface that (i) supports the provision of real-time information in terms of rates and room availability, (ii) supports the business model lacking on-site receptions and (iii) allows all reservations to be made and administered on the Internet (both by customers and the personnel).
- Full automation of many management functions and tasks relating to service and maintenance. High flexibility in terms of continued system development/modifications: to make it easily extendable.

The Future of the Company

Omena Hotels Ltd demonstrates a great potential for substantial growth and profitability in the next few years. The budget hotels constitute the growth driver in the European hotel industry today, and with good partners the company can turn its competitive advantages into a major financial success. The fact that the concept is working and accepted by the market has been shown not only by the high, and growing, sales figures, but also by an online consumer survey conducted already in 2004 among current and prospective customers of Omena. The objective of the survey, which was completed by 2728 respondents, was to evaluate whether and how well the new accommodation concept satisfies the needs and wants of today's Finnish hotel guests, and to find out how Omena Hotels should market, extend or revise its concept and the services offered. Overall, the findings indicated that the product offered by the company is in line with what the customers look for in a hotel. The value-adding elements highlighted in Omena's business model are indeed perceived as rewarding, and at the same time the market indicated a surprisingly high tolerance with the issues expected to make people sceptical towards and hesitant about the concept (such as the lack of on-site receptions and personnel). Somewhat surprisingly, both business and leisure travellers found the concept appealing. An overwhelming majority of the respondents had been attracted by the low room rates. Of those who had stayed at an Omena hotel, 92.5% responded that they definitely or likely will return, and only 1.4% said 'unlikely or definitely not'. Of those who had stayed at the hotel, 89.9% stated that they would recommend it to their friends.

Introducing an entirely new concept in a highly conservative sector involves, however, not only opportunities, but also considerable risks. As a new, privately owned hotel chain and a start-up company, Omena Hotels has faced major challenges during the first years of operation, and the future certainly holds further significant risks.

The company's operations in Finland are expected to generate a turnover of approximately €5.5 million in 2007, with turnover growing at significant rates in the next few years. For Omena Hotels, the real growth opportunities can, however, be found outside Finland's borders. Accordingly, the company aims at starting an ambitious expansion abroad (initially into the nearby markets) from 2008 onwards. In order to reap significant – and important – first mover advantages, the hotel chain should expand rapidly in the next few years, but as for any start-up company, the considerable investment cost which directly affect the free cash flow constitute a critical issue in the growth strategy. Although the existing Omena hotels have reached their break-even occupancy rates surprisingly fast, any hotel is unlikely to be profitable right from the start. Consequently, financing will be needed through industry partners or venture capital firms in the near future to facilitate a rapid expansion.

Likewise, the direct distribution strategy chosen by Omena is a significant challenge to a start-up company, especially in the hotel business which is far from local in nature. Omena Hotels is faced with the challenge of creating awareness of its offerings and its online marketplace (http://www.omena.com) and stimulating demand as an independent hotel chain that does not, at this point, participate in any global distribution systems. This requires, typically, massive and aggressive initial marketing efforts and a substantial advertising and business promotion budget – something that typically constitutes a problem for a start-up company.

As far as the prospective first mover advantages are concerned, there is an apparent risk – or even likelihood – that larger established hotel chains with significant financial resources introduce new brands with comparable or identical concepts targeting the same customer segments, thus potentially prevent Omena Hotels from fully exploiting its obvious competitive advantages and reaching its full potential on all target markets.

An alternative, yet currently not used, path to a rapid expansion is offered by a franchising strategy, where independent hotels with scarce resources and deficient marketing and management functions transform their current, traditional operations by adopting the Omena concept, technologies and brand. A franchising strategy seems attractive especially in smaller cities where small units are to be preferred, and the occupancy rates and price levels (and thus the expected profitability per unit) tend to be lower than in the larger cities. To this end, Omena aims at internalizing – in part or in full – the technological solutions and information systems currently in use, while at the same time developing new system integrations that can support Omena's operations and business model (being able to manage all functions through a central system and server) as well as enhance its competitiveness.

Key Conclusions

- Omena has introduced a non-frills non employees on site hotel concept.
- Omena uses a proprietary reservation and hotel management system which the company has designed and built from scratch in order to generate a solution that is tailor-made for its exceptional business model.
- Omena Hotels is using innovation in ICT and e-commerce to develop its competitiveness.
- Companies that are able to exploit, in full, the many potential benefits electronic channels and ICT can achieve competitive advantages.

Review and Discussion Questions

- How can a hotel operate without staff on the premises?
- What challenges does this raise for the company and how can technology address those challenges?
- Can hotels adopt a direct only distribution strategy?
- What technological solutions can support customer satisfaction in hotels?

References and Further Reading

Buhalis, D., & Main, H. (1998). Information technology in peripheral small and medium hospitality enterprises: Strategic analysis and critical factors. *International Journal of Contemporary Hospitality Management*, 10 (5), 198–202.

Kim, W.C., & Mauborgne, R. (2005). *Blue ocean strategy: How to create uncontested market space and make the competition irrelevant*. Harvard: Harvard Business School Press.

Sheldon, P.J. (1997). *Tourism information technology*. Wallingford, UK: CAB International.

Werthner, H., & Klein, S. (1999). *Information technology and tourism – A challenging relationship*. Vienna: Springer-Verlag.

Company's website: http://www.omena.com.

5

Carnival City: valuating guests in the gaming industry

Cyril Francis

Learning Objectives

- Demonstrate how technology can be used in a casino environment.
- Illustrate how technology can facilitate the operation of a cashless casino.
- Explain how ICT can assist the identification and service of valuable customers.

Introduction and Company Development

Carnival City Casino, which is part of Sun International South Africa, is situated in the financial capital of South Africa, Gauteng. Sun International (SI) has been the only gambling provider in South Africa since the previous government's classification of the so-called TBVC states (Transkei, Bophutaswane, Venda en Ciskei) from 1979 to the early 1990s. It all started with Sol Kernzer's ultimate dream – Sun City, the Kingdom of Pleasure.

With the introduction of the New Gambling Act no. 33 of 1996, 40 casinos were earmarked for South Africa across the 9 provinces. Carnival City is one of the twelve casinos owned and operated by Sun Internatinal. Situated in Gauteng on the East Rand, with a gambling potential of €435 million, this casino is ranked number 3 with an annual turnover of €87.05 million. In 2005, the industry grew by 14% in Gauteng, with Carnival City recording a growth of 22%.

The casino operating environment is highly regulated in South Africa, according to the prescriptions of the Act and hefty penalties are imposed to transgressors. Technology plays an important part in the whole process as all slot machines across the country are linked to the office of the national Gambling Board.

Sun International (SI) is a world leader in casino technology. The combination of its smart-card base, casino operations and its loyalty programme confers a big advantage over its local and foreign competitors. This bodes well for global expansion (*Financial Mail*, 4 February 2005).

Main Product Offering and Value Added

Carnival City's vision is 'To be the most admired casino in Southern Africa' and to live up to their dream, they strive to provide the 'ultimate gaming experience' to their customer base. The Carnival City product consists of a Carnival Club Hotel (a 105 room 4 star hotel); 1750 Slot machines; 60 High-tech tables ranging from Easy Poker, Magic Poker, Let it Ride Poker, American Roulette, Black Jack, Diamond Rush Black Jack, Single Deck Black Jack, Perfect Pairs Black Jack, Punto Banco and Midi Punto Banco; 6 Quality restaurants and a number of fast food outlets; 2 concert/theatre and conference venues; a Magic Company for kids' entertainment; and a number of bars.

Carnival City offers a most valued guest (MVG) loyalty programme, which was introduced in the year 2000. This system enables punters to earn points towards fabulous rewards and benefits at all Sun International casinos and resorts. For every €54 played on the slot machines customers earn 1 MVG point and on the tables, for every €272 bet they accumulate another MVG point. The system also allows you to move up in status from a maroon card, to silver, gold and ultimately platinum. Points continue to accumulate and are valid for a 12-month period only.

The gambling industry in Gauteng is very competitive. Amongst the four big casinos Carnival City ranks third. The others are: Montecasino (turnover of €130 million annually); Emperors Palace (turnover of €108 million annually); and Gold Reef City (turnover of €65 million annually). Their products are all very similar and therefore continuous rivalry takes place amongst these casinos. Casinos out-smart one another by applying more products and offering innovations on a regular basis.

Carnival City's success can be channelled towards their total customer care and commitment which is part of their business philosophy. This is further strengthened by the visibility of management on the casino floor, in building rapport and relationships with their clientele.

Business Model

Carnival City's promise of the ultimate entertainment experience revolves around a product offering that will fulfil the needs and desires of punters and their entire family. While adults are gambling, there is more than enough for the younger kids to do.

Carnival City's target market is basically from the East Rand, predominantly Afrikaan-speaking, between the ages of 20 and 55. This includes both sexes, with a phenomenal increase in female punters. Due to its location in a less affluent area, it takes a lot of creative marketing to lure people from other areas to Carnival City. The Asian market, both locally and internationally, is growing at a tremendous rate.

Suppliers of essential products to Carnival City range from slot machines, to guest supplies for the hotel, to food and beverage items and many more. They develop preferred relationships with most of their suppliers and in doing so they benefit from costing savings and preferential arrangements. They also have exclusive arrangements with their slot machine and gaming manufacturers that will provide certain equipment to Carnival City and Sun

International Casinos exclusively. This gives them a reasonable lead time over their nearest competitors.

As Carnival City is part of Sun International, it is a listed public company with the highest percentage of black economic empowerment (BEE) as stipulated by the New National Gambling Act.

Sun International as a gambling operator is a very successful company as outlined in their 2005 financial summary which includes:

Revenue	€563,755,660
Direct costs	€237,073,243
Gross profit	€326,601,098
Indirect costs	€143,288,469
Operating profit	€155,375,370
Profit after tax	€104,014,399

Carnival City is the third highest contributor to the Sun International financial success, with only Grande West Casino (Cape Town) and Sun City (North West Province) out-performing them.

Technological and Business Innovation

Carnival City and some of the Sun International casinos are the only cashless casinos in the country. The system enables punters to use a smart credit card size, gaming technological tool that will enable punters to play any machine at anytime during their visit. Punters simply load money onto the card and the smart card ship records the value loaded onto the card. The same system interface with the most valued guests (MVG) programme, where the smart card chip will contain the following information on the systems database: the demographic information of the punter; what level or status the punter has; how often the punter had visited the casino in the last month; what machines or tables the punter has played during his/her last visit; what amounts of money the punter gained or lost over a period.

At Carnival City 20% of its punters contribute 80% of its revenue. A high percentage of the platinum and gold MVG cardholders spend on average €54,460 per visit, which is a major source of revenue for the casino. The average punter at Carnival City spends €32.4 per visit. Therefore, the platinum and gold cardholders are treated like royalty with complimentary accommodation, food and beverages, transfers to and from the casino and other personal services.

The MVG system provides Carnival City with a tremendous information database for marketing and promotional activities, such as text message invitations, mail-shots or simply keeping contact with your valued punters.

The advanced technology that enables the cashless system and MVG programme to interface, supports Carnival City to have promotional cash draws where a punter can win a jackpot of any amount by simply playing a slot machine. No winning combination need to be recorded for the punter to enjoy this benefit. This process has been taken a step further by including a concept called 'winner's circle', where 10 slots machines are linked next to one another and if any person within that circle wins a mystery jackpot, all the other punters will receive a consolation prize.

Technology is also crucial in the area of controlling the gaming operation of all slot machines and tables (how they function, when they pay out and the amount). The South African Bureau of Standards (SABS) has also developed an electronic device which is inserted into all slot machines to prevent casino operates from manipulating pay-outs. All pay-outs are strictly monitored and controlled by the National Gambling Board. The area of security is also highly monitored and regulated at Carnival City with 24/7 surveillance of playing areas, cash-up areas and the physical bank on the premises. The entire premises is under surveillance 24/7. This is a crucial aspect with regard to the punter experience.

This advanced technology is Carnival City's greatest competitive advantage and gives them a 4–5 year lead time on the rest of the other casinos in Gauteng. The other casinos are almost not in a position to copy this technology due to the high investment cost involved.

Key Challenges for the Future

Advanced technology remains Carnival City's key competitive advantage. This is enabled by their present technological infrastructure, which in future will have to be improved, for them to remain ahead of their competitors. The current ICT system is structured to deal with: facilitating; supporting; user facing and guest facing; linking with MVG services; gaming technology services; hospitality technology services; guest technology services; back of house business system services; back of house desktop and printing services; information security services; enterprise system services; network services; infrastructure services and service management services. Figure 5.1 illustrates the characteristics of the system.

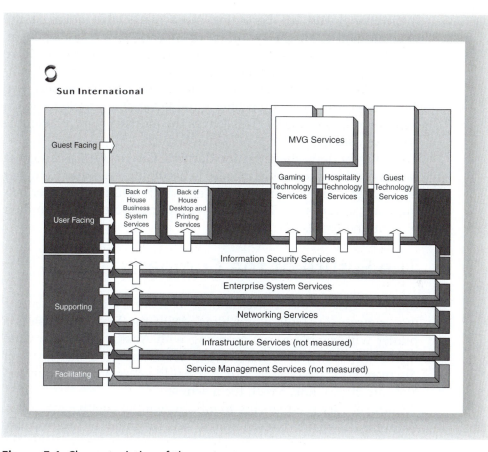

Figure 5.1 Characteristics of the system
Source: Sun International SA (http://www.suninternational.co.za)

Figure 5.1 illustrates the business service relationship between Sun International and its contracted service providers in their business model where technology plays an important role. The first band outlines the nine key business service units (as outlined in the previous paragraph) and how these services are facilitated. The second band outlines the supporting units that are crucial to the successful execution of these services. The third band outlines the user facing operations to be executed to achieve the desired service delivery. The final band outlines the gaming (core gaming systems), hospitality (operational services and functions) and most valued guest services (measuring guest satisfaction) to ensure that all customers and guests receive the services they expect from an operator such as Carnival City.

The biggest challenge for management at Carnival City is the lack of skilled employees in the various sectors of the business. Most of the skilled employees in the industry are trained at Sun

International and are becoming more marketable amongst the other casinos due to their shortage of appropriately trained people. Due to the fast pace of business operations, casinos do not have the time to properly train senior members of staff or for that matter, any level of staff due to the rigid regulations of the new Act. The easiest way to obtain properly trained staff is simply to poach them from other casinos. This leaves the industry very vulnerable and increases the shortage of skilled labour.

Another serious challenge for Carnival City, as well as for other casinos is that disposable income is becoming less, due to higher interest rates and commodity prices, which results in smaller bettings and fewer visits. This will have a remarkable impact on their bottom-line profits.

The Future of the Company

Carnival City is the first casino in the country to introduce the new concept of 'Hollywood Slots'. With the Hollywood slots a punter will be able to get grooving with Austin Powers in Gold member™, or win monster payouts on Young Frankenstein™, or discover your destiny as Magic 8 Ball™ reveals all! Hollywood Slots are 20 pay-line, 5 reel, 10c machines.

Carnival City is advancing to introduce more creative machines, with greater visual presentations, accompanied by appropriate sound and movement activities to create 'visual – real' effects. Technology will continue to be critical for the operations and strategy of the company.

Key Conclusions

- Carnival City uses a comprehensive information database for marketing and promotional activities.
- Technology is crucial in the area of controlling the gaming operation of all slot machines and tables.
- Technology also plays a critical role for security.

Review and Discussion Questions

- What are the unique ICT needs for casinos?
- What are the different layers of technology that are used in the Carnival City and why?
- How can Casinos use ICTs for competitive advantage?

References and Further Reading

Litchko, J.P. (2004). *KNOW ICT security: Secure ICT systems, casino style*. Kensington: KNOW Book Publishing.

Lucas, A.F., & Bowen, J.T. (2002). Measuring the effectiveness of casino promotions. *International Journal of Hospitality Management*, 21 (2), 189–202.

Lucas, A.F., Dunn, W.T., Roehl, W.S., & Wolcott, G.M. (2004). Evaluating slot machine performance: A performance-potential model. *International Journal of Hospitality Management*, 23 (2), 103–121.

Scheri, S.R. (2005). *The Casino's most valued chip: How technology transformed the gaming industry*. Palo Alto: Institute for the history of Technology.

Company's website: http://www.suninternational.co.za.

Company's website: http://www.carnivalcity.co.za.

Interview with Riaan van Rooyen, General Manager (Carnival City).

6

Hotel Sallerhof: innovations in interaction

Roman Egger and Leonhard Wörndl

Learning Objectives

- Demonstrate how technology can be used by small businesses.
- Illustrate how technology can provide competitive advantage to small hotels.
- Explain how small hotels can manage multi-distribution channels.

Introduction

Tourism in Austria consists primarily of small and medium-sized tourism businesses (SMTEs) and therefore has naturally a highly heterogeneous structure. In addition to their size, SMTEs are also characterized by their independence, flexibility, seasonality, family ownership and management (Buhalis, 2003), and frequently by their geographical isolation. This often leads to traditional management practices which are characterized by short-term perspectives, a lack of willingness to cooperate and a reluctance to adopt Information and Communication Technologies (ICTs). Although there are big differences in quality and quantity of information and services provided online, nowadays almost every Austrian hotel has its own website.

Long before the Internet-boom started in the Austrian tourism industry, one Salzburg hotel manager was already communicating with his guests through the web. Since that time he has been permanently trying new strategies and tools to increase his online success. A comparison between his website and that of his competitors shows that he is still one step ahead. During the whole 2007 summer season he reached a 100% occupancy rate and he is convinced that the main reason for that success is his consequent improvement of e-business strategies.

Main Products and Value Added

The Hotel Sallerhof is a family run B&B in a small village, about 10 kilometres south of the city of Salzburg. Due to its vicinity to the city area, tourists still recognize it as a Salzburg hotel. Because of its accessibility, the Sallerhof has some major disadvantages compared to typical Salzburg city hotels. Public transportation to the city centre and to the most popular tourism sites is limited as far as frequency (2 busses per hour), commodity and operation hours (last bus at 11 p.m.) is concerned. The Hotel Sallerhof is very attractive for tourists arriving by car, being located near the exit from one of Europe's most important highways, which connects the areas north of the Alps (e.g. Germany and the Netherlands) with those in the south (e.g. Italy and Croatia). The Sallerhof can be reached within a 15 minute ride by taxi from the Salzburg Airport. The distance from the train station is about 10 kilometres, public transportation is available.

In 1974 the Sallerhof was opened as a 3-star B&B by the father of the present owner, who succeeded his father in 1989. The Hotel

Sallerhof has 38 beds and through the quality of the rooms and the service being constantly improved it has retained its three star rating. It represents a typical Austrian tourism SMTE.

When it opened, the B&B Hotel Sallerhof only offered accommodation and breakfast. The majority of the guests were walk-ins or regular guests and the local destination management organization (DMO) was an important marketing partner sending in new tourists. Nowadays, the Sallerhof also offers packages including not only lodging and breakfast, but also additional services which are typically requested by guests visiting Salzburg.

Technological and Business Innovation

The Sallerhof was among the first hotels in the Salzburg area offering Internet services like email and World Wide Web (www) for business communication and marketing. In the 1990s when Compuserve was the first email service available in Austria, the Sallerhof started not only sending and receiving emails but also collecting email addresses. It was the first 3-star hotel with a text-based website in the Salzburg area, launched in 1993. Since then the management of the hotel has been permanently improving and extending its Internet services. Consequently, as shown in Table 6.1, the guest structure of the Sallerhof is unique and differs from that of the Salzburg region, by being much more international, due to the broader coverage of the Internet as a marketing tool and distribution channel. The share of Sallerhof guests coming from overseas countries is significantly higher than that of the city of Salzburg. The logfile of the www.sallerhof.at website shows a similar structure as the room-nights of the hotel.

As another very positive result of the consistent adoption of eTourism strategies, the Sallerhof reached a 100% occupancy rate in the 2007 season. Due to its precise statistics it is known that the hotel guests can basically be divided into two groups. There is a share of 40% of repeat visitors and guests being recommended. From the 60% of the new guests that come every year about 95% do their booking or reservation through the Internet. Fifty percent of these are acquired through search engines. These customers finally book through the hotels' own booking engine which is provided by Feratel (see Case 24). Another 40% find their way to the Sallerhof website through links and 10% book through one of the intermediaries the Sallerhof is cooperating with. There is only

Table 6.1 Room-nights 2005 by Nationality of guests, Hotel Sallerhof compared with City of Salzburg

Country	Sallerhof		Logfile (Visits) %	City of Salzburg	
	Roomnights	%		Roomnights	%
USA	1,343	17.8	13.53	173,563	9.21
Italy	1,119	14.8	13.84	163,806	8.69
UK	928	12.3	5.27	116,625	6.19
Austria	879	11.6	7.87	486,710	25.82
Germany	654	8.7	8.76	352,428	18.70
Canada	420	5.6	2.89	18,319	0.97
France	301	4.0	6.05	39,553	2.10
Australia	294	3.9	1.51	28,341	1.50
Netherlands	185	2.4	4.50	26,652	1.41
Belgium	157	2.1	3.37	12,296	0.65
Spain	131	1.7	3.89	38,711	2.05
Ireland	119	1.6	0.33	12,788	0.68
Switzerland	109	1.4	1.44	51,032	2.71
Hungary	87	1.2	3.97	12,411	0.66
Sweden	72	1.0	0.78	10,883	0.58
Greece	42	0.6	0.37	12,400	0.66
Poland	14	0.2	3.23	6,399	0.34
Others	700	9.3	18.40	321,933	17.08
Total	7,554	100.0	100.00	1884,850	100.00

a very small number of new customers left that do their booking by letter or by telephone. The contribution of the local DMO to the bookings of the hotel is almost zero.

eMediaries like Hotel.de, Venere.com, booking.com, HRS.com and some more, are mainly used for offering last minute deals. In 2002 about 2% of the new customers were acquired through this channel. Now eMediaries account for 10% with raising tendency. The hotel started with four to five partnerships, trying out and testing them constantly. The most valuable intermediaries were identified. However the dynamic development of the market makes it necessary for the Sallerhof to permanently search for new partnerships, applying the trial and error principle.

The constant enhancement of the Internet as a distribution channel has initiated a change in marketing as well as product development and the implementation of some basic strategies of customer relationship management. Through the hotel website or after their arrival, guests staying between three and five nights can book packages including elements like concerts, a Sound of Music tour, a candlelight dinner, a mountain excursion with a famous cable car or a visit to a nearby salt mine. These pre-customized products turned out to be very successful for the following reasons.

Recommendation of Available Services and Products

The adoption of the Internet as a marketing and distribution channel by almost all tourism companies in Salzburg makes it very difficult for a customer to find relevant information for his individual needs. The variety of available products makes it hard to choose and plan a trip in detail. A tourist who visits the place for the first time does not know which products can be combined, nor does he have information about how to move around when distant sites are visited. For most tourists using the Internet for travel prepar-ation, the overload of offers is perceived more like a burden than an assistance. Tourists therefore really appreciate the individual recommendations given by the Sallerhof.

There is a growing number of low-cost airlines that connect Salzburg with the European markets. They bring in more and more tourists, who do not only book their tickets online, but also search for other services like accommodation, tickets for concerts or theatre, or sightseeing tours in the internet. A single website, providing information about all these attractions and activities, is an additional help for guests with limited time for travel preparation. The packages that the Sallerhof offers include many of these attractions which require reservations and bookings. The change of consumer behaviour towards last minute bookings does not leave tourists much time for travel preparations. Therefore predefined packages are highly appreciated by these customers. The big variety of services offered on the website gives the online visitor the impression that the hotel is the key to all attractions and leisure activities of the destination. This creates a benefit and makes the website and the hotel more attractive.

The predefined holiday packages are a managerial challenge for the hotel staff because reservations have to be made and transportation has to be organized to be quite flexible, depending on the individual plans of the guests. Still, the Sallerhof considers these additional tasks a chance to raise profits as packages have become an additional income through commissions paid by the tour operators or ticket agencies, which act in a very competitive environment. Due to the permanent business relationships between the hotel and the different leisure and tour companies, the Sallerhof guests have reached the status of privileged tourists and they are attended to more carefully than the usual guest. Individual services, like concert tickets or city tours that are booked as a part or without a special package can be offered to the guest at the same price as if they would purchase it directly at the theatre or from the tour operator. As an intermediary, the Sallerhof gets quite an attractive commission that is a welcome contribution to its revenue. To the tourist this appears like a free service from the hotel, which they perceive as a highly welcome benefit.

Special Functionality of the Website

As mentioned before, the website of the Hotel Sallerhof is its main distribution channel and offers tools and features that exceed the typical functionality of an SMTE hotel website and even most big hotels in the area.

- *Languages*: At present the Sallerhof offers its services in 11 different languages, among which are Russian and Slovenian. Both markets are considered as high potentials for the Austrian tourism within the next few years. Although many Austrian hotels offer only limited parts of their websites in foreign languages, the Sallerhof has translated most of its contents. A Japanese version of the website will be online within the next months. Although the hotel's staff is only able to handle English and Italian requests without external help, no complaints were perceived by visitors. To limit the languages for necessary one to one communication, the online visitor is asked on each contact form to choose the preferred language among German, English or Italian. For the customers this seems to be acceptable. The most important information can be obtained in their mother tongue, but they have to communicate in one of the three offered languages.
- *Integration of hotel videos*: The hotel Sallerhof offers a variety of videos in which the hotel as well as the most important tourism sites and tours in the surrounding area are presented. These videos are not only available on the website itself but also in the in-house TV system. This enables the guest to get information about popular activities in the destination not only before starting the trip but also after the arrival in the room. This service has become a very powerful sales tool for tours, concert tickets and other programmes that are sold at the reception.
- *Credit card payment reduces no-shows*: Since 2005 it is required to pay a deposit of €20 by credit card if one books online via the

website. Therefore an SSL encryption had to be implemented which caused additional expenses. At the same time the number of 'no-shows' decreased to almost zero. Furthermore the terms of cancellation were included in every reply made to an email request. It was interesting to see that these enhanced consumers' trust and stimulated paying by credit card.

- *Customers want 'information only'*: Through the observation of the online behaviour of the Sallerhof guests it is evident that the number of requests significantly grew as soon as all request or reservation forms were clearly titled as 'non-binding'. This proves that customers appreciate online forms which absolutely clarify that they are sending an unbinding request and not a binding reservation after which troublesome discussions might occur.

Web marketing

The Sallerhof uses different web marketing strategies especially for in-site promotion:

- *Search engines – link strategy*: The Sallerhof is constantly trying to use the potential of search engines for site promotion. It has reached a page one ranking for many of its preferred keywords. Due to its importance for search engines a great effort was put on link popularity and the number of links that lead to the Sallerhof website could be raised. Although the figures cannot be taken as absolute numbers (Google is known for not showing real numbers) the comparison in terms of link popularity with three similar hotels in the surrounding area shows the link prominence of Sallerhof (Table 6.2).
- *Email marketing*: The Sallerhof has tried several email marketing strategies from which two turned out to be most effective. Two weeks after making a request, the guest gets information about tourism attractions in the city of Salzburg. The hotel owner is convinced that this helps to persuade guests who have not yet decided where to stay, to make their decision in favour of the Sallerhof. One month after the departure every guest gets a friendly and personal email in which the hotel asks for recommendations in the online guestbook as well as for feedback and suggestions for improvement.
- *The power of rating systems*: The Sallerhof participates in several platforms, some of them providing rating systems. Because of the growing importance of these systems, the Sallerhof actively encourages all visitors of the website to vote for its service.

Table 6.2 Total number of links to homepage analysed in a link popularity check by www.marketleap.com in July 2006

Hotels	Number of links
www.sallerhof.at	3584
www.simmerlwirt.at	59
www.hoteluntersberg.at	118
www.schlosswirt-anif.com	164

Thereby the hotel Sallerhof won the 'Best B&B award' in 2004, 2005 as well as in 2007 which resulted in a strong increase in online bookings.

- *Measuring online success*: A core application for all marketing activities of the Sallerhof is the logfile and benchmarking tool 'Checkeffect' (detailed description can be found in Case 33). Checkeffect is a sophisticated logfile analysis tool as well as a system to benchmark online success with other comparable hotels. The system enables the Hotel Sallerhof not only to get statistics about online visitors but also to evaluate all marketing activities, links and platforms used to increase the hotel's online popularity. Not only the number of online visitors that come through a certain source like google.com or bedandbreakfast.com, are identified but also the quality of the traffic can be evaluated. The Checkeffect system counts the number of visitors and tracks each one through the website to see if a request was made. The tool measures the actual value of each paid link, by recording the number of requests which were initiated by a specific referrer.

The Future of the Company

The Sallerhof management is convinced that only high quality tourism products can be sold online, as well as offline. Therefore the hotel was renovated and although it will still be marketed as a 3-star hotel, quality will come up to a 4-star standard. All rooms will be equipped with LAN access, whilst additional internet terminals for guests will be offered in the lobby. Also, the website will be made available in Swedish and Chinese to attract more guests from these markets.

Key Conclusions

- Small hotels can use innovative technologies to approach and serve their clients.
- Innovative technologies do not always require huge investments.
- Small hotels that fail to understand the opportunities ICTs bring will face a competitive disadvantage.

Review and Discussion Questions

- How can small hotels use ICTs to compete with hotel chains?
- What tools should small hotels use to serve their customers?
- How can small hotels select third-party distributors?

Further Reading

Buhalis, D. (2003). *eTourism: Information technology for strategic tourism management*. London: Pearson (Financial Times/Prentice Hall).

Buhalis, D., & Egger, R. (2006). Informations- und Kom munikationstechnologien als Mittel zur Prozess- und Produktinnovation für den Unternehmer. In M. Peters, & B. Pikkemaat (Eds.), *Innovationen im Tourismus* (pp. 163–176). Berlin: ESV Verlag.

O'Connor, P., & Frew, A.J. (2002). The future of hotel electronic distribution. *Cornell Hotel and Restaurant Administration Quarterly*, 43 (3), 33–45.

Peters, W.D. (2005). *A View on the Merchant Model*. Retrieved from http://www.hospitalitynet.org/news/4022608.html.

Statistik Austria (2006). *Tourismus in Österreich*. Vienna: Eigenverlag.

United Nations World Tourism Organization (UNWTO) (2006). *World tourism barometer*, 4 (2).

Company's website: http://www.sallerhof.com.

Case

7

'Emmantina' and 'Palmyra Beach' Hotels: distribution for independent hotels

Konstantina Kaldis and Emmanouil Kaldis

Learning Objectives

- Demonstrate how individual hotels can effectively organise a competitive marketing strategy through e-distribution.
- Appreciate yield and revenue management through the hotels' own website, partnerships with third-party websites and Global Distribution Systems (GDS) representation.
- Explain how individual hotels can manage multi-distribution channels.
- Illustrate how small hotels can design their web sites to offer content and be optimized for search engines.

Introduction and Company Development

The 'Emmantina' and 'Palmyra Beach' hotels are situated in Glyfada, a coastal suburb of Athens, in Greece. Glyfada is often referred to as the Athenian Riviera, a seaside resort only 15 km from the centre of Athens. The hotels are just 100 metres from the commercial centre of Glyfada and the beach and 1 km from the Athens Golf Course.

Many tourism related companies operate in the area of Glyfada. There are 15 hotels, nine of which are 4-star hotels. Glyfada hotels also compete with other hotels in the overall coastal area (a total distance of approximately 70 km) with a total number of 136 hotels extending from the Port of Piraeus to Cape Sounion.

Over the past few years Glyfada's tourism is challenged. Various factors have adversely affected tourism demand, the major being the relocation of the Athens airport. The opportunity for the upgrading of the area has not been exploited to its fullest, as the destination has not been successfully re-promoted to attract new market segments for leisure and business tourism.

This factor, in an environment of heightened competition, has necessitated an effective and optimised e-strategy, not only for the promotion of the hotel's facilities and services, but also for the overall marketing of the destination.

Main Products/Offerings and Value Added

'Emmantina' and 'Palmyra Beach' hotels (will now be referred to in the text as 'the Hotel') offer accommodation, alimentation, conference and banqueting services. They are two medium sized 4-star hotels, with 80 and 56 rooms respectively. They have common proprietorship and management and are family-owned. The strategic goal of the company is to offer comprehensive and high-quality accommodation services to its clients. Due to the strategic location of the hotel, close to the centre of Athens and the seaside, the company has the ability to address the needs of an extended variety of markets. Main customer target groups are foreigners and Greeks, tourists and business travellers.

Business Model

In an environment of constant change, high levels of competition and increased expectations by customers, the management has set the e-distribution strategy and development as a priority. It is acknowledged that an electronic distribution strategy is critical. The term distribution involves the selection and operation of channels by which a company distributes its products to its markets (Holloway & Robinson, 1995). The main target would be the development of the hotel in this sector. Rather than trying to adapt and strive to keep up with the pace of technological changes in the tourism industry, the company allocates all those resources necessary to aim for leadership in the field of electronic distribution and uses than as a tool to strike a major competitive advantage in the industry among competitors. Its aim is to become a role-model company for others.

Technological and Business Innovation

The first step is the development of the e-marketing department and the appointment of a qualified employee to take care of the e-distribution function of the hotel. Thereafter, three key factors and areas of interest are pinpointed for the e-distribution of hotels:

- The hotels' website
- Partnerships with third party websites
- Global Distribution Systems (GDS) representation

Hotel Website

The proprietary website of the hotel is promoted in all communication material of the hotel and acts as a point of reference to guests by providing pre-purchase information and facilitating consumer decision-making. It is considered by the administration to be the basis for the hotels' Internet marketing strategy. It was decided to build a new website for each hotel with all the parameters that would optimise its potential for successful promotion and revenue generation (Briggs, 2001).

Design for content: emphasis is put on offering as much pre-travel information as possible. It is of major importance that the website provides useful and abundant content; descriptive information about the hotels' services and facilities, as well as information concerning the destination. A well designed content creates a clear picture of the hotel that will correspond to customers' expectations. Both leisure and business travellers tend to search the web for resort information. During their search they may end up browsing the hotels' website as it will be providing the information that they are looking for. The website assists travellers in evaluating whether services, price, hotel category and hotel ambience match desirable characteristics. Abundant pictures are placed next to the text to facilitate reading and make web pages more attractive. An electronic brochure is made available, clear contact information is provided, as well as useful maps and location information. Finally, in developing the website content, Search Engine Optimization (SEO) is also considered especially for the first page of the website. Therefore specific keywords are selected and are supported by content.

Design for interactivity: email capture is enabled. Customers may opt in to provide the hotel with their email address. In this way they can receive hotel news, information about new services and facilities, and most importantly special offers. It has been decided that all email and other queries of the hotel must be dealt with within 24 hours. Virtual tours, that enable surfers to virtually navigate through the hotel's premises, are also available.

Design for dynamics: the website is constructed by using a fully dynamic, rather than static, platform, based on the 'php' programming language. This enables management to change the hotel content with great ease. The content management system of the website, which has been developed by the company who has undertaken the building of the site, facilitates the uploading of information about local events, cultural festivities and sport contests. Special offers can be created and instantly uploaded to provide guests with the most current information and instantly respond to market conditions diverting demand towards the low season.

Design for yield and revenue generation: the online reservations function is of outmost importance and is made available in the main menu, which appears in all pages. Therefore, while browsing the site, the potential customer is able to receive a quote for a stay on desirable dates. It addresses the need of customers to instantly receive confirmation of their booking. An external company, Oceanic Consultancy Co. Ltd, seamlessly powers this function on a commission basis, by providing the ASP based software 'Globekey', required to enable direct online sales securely.

Design for promotion: in order to promote the website a search engine submission tool is purchased. The main functionality of this tool is the automatic URL submission to any search engine. It can also provide guidance for search engine optimisation. Furthermore, banner marketing activities of selected websites are pursued and search engine advertising is undertaken. Link exchanges are promoted in order to increase traffic and popularity of the site. Another tactic used is the submission of the property in both local and international electronic directories, like in.gr, flash.gr, yahoo, msn.

Design for accessibility: taking possible target groups into consideration it is acknowledged that it is necessary to address many different people in different countries. A multilingual site serves as an important tool in penetrating different markets, simply by addressing the audience in its own language. It also enables the website to be promoted on search engines of different countries.

Partner Websites

Through the disintermediation and re-intermediation processes that takes place with the emergence of the Internet, many companies have developed sites and portals that either act as a catalogue by promoting hotel details or generate revenue for hotels by enabling reservations. Partner site selection can be a strenuous process as it is difficult to assess the quality, integrity and revenue potential of a prospective partner site. Currently the three most important key partners include, Expedia, HRS and Booking.com. There are several issues in the strategy for developing and selecting partnerships. A major issue is which pricing policy to pursue online bookings. Internet users browse through several sites not only to select a hotel at their chosen location but also to compare offers for a certain hotel through several sites. Rate parity demands clear e-marketing strategy from the hotel and continuous monitoring as it frequently relies on third parties, making it difficult to maintain and control.

Two main third party models exist. The first model is on a commission basis. The partner promotes the hotel's commissionable rates, and the hotel pays the intermediary at the agreed percentage on revenue produced. The intermediary provides the hotel with necessary guest details to secure the reservation. The guest pays the hotel directly. The second model is the merchant model, by which the hotel provides the partner with net rates. The intermediary promotes the hotel directly or through other partners by adding a mark-up margin, and also by promoting it as a package deal with other supplementary services. The partner only provides the hotel with basic reservation details. The intermediary pays the hotel at agreed intervals. Price parity can be an issue in this case, as the hotel has no control or knowledge on the actual rate rooms are being sold.

Maintaining an up-to-date image and unique profile of the hotel throughout the WWW is also a critical challenge, as it is important to maintain brand integrity and rate parity. Emphasis on genuine and honest information is imperative, especially now that websites enabling online reviewing by travellers is on the increase. A satisfied or unsatisfied guest currently has a much louder voice.

Another issue is the assessment of prospective partners. Not only is it costly and time consuming to register to a new site, but it is also critical to constantly maintain and control this site. Addressing the above issue the company has decided to pursue the following strategy. At a strategic level the management has chosen to maintain rate parity and price integrity in order not to confuse the public and to insure confidence in the hotel. This also assists in maintaining important partnerships with third-party sites, as each one faces equal opportunities to produce revenue.

The management sets five main assessment criteria for the evaluation of partners. A basic criterion is the popularity of the intermediary with the target audience and revenue generation capability. Secondly, to ensure correctness of property details, the responsiveness of the partner and easiness in communication is taken into consideration. Also search engine performance, as well as the user-friendliness of the booking engine, is evaluated. Lastly, the associated costs are reviewed.

Selection of GDS Provider

GDSs are one of the major drivers of information technologies in tourism (Cooper *et al.*, 1998). Listing in the GDS is today a simpler and less costly task in comparison to a few years ago. Major representation companies are building new products to target the needs of independent and small- to medium-sized hotels. Listing in all GDS is very important as it enables the hotel to be booked by travel agencies around the world. The company has conducted market research in order to select an appropriate representation company that would list the properties in the GDS. The decision was based on the following criteria:

- Ability to list the hotel in all GDS
- User friendly and flexibility of platform used by the hotel

- Partnerships of the representation company with other major websites
- Participation of the representation company in consortia (negotiated rate agreements)
- Total cost (initial fee, monthly fees, and transaction fees)
- Marketing activities pursued to promote the hotel entry code in the GDS
- Technology used.

Key Challenges for the Future

By signing room allotment agreements and enabling instant bookings to third parties and GDS, the hotel strives to effectively manage these on a day-to-day basis. A key future challenge is to streamline allocation by using a common platform to manage all these channels and effectively apply yield management techniques. Following this step, the hotel plans to integrate the online reservation functionality of its proprietary website with its Property Management System (namely the Protel Hotel Software), bypassing commissions paid to the third party booking engine.

Another challenge the hotel faces is the need to constantly keep its website up-to-date by providing applicable special offers and current resort information. It is also important to exploit its online customer base, by using the email addresses provided by customers from the website or other sources. The hotel also aims to penetrate new markets by using a multilingual approach. Overall as the e-distribution market constantly changes it is imperative to keep up with the new developments.

Conclusion

From May 2005 until May 2006 it was estimated that 19.50% of the total room turnover derived from electronic sources, of which 2% derived from the GDS, 5% from the proprietary web site and 12.50% from partner sites. It is important to mention that revenue from the proprietary website is considerably understated, as many customers deriving from this source actually prefer to use alternative reservation methods (telephone, email, fax, etc.) rather than booking directly online.

The e-distribution function stands to become one of the competitive advantages of the hotel. The organizational structure is adapted to reflect these changes in the marketing department. The appointment of a skilled employee to handle this function is critical. Those hotels who understand the increasing dynamics of the Internet and e-distribution stand to win a major market share, a great competitive advantage in an era of increased competition.

Key Conclusions

- Small hotels should coordinate their e-distribution strategies to gain a competitive advantage.
- The proprietary website of the hotel should be regarded as the online image of the hotel, an important source of information to existing and prospective customers, as well as a source of revenue.
- Partner websites need to be managed to ensure price parity and brand integrity.

Review and Discussion Questions

- How can individual hotels negotiate with powerful third party distributors?
- Which are the main criteria used to select distributors?
- How should a small hotel organize its e-marketing strategy?

References and Further Reading

Briggs, S. (2001). *Successful web marketing for the tourism and leisure sectors*. London: Kogan Page Limited.

Carrol, B., & Siguaw, J. (2003). Evolution in electronic distribution: Effects on hotels and intermediaries. *Cornell Hotel and Restaurant Administration Quarterly*, 3 (5), 3–20.

Choosing a Reservation Representation Company. Part 1. Retrieved from http://www.burns-htc.com/Articles/Choosing_a_Reservation_Rep_Company_Part_1.htm.

Choosing a Reservation Representation Company. Part 2. Retrieved from http://www.burns-htc.com/Articles/Choosing_a_Reservation_Rep_Company_Part_2.htm.

Cooper, C., Fletcher, J., Gilbert, D., & Wanhill, S. (1998). *Tourism principles and practices*. New York: Addison Wesley Longman.

Holloway, C., & Robinson, C. (1995). *Marketing for tourism.* London: Longman Group Limited.

O'Connor, P. (2003). On-line pricing: An analysis of hotel-company practices. *Cornell Hotel and Restaurant Administration Quarterly*, February, 88–96.

Time for Change: The Evolution of Electronic Distribution and Central Reservations Management is for Real. Retrieved from http://www.burns-htc.com/Articles/Time_for_change.htm.

Company's website: http://www.emmantina.gr.

8

Orbis On Line: Internet distribution strategies for a regional hotel group

Miroslaw Nalazek

Learning Objectives

- Demonstrate how regional hospitality groups can take advantage of the Internet.
- Appreciate the need to develop new distribution strategy as a result of the Internet induced transparency.
- Explain how technology can assist organizations to operationalize their distribution strategies.

Introduction

Information technologies have brought dramatic changes to the way tourist products are distributed. Internet channels are bringing not only new opportunities, but also threats, to suppliers. In the new competitive environment the balance of power is shifting towards customers who are now easily able to find the best offerings easily. New intermediaries in the shape of online travel agencies have emerged as a very powerful, if expensive, distribution channel. All this necessitates a new approach to distribution strategies by the hotel sector. The challenge is how to keep distribution costs as low as possible, how to maximize potential reach and exposure, and how to maintain control over proprietary products.

This case study shows how the regional hotel group – Orbis Hotels Group – developed, as part of their new distribution strategy, the system 'Orbis On Line', which enables Orbis to control its offerings and use new web channels to successfully market products.

Orbis Hotel Group

Orbis S.A. operating under the name Orbis Hotel Group with headquarters in Warsaw, Poland, is the largest hotel network in Central-Eastern Europe. It is operating under the brands Sofitel, Novotel, Mercure, Ibis, Orbis Hotels and Etap. Currently the group manages 64 hotels in Poland and one in Lithuania. By 2009 the company plans to expand the number of hotels to 82 especially in economy segment (mainly Ibis and Etap brands). Orbis S.A. is also a major shareholder of Orbis Travel, a travel agency network and tour operator, as well as Orbis Transport the bus operator. Orbis S.A. has been listed on the Warsaw Stock Exchange since 1997. Its major stockholder and partner is Accor Group, one of the biggest hotel groups in the world.

Why a New Approach to Distribution was Needed

The expansion of the Internet has dramatically changed the traditional distribution model of hotel services dramatically. Four to five years ago hoteliers were desperate for any business through any channel, due to low occupancy rates resulting from the slow economy and other global factors such as 9/11 terrorist attacks and SARS.

Online travel agencies' promises to bring new incremental revenue was welcomed even if it meant deep discounts from the rack rates as it meant covering, at least partially, overhead expenses. Orbis Hotels were no exception. Most of them entered into merchant contracts with many online travel agencies, both Polish and international.

However, soon so-called Internet rates, which supposedly were limited to only certain segments of the market, became widely available. For example, all three major horizontal portals in Poland: www.onet.pl, www.interia.pl and www.wp.pl were offering discounted rates at most Orbis hotels to everybody with no restrictions or limitations. They were also available through travel sites such as www.odkryjposlke.pl, www.staypoland.pl and many other Polish and foreign sites. Instead of an additional channel, online travel agents became the primary web channel for many Orbis hotels. What made the situation worse was that each hotel could have a direct contract with the same online travel agency. The competition was not only with non-Orbis hotels, but also in some cases with other Orbis hotels in the same locations. The result was that some hotels were selling rooms with discounts 30–50% on rack rates. With 30% or more of revenues from the sales of a room going to intermediaries and increasing share of sales of online travel agencies it was clear that average daily rates (ADR) would have to fall and negatively affect the profits of hotels and the whole Group.

Another problem which emerged in connection with Internet channels was inconsistency in rates between various channels. The differences between rates for the same product could reach 20–30% depending on the channel the customer was using. This was not only Orbis hotels' problem. According to a KPMG survey (KPMG, 2005) only 1% of the hotels surveyed had consistent rates across all distribution channels. The survey was conducted with over 330 hotels in 16 countries in February 2005.

New Distribution Strategy

To eliminate these problems and secure competitive advantage on the market, in 2003, Orbis Hotel Group adopted a new distribution strategy.

First, as a way of lowering the distribution costs, the Group decided to increase direct sales through its own website. The distribution cost in this case is a fraction of what it was through traditional channels such as GDS, online travel agents and other systems such as Utell (Starkov, 2002; Buhalis, 2003). An additional advantage of direct distribution is lessening the dependency on those expensive channels and gaining better control over Orbis' own products. The reservation process is an important opportunity to gather information about the customer and to build a relationship with him. Some authors claim that given its benefits, other channels will become ultimately obsolete.

Second, the strategy called for the introduction of an advanced revenue management system for all hotels to increase revenues and profitability. The system will optimize revenues by managing rates and their availability based on historical and actual demand. The main market segment for most of Orbis hotels are corporate clients. The demand from that segment is characterized by fluctuations. Therefore it is very important to sell inventory to other segments when corporate clients demand is low.

Thirdly, the situation where the same rates category was different in some channels from the others was considered as detrimental to building customer confidence and their loyalty. It was decided, then, that rates should be consistent through all channels irrespective whether it is direct or indirect sale. The best rate on Orbis' own website should be guaranteed.

Implementation of the above tasks required the introduction of a new ICT system, which would combine the functions of a reservation system both for direct and indirect sales provide a revenue management system with the functionality to control all rates in different channels.

How the Orbis On Line System Helps to Implement the New Distribution Strategy

The Orbis On Line system (www.orbisonline.pl) was developed by a local ICT company in two phases. In the first phase, which lasted 9 months, an Internet reservation system both for individual and corporate clients was developed along with several interfaces to other Orbis systems, and started its operation in June 2004. Within 15 months other modules of the system were added so by the end of 2005, full functionality was in place. Today Orbis On Line serves not only as an Internet reservation channel and revenue management system but also as a distribution platform fully integrated with other key applications of the Orbis group, such as a central database of all hotels, a corporate client database as well as outside systems like a credit card authorization centre.

The design of Orbis On Line system is modular so it can be easily adapted to changing business needs of the company in the future.

Direct Sales Modules

Direct distribution is done through two modules: for individual clients and for corporate clients. The user interface for individual clients is in Polish and also in English, French, German and Russian. In addition to standard searching and booking capabilities, users may register in the system so that their personal details are kept in the system database and can be used for future reservations. When designing the module the priority was on a balance between simplicity and functionality. After selecting the hotel, the individual user can finalize the booking in just two steps while having options for additional functions such as invoice printing, credit card payment, instant confirmation printing, etc.

Access to the system by corporate clients (also public administration) is only possible with authentication (user name and the password). The system keeps data from several thousands of contracts signed by Orbis Group with Polish and foreign firms. Details of contracts (special rates, payment conditions, etc.) are kept in a separate application and are updated in the Orbis On Line system on a daily basis through a dedicated interface. Corporate users can book hotels in Orbis On Line either at negotiated rates or any rates available to individual clients. The user interface is in Polish or English. Each corporate client has access to all their own bookings and can review previous bookings and manage (change or cancel) those that are pending.

Orbis On Line was very positively received by corporate clients since it meant substantial cost savings and better control of travel expenditures.

Revenue Management Module

To adapt room availability to changing demand, different rate categories were created. Allocations of inventory of each room type to those categories, both long and short term (1 month), are done with a dedicated revenue management module. Any price or availability changes resulting from changing market conditions can be immediately accessed.

Revenue management is especially important for hotels of upper categories as often more than 20 different rates are available, across

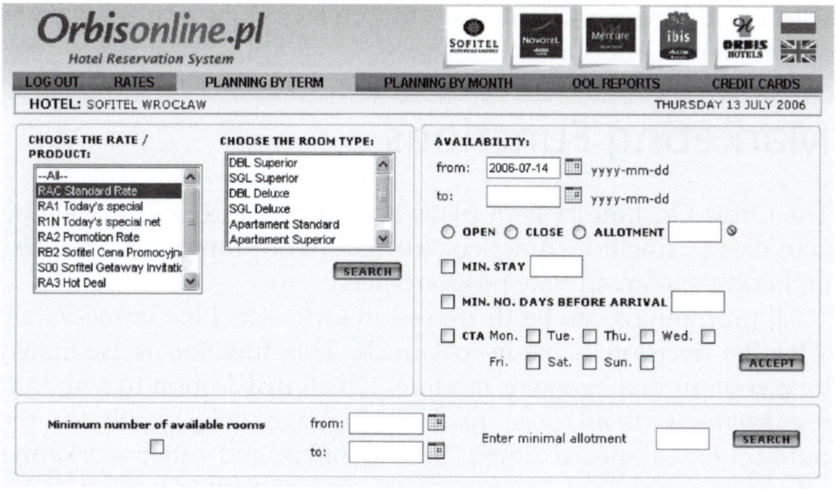

Figure 8.1 Revenue management module
Source: www.orbisonline.pl

several room types. Hotels of lower categories usually apply 1–2 rate categories; therefore revenue management is less complicated.

In addition to room availability hotels can create hotel packages, stipulate minimum days required prior to arrival and close certain days of the week (so-called 'closed to arrival' function). In Figure 8.1 the screen with long-term planning of availability is displayed.

Online Travel Agents' Interface – Price Control Function

To solve the problem of inconsistency of rates in different distribution channels it was decided to produce an application that would store all rates for all hotels and allow for their management online, directly by hotels. This so-called 'Central Price List', also represents the single source of information on rates for online travel agents (web agents). Rates are uploaded on daily basis in the form of XML structured messages and then imported to web agents' systems.

The interface has also another very important function – it provides web agents with room inventory availability in all hotels so that their respective systems can display real time availability and confirm bookings made in those systems; effectively enabling Orbis On Line to act as a gateway for online travel agents.

In order to simplify the management of web agent channels on an ongoing basis and therefore reduce costs, only those agents who could develop an interface to Orbis On Line were invited to partner with Orbis Group.

Marketing Functions

The Orbis On Line system plays an important role in marketing activities as it includes functions such as online promotions, statistics gathering and an affiliate programmes.

All promotions can be displayed in Orbis On Line immediately after the decision is made to launch. This function is facilitated by a content management module, which in addition to standard management of all texts in five languages also facilitates the publication of special offers. Special offers and other marketing information are sent via newsletter and distributed to all registered customers in order to increase their loyalty.

All important statistics regarding the usage of Orbis On Line site are captured by a special third-party programme. They provide very valuable marketing information on usage of the site: time spent, behavioural patterns, user's profile, relative popularity of offers and/or sections, key words users use to search for Orbis hotels, etc. This programme also identifies how well the Orbis On Line website is positioned in various search engines.

The affiliate programme allows all interested parties to offer Orbis hotels on their sites. The benefit for Orbis Hotels is obvious – they can substantially increase the reach of their offer. For Orbis partners the benefit is financial as they receive commission when the customer actually makes the booking.

Synopsis and Challenges for the Future

Orbis On Line's innovative approach to its distribution model gives the company significant competitive advantage. Complex revenue management, rates control and marketing activities contribute to increase ADR and profitability of the Group.

However, continuous development of the system is necessary for maintaining its leading position. To achieve this, Orbis Group has outlined a number of key actions. These include improvement of technology, further extension of services available to corporate and individual users as well as travel agents, and expansion of partnership programs (placing links on other tourism and non-tourism portals).

Key Conclusions

- Travel intermediaries and hotel groups need to take advantage of the emerging technologies.
- Distribution strategies need to take advantage of the Internet and explore the full potential for organizations to strengthen their competitiveness.
- Interconnectivity with partners should be fully automated to ensure interoperability and efficiency.

Review and Discussion Questions

- How can distribution strategies support the competitiveness of hotel groups?
- What technologies are required to maximize the distribution potential?
- Why is revenue management important for hotel groups?

References and Further Reading

Buhalis, D. (2003). *eTourism: Information technology for strategic tourism management*. Harlow: Prentice Hall.

Connoly, D. *What's Your Hotel Distribution Strategy?* Retrieved from http://www.hftp.org/members/bottomline/backissues/2001/DEC01–JAN02/distr.htm.

KPMG Hotel Distribution Survey 2005. Retrieved from http://www.kpmg.com.

Orbis Annual Reports 2003, 2004 and 2005.

Starkov, M. (2002). *The Internet: Hotelier's Best Ally or Worst Enemy?* Retrieved from http://www.hospitalitybusiness.com.

Company's website: http://www.orbisonline.pl.

Conclusion of Hospitality Section

Both international hotel chains and SMTEs increasingly use ICTs to implement strategic and operative objectives. The Internet has now penetrated all major fields of life and business in our society, and is of interest for both consumers and providers. It thus constitutes a medium that is being used more and more, and hence acquiring more and more importance. Online marketing, whether direct, via an online travel agency or via a destination website, is thus of huge importance for large and small enterprises, both directly and indirectly.

Alongside the use for distribution and marketing purposes, ICTs have become a major factor in the hospitality industry in both the front office and the back office area. Property management systems and central reservation systems in large decentralized units manage information about room availability, prices, categories and status, customer data, personnel data, wage payment and bookkeeping data. The technological developments in recent years have produced numerous solutions for improving process efficiency, enhancing internal and cross-business coordination and ensuing communication with the customer via a large number of information and distribution channels. The effectiveness in using ICTs and online distribution channels will increasingly determine the ability of hotels to manage their inventory and rates effectively.

Part Two

Intermediaries
Dimitrios Buhalis
Roman Egger

Introduction

While for a tourism supplier the production of the service is at the centre of his activities, the distribution of third-party services constitutes the core business of an intermediary. Hence intermediaries act for a producer to market the products to end customers or other intermediaries. Traditionally, intermediaries of the travel industry have been outbound and inbound travel agencies and tour operators. However, there was a sudden change in the market structures following the rise of the Internet in the late 1990s. The Internet restructured the entire touristic value chain, forcing the existing intermediaries to take up the new medium and to develop corresponding business models.

While the value chain in the old economy can be regarded as a sequence of linear sub-processes, in the new economy these processes are carried out simultaneously by a number of different networks. This structure permits a free configuration of the value chain, with company-internal and external processes being supported by intranets and extranets. Therefore, the use of the Internet in the field of tourism can no longer be regarded as a supplementary independent application, but instead it must be integrated along the entire value chain (Porter 2001). While in classical economics, commerce is regarded as having four basic functions, namely spatial, temporal, quantitative and qualitative transformation, the Internet is capable of supporting and unbundling all functions. This allows the possibility of outsourcing functions and processes to suppliers outside the trade. These issues form the basis of the emerging trends described as dynamic intermediation, disintermediation and reintermediation.

The unbundling of individual functions creates specialized enterprises whose core competence means that efficiency and cost benefits can be achieved. Chircu and Kauffman (2000) defined the term intermediation as the entry of a new enterprise in the value chain in order to establish a link between customers and providers, either as a provider of new and innovatory services or as competitor to existing intermediaries. Intermediaries play an important economic role, both on physical markets and on information markets. The intermediary acts to secure quality and variety, and offers product-specific information. The intermediation costs arising must naturally be added to the production cost and as a consequence increase price and make competition more difficult.

The WWW has offered a new distribution alternative alongside the three existing channels of face-to-face, catalogue and telephone sales. Nowadays, Internet users are able to search the net on their own, to compare and book offers at any time they choose from any location around the world. Greater transparency and lower transaction costs in the Internet economy result in a shifting of market forces towards the customer (empowerment). Today, the Internet can provide tourists with better information than travel agencies were able to do only a few years ago. This fact is changing the process of purchase decisions dramatically. Direct contact with the provider of services may render the route via the intermediary obsolete. Falling transaction and interaction costs reduce the role of the intermediaries and can lead to disintermediation. In the context of tourism, this mainly affects tour operators, travel agencies and the GDS. The trend towards disintermediation is driven both by the suppliers and by the consumers, and implemented by what are known as cybermediaries. These enter the electronic marketplace and make the exchange between purchasers and sellers easier, the purchasers being either private persons (B2C) or companies (B2B) (Egger, 2005; Morris & Morris, 2002; Buhalis & Licata, 2002).

The direct contact to the customer aimed at by disintermediation however leads to new uncertainty and market confusion. As a result, several new intermediaries and online travel agencies aggregate tourism products and provide transparency among the multitude of offerings (Case 9: Lastminute.com; Case 10: Wotif; Case 11: A2Z Professionals Travel). Amongst the new e-mediaries there are also numerous providers that belong to enterprises outside the trade. These providers often have many years of e-business know-how and have a powerful financial background. Expedia (Case 10), a system developed by Microsoft, has had a very rapid growth, demonstrating that the new major e-mediaries constitute not only a stronger competition but are also able to displace many companies with years of experience in tourism, such as American Express and Rosenbluth Travel (Buhalis, 2003). Some travel-intermediaries are still fighting today for their spot on the online market. The following case studies illustrate how travel organizers use ICTs to coordinate their processes, communicate interactively with their stakeholders, make strategic management decisions and profit from new sources of income (Case 12: ITWG; Case 13: Incoming Partners; Case 16: TUI).

The Internet is also forcing GDSs and switch companies to reconsider their business models. For instance, Travelocity.com was purchased by Sabre in order to establish contact with customers and to counteract tendencies towards disintermediation (Palmer, 1999). In this respect, reintermediation is regarded as:

> *the process through which an once disintermediated player is able to re-enter the value chain that supports buyer-seller transactions. Reintermediation occurs when the traditional player in the marketplace is able to adopt new and innovative ways for conducting transactions, often enhanced by the applications of ICT, and thus effectively fight back against other competitors that have created the pressures for disintermediation* (Chircu & Kauffman, 2000)

The risk for intermediaries in this connection appears not to be disintermediation but possibly the failure to achieve reintermediation in time (Egger, 2005). Evidence from the Scandinavian countries demonstrate that tour operators have re-emerged as key players in the marketplace, once they were able to apply ICTs and eCommerce effectively.

The huge success of the Internet has also produced new and up-to-now non-existent forms of intermediaries. Metamediaries like travel meta-search engines (TSEs) and 'infomediaries' appear between suppliers and consumers to aggregate and filter out relevant and pertinent information from the wealth of material. TSEs like Sidestep (Case 14), Mobissimo and Kayak enable customers to compare offers and prices by carrying out live queries to suppliers, consolidators and online agencies and presenting the results transparently. Numerous infomediaries such as Tripadvisor and HolidayCheck (Case 15) successfully implement a Web 2.0 approach and integrate the users as producers of trusted content. Tourists use the intermediaries' portals to report on their travel experiences, describe offers and evaluate tourism products and services.

In a buyer's market, it is necessary to be present in the communication channels used by consumers. Alongside online travel agencies, which have adapted their business model to become hardly distinguishable from tour operators, Internet portals (e.g. Yahoo! Travel) and vertical portals (e.g. ski.com, golf.com) have also specialized in the tourism sector. They provide information or theme-focused access to tourism providers. Auction platforms such as eBay have also become attractive for tourism products over the last few years. The complexity and variety of the travel market therefore require new intermediaries who offer solutions in multi-channel management (Case 17: Cultuzz) and coordinate processes in order to make economical use of the variety of marketing possibilities. The intermediate trade in the tourist sector, driven by the rapid development of ICTs, in particular on the Internet, has undergone dramatic changes and increased in dynamism. For this reason, intermediaries will in future need more than ever a high degree of flexibility and willingness to innovate. In addition, a decisive factor will be the clear communication of customer value-added benefits and a dynamic interaction with all stakeholders.

These changes force intermediaries to rethink their business model and to take drastic actions in re-developing their value chains. They disintermediate all other intermediaries that are adding cost to the production and distribution. For example, tour operators aim to sell their packages directly bypassing travel agencies. They also dis-bundle their packages and sell individual components. On the other hand travel agencies dynamically package tour products and support the development of customized packages, disintermediating tour operators. Electronic intermediaries are also emerging dynamically and challenge traditional distributors. For example, Expedia and Lastminute.com are now challenging the business models of Thomson and Thomas Cook, forcing them to rethink their operations and strategies. Auctions sites such as eBay.com, price comparison sites such as Kelkoo and Kayak.com; price reversing sites such as Priceline.com and price prediction sites such as farecast.com also provide a great challenge for the pricing strategies of both suppliers and intermediaries. In addition Web 2.0 or Travel 2.0 providers such as Tripadvisor.com, IGOUGO.com and Wayn.com also enableconsumers to interact and to offer peer-to-peer advice. At a time of a very volatile environment in the marketplace, tourism intermediaries are forced to readdress both their revenue and cost bases as well as to re-evaluate all partnerships and value chains.

References and Further Reading

Buhalis, D. (2003). *eTourism: Information technology for strategic tourism management*. Pearson: Financial Times/Prentice Hall.

Buhalis, D., & Licata, C.M. (2002). The future of eTourism intermediaries. *Tourism Management*, 23, 207–220.

Chircu, A., & Kauffman, R. (2000). Reintermediation strategies in business-to-business electronic commerce. *International Journal of Electronic Commerce*, 4, 7–42.

Egger, R. (2005). *Grundlagen des eTourism: Informations- und Kom munikationstechnologien im Tourismus*. Aachen: Shaker Verlag.

Gellman, R. (1996). Disintermediation and the Internet. *Government Information Quarterly*, 1, 1–8.

Morris, L., & Morris, J. (2002). The changing role of the middlemen in the distribution of personal computers. *Journal of Retailing and Consumer Services*, 9, 97–105.

O'Connor, P. (2004). *Using computers in hospitality*. London: Thomson.

Österreich Werbung. (2007). Web 2.0 im Internet. Abgerufen am 29.05.2007. Erreichbar unter [http://www.austriatourism. com/scms/media.php/8998/Web20_summary.pdf].

Palmer, A., & McCole, P. (1999). The virtual re-indermediation of travel services: A conceptual framework and empirical investigation. *International Journal of Contemporary Hospitality Management*, 6 (1), 33–47.

Palmer, A., & McCole, P. (2000). The role of electronic commerce in creating virtual tourism destination marketing organisations. *International Journal of Contemporary Hospitality Management*, 12 (3), 198–204.

Porter, M. (2001). Strategy and the Internet. *Harvard Business Review*, 63–78.

Case

9

Lastminute.com: from reservation system to lifestyle portal

Dimitrios Buhalis and Senem Yazici-Malkoclar

Learning Objectives

- Demonstrate how intermediation has changed in the tourism industry.
- Appreciate the concept of value-added services in intermediation.
- Explore how travel intermediaries have gone through major concentration in the marketplace.
- Explain how advanced intermediaries deal with consumers online.
- Understand the issues related to company integration, following mergers and acquisitions.

Introduction

In October 1998 Brent Hoberman and Martha Lane Fox launched lastminute.com in the UK. Using the Internet they match suppliers' inventory with consumer last-minute demand. Lastminute.com works with a range of suppliers in the travel, entertainment and gift industries and is dedicated to bringing its customers attractive products and services. In 2005, it operated directly in 14 European countries and participated in 3 international joint ventures, providing travel and leisure inspirations and solutions to customers. In 2006 it was bought by the Travelocity/SABRE group to assist the group to expand their operations in Europe.

Hoberman and Lane Fox created the lastminute.com in their living room in London. As a strategy and technology consultant, Hoberman realized the big gap in the travel industry. Tourism operates on a dynamic structure and its specific characteristics make it different to other industries. Products are perishable and hotel rooms or airline products cannot be stored for sale the next day. Each day, unsold hotel room and airline seat sales are lost for ever. It is exactly the same for theatre tickets and many other similar services. That was the starting point of their dreams, which was to provide travel products at short notice and cheap prices to customers by using a dynamic website. The idea was to sell online seats and hotel rooms just a couple of days before departure at affordable prices. Lastminute.com developed a different approach to consumer behaviour, allowing impulse decisions at the last minute.

Hoberman and Lane Fox had a difficult time in raising financial capital to start up their business. The idea was unusual and hard-nosed financiers were difficult to persuade. However, they managed to raise £600,000 from Lane Fox's family and other financial sources and had a website live in 3 months. After they launched the website, they managed to obtain $1.5 million in seed money from investors in exchange for 40% of the equity in the firm.

Differentiating Travel Intermediation

From its origins Lastminute.com has been seeking to differentiate itself by packaging and delivering products and services in convenient, novel and distinctive ways. The company has been successful in developing a distinctive and widely recognized brand, which is intended to communicate spontaneity and a sense of adventure to a youthful target demographic. Lastminute.com has never expressed desire to become a normal travel agency website like others. The main objective was to build a lifestyle portal and distribution channel which was used every day for all their clients' leisure and travel needs. Gradually lastminute.com also developed solutions for the travel trade, especially after purchasing holidayautos.com and medhotels.com. Table 9.1 shows the Lastminute.com mission statement, values and 'leadership DNA'.

Table 9.1 Lastminute.com mission statement, value and 'DNA'

Lastminute.com Mission	'To strengthen our position as the number one e-commerce lifestyle player by delighting our customers with great-value inspiration and solutions.'
Lastminute.com Values	**Passion:** To display unprompted determination and figure boundless enthusiasm for work and the company. Drive and strong feelings of emotion are contagious to everyone around.
	Innovation: To question the status quo, generate and pursue creative ideas. To take intelligent risks and not to be afraid of making mistakes.
	Agility: To make tough, timely decisions while keeping quality and accuracy in mind. Be 'urgent', flexible and resourceful, overcoming obstacles to make things happen.
	Customer focus: To be optimistic, trustworthy and committed. To anticipate the customer's needs and concerns, and work to exceed expectations.
	Integrity: To enable the customer to make better, informed choices by providing straight-talking advice and useful information. To follow through on commitments giving customers and fellow employees consistent and honest guidance. To keep things simple.
	Fun: To create an environment which excites, inspires and motivates those around. To keep good humour, be 'human' and 'real', and respect the work/life balance.
Lastminute.com Leadership DNA	**Trustworthiness, transparency and openness:** To insist on honesty, integrity and openness. **Raise the bar:** To increase our standards of performance and strive for values. **Lead by example:** To inspire excellence and consistently demonstrate our values. **One voice:** To embrace 'collective' responsibility. **Bring me solutions:** To identify a problem is important, but to find the solutions is far more valuable. **No silos:** It is not 'their' problem: it's 'our' problem. The obligation to care: To truly care about the business and our colleagues

Sources: Adapted from Lastminute.com Annual Reports (2000–2005)

Lastminute.com has relationships with over 9300 suppliers, including scheduled airlines, hotels, package tour operators, theatre, sports and entertainment promoters, restaurants, speciality service providers, gift suppliers and car hire, both in the UK and internationally. Examples of supplier relationships include Lufthansa, Air France, Alitalia, British Midland, UNITED Airlines, Virgin Atlantic Airways, Starwood Hotels and Resorts Worldwide, The Savoy Group, Sol Melia, Kempinski Hotels, English National Ballet, The Royal Albert Hall and Conran Restaurants. Another development was a new partnership deal with Disneyland Resort Paris, also offering customers hotel accommodation and theme park tickets for Europe's number one tourist theme park. All seven of the themed Disney Hotels could be booked through lastminute.com, together with unlimited entry to the theme parks.

Lastminute.com carries almost no inventory risk, selling perishable inventory for its suppliers, and, where appropriate, protects suppliers' brand names until after purchase. To achieve this it is of utmost importance to continually expand the inventory sourced from high quality suppliers across the entire range of goods and services. Figure 9.1 shows the relationship between customer and

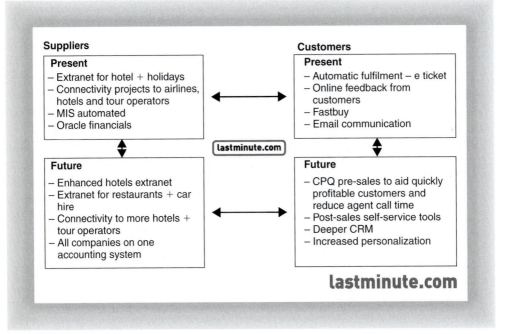

Figure 9.1 Lastminute.com business plan
Source: Hoberman and Fox (2003)

supplier of Lastminute.com. Their business plan was based on delivering the right product at the right time to the right customer at a reasonable (not necessarily cheapest) price range by using the right technology.

The best way to reach the right customer was a differentiated marketing and sales approach. Lastminute.com had an aggressive marketing strategy especially in the UK that used a range of media and public relationships. Lastminute.com became a household name in less than 2 years, thanks to its strong branding and media coverage. The main tool of the marketing is the weekly newsletter, which shows all deals and news in a highly segmented and contemporary style. Figure 9.2 shows the newsletter circle marketing benefits of customer decision-making process and shows current subscribers in 2003. On 31st December 2004, Lastminute.com had over 9.8 million subscribers to its weekly newsletter and it increased to 10.3 million subscribers at the end of March 2005. The number of cumulative customer was 6.3 million in December 2004 which grew up to 7.2 million in March 2005.

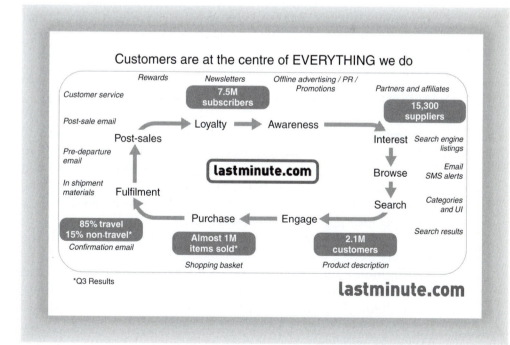

Figure 9.2 The newsletter circle of marketing
Source: Hoberman and Fox (2003)

Figure 9.3 Effective and sustainable marketing techniques
Source: Hoberman (2004)

Lastminute.com has epitomized the 'cool marketing' for their strategy. They used effective and sustainable marketing techniques which are shown in Figure 9.3 to encourage people to 'do something' and to respond on impulse. The advertisements included irreverent lines, contemporary and often controversial messages and striking images on branded buses to drive round key UK and French cities and billboard advertising in tube and train stations.

Business and Technology Innovations

A number of innovations were clearly evident in Lastminute. com development. In June 2004, Lastminute.com had launched an exciting new service through the O2 mobile network that enabled leisure-seekers to locate various deals through their mobile phone using the latest mobile location technology. Technology was a key aspect to keep prices down and reach customers fast and easy (Figure 9.4). The system enabled customers to interact with the company using a wide range of technologies.

Lastminute.com also developed their distribution channels and mechanism beyond the Internet adopting e-shops, IDTV (interactive digital TV e.g. Sky), PDA (personal digital assistants) and mobile phones, airport kiosks, white label solutions (e.g. Tesco), BT kiosks and voice recognition technology (Hoberman & Fox, 2003). Figure 9.5 shows some examples of technological devices Lastminute.com used for distributing products.

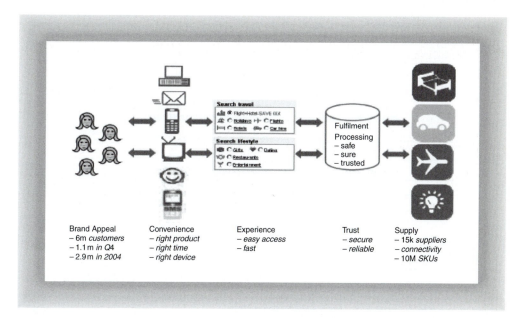

Figure 9.4 Lastminute.com technology platform
Source: Hoberman (2004)

Figure 9.5 Lastminute.com technology device
Source: Hoberman and Fox (2003)

Growing to a Pan European Business

The growth of Lastminute.com has been meteoric. Lastminute.com had just three recorded customers in October 1998. In October 1999,

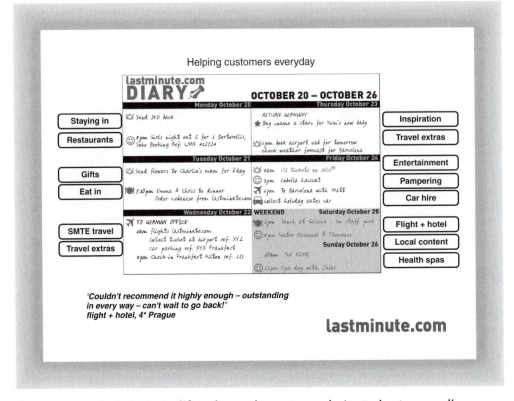

Figure 9.6 Lastminute.com lifestyle product approach: Lastminute.com diary
Sources: Recommended Offer for Online Travel Corporation Plc, Lastminute.com analyst presentation, 3 March 2003

it was voted 'Best UK Internet start-up' by management consultants Bain & Company and *Management Today* magazine. Floated in March 2000, the company had grown to 165 employees and the business had moved to offices in Oxford Circus. Lastminute.com became Europe's leading independent travel and leisure business which sell package holidays on behalf of 250 third-party tour operators. It was the first company that offered customers the opportunity to dynamically package a unique holiday experience, combining any flight with any hotel room and rental car. Figure 9.6 shows that Lastminute.com had a unique lifestyle proposition offering tickets to shows, gigs, festivals and theme-parks as well as leisure experiences, DVDs, restaurants and gifts. The main idea was that customers must use Lastminute.com for their everyday travel and leisure needs. They have created a Lastminute.com diary to show how easy it is to use the portal for different purposes in one day.

To consolidate its position in Europe, Lastminute.com grew rapidly through a number of acquisitions, making it one of the leading online players with a diverse portfolio. The group as it stood in 2005 had great inventory diversity and excellent relationships with suppliers. It also had access to more than 10 million customers around Europe that regularly used the service for a variety of leisure and business products. Lastminute.com had satellite offices in Ireland, Sweden, Australia and the Netherlands and joint ventures in Japan and UAE. It employed 2000 people globally, with its head office in London housing 350 of them. Lastminute.com is one of the top two most visited travel agency websites in the UK, with an average of 6 million unique site visitors monthly and receives most site hits on a Sunday, with almost 18% of overall visitors logging on that day.

In 2006, the company had over 9.8 million registered subscribers in Europe. Lastminute.com aims to be the global marketplace for all last minute services and transactions. Following the success of the UK site, localized versions of the website have since been launched in France, Germany, Sweden, Italy, Spain, the Netherlands, Australia, New Zealand and South Africa. This growing multinational presence will give the company the ability to develop and further strengthen the Lastminute.com brand. Lastminute.com seeks to differentiate itself by generating some of the lowest prices for many travel and entertainment deals, and by packaging and delivering products and services, such as restaurant reservations, entertainment tickets and gifts, in convenient, novel and distinctive ways. It also aims to inspire its customers to try something different. Hence, Lastminute.com aims at creating the one-stop shop for all last minute needs.

Figure 9.7 demonstrates that a number of trends in travel, technology and lifestyle are best supplied by the Lastminute.com offering, demonstrating that the company has a promising future. Their mission statement suggests

> *lastminute.com encourages spontaneous, romantic and sometimes adventurous behaviour by offering people the chance to live their dreams at unbeatable prices!*

This clearly defines their business as a life style portal offering a wide range of products and services to people that impulse purchasing. Although tourism products dominate the site, several additional products are available including meals delivered at home, gifts including electronics and underwear and insurance. The company has developed a distinctive brand, which communicates spontaneity and a sense of adventure, attracting a loyal community of registered subscribers that use the Lastminute.com's

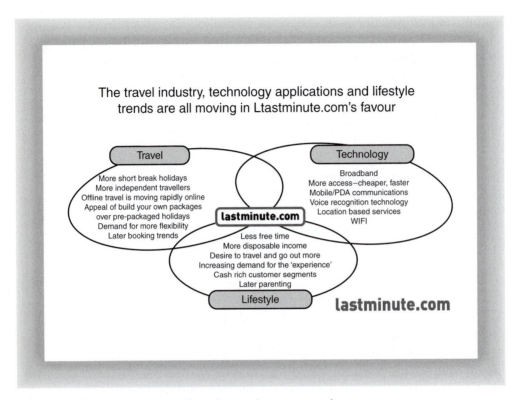

Figure 9.7 Lastminute.com lifestyle product approach
Source: Recommended Offer for Online Travel Corporation Plc, Lastminute.com analyst presentation, 3 March 2003

website and have submitted their email addresses and other data to receive weekly emails.

The Future of the Company

Between 2000 and 2004, Lastminute.com purchased 14 businesses to gain scale and presence throughout Europe and also to expand its value chain backwards (by enhancing inventory and its value) and forward (by accessing more consumers in Europe). Figure 9.8 shows that Lastminute.com now owns and operates online brands including holidayautos.com, travelprice.com, degriftour.com, travel select.com, travel4less.co.uk, eXhilaration.co.uk, medhotels.com, first-option.co.uk, gemstonetravel.com, onlinetravel.com and last-minute.de. Recent acquisitions have given Lastminute.com scale but have also made the organization more complex. Figure 9.8 summarizes Lastminute.com's acquisition trail and demonstrates how the company gained size in such a short period of time.

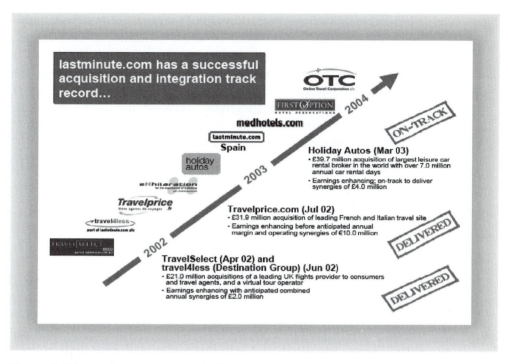

Figure 9.8 Lastminute.com acquisitions
Source: Recommended Offer for Online Travel Corporation Plc, Lastminute.com analyst presentation, 3 March 2004

Acquisition of Lastminute.com by Travelocity Europe

In July 2005 Travelocity acquired Lastminute.com Plc in order to expand and grow in the European Market. The acquisition was made by Travelocity Europe Ltd, an indirect subsidiary of Sabre Holdings. In a move aimed at creating Europe's largest online travel service company, Travelocity.com offered approximately £577 million (US$1.1 billion) paying 165p a share. The acquisition price for the shares in Lastminute.com and the redemption price payable in respect of Lastminute.com's bonds equates to an equity value of approximately £577 million and an enterprise value of approximately £584 million, including gross debt as at 20 July 2005 of approximately £79 million and estimated cash at bank in hand at 14 July 2005 of approximately £72 million. Hoberman, who remained as chief executive, received just over £26 million for his 15.8 million shares, while Lane Fox's stake of 8.2 million shares was worth around £13.5 million.

For Travelocity the integration with Lastminute.com offered strategic, financial and operational benefits, including a good launch pad for Sabre's wholesale initiatives in Europe. Holiday Autos is the world's largest leisure car rental broker and MedHotels is the leading UK wholesaler for Mediterranean resort hotels. Leveraging Lastminute.com's broad merchant content for Sabre agencies also enables expansion of their product type. Travelocity claimed the strategic benefits of the merger as:

- Creates a leading position in Europe;
- Global supplier value proposition;
- Complementary supplier relationships;
- Significant combined brand power;
- Strong management team;
- Excellent cultural fit and entrepreneurial spirit.

The combined force of Lastminute.com and Travelocity will mean fierce competition for IAC's Expedia and Cendant. This move places them at a competitive advantage because they are now penetrating all key channels of travel online and offline around the world. The acquisition of Lastminute.com will also help Sabre's negotiating position with global airline and hotel companies, creating cheaper prices which it could then pass on to customers. Its high brand recognition, supplier relationships (currently around 13,600) and the size of its user base are considerable assets for Travelocity.

The company announced that with the closing of the acquisition, Lastminute.com will be the lead brand for Travelocity in most of Europe, and is expected to continue expanding. Travelocity will support multiple brands where it makes sense, with the intent of sharing underlying infrastructure, technology and supply to drive cost savings. Some of the benefits the companies expect to achieve include offering a wide range of discounted hotels through Travelocity's net rate hotel program to Lastminute.com customers, sharing best-in-class technology capabilities globally, and providing expanded European travel options for Travelocity customers over time. Additionally, Sabre Holdings' agency partners may gain additional European travel options that are a part of the Lastminute.com portfolio.

Conclusion

Travel companies try to strengthen their off-line and online presence in the marketplace. Lastminute.com emerged from nowhere to become one of the key players in the online travel market and a household brand in only few years. It facilitated the transformation of the tourism industry through the introduction of dynamic packaging and emerged as a key player in the marketplace through its differentiation and lifestyle concepts. Travelocity saw the uniqueness of Lastminute.com and bought it to expand its entire network. After combining Travelocity and Lastminute.com a number of market, with technological and cultural challenges emerge. Despite the rapid developments in the industry, travel is still a dynamic and the fastest changing industry, with new ideas and consumers demands always reshaping the industry. The combined Travelocity/Lastminute.com will be gaining more powerful place in the European market. The future of the travel industry is unknown but it is becoming increasingly obvious that integration and merger will be controlled by large, integrated US-based companies in the future.

References and Further Reading

Hoberman, B., & Fox, M.L. (2003). *Vision and Potential Growth Lastminute.com Analyst Presentation*, Lastminute.com Investor Relation, Retrieved from http://www.hugin.info/131840/R/925314/125915.pdf.

Hoberman, B. (2004). *Solid Platform Growth Lastminute.com Analyst Presentation*, Lastminute.com Investor Relation, Retrieved from http://www.hugin.info/131840/R/970300/141967.pdf.

Lastminute.com Annual Reports. (2000–2005), Retrieved from http://www.cws.huginonline.com/L/131840/reports.html.

Lastminute.com General Press Release (2000–2005). *Lastminute.com Investor Relation*, Retrieved from http://www.cws.huginonline.com/L/131840/financial_releases.html.

http://www.sabre.com.

http://www.travelocity.com.

Company's website: http://www.lastminute.com.

10

Wotif.com: last minute selling of distressed accommodation inventory

Paul Weeks and Charles Tee

Learning Objectives

- Demonstrate how last minute distressed inventory intermediation has become mainstream in the tourism industry.
- Appreciate the role of bed banks for the tourism industry.
- Explore how competitive the travel intermediaries market has become.
- Explain the business model of Wotif.com.
- Understand the challenges related to online distribution of distressed inventory.

Introduction

In recent years, an increasing number of Web-based businesses have specialized in selling service products such as airline seats and hotel roomnights. As online service intermediaries (e-mediaries), these firms have successfully gained the interest and patronage of service customers because they are able to offer substantial benefits to the customer, such as a number of choices, convenience and value for money. For the sellers, such as airlines and hotels, these firms help increase the effectiveness and efficiency of distribution, which, in a service context, is a major determinant of the business success of a service provider (La & Kandampully, 2002). This case study focuses on one such organization: Wotif.com, a specialist in last minute selling of distressed accommodation inventory in Australia and the surrounding Asian region.

Company Development

Beginning with a few hotel properties in 2000, Wotif.com was born in Brisbane and serviced the Australian accommodation market. Instead of coving all sectors within tourism industries, Wotif.com chose to limit its reach to the accommodation sector. This company was one of the first to identify a market for distressed room inventory and initially allowed online customer to buy one week ahead. In contrast to other online e-mediaries at the time, such as lastminute.com and webjet.com.au, Wotif.com created a hotel price matrix, which provided the added benefit for travellers to see a range of days/prices, rather than the traditional static total nights/total booking cost scenario. The ability of Wotif.com to tap into volatile rooms inventory (selling 7 days prior) meant that they could provide genuinely heavily discounted rooms to both inventory generators (accommodation suppliers) and potential customers.

Starting with the hotel sector, within the first 12 months, Wotif.com had expanded into other alternative accommodation, such as bed and breakfasts, apartments, guesthouses and motels.

Over the next 2 or 3 years, the company expanded into Europe (opening its London office in 2001), and embedded a more advanced search facility into its web portal, enabling customers to search by a variety of categories, such as price, star rating, destination, and extended its booking period to 14 days out. By the end of 2003, the company was selling inventory on 20 countries, from the US through to Europe, including Asia and New Zealand (Wotif.com History, 2006).

By 2006, Wotif.com's portfolio included over 6000 hotels, motels, serviced apartments, resorts and guesthouses in 36 countries (from Austria, Hungary, Portugal to Vietnam). The company has major regional offices in Canada, New Zealand, Malaysia, Singapore and the United Kingdom; its headquarters are still in Brisbane, Australia. The properties can be booked online or through its call centre which operates 24 hours a day, 7 days a week. The company also announced that it would yet again extend its booking period, this time to 28 days.

Main Products/Offerings and Value Added

Wotif.com's business started with the servicing of the accommodation needs of the Australian traveller within Australia. It has since evolved to offer international accommodation options and also opened up to service the needs of travellers internationally.

Accommodation properties discount their full-rate rooms, uploading these rates onto Wotif.com's website to target travellers looking for short-term bargains. Of the AU$10 billion Australian accommodation market, in 2006 Wotif.com commands a 5% market share (AU$250 million). Online market growth by online websites excluding that of hotel's own websites' competitors is close to 30% per year. For the online accommodation market in Australia, Wotif.com has 50% of the online booking market and 70% of the last-minute market for accommodation booked within 14 days of travel. It generates 36% of all online accommodation sales emanating from Australia.

Given the extension to its booking period (in 2006, 28 days out), the company is now vying for business with other online travel portals, who sell their hotel accommodation allotment on longer lead times, but at higher prices, than the 'last-minute' market. For the inventory generators (accommodation sector businesses) this alleviates the problem of unoccupied rooms, when supply exceeds demand; for the traveller it allows them to find and book real-time last-minute deals at heavily discounted prices.

There are few Australian accommodation websites operating a service identical to that of Wotif.com. Examples of Wotif.com's main competitors include ratestogo.com and readyrooms.com; the former plies their trade more internationally than does Wotif.com, and the latter is a subsidiary of Qantas, using the competitive power of such a large organization to leverage its offerings. One interesting point here is that ratestogo.com has created a 'member' category of booking, allowing its 'members' to gain reward points if they book with ratestogo.com, redeemable for other ratestogo.com properties.

There are other online e-mediaries that sell a range of product to their customers; Lastminute.com for example offers not just accommodation, but 'holidays, hotels, restaurants, entertainment, gifts, experiences' (Lastminute.com, 2006).

Business Model

In 2006, annual revenues of AU$360 million, with 2 million user sessions and 110,000 bookings per month (Timson, 2006) has meant that the company has been in the process of rapid expansion. With such an expansion, the focus has been on the strategic direction of the company and its move into the Asian market.

Wotif.com customers come from a range of markets, including short-term travellers looking for a cheap stop-over rate to corporate clients who regularly use Wotif.com to make booking for their management and staff. There is a clear split between the leisure and business markets: 50:50. According to the Wotif.com figures (Wotif.com, 2006), the average Wotif.com booking was for a total of AU$265 (AU$147 per room per night), staying an average 1.5 nights, in a 4 or 4 and a half star property, booked 6 days in advance.

Wotif.com contracts with a number of accommodation sector suppliers who provide the company with an allotment of rooms that Wotif.com can sell at heavily discounted prices. The hotel can access the current take-up of rooms, and make their own tactical decisions as to whether they will increase or decrease allotments. Rather than being part of a larger organization (such as Lastminute. com, which is part of the Travelocity/Sabre group), Wotif.com identifies and markets its unique product to most of the better know hotel chains and independents. These include Accor, Choice, Hilton, Radisson, Days Inn and Starwood.

The e-mediary model (Figure 10.1) suggests a close relationship between inventory generators and e-mediaries, such as Wotif.com. In the case of this company, because its focus is limited to the accommodation sector, this symbiotic relationship is critical to the ongoing well-being of Wotif.com. Instead of focusing on the ability to contract highly discounted rate from its hotel partners, Wotif.com acknowledges the impact that service has in the interaction: customers will evaluate the service quality of both Wotif.com and its partners through the users' experiences whilst using the Wotif.com booking portal.

There are two key aspects to the company's vision: the online experience and customer service. Scalability of operations is a

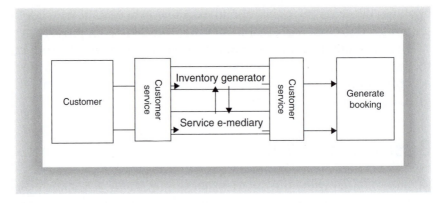

Figure 10.1 The e-mediary model

crucial aspect of Wotif.com's business operations. Given that the accommodation sector experiences peaks and troughs of booking activity, Wotif.com has focused very much on the experience of the user and the ability to provide consistent quality service interactions regardless of the traffic on the company's website (Timson, 2006). In order to accomplish the Wotif.com vision, new technology and a change in culture has been implemented in the company.

Technological and Business Innovation

The company has seen a huge increase in its Internet activity since it began in 2000. The move from allowing bookings 7 days prior to 28 days out, has generated a far greater market than had originally been anticipated. In order to cope with the increase (servicing 7000 customers online simultaneously [Timson, 2006]), the company has moved away from a Windows-based infrastructure to one using open source, where the company can take full advantage of new, improved and faster hardware.

The eight new 64-bit Sun Microsystems servers have been installed in their host centre in Adelaide, after heavy-load testing. The system can now accommodate a variety of software options, from open source, open standard through to proprietary brands (Timson, 2006).

The 38-people-strong ICT team monitors and controls the website, using Java and J2EE for web development. Most of the offices around the world still run Windows-based machines using Microsoft Office and ancillary programs. One of the key features of Wotif.com is that there is no requirement to take personal details or lock customers into a customer relationship management system (CRM). Wotif.com's vision is that customers will keep coming back to the company because it offers the best prices, the broadest range of accommodation options and has the most user-friendly interface (Timson, 2006).

Key Challenges for the Future

Wotif.com is one of only a handful of e-mediaries that service only the accommodation sector. This could be seen as a competitive disadvantage, due to its narrow portfolio, even though it accounts for some 6000 properties in 35 countries. By comparison, most of the other e-mediaries offer a range of products, from flights, to car hire to tour bookings at destination regions.

The highly competitive nature of the Internet, especially within the travel market, is a challenge for this company. The growth of the Internet, increasing use of e-commerce and the B2C sector mean that Wotif.com must focus clearly on its current markets and continue to deliver a fast user experience to its customers.

Other key challenges facing Wotif.com include:

- *Possible mergers and acquisitions*: At this stage, Wotif.com is a single entity, but this does not preclude future mergers with larger, product compatible organizations.
- *Globalization*: In 2006, Wotif.com focused its business on the Australasian region. However, there are plans to broaden its reach into Europe and the Americas, bringing it into competition with other established e-mediaries.
- *Quality control of inventory*: This is a crucial element of any e-mediary, but more so for a business that primarily focuses on the accommodation sector. Quality of its product offering is mandatory, through strict control criteria, and often through personal visits to inventory generators by its staff.
- *Scability*: This has been suggested as a key component of Wotif. com's operational strategy. Being able to constantly monitor fluctuations in both the supply and demand of hotel rooms requires both a managerial and technological solution.
- *Interconnection*: With both other e-mediaries (cooperative strategies) and other partners. This enables the company to broaden its product base and to ensure its future sustainability.

The Future of the Company

Over the past six years, Wotif.com has proved itself as a highly regarded force within the online travel market. Whilst focusing on distressed inventory and keeping bookings narrow (to 28 days out), it has been able to expand its supplier base, whilst also continuing to heavily discount room allotments.

In September 2005, the company announced that it would list on the Australian Stock Exchange. An initial public offering (IPO) has been lodged, together with a prospectus (available from the Wotif. com website). The company would still be owned by its current shareholders, and its CEO, who will hold 25.1% of shares post the IPO (Scoop Independent News, 2006).

In another move, Wotif.com has entered a partnership with an New Zealand company called Yourbiz.co.nz, with the intention of expanding its market reach outside Australia and Asia. Yourbiz is an online resource for small to medium businesses in NZ, many of whom will benefit from Wotif's involvement through better buying power for accommodation.

Overall, Wotif.com is a healthy, viable and sustainable organization. It is industry focused with advanced technology inter-woven into a forward-looking management perspective and business structure.

Key Conclusions

- Distributing last minute distressed inventory online is a key function of the Internet.
- Principals are now able to show real time prices and availability and follow their demand and supply function much closer.
- Hospitality intermediation has changed the industry dramatically.
- Competition is fierce and margins are becoming tight.
- Wotif.com has emerged as a global hotel distributor.

Review and Discussion Questions

- What is the unique selling point of Wotif.com?
- Discuss how Wotif.com can add value to its offerings.
- Explore the sources of competitive advantage for Wotif.com.
- How can Wotif.com improve its profitability?

References and Further Reading

La, K.V., & Kandampully, J. (2002). Electronic retailing and distribution of services: Cyber intermediaries that serve customers and service providers. *Managing Service Quality*, 12 (2), 100–116.

Lastminute.com (2006). *Lastminute.com Catalogue*. Retrieved 4 April 2006 from http://www.au.lastminute.com/lmn/pso/catalog.

Scoop Independent News (2006). *Wotif.com Announces Partnership with Yourbiz, 7th April 2006*, Retrieved 10 April 2006 from http://www.scoop.co.nz/stories.

Timson, L. (2006). Straight from the open source, *Sydney Morning Herald*, Tuesday, 4 April, p. 26.

Wotif.com (2006). *Our History*, Retrieved 12 March 2006 from http://info.wotif.com/about_our_history.

http://www.HolidayCity.com.

http://www.ratestogo.com.

http://www.readyrooms.com.

http://www.Asiarooms.com.

http://www.asiatravel.com.

Company's website: http://www.wotif.com.

Case

11

A2Z Professional Travel Ltd: online travel agency in Thailand

Pongsak Hoontrakul and Sunil Sahadev

Learning Objectives

- Demonstrate how a destination-based intermediary can provide products and services.
- Appreciate the role of destination-based intermediaries as B2B and B2C players.
- Explore the value-added services offered by a destination-based intermediary.
- Explain the business model of A2Z.
- Understand the future challenges emerging for online distribution.

Introduction

Thailand is one of the most favourite tourist destinations in the world. It is estimated that about 10 million tourists visit Thailand every year. Due to certain unforeseen events like the SARS outbreak and the Tsunami, the expected growth rate in tourist arrivals has not materialized over the last two years. However, the World Travel and Tourism Council (WTTC) forecasts a bright future for Thailand tourism in the next decade. Presently, the earnings from tourism contribute about 11% of the GDP of Thailand and are expected to increase to about 14% in 4–5 years.

A2Z Professional Travel Ltd (or A2Z) is an online travel intermediary based in Bangkok, Thailand (www.A2Z-ProTravel.com). It offers various travel-related services to both tourists and other travel agencies all over the world since its inception in 2002. Through its network of websites, the firm enables tourists and travellers to search and book rooms in hotels spread across Thailand. The firm practically offers an one-stop service that covers all needs, such as airport transfer, car rental, flight reservation, tourist guide, travel advisory, customized and familiarization trip arrangements, etc. To the potential tourist, it is best known for hotel bookings because it represents more than 1000 independently owned and operated (IOO) hotels in Thailand. The www.A2Z-Protravel.com, which is the company site, was founded in 2002 as an offshoot from Taipan1.com Ltd; a Bangkok based website that carried interesting travelogues about various locations in Thailand. This website attracted many prospective visitors who were interested in travelling to Thailand to enjoy the beautiful scenery and climate. Presently the company employs about 30 people. No agency is involved in collecting reliable data about the on-line travel industry in Thailand and hence it is difficult to estimate the relative market shares of the major players. Yet, A2Z professional travel undertook 25,000 room night bookings in 2004, with compound growth rate at 70%.

Key Products and Services and Value Added

World wide, in the travel and tourism industry, apart from the eventual service provider, firms that connect the end-customer to the service provider, like travel agents, also play an important role. This is because of the peculiar nature of the tourism product and the large geographical distance that separates the eventual service provider from the end-user.

A2Z offers services in both the B2C as well as B2B domains. Presently its major thrust is in the B2C domain where through its popular websites, A2Z offers its potential customers opportunities to search and book rooms in about 1000 IOOs properties across Thailand. Morethailand.com, the most popular among these websites, has grown to become a very popular brand among tourists and hoteliers in Thailand.

By relying on morethailand.com (homepage shown in Figure 11.1) or the other websites of A2Z protravel, customers benefit immensely in terms of the variety of choice that becomes available to them. This is because morethailand.com and other associated websites feature mostly IOO hotels. These hotels are comparatively less expensive and offer some exotic choices compared to large hotel chains. Morethailand.com prominently features IOO hotels which would otherwise be missed out on the GDS and large travel agency networks. For tourists located at geographically distant locations, information about and an opportunity to book in such IOO hotels provide an attractive proposition. Often, the tourists also receive considerable discounts from morethailand.com for rooms booked.

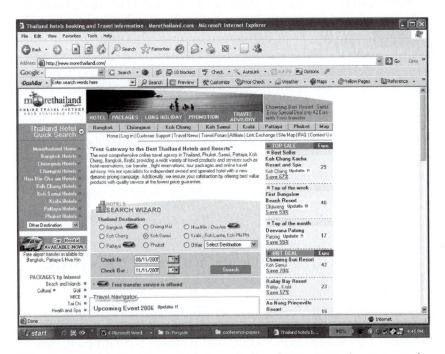

Figure 11.1 The homepage of morethailand.com, B2C site targeted inbound travellers

For these IOOs, having an effective presence in the online market is otherwise quite unviable and unlike travel wholesalers, morethailand.com does not demand a heavy discount from the IOOs. Compared to about 50–60% discount estimated by some travel wholesalers, morethailand.com charges less than 30% as discount. Thus, both ends of the stakeholder chain – the customers as well as the supplier – are in a win-win position if they choose to associate with morethailand.com.

B2B Offerings

While the B2C initiative of A2Z is being established, an expansion into the B2B domain is being contemplated. This involves linkages with the similar businesses units, from the travel distribution value chain that operate from different markets or offering complimentary products. With B2B operations A2Z would be able to access new markets, while the technology enabled interconnectivity options would provide operational efficiencies and scalability. Two types of B2B partnerships are contemplated: (i) Distribution partnerships with travel service providers with own distribution network and technology infrastructure, for the distribution of Thai-based travel products (e.g. MakeMyTrip.com, SunHotel.com) and (ii) Supplier partnerships with major B2B suppliers, for the supply of the hotel inventory from outside Thailand (e.g. HotelBeds.com, GHRS.com). This is enabled through the development of two major technology platforms: (i) The XML Interface, where the system uses the XML language to interact with the partner system and the inventory data is exchanged on a real time basis and (ii) Web services where ubiquitous technologies like XML, SOAP, etc. are used and is a cost effective solution that offers high flexibility and reusability.

Distribution partnerships imply using the existing aggregated inventory of A2Z pro travel to strike deals with large buyers like tour operators and travel agents in Europe and USA. Typically, it is not convenient or economical for the tour operators and travel agents based out of Europe or other developed countries to directly contact these small IOO hotels in Thailand; though such small but beautiful properties are in high demand in developed countries. Here the main advantage that A2Z enjoys is its existing network and the local knowledge that it has so assiduously built over the past several years. This network of relationships gives A2Z pro travel a competitive edge over its main competitors. Distribution partnerships are contemplated with (i) on-line travel retailers,

(ii) B2B distributors and (iii) off-line travel agents. The business structure for the distribution side partnerships is shown in Figure 11.2.

In addition, A2Z also operates the outbound travel division targeting the customers from Thailand and other nearby locations. The service is offered under the MoreCityHotels.com brand. A2Z relies on the supply from major B2B suppliers providing service for the targeted locations. Real time connectivity is established with the service providers with the help of XML interface and web services. The website – www.MoreCityHotels.com is used for this purpose. The business structure for the outbound division is shown in Figure 11.3.

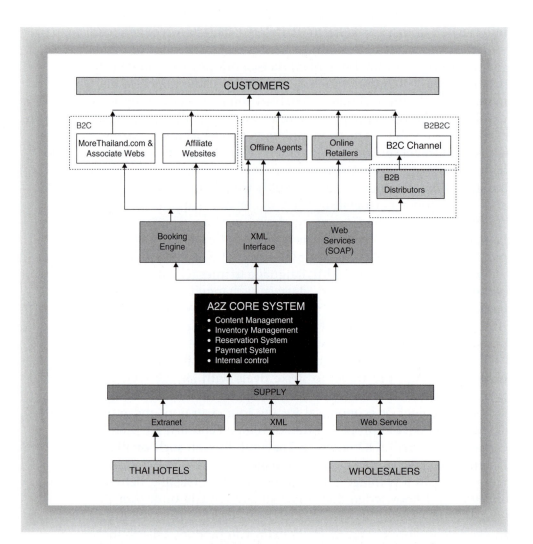

Figure 11.2 B2C and B2B2C business concept and charts for www.A2Z-ProTravel.com

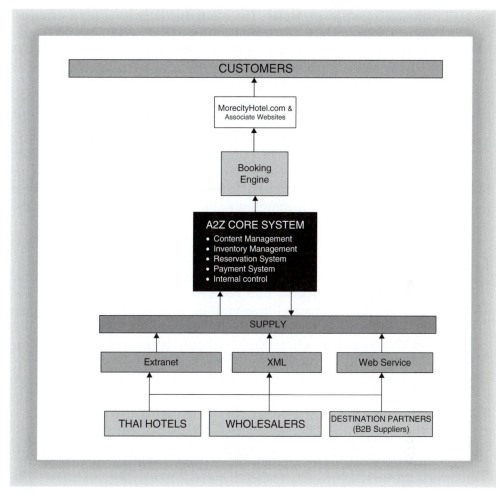

Figure 11.3 The business concept of www.MoreCityHotel.com for outbound travellers

Business Model

The intermediary enters into a contract/agreement with hotels in a particular destination based on which the names, descriptions and room rents of the hotel are included in the website. The hotel offers rooms at the rate indicated in the website to any customer who makes the inquiry through the website. Normally, the rates displayed in the website would be a bit less than the walk-in rates charged by the hotels. Customers can search and book a room matching their requirements through the website of the e-intermediary where a large number of hotels is displayed. The customer can book through the booking engine in the website and the full amount is passed on to the hotel three days before the customer is due to arrive in the hotel. The e-intermediary receives a commission/profit for each room booked through their website. There are of course certain instances of bookings where certain hotels would always reserve certain rooms for the website whose availability can be instantly confirmed.

The main cost for the e-intermediaries is to maintain staff for the back office activities and promotion of their websites. The marketing activities include search engine optimization, email marketing and other means of off-line promotion. Hotels which find it costlier to have electronic interfaces can easily make themselves available to a global audience through the Internet by contracting with these e-intermediaries. Customers also benefit since they can search and book rooms at affordable rates.

To understand the position of A2Z in the B2C domain, it is important to analyse the travel intermediary sector of Thailand. Figure 11.4 depicts the various channels through which a potential tourist can book rooms in a hotel in Thailand. Of these, the first and the second channel involving the wholesaler, the travel agent and/or the tour operator is the most established and popular one in Thailand. The wholesalers, typically based out of Europe, are large intermediaries with links to several hotels and several travel agents. The wholesalers demand huge discounts (often up to 60%) from the hotels as they deal with big volumes. A part of this

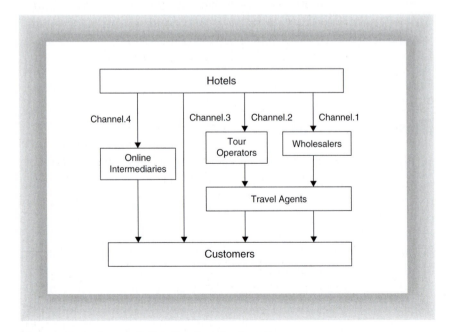

Figure 11.4 Channel distribution for hotels

discount is passed on to the travel agent who is in direct contact with the customer. The wholesalers are very powerful in the market primarily due to the huge volume they handle and also due to the supply experienced. About 70% of the hotels are highly reliant on the wholesalers for their marketing effort. The international travel wholesalers such as LTU, TUI and Thomas Cook enjoy oligopsony, especially in getting large chunks of rooms at a low cost.

The third channel, that is the direct channel or walk-ins, are not very practicable to depend upon, particularly for large hotels with more than 200 rooms. This is because it is impossible to create awareness about the hotel when there is a huge geographical barrier between the tourist and the hotel. But some rooms (less than 10%) get sold directly.

The on-line channel, depicted as the fourth route, is expected to be the channel of the future and comprises of a variety of channels like global distribution systems (GDS), on-line portals of large chains like Best Western or Holiday Inn, on-line travel agents who operate on a global basis, as well as on-line travel agents with a regional presence. The GDSs like SABRE, Amadeus, WorldSpan and Galileo have been in existence since the late 1970s. These systems span the entire world and enable travel agencies to book airline tickets or hotel rooms anywhere in the world. Large global intermediaries like expedia.com, orbitz.com, Travelocity.com, hotels.com often get inventory from GDS and have a worldwide presence. They enable customers anywhere in the world to search for and book rooms. Another type of on-line travel intermediaries are the global marketing representatives such as Utell.com, Best Western, Concorde, etc. These companies cater to IOO hotels not large enough to invest in being a part of the GDSs.

The latest entrants in this field are e-intermediaries that operate exclusively through the Internet. The new intermediaries normally concentrate on particular regions and cater to small or independent hotels. These intermediaries basically provide a much cheaper and easier way for hotels to sell their rooms through cyberspace. Some of the main players in this field in Thailand, apart from morethailand.com, are asiatravel.com, sawadee.com, phuket.com and hotels-Thailand.com. The emergence of e-intermediaries as a strong contender against off-line travel wholesalers and consolidators can be attributed to several technological and market-related factors. With the rapid expansion of the Internet in the developed countries – the prime market for Thailand – the advantage enjoyed by the travel wholesalers due to their close proximity to the customers has been blunted to a large extent. In addition, e-intermediaries have considerably less operating costs than the large travel wholesalers located in some of the most expensive cities with a large employee contingent. e-Intermediaries are thus expected to match the travel wholesalers in terms of the discounts charged to hotels.

Future Challenges

A2Z pro travel use search engine optimization (SEO) and search engine-marketing (SEM) gearing toward search engines like Google. com, Yahoo.com and msn.com to drive traffic to its websites. This is a constant process and involves the full time attention of four staff members of A2Z pro travel. The visitor to inquiry ratio is estimated to be about 5%. The primary aim of SEO is to keep the company's websites in the first 10 positions in the output screen, when the customers type the most popular key words in the three search engines. Presently there are 20 websites for the company and each website contributes directly and indirectly to the traffic. Together, all the 20 websites generate around 22,000 hits and 5000 unique visitors per day. Maintaining 20 websites is part of a well thought out strategy. Except morethailand.com, the other websites are primarily information providers. Most of these allied websites also serve the purpose of increasing the company's visibility when potential customers search using destinations as key words in search engines.

The online travel intermediary market is evolving. A2Z pro travel is in the process of consolidating its position as well as trying to expand into other markets. The biggest challenge for A2Z pro travel remains the existence of large travel wholesalers in the market. The legacy of the travel wholesalers makes it difficult for A2Z pro travel to expand its model rapidly across Thailand. Hotels are far too attached to travel wholesalers and consider it quite risky to develop a committed relationship with A2Z pro travel.

Despite the obvious advantage offered by the A2Z pro travel's business model in the B2C segment, it is yet to enjoy widespread adoption. The main hindrance is that Thai hoteliers prefer to sell their rooms through commitment contracts through the 'merchant model' where they are paid in advance for those rooms, though at a significant discount. A large number of rooms in a hotel are sold out in advance through this manner, thereby relieving the hotels of any responsibility to market their rooms and reducing their risk. On-line intermediaries on the other hand mostly follow a 'commission model' where hotels are not paid upfront before the rooms are sold. Thus, hotels are not assured of a certain occupancy rate and are not offered any guarantees of revenue. Many small hotels fall prey to the lure of committed cash, paying little attention to profitability and embrace travel wholesalers rather than e-intermediaries.

Even when profitability is emphasized over cash flows, occupancy rate remains the major concern for most of the hotels. High occupancy supports the food and beverage business in the property. Hotels therefore offer better terms to intermediaries that bring greater customer inquiries. It is hence imperative for A2Z pro travel to build up customer interest in its sites like morethailand.com to survive and grow in the market. The number of hits received at its websites and the resultant bookings are considered to be the key success factor by A2Z-ProTravel.com.

Conclusions

The biggest challenge for the A2Z management is therefore to convince the small hoteliers of the viability and utility of the model. The hoteliers have to be convinced that this model will definitely work and also that it can be relied upon. Presently a series of relationship building programmes are being held to convince the hoteliers to give more prominence to A2Z pro travel. The company conducts several business meetings in which hoteliers are invited to attend.

The company has invested more than €80,000 for the migration of the system to the new platform. A2Z set the modest target of 10,000 transactions for the B2B project during its initial phase of operation in 2006. The challenge for A2Z is to sustain the first mover advantage, in offering the technology based distribution options through coherent strategies that optimizes the potential of the platform.

Onward distribution may involve major players such as expedia.com, travelocity.com via online connectivity. But securing partners from similar online travel agents in each country such as HotelBeds.com in Spain, MakeMyTrip.com in India, Ctrip.com in China may be the key to success since it would leverage on Internet network benefits of open travel alliance system.

Key Conclusions

- Destination based intermediaries can add value and distribute a wide range of products.
- In developing markets it is still difficult to convince suppliers to work with Internet intermediaries.
- As the technology cost is quite high it is often difficult for companies to invest heavily especially in the beginning.
- Destination based intermediaries need to have a wide B2B and B2C distribution mix.

Review and Discussion Questions

- What is the unique selling point of a destination based intermediary?
- Discuss how a destination based intermediary can add value to its offerings.
- Explore what are the sources of competitive advantage for destination based intermediaries.
- How can a destination based intermediary improve its profitability?

References and Further Reading

Buhalis, D., & Licata, C.M. (2002). The future of eTourism intermediaries. *Tourism Management*, 23, 207–220.

Cooper, C., Fletcher, J., Gilbert, D., & Wanhill, S. (1998). *Tourism principles and practice*. Essex: Pearson.

Hoontrakul, P. (2004). *Value Revelation in Differentiated Goods for Travel Industry, Discussion Paper*. Sasin of Chulalongkorn University. Bangkok. Retrieved from http://www.Pongsak.Hoontrakul.com.

Jensen, M.C., & Meckling, W.H. (1976). Theory of the firm: Managerial behavior, agency costs and ownership structure. *Journal of Financial Economics*, 3, 303–360.

http://www.morethailand.com.

http://www.tat.or.th.

http://www.world-tourism.org.

Company's website: http://www.a2zprotravel.com.

Case

12

ITWG: increasing intermediated flows

Immacolata Vellecco and Maria Immacolata Simeon

Learning Objectives

- Demonstrate how a destination based intermediary can provide products and services – with an example from Italy.
- Appreciate how a hotel based intermediary can become a destination based intermediary.
- Demonstrate the recent growth in Internet bookings.
- Explain the business model of ITWG.

Introduction

ITWG (short for Italian Tourist Web Guide) started as an Internet site in 1996. At the beginning the site was a promotional show-case for hotels. Then in 2000 – when ITWG.com was started up as a limited company – it became an on-line tour operator specializing in incoming tourism. ITWG was one of the first companies in Italy to promote tourism over the Internet, a type of business that developed and spread relatively late in Italy compared with other countries. In 2000 the firm, with its head office in Tuscany (at Lucca and Prato), was started up with an initial financing of €250,000 and then consolidated with a further injection of €250,000.

Organization

The four founder members are the brothers Paolo and Carlo Nardini, Renato Berti and Luca Menni. When they came together to start up the business project, the Nardini brothers were working in the ICT sector, Berti in travel publishing and Menni in marketing.

Since 2001 ITWG has changed its corporate status from a limited company to a public company. Apart from a few private individuals (all operational managers), the main stakeholders are:

- The E-venture firm that permitted its start-up through the EuroVenture European investment fund;
- Serenissima Infracom S.A., a company that offers advanced-technology solutions in the field of telecommunications and the Internet, controlled by the Società Autostrade Brescia-Padova.

At that time the Italian tourist intermediation market was dominated by outgoing operators (Petrillo, 2002). Moreover, the sector was beginning to show signs of crisis and instability, with considerable levels of company mergers and acquisitions; due partly to the change in consumer preferences that appeared geared towards a higher degree of personalized travel arrangements compared with those of standardized tourist packages. Realizing the extraordinary potential of the Internet as a chance to market Italy's tourist attractions successfully worldwide, ITWG entered the new business which, by extending the 'arc of integration' in the supply chain (Frohlich & Westbrook, 2001) it allowed the value produced by the two successive intermediation steps to be captured.

ITWG performs both the functions of a tour operator by putting together the holiday package, and that of a travel agency. It currently has 19 employees.

Products and Services

The main product supplied by ITWG is Italian travel inventory. Foreign tourists may make up their travel according to their specific preferences. For example, a stay at thermal baths may be combined with a visit to an art city, a seaside stay with a gastronomic itinerary. For business tourism, ITWG offers a calendar of trade fairs in various Italian cities. The search for the location may proceed by town, city, by region or by theme, with the possibility of obtaining concise information on the history, art heritage and sights in each location, as well hints on shopping and cuisine, on nightlife, on how to reach places. A forum allows users to share their travel experiences.

The holiday packages proposed are original products formulated exclusively by Italian Tourist Web Guide (ITWG) and continually updated with special offers. The firm supplies only high-quality services. As a member of the Italian Federation of Travel and Tourist Agencies (FIAVET), ITWG is responsible for the consumers to the holidays that it organizes and sells itself (as laid down by the EC Directive). Payment may be made in advance on-line with a credit card, although the latter may also be used only as the reservation guarantee and debited in the hotel on departure. Payment may also be made in the traditional fashion (bank transfer or postal money order within 3 days of booking).

The main service supplied by ITWG is hotel booking, which the company offers directly, without intermediaries. In addition, there is the booking of flights and other travel tickets, and car rental which is provided by their link with Avis Rent A Car System (Avis). ITWG targets both Italian and foreign tourists, which is why the portal was created in five languages. The main users of e-reservation are Italian (25%), British (13.5%) and American (12.5%) customers.

Since 2002 ITWG has also been linked to the hotel chain Italy Hotel Club which numbers over 40 and 4- and 3-star hotels throughout Italy. ITWG facilitates their promotional business (printing and international distribution of the hotel guide, promotion and booking at the site http://www.italyhotelclub.com). In this way, ITWG confirms the trend, extensively verified by research on the tourist industry, of tour operators expanding the control of hotel businesses (Medina-Muñoz *et al.*, 2003).

Hotels that are part of the chain are classified into four types, identified by four colours. The Business type (red) offers appropriate infrastructures and services for satisfying the needs of business such as meetings and conferences; the Holiday type (blue) identifies structures situated in sites of outstanding natural beauty; the

Art type (yellow) meets the needs of those staying in Italy's art cities and wishing to discover the immense historical and cultural heritage; the Relax type (green) hosts tourists seeking tranquillity, oriented towards well-being and body care.

The on-line booking system developed allows hotels to interact directly with the system, constantly updating availability and prices using an Internet back-office procedure created in-house. The booking is made on-line; it requires no further confirmation and the customer can print the booking voucher immediately.

The system may also be used in application service provider mode, from other sites and portals and by hotel chains, thereby reducing the need to develop internally the information systems and professional skills to manage them (Kern *et al.*, 2002). A B2B section dedicated to travel agencies allows the agencies, or foreign operators, to book a hotel or tourist package in Italy on behalf of their customers and duly receive the equivalent commission to that of traditional channels, yet with two advantages: there is no fixed affiliation cost and no need to have dedicated terminals like most existing systems.

As to the technology, the adoption of Pegasus and the agreement with GDS Galileo Italia (Galileo Italia, 2006), which is currently part of Cendant travel distribution services, have considerably increased the visibility of the portal in the web.

ITWG styles itself as a 'business node' (Rayman Bacchus & Molina, 2001). It is linked by many other sites and is considered one of the main points of reference for tourism in Italy, not only for tourists but also over 4000 travel agencies.

Growth to a Major Player

The company has recorded rapid success: in 2000 (the first year it operated as tour operator) it handled 8464 bookings amounting to €2,958,672. As early as 2001 ITWG recorded 500,000 visitors a month (AITech-Assinform, 2006) and managed to sell hotel stays worth more than €7 million. In 2003 over 76,000 hotel nights were sold, amounting to €8.2 million overall, while for 2004 a growth rate of 35% was registered.

The company's rapid growth may be viewed within the trend of rapid Internet diffusion both globally and in Italy, which has made up the initial lag behind other countries. Online tourism in 2005 accounted for 43% of total Internet sales in Italy (*Marketpress*, 2006). Total sales of tourist products increased from €300 million in 2003 to €800 million in 2004 and €1200 million in 2005 (*Marketpress*, 2006). Nevertheless growth has been steady despite moments of

Table 12.1 Bookings and values trends

Year	Bookings	Value (€)
2000	8,494	2,958,672
2001	22,737	7,222,113
2002	28,439	8,600,000
2003	29,069	8,265,000
2004	38,991	10,478,804
2005	42,885	11,535,609

Sources: AlTech-Assinform (2006), ITWG.com S.p.A.

severe crisis (due to international political events) which have characterized recent years: the year 2005 saw 42,885 bookings (105,435 overnight stays) amounting to €11,535,609 (ITWG.com source). Table 12.1 demonstrates the booking and value trends.

Consolidation and Future Challenges

On the Italian market in 2005, ITWG ranked among the top 20 virtual operators and, of these, among the top 5 'pure players' (Marketpress, 2006). This ranking may well be maintained and consolidated, provided that the firm's technological strategy retains the capacity to keep pace with both innovation dynamics and technology diffusion.

Constant contact needs to be maintained with the hotels and other service providers to ensure the level of quality expected by the customer and the benefits of a favourable price/quality ratio. Monitoring of consumer preferences vis-à-vis itineraries and tourist destinations will also permit holiday package proposals to be periodically updated.

The company strategy is to increase the number of strategic agreements as well as segment and diversify its tourist supply to increase intermediate flows and relative income. The commercial partnership with Ryan Air, the leading low-cost airline company, became operative in 2005. It proposes ITWG.com tourist packages directly on its own Internet site devoted to 'breaks' (http://www.activity-breaks.com).

Besides broadening its commercial partnerships (which will involve other low-cost airlines, other GDSs and Networks of travel agencies interested in proposing ITWG.com holiday solutions to their customers) there is the segmentation of tourist suppliers with the development of thematic channels. The first two thematic channels opened in 2006 were:

- http://www.business.itwg.com, a channel devoted exclusively to firms where preferential rates are presented to business travellers;
- http://www.benessere.itwg.com, a channel devoted to stays at spa, thermal baths, hotels and health farms in Italy.

Conclusions

The Internet is a great chance for growth new ventures start up. Fast growing markets require fast growth-oriented strategic management, as in the case of ITWG. Technology does not ensure business development by itself, although it is a very substantial asset. If technology is merely used to deliver services, newcomers can easily imitate the business and competitive advantage will be eroded as technology spreads out.

Creating service value through technology requires a never ending innovation strategy, and the business vision has to be oriented towards the enlargement of the network and the business scope. In the case of ITWG, special attention is paid to strategic partnerships which are able to increase visibility on the web and to raise intermediated flows and income in order to enlarge the business scope, whereas high quality services and specialization towards tourist targets can help consolidation and balance high dynamic market risks.

Acknowledgment

The authors acknowledge the precious contribution of Luca Menni, marketing director of ITWG.com, who kindly supplied updated data and information about the company.

Key Conclusions

- Although Internet bookings have increased dramatically there is huge competition increasing from around the world.
- It is critical for destination-based intermediaries to improve their interoperability with suppliers and distributors to enhance efficiency.
- Creating service value through technology requires a never-ending innovation strategy.

Review and Discussion Questions

- How can a destination-based intermediary based in Italy improve its profitability?
- How can a destination-based intermediary compete with the global intermediaries?
- Discuss how a destination-based intermediary can collaborate with affiliates and on-ward distributors.
- Explore how destination-based intermediaries can improve their interoperability with suppliers and affiliates.

References and Further Reading

AITech-Assinform. Retrieved 10 January 2006 from http://www.aitech-assinform.it/casibusiness/02.asp.

Buhalis, D., & Licata, M.C. (2002). The future eTourism inter-mediaries. *Tourism Management*, 23 (3), 207–220.

Frohlich, M.T., & Westbrook, R. (2001). Arcs of integration: An international study of supply chain strategies. *Journal of Operation Management*, 19 (2), 185–200.

Galileo Italia. Retrieved 17 March 2006 from http://www.galileoitalia.com/Galileo_ITWG.htm.

Kern, T., Kreijger, J., & Willcocks, L. (2002). Exploring ASP as sourcing strategy: Theoretical perspectives, propositions for practice. *Journal of Strategic Information Systems*, 11 (2), 153–177.

Marketpress. Retrieved 23 March 2006 from http://www.marketpress.info.

Medina-Muñoz, R.D., Medina-Muñoz, D.R., & García-Falcón, J.M. (2003). Understanding European tour operators' control on accommodation companies: An empirical evidence. *Tourism Management*, 24 (2), 135–147.

Ordanini, A., & Pol, A. (2001). Infomediation and competive advantage in B2b digital marketplaces. *European Management Journal*, 19 (3), 276–285.

Petrillo, C.S. (2002). Position and strategic choices of Italian tour operators in European competition. *Tourism*, 50 (1), 51–66.

Rayman Bacchus, L., & Molina, A. (2001). Internet-based tourism services: Business issues and trends. *Futures*, 33 (7), 589–605.

Company's website: www.itwg.com.

13

Incoming Partners: integrating operations

Rodolfo Baggio

Learning Objectives

- Demonstrate how an incoming agent can take advantage of the Internet for distributing their products.
- Explore technological and business innovations essential for incoming agents.
- Illustrate the system architecture for an incoming agent.
- Explain the functions of technology for incoming agencies.

Introduction

The role of intermediaries has been scrutinized since the very beginning of what is commonly known as the 'Internet revolution'. Despite the many disbelievers, mainly in popular press, an electronic mediation role has been recognized, since then, as important in many instances. It was thought, in fact, that technology would have been able to enable (Sarkar *et al.*, 1995):

> *new types of economies of scale, scope, and knowledge by intermediaries, leading to the rapid evolution of many new forms of cybermediaries who are interposing themselves between producers and consumers.*

The travel and tourism sector, rather obviously, has shared the same considerations (Dilworth, 1996):

> *The perceived threat of the Internet for travel agents has also blinded many to the possible benefits that can be gained through this new technology. In their role as information consultants, many agents now have access to a far wider audience than they have had traditionally. While the battle for market share on the Internet will probably only leave room for several cybermediaries of the TravelWeb type, there may still be demand for focused cybermediaries.*

Basically, this is the reconfirmation of the role of intermediaries in a market, revisited by taking into account the possibilities offered by the new technologies. This role, as known to classical economic theories, becomes a crucial one when considering the global nature of the tourism marketplace (Spulber, 1999). This is, with hindsight, what has happened as a result of the huge diffusion of the Internet.

Since then, however, it has been recognized that a crucial success factor for an intermediary in the newly formed electronic commerce space is a good and effective capability to foster:

> *roles that will include aggregating information goods, providing trust relationships and ensuring the integrity of the market, matching customers and suppliers, and providing marketing information to suppliers (Bailey & Bakos, 1997).*

The Company and the Products

An example of such new intermediaries is Incoming Partners, an Italian tour operator based in Milan. The company was founded in 1999 from a branch of the incoming department of a larger travel agency. Its staff of five people make it the typical representative of those small enterprises which form the vast majority of the European tourism sector.

From the beginning, the company has chosen to offer its services to other companies, on a B2B basis, not to single individuals. The clients are tour operators and travel agencies as well as travel departments of large corporations. The programmes that Incoming Partners offer cover mainly the northern part of Italy and, in particular, the art cities. In this context, a wide range of packages and personalized services form the catalogue proposed to actual or potential customers.

A typical list is the following:

- Hotel stays, including customized transfers, tour packages, special arrangements and personalized assistance to travellers;
- Congresses, meetings, events, or complementary activities for these such as pre- and post-event tours, gala dinners, private concerts or shows.

Additionally, Incoming Partners is authorized to book and sell La Scala and Teatro degli Arcimboldi tickets. Recently it has also been appointed as booking centre for Viscontea, the electric boat sailing the Naviglio Grande, the Big Canal that was made navigable by Leonardo da Vinci and flows from Milan into the Ticino river.

Technological and Business Innovation

Since its foundation, the company has deemed crucial, for its business, to make extensive use of information and communication technologies. The first project, therefore, has been the design and implementation of a system geared towards the full automation of all operational activities.

After a survey and an analysis of the products available on the market, it was decided to start the development of a customized system. The company thought that all the available packages were too 'admin oriented'. They provided good and extensive capabilities of managing invoices, balance sheets and so forth, but were inadequate functionalities for supporting actual operations.

The system has a very simple logical architecture (Figure 13.1). It rests on three databases: customers, suppliers and users, containing all the data needed for day-to-day activities. A connection to the Internet allows the interaction with the company website and the management of the communications with customers and suppliers. The access to the databases and to the different functions is provided by a user interface and an authorization layer. The whole

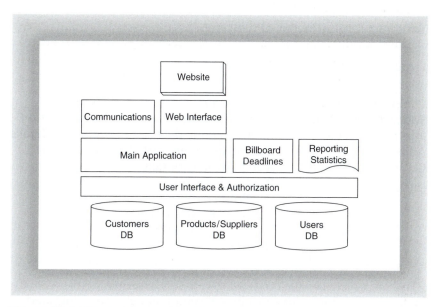

Figure 13.1 The system architecture

system is based on Microsoft Access, chosen for its convenience, ease of use and for the wide availability of suitable programming skills in the market.

The databases contain all the necessary operational information; a schematic list is given in Table 13.1.

The main functions available are the following:

- Contracts with suppliers and customers;
- Offers, price estimates and quotations;
- Deadlines management (billboard);
- Booking (both from customers and towards suppliers);
- Confirmations, invoicing;
- Payments management, alerts;
- Communications with customers and suppliers;
- Reporting and statistical analyses;
- Mailings and promotional activities.

As Michele Mondolfo (the company's owner) states, the main philosophy behind the whole development has been the old maxim: a place for everything and everything in its place. This translates into a special care taken in assuring the absence of any duplication or redundancy. The database structures are fully normalized thus eliminating potential anomalies during the data operations. All data are inserted only once and reused internally according to the different needs. Standard elements such as zip

Table 13.1 Logical layout of the company databases

Customers	Suppliers	Users
Company name	Brand name	Name
Basic company data	Company name	Organization
Internal contacts	Basic company data	Contact details
Administrative details	Operative details, pictures	Access rights
Comments, remarks	Administrative details	
History	Product inventory (allotments)	
	Costs (and resale prices)	
	Comments, remarks	
	History	

codes, bank codes, city-province-region lists, etc. are contained in specific tables and do not need any further editing.

Well aware of the renowned 'IT productivity paradox' and its possible overcomes (Dos Santos & Sussman, 2000) and applying in full the idea of avoiding redundancies and mishandlings, the system has been designed to provide an integrated environment allowing the complete automation of repetitive activities while leaving room for intervention in special cases. More than just an operational support, the Incoming Partner application is a real knowledge repository.

What characterizes the application, and is considered its main strength, is an 'obsessive' care for detail. For example, the meeting capabilities of a hotel are described by recording all the rooms with all possible configurations, equipment and capacities. The list continues with pictures and details on the surroundings (spaces, furniture, lights, windows, etc.) along with the comments regarding the suitability for different types of usage and the evaluation of the strengths and weaknesses of the resource. All the suppliers used by the company and all the customers are treated with this richness of details. This particular aspect gives the system a much wider and more important function within the organization. The capability of easily finding, at all times, the best possible match between the customer needs and expectations and the proposal made is a real possibility and not only a wishful option.

The website: www.incomingpartners.it (Figure 13.2) is an important complement to the system. It is built with the objective of being a communication and operational instrument directed to

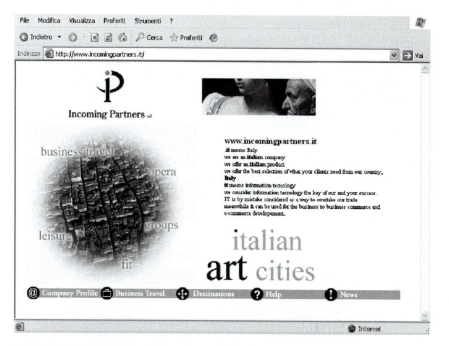

Figure 13.2 Incoming Partners website home page
Source: http://www.incomingpartners.it

the customers. Apart from a simple presentation of the company and its products, the main area is the one dedicated to authorized clients. The base system gives the possibility to decide what information or details should be extracted and published online. The selected data are then uploaded by ftp. Users of the online area (restricted and password protected) have the possibility to browse the characteristics of the different items (Figure 13.3) and packages constituting the company's offering and fill in a request for quotation.

All the resources and the expertise of the company are available through a unified platform. This ensemble of integrated applications provides an example of how Internet, intranet and extranet tools may co-exist. They form a seamless system in which the different types of users find effective and efficient capabilities able to meet their informational and operational needs.

Key Challenges for the Future

The contribution given to the company's business by the whole system is very difficult to evaluate since there are no terms for

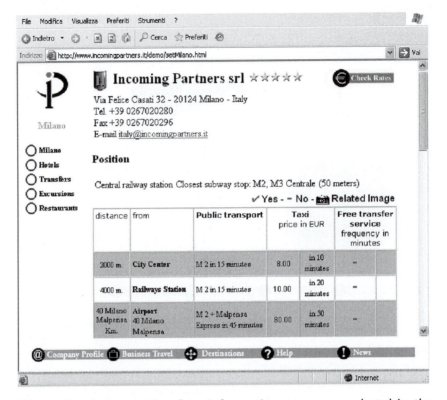

Figure 13.3 An example of an information screen on a hotel in the restricted area of Incoming Partners website
Source: http://www.incomingpartners.it

comparison. The company has always operated with it. It is one of the main contributors to the good performance in sales and revenues and for their increase in the last 3 years.

An estimate, done by the owner and based on his experience in the field, is that the usage of more 'offline traditional' methods would have required more than twice as many human and financial resources to satisfy the same transaction volumes. More importantly, the very low error rate contributes to very good levels of customers satisfaction with the service provided. The efficiency and effectiveness of the solution adopted helps in saving a good amount of time which can be used for those field inspections that greatly contribute to the accuracy and updating of the information in the knowledge repository.

The possibility to find information very quickly and data and the connection with fast communication systems gives also a good capacity to react to last-minute unexpected events and to rearrange packages in very short times; again an effective contribution to the overall satisfaction of the customers. Given these results, no special plans have been made with regards to the technical supports for the company's business. All the main efforts go in conceiving new services and products. The future activities foresee the ongoing maintenance and care for the information base and the constant updating to new forms of communications (mobile phones) with customers and suppliers.

The Future of the Company

The technological infrastructure developed so far is an important basis for the future plans of the company. Two are the main lines of development: The first concerns the reinforcement and the expansion of the present B2B activities. The second one consists of developing partnerships aimed at providing tourism services to support important events such as international fairs, art exhibitions or sport competitions occurring in northern Italy – Milan, in particular. New services or products will have, if needed, dedicated subsystems. For example, a website (www.navigamilano.it) for the operations connected with the booking centre for the Viscontea boat is under development. Being directed also to the general public, the new services will have the possibility of direct online (credit card) bookings and payments. The implementation of these functions is forthcoming.

In conclusion, Incoming Partners represents a good example of how, with relatively limited resources, good results can be obtained with an integrated system, designed with clear objectives in mind and fully geared towards the efficiency and effectiveness of day-to-day operations.

Key Conclusions

- Incoming agencies have benefited greatly from the Internet revolution.
- A comprehensive system can support the competitiveness of incoming agencies.
- Different systems are required for B2B and B2C solutions.

Review and Discussion Questions

- Discuss the structure of an integrated incoming agency system.
- How can an incoming agency use their systems to improve their efficiency and profitability?
- Discuss how an incoming agency can connect their systems with affiliates and on-ward distributors.
- Explore how destination-based intermediaries improve their interoperability with suppliers and affiliates.

References and Further Reading

Antonioli Corigliano, M., & Baggio, R. (2004). Italian tourism on the Internet – new business models. In K. Weiermair, & C. Mathies (Eds.), *The tourism and leisure industry – shaping the future* (pp. 301–316). New York: The Haworth Press.

Bailey, J.P., & Bakos, Y. (1997). An exploratory study of the emerging role of electronic intermediaries. *International Journal of Electronic Commerce*, 1 (3), 7–20.

Buhalis, D., & Laws, E. (Eds.) (2001). *Tourism distribution channels: Practices, issues and transformation*. London: Thomson.

Buhalis, D., & Licata, M. (2002). The future eTourism intermediaries. *Tourism Management*, 23, 207–220.

Dilworth, J. (1996). *The Travel Industry Response to the WWW. – Towards a Travel Distribution Revolution*. Retrieved February 2006 from http://www.dilworth.org/travel.

Dos Santos, B., & Sussman, L. (2000). Improving the return on IT investment: The productivity paradox. *International Journal of Information Management*, 20 (6), 429–440.

ECTAA – Group of National Travel Agents' and Tour Operators' Associations within the EU: http://www.ectaa.org.

Sarkar, M.B., Butler, B., & Steinfield, C. (1995). Intermediaries and cybermediaries: A continuing role for mediating players in the electronic marketplace. *Journal of Computer-Mediated Communication*, 1 (3). Retrieved December 2005 from http://jcmc.huji.ac.il/vol1/issue3/sarkar.html.

Spulber, D.F. (1999). *Market microstructure: Intermediaries and the theory of the firm*. Cambridge: Cambridge University Press.

World Travel & Tourism Council: http://www.wttc.org.

Company's website: http://www.incomingpartners.it.

14

SideStep: travel meta-search engine

Young A Park and Ulrike Gretzel

Learning Objectives

- Demonstrate that travel search engines (TSEs) or meta-search engines, are a new breed of online intermediaries.
- Explain that TSEs have the potential to fundamentally change the travel distribution landscape.
- Explore technological and business innovations essential for TSEs.

Introduction

Travel search engines (TSEs), frequently also called meta-search engines, are a new breed of online intermediaries that have the potential to fundamentally change the travel distribution landscape. TSEs like SideStep, Kayak and Mobissimo provide consumers with a comprehensive selection of choices and price comparison opportunities by simultaneously conducting live-availability searches on the websites of online agencies, consolidators and suppliers. SideStep, Inc. is currently the leading TSE in the United States with headquarters in California. SideStep was founded in late 1999, with $17 million in private funding, and has been profitable every year since. Initially, SideStep focused on developing search engine technology for travel, a vertical market that was not served well by general purpose search engines. However, as the technology matured and competitors emerged, SideStep started concentrating more on alliance formation to increase the number of databases it can search. SideStep currently has alliances with leading travel companies such as JetBlue, American Airlines, Hyatt, Orbitz, National Leisure Group and Thrifty Car Rental and continues to expand its alliance base. In 2005, SideStep signed a distribution agreement with Hilton Hotels and later that year announced an agreement to provide the search results for the Amazon.com travel store. SideStep has been named one of *Time* Magazine's '50 Coolest Web Sites' and declared 'Best of the Web' by both *Forbes* and *BusinessWeek Online*.

Main Products

SideStep's main offering is its meta-search engine (Figure 14.1). It searches an extensive number of travel sites including airlines, hotels, and rental car companies, plus online travel agencies and consolidators. Not included in SideStep's comprehensive network of alliances are Expedia and Travelocity, which means SideStep users do not get to see prices from two of the industry's biggest online travel agents. To overcome this apparent disadvantage, SideStep offers a toolbar that users can download and install on their browser (Figure 14.2). When they search for travel deals on non-partner sites, the toolbar displaying the SideStep search results stays open and allows for direct-price comparisons. Another core feature of SideStep is SmartSortSM, which allows users to customize search results by filtering results based on criteria such as price, star rating, distance, amenities or departure time, number of stops and airline in the case of flights. SideStep has also launched search tools and sorting

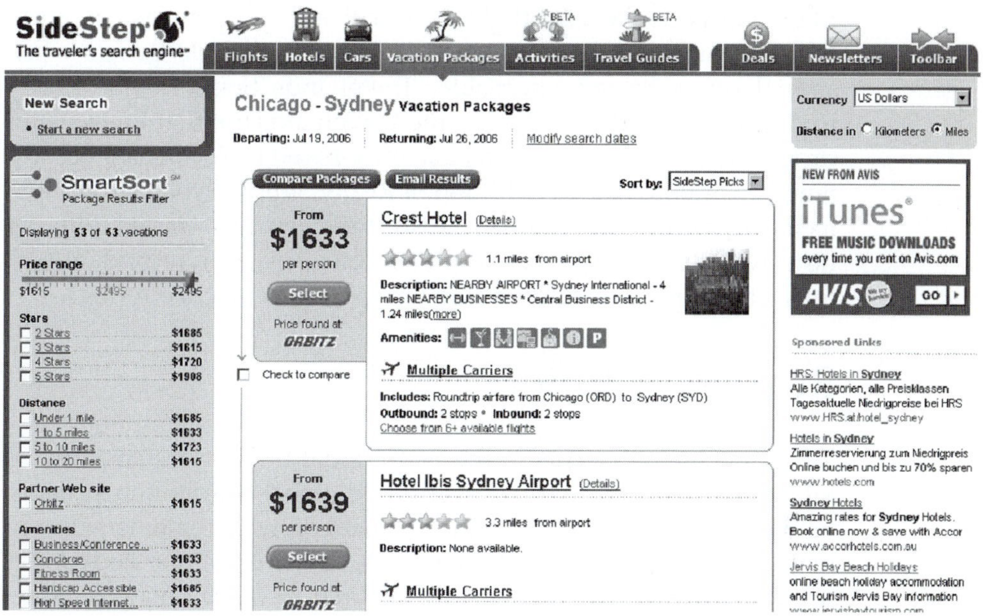

Figure 14.1 SideStep search results
Source: www.sidestep.com

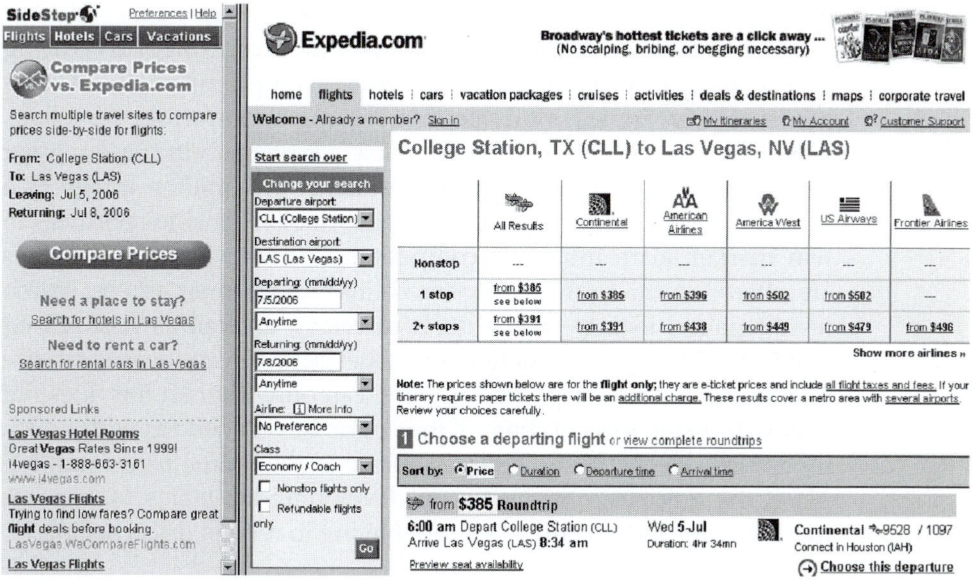

Figure 14.2 SideStep Toolbar
Source: www.sidestep.com

mechanisms for vacation packages as well as for activities. Further, the Travel Deals directory offers consumers a comprehensive collection of hundreds of bargains from popular travel companies. The directory is easy to browse, with deals grouped in categories that range from international flights to resort and spa getaways. In addition, SideStep features two email newsletters that alert users when special offers become available. TravelFinds Special is a weekly update on travel deals whereas the TravelFinds Spotlight newsletter provides monthly destination or activity-based travel deals. Recently, SideStep announced the addition of Really Simple Syndication (RSS) feeds of current travel deals. Also, SideStep has started offering hotel reviews powered by TravelPost.com. This is an important step towards adding even more value to SideStep's current offerings.

Business Model

The only channel agents in the pre-Internet travel value chain were intermediaries such as travel agents and global distribution systems. However, these structures radically changed with the emergence of new eMediaries (Buhalis & Licata, 2002). TSEs moved one step further up the travel distribution chain compared to other online intermediaries and can be seen as 'metamediaries'; that is, they aggregate offerings from suppliers, intermediaries and infomediaries such as TravelPost.com. In contrast to the commission-based business models that are prevalent for intermediaries, metamediaries like SideStep generate revenues through referral fees and advertising. Advertising in SideStep's TravelFinds email newsletters, for example, allows companies to drive incremental sales by reaching opportunistic travellers. Advertisements on SideStep.com enable suppliers to increase market share within SideStep's substantial audience (4.7 million travellers a month). Marketing through the SideStep toolbar enables partners to win market share from key competitors. Advertising opportunities are offered in the form of sponsored links and banner ads on search results pages, listings in the deals directory, as well as customized emails to Sidestep's newsletter subscriber base. Given the importance of alliances for SideStep, the company can only flourish if it does not encroach on the market share of the online travel agencies with which it partners. Hence for SideStep to thrive in the online travel marketplace, the emphasis has to be on developing strategies to increase market share and revenues without having to rely on direct selling.

Technological and Business Innovation

SideStep's flagship product is its travel search engine technology, available to consumers through both the SideStep.com website and the SideStep toolbar. While traditional search engines (e.g. Google) were built to handle information that is fairly static, SideStep was designed to handle highly fluid data. In the travel industry, pricing and inventory availability are in constant flux. For instance, there are more than 1 million price and availability changes in the airline sector alone on any given day. SideStep's core technology is optimized for this shifting data landscape, enabling SideStep to pull together dynamic information from numerous sources in ways that conventional search engines cannot. This technology allows SideStep to offer value to intermediaries, suppliers and customers. The value proposition of SideStep for intermediaries lies mostly in gaining greater exposure to consumers while retaining control over bookings and thus commissions. In contrast, from the suppliers' perspective, SideStep offers added distribution, consolidated aggregation through its vacation packages search, as well as increased customer loyalty through direct customer handling. It also provides suppliers with low-cost distribution, which is especially attractive for cash-strapped airlines searching for ways to avoid the higher commissions charged by online travel agencies like Expedia. However, some suppliers are concerned that TSEs like SideStep will destroy their brands because their comparison capabilities encourage consumers to focus only on price. SideStep adds value for the consumer by offering an one-stop search model, enriched content, and a user-friendly interface. In addition, it enhances comparison shopping, which has been identified by Keeney (1999) as one of the core added values of Internet commerce.

Key Challenges

The technology itself provides little sustainable competitive advantage as it can be easily copied. Although SideStep initially benefited from being a first-mover in the travel distribution market, competitors like Kayak and Mobissimo as well as Yahoo! Farechase emerged quickly. According to Wynne *et al.* (2001), control in the electronic travel distribution channel is essential and there is room for only a few of such 'magnets' that will essentially concentrate travel information, reduce search costs and facilitate transactions for the entire market. SideStep's direct competitors have also started providing additional functions on their websites to increase the value of the search technology. Mobissimo, for instance, offers a travel blog section featuring travel news and tips. Besides providing its users with email alerts, RSS feeds and a bot, which is a software program that can execute search commands and can be added to one's AOL IM buddy list, Kayak includes a trip idea section that allows users to be inspired by most recent searches for specific points of origin. One can also create a trip idea and share it with family and friends. Further, in late 2005 Kayak started offering a service for complex flight itineraries with beta testing of multi-city search that helps consumers find travel savings for even the most complicated itineraries. Competition could also emerge from online travel agencies and global distribution systems if they adopt comparison shopping tools. A recent Eyefortravel study (EyeforTravel, 2005) indicates that whereas travel suppliers see TSEs as marketing tools that help them drive even more traffic to their already increasingly used websites, online travel agencies consider them to be competitors and plan to compete with them by increasing the search capabilities on their sites. Online travel agencies have the clear advantage of being better established in the market, dominating customer satisfaction and customer acquisition, and, according to a study by Nielsen/NetRatings (2005), attracting the majority of online travel shoppers through their well-trusted brand names. A recent study by Park and Gretzel (2006) also found little awareness of TSEs while brand recognition is extremely high for the major online travel agencies. Further, trust was found as a major factor that drives TSE adoption, and SideStep has yet to gain it. In addition to winning over consumers, SideStep will also have to continue to convince its partners of its value. Jupiter Research (2005) reports that supplier websites have not yet seen their sales significantly impacted by TSEs.

Future of the Company

Not everyone is convinced that SideStep will be able to overcome the higher name recognition and deeper pockets of established online travel agencies and to use travel suppliers' growing power in the market to its advantage. Keeping up with rapidly changing technology and better understanding customer needs will be key for SideStep's success. Greater customization and personalization of its offerings and continuously tracking customer needs through mining the searches conducted on its website could provide the necessary competitive edge over other TSEs as well as online travel agencies. Value could also be added by allowing users to create accounts and, thus, be able to refer to previous searches or simultaneously manage results for multiple trips. What is also often overlooked in the context of comparison-shopping is that while consumers value time savings provided by comparison tools, they also want to enjoy the shopping experience (Marmorstein *et al.*, 1992). More engaging content and increased interactivity as well as additional support in the decision-making process, for example through recommendations, could enhance the enjoyment value of the SideStep website. Moreover, increasing its brand recognition and expansion into markets other than the ones currently served could provide SideStep with the momentum necessary to counter competitive forces in the travel marketplace. For instance, SideStep has recently added cruises and private jets to its searchable offerings and is expected to continue the expansion of its product line. Finally, as services provided through mobile devices gain importance, it will become ever more critical for SideStep to consider developing mCommerce solutions for travel distribution.

Key Conclusions

- TSEs move up the travel distribution chain to become 'metamediaries'.
- From the suppliers' perspective, SideStep offers added distribution, consolidated aggregation through its vacation packages search, as well as increased customer loyalty through direct customer handling.
- Some suppliers are concerned that TSEs destroy brands because their comparison capabilities encourage consumers to focus only on price.

Review and Discussion Questions

- What is the value that TSEs offer to each stakeholder?
- What is the impact of TSEs to brands?
- How can suppliers take advantage of TSEs?
- What is the impact of TSEs to revenue and revenue management?

References and Further Reading

Buhalis, D., & Laws, E. (2001). *Tourism distribution channels.* London: Continuum.

Buhalis, D., & Licata, M.C. (2002). The future eTourism intermediaries. *Tourism Management*, 23, 207–220.

EyeforTravel (2005). *A Strategic Analysis of the Travel Search Engine (TSE) Market*. Retrieved 2 September 2005 from http://www.eyefortravel.com/reports.asp.

Jupiter Research (2005). *US Travel Consumer Survey 2005*. Retrieved 25 August 2005 from http://www.jupiterresearch.com.

Keeney, R.L. (1999). The value of Internet commerce to the customer. *Management Science*, 45 (4), 533–542.

Marmorstein, H., Grewal, D., & Fishe, R. (1992). The value of time spent in price-comparison shopping: Survey and experimental evidence. *Journal of Consumer Research*, 19 (1), 52–61.

Nielsen/NetRatings (2005). *Press Release June 21 2005*. Retrieved 3 March 2006 from http://www.nielsen-netratings.com/pr/pr_050621.pdf.

Park, Y., & Gretzel, U. (2006). Evaluation of emerging technologies in tourism: The case of travel search engines. In M. Hitz, M. Sigala, & J. Murphy (Eds.), *Information and communication technologies in tourism 2006* (pp. 371–382). Vienna: Springer Verlag.

Pearce, D.G., & Schott, S. (2005). Tourism distribution channels: The visitors' perspective. *Journal of Travel Research*, 44 (August), 50–63.

Werthner, H., & Klein, S. (1999). ICT and the changing landscape of global tourism distribution. *Electronic Markets*, 9 (4), 256–262.

Wynne, C., Berthon, P., Pitt, L., Ewing, M., & Napoli, J. (2001). The impact of the Internet on the distribution value chain: The case of the South African tourism industry. *International Marketing Review*, 18 (4), 420–431.

Eyefortravel.com.

Company's website: http://www.Sidestep.com.

15

HolidayCheck: rendering holiday impressions

Axel Jockwer and Constanze Russ-Mohl

Learning Objectives

- Demonstrate the importance of Travel 2.0 through user generated content such as hotel reviews.
- Illustrate the value of hotel reviews online.
- Explain the business model of a hotel reviews site.
- Explore the technological and business innovations essential for hotel reviews sites.

Introduction and Company Development

Markus Schott and a couple of friends started HolidayCheck AG in 1999, as the idea behind evolved from a personal experience. Schott was about to book a vacation online and missed honest information, other than what the brochure could offer him. He found a private Canadian webpage with some personal hotel reviews, trusted the information he got and enjoyed a wonderful holiday. The idea was born. At the time it was a student's hobby without any commercial intentions, since nobody believed the project would ever be this successful.

HolidayCheck started off receiving about three reviews per day. After RTL television, one of Germany's largest TV-stations, reported on HolidayCheck's website in 2003, introducing the content as extremely helpful, the servers broke down. Indeed, people cared for HolidayCheck's product. To meet the new higher demands HolidayCheck started expanding. Until the summer of 2004. HolidayCheck could just cover its expenses by linking to affiliated travel agencies.

Today HolidayCheck runs its own online travel agency with 54 employees, 74 freelancers and interns, these numbers constantly growing. It is now the leading German-speaking hotel review platform. Depending on the season, 500–1500 hotel reviews are submitted per day. Compared to competitors on the German market like votello.de, cooleferien.com or hotelkritiken.de, HolidayCheck possesses not only the most, but also the most relevant, content for tourists originating from the German-speaking countries (Peter, 2006). International competitors are entering the German market. Tripadvisor, for example, also offers hotel reviews in German. Their data bank contains 5 million reviews, but mainly in English. HolidayCheck's main advantage lies in the German content, oriented on German's travel destinations, sorted and structured in a concise German way.

HolidayCheck definitely became the benchmark in the hotel review business (Beier *et al.*, 2006). For international markets HolidayCheck still offers limited content. It has to compete with huge platforms like Tripadvisor's with a total of 10 million reviews[1] in English and other languages.

---

[1]Tripadvisor's terms for a review are different. Here any entry for a hotel (e.g. photo, forum statement) is considered a review.

Main Products/Offerings and Value Added

People are regularly willing to spend large amounts of money for their vacations, but it is often hard for them to receive adequate information, especially when they plan to book over the Internet. HolidayCheck fills this niche by delivering hotel reviews, travel tips and holiday pictures contributed by a very trustworthy group – the users themselves. HolidayCheck offers free of charge, authentic, user-generated information about travel destinations, in order to provide tourists with a better choice for a well-suited vacation.

The company profits from selling vacations to the reviewed hotels. The travellers are satisfied with their vacation, because they Were able to research and evaluate the destination in advance. HolidayCheck users know before they book whether the hotel is rather for singles or families, what the food is like, whether the beach is pebbly or fine sand, the pool is just perfect for children, or mostly overcrowded, etc. HolidayCheck becomes part of the booking process and may be used for the next holiday again.

The HolidayCheck concept works. It is all about trustworthy information and knowledge. The huge databank with currently more than 660,000 worldwide hotel reviews, 240,000 holiday pictures, 25,000 travel tips and 740,000 forum entries is HolidayCheck's pride and comparative advantage to other travel agencies in the German-speaking area.

Users submit their holiday impressions because they want to share their travel experiences with other people and be part of a traveller community. HolidayCheck provides them a platform for that. At the same time this platform serves as a databank for tourists in search of information and offers concerning future travel plans.

The company always relied strongly on mouth-to-mouth propaganda, as a channel for trusted information. Contrary to its competitors, HolidayCheck never had to invest in expensive publicity. Instead the media engage HolidayCheck for expert interviews on travel subjects generating lots of publicity.

Business Model

Value Chain

According to Michael Porter's (1985) definition, HolidayCheck's value-adding activity is collecting, organizing and checking the quality of the incoming reviews, pictures, videos, tips, postings and reports (content management). The company then links these to travel offers, and thus sells vacations for different tour operators, collecting their commissions.

Customers

HolidayCheck attracts customers in search of providing and receiving travel information via Internet. About 55% of the German population over years of age uses the Internet (AGOF, 2006), mainly for communicative and informative reasons. Information about vacationing is placed number one on the list of online requested products in Germany (AGOF, 2005). The HolidayCheck customer can be found within these reference points. There are three types of customers:

- *Visitors*: Just looking at the page and searching for information.
- *Users*: Providing the content.
- *Bookers*: HolidayCheck's main source of revenue.

The whole portal is now mainly financed by the revenues from bookings (HolidayCheck, 2005) fulfilled by a proper online travel agency. The latter is specialized in selling packaged holidays to typical German, Swiss and Austrian holiday destinations.

In order to fully cover the market, selling travel and the possibility to review hotels is combined with a partner program. Any person with a webpage can integrate part of the HolidayCheck-content and thus become a partner. If a vacation is booked via this partner's website, the data transmitted to HolidayCheck include a code stating the sale by the partner organization. HolidayCheck then transfers parts of the commission to the partner's bank account. This way the company reaches a greater range of customers. It's in the partner's interest to locate and promote content, since he will be able to earn money this way. So far HolidayCheck has generated 1700 partners.

Suppliers

In case of HolidayCheck, the suppliers are also the customers. Users provide information through different available channels, hotel reviews, holiday pictures, forum entries, travel reports for the travel magazine. They become customers, when they search for information or book a vacation. The tour operators provide the vacation, but are at the same time customers, since they pay for HolidayCheck's services for acting as their agent.

Stakeholders

Stakeholders of HolidayCheck are tourists, tour operators, partners, hotels, media, travel insurances, rental cars, and of course its employees and shareholders (Tomorrow-Focus and the founders).

Profitability

HolidayCheck is, despite its age, already profitable. The concept of linking reviewed information directly to travel offers works. People who feel well informed are also willing to spend more on their vacation. The travel agency is busy handling more than 600 daily booking requests. The average booking amount is relatively higher than for other online travel agents. The company is in constantly searching for new travel agents; it is permanently expanding. Additionally, it can also make a profit with the number of page impressions when selling advertising space. HolidayCheck constantly has more than 3 million page impressions per day. With the growing amount of users and visitors this number increases too.

Technological and Business Innovation

Reviews are exclusively written by the users. Proper editorials are reduced to travel service information, a newsletter, an online magazine and some additional tips. This guarantees a maximum of independence and authenticity. In order to serve these purposes HolidayCheck's hotel reviewing IT is strongly linked to highly qualified and experienced manpower. The company uses its own optimized procedure. Since it is a browser-based remote data bank, HolidayCheck members are able to connect from anywhere. This is not just a social contribution but also a practical advantage insofar as the composition of the content team can reflect the different user groups, for example families with small children. Parents are able to work from home. Each of the entered reviews is first scanned by a computer routine developed by HolidayCheck IT that assigns the review to a certain category. It is then double-checked by a member of the content team. The intended purpose of this procedure is to be able to identify any fakes and reviews posted by hoteliers or tour operators themselves. This is very important for HolidayCheck's philosophy: to be an authentic and honest platform created by travellers for travellers. This trust is HolidayCheck's most important marketing tool. They sell vacations, even though they also place critical reviews online; in other words not just by transmitting only positive information, but also the negative parts. So HolidayCheck is successful because it combines the advantages of a reasonably priced online travel agency and a great variety of travel offers with multiple personal experiences that another travel agent cannot deliver, since information is passed directly from the exact same type of vacationer, e.g. pensioner to pensioner.

Key Challenges for the Future

HolidayCheck is a growing enterprise; its success is based on high quality standards. This is a great challenge for many reasons. First of all, the Internet market is on the rise, as is the information provided there. Since HolidayCheck attracts customers that trust online reviews, it remains important that the value of the reviews remains assured. Preserving honesty will be the key to future success. Only in this way HolidayCheck can remain a trusted brand and hotel reviews the successful marketing tool for selling travel.

Fake reviews need to be identified and blocked in advance through a little detective work. A specially developed computer program identifies where the computer is located that the user submitted the review from and the wording he used. Then a content manager reads the review to see whether there are any conspicuous comments that could identify the review as fake. A whole catalogue of hints how to identify fake reviews using the information in the reviews has been designed. So far HolidayCheck has been very good at it, as proven by different tests in the media (Lück, 2005; Peter, 2006). The real challenge comes with the company's expansion through internationalization, the year's release of the English and French websites and the thereby larger amount of incoming reviews will all have to be double checked. The chance of overlooking a fake review becomes higher as more reviews are published.

The second issue is the security of the transmitted data. For the customers' safety these processes have been approved by the strict German Technical Inspection Agency (TÜV).

Concerning the hotel reviews, HolidayCheck needs to be aware of emerging competition. The idea of finding the right place for a vacation by first choosing a suited hotel is a success.

Principally, any online travel agency could take hold of the hotel reviews, but then book using their own agency which would leave HolidayCheck as their aid in selling travel without any returns.

Internationally renowned online agencies started platforms for hotel reviews. Therefore it is very important for HolidayCheck to quickly win over strong affiliates with their partner program. The wider the range of HolidayCheck, the harder and less attractive it will be for competitors to enter the market.

The Company's Future

As shown by VIR (Verband Internet Reisevertrieb, 2006 [Association for Internet Marketing]) at the ITB (International Tourism Convention) in Berlin, the online travel market is expected to grow fast. By 2015 40–80% of all vacations are to be booked online. In 2006 only 17% of all vacations were booked electronically and 70–80% of all information concerning travel destinations is researched online.

Going along with the trend, HolidayCheck is on its way to become an international company. The English and French web pages were launched in 2006, containing the basic services: hotel reviews, holiday pictures and booking features. This way the range of customers is to be expanded first, before HolidayCheck also starts to cooperate with tour operators from these countries. Absolutely no promotion has been done for making these websites known so far. But the international pages already generate 40,000 visits and several reviews every day.

Key Conclusions

- For a Travel 2.0 site to be successful there must be critical mass in content.
- User generated hotel reviews add value to consumers.
- Hotel reviews can assist travel organizations to sell additional products.
- There is great competition emerging in the Travel 2.0 space.

Review and Discussion Questions

- How trusted are hotel review sites?
- What is the competitive advantage of HolidayCheck versus Tripadvisor and other competitors?
- How can hotel review sites maintain the objectivity of reviews?

References and Further Reading

AGOF (2005). *Berichtsband – Zusammenfassung zur Internet Facts 2005-II*. Retrieved 26 June 2006 from http://www.agof.de/index.download.b0f9855d4ad405c20440b218ccafc8fa.pdf.

Beier, A.-C., Bunzel, S., Däge, S., Nürnberger, T., Theos, K., & Weinert, M. (2006). *Touristische Bewertungsplattformen im Fokus*. Hochschule Heilbronn Studiengang Tourismus-betriebswirtschaft.

HolidayCheck (2005). *Jahresbericht*. Kreuzlingen.

Lück, Simone (2005). Tester im Test. *ADACtraveller*, 1.12, 36–38.

Peter, D. (2006). Hotels: Die Tops und Flops. *Clever Reisen*, 3, 36–38.

Porter, M.E. (1985). *Competitive advantage: Creating and sustaining superior performance*. New York: The Free Press.

Verband Internet Reisevertrieb (2006). *Die Zukunft bucht online*. Berlin: ITB.

Company's website: http://www.holidaycheck.com.

16

TUI: integrating destination information

Alexis Papathanassis

Learning Objectives

- Demonstrate how tour operators place high demands on Information and Communication Technologys (ICTs).
- Illustrate how tour operators can take advantage of an ICT platform to address market challenges.
- Explain how the tour operating business model has changed as a result of ICTs.
- Demonstrate that successful e-commerce requires an equivalent competence in terms of 'e-production' and 'e-infrastructure' to support it.

Introduction

Tour operating is one of the most complex forms of intermediary, placing high demands on Information and Communication Technologies (ICTs). The ICT platform of a modern tour operator does not only bear the weight of daily operations, but is also crucial for addressing the future's challenges. More frequently than desired, the migration towards an 'e-enabled' business model is perceived as, and limited to, the development of web-presence. In reality, this is only part of the story. Successful e-commerce requires an equivalent competence in terms of 'e-production' and 'e-infrastructure' to support it. The following case study aims at illustrating this notion, as well as highlighting how challenging it can be; more in an organizational than a technological sense.

Company Background

The Touristik Union International (TUI) is arguably the largest tourism group in Europe. Together with Thomas Cook, the Rewe Group, First Choice and MyTravel, they comprise the 'big five' of European packaged tourism. Cumulatively, they produced a turnover of €33.5 billion during 2004 (Krane, 2005). Nowadays, they enjoy the lion's share in the sector, their market share ranging from 50% to 70% in all the major European source markets (Papathanassis, 2004). TUI has practically become a synonym for the fully integrated tourism group. The 'World of TUI' enjoys a strong presence throughout the entire international holiday supply and distribution chain. According to the group's latest published profile, TUI employs some 57,000 people worldwide, supporting the group's international value chain (Table 16.1).

Table 16.1 TUI's organizational profile

3,200 travel agencies, 50 websites, and a TV channel	Retail
79 tour operator brands in 18 source markets	Tour operating
Fleet of 100 aircrafts	Transport
37 destination management companies (DMCs) and rep services in 70 countries	In-resort
285 (own) hotels, amounting to some 165,000 beds	Accommodation

TUI and Information Intensity

Next to the finance sector, tourism is characterized by a relatively high degree of information intensity. A spontaneous visit to the average neighbourhood travel agency and a look at the vast amount of holiday brochures available will no doubt confirm this assertion. For a tourism conglomerate the size of TUI, collecting, transforming and publishing content (e.g. hotel descriptions, resort information, photos, images) is a formidable task. Alone in Germany, the brand TUI offers no less than 25 different brochures, some of them containing more than 300 pages. This level of information intensity is evident for the rest of the 'big five' as well. For example, Thomas Cook publishes approximately 40 different brochures throughout their main European source markets (Liedtke, 2002). It is worth considering that such brochures are published in multiple price- and/or season-relevant editions. At this point, it is also worth remembering that holiday brochures are not the only distribution medium. Internet sites, TV channels and call centres also utilize content.

During the post-merger integration phase between TUI and Thomson, it was estimated that if the content was to be collected centrally on behalf of the group's major source markets, it would require the ongoing capturing, verification and updating of:

• Approximately 1000 information elements per accommodation unit (hotels, apartments, etc.);
• For a total of 12,000 accommodation units.

Maintaining this magnitude of content-handling operations is a logistical and financing challenge, thus rendering aligned processes and systems an absolute necessity.

Towards a Platform Strategy

During the late 1990s, TUI, then known as Preussag, embarked in a series of horizontal acquisitions across various European source markets. Amongst others, the acquisition of the Thomson Travel Group in the UK, which also included the Swedish-based Scandinavian tour operator Fritidsresor, can be described as a key milestone in the group's history. Consistently proceeding with the 'shopping trip' around Europe, including the take-over of Nouvelles Frontieres in France, TUI gradually migrated from being a vertically integrated tourism group to gaining the status of a pan-European tourism conglomerate.

In her business classic *When Giants Learn How To Dance*, Rosabeth Moss-Kanter (1989) argued that, in the face of increasing global competition, large corporations need to become lean, flexible, efficient and synergy-oriented. And indeed, in the face of source-market demand volatility, attributed to an array of political and economic events, 'holiday giants', such as TUI, need to 'learn how to dance'. The conception and implementation of TUI's platform strategy aimed at achieving exactly that. Namely, consolidating its destination-, carrier- and infrastructure-related operations to achieve synergies, while at the same time using this integrated operational platform to individually serve its international portfolio of source markets and tour operator brands. For the lack of a better analogy, this reflects a strategy borrowed from the automobile industry, the basic idea being the creation and standardization of different holiday modules (i.e. flight, accommodation), which can be packaged in different ways and sold under different brands in a pan-European scale (Blohm & Schneidewind, 2002).

The main synergy levels related to the adoption of such a setup are:

- *Risk-sharing*: Capacity exchanges between the different source-market organizations in order to normalize national demand fluctuations and to compensate for capacity-forecasting errors (especially for own and contractually committed hotel capacities). In other words, if one of the group's tour operators experience bed capacity utilization difficulties in their own source market, making them available to their European sister companies with a need for extra bed capacities, presents a win-win situation. Such an approach utilizes the horizontal dimension of the group and aims at reducing capacity risk by sharing it across source markets.
- *Pooled purchasing*: Centralizing and consolidating hotel contracting operations at a group-level improves the bargaining position against suppliers and allows volume-related discounts.
- *'Capture-Once, Publish Everywhere' (COPE)*: This level is concerned with content-related operations. Content refers to textual descriptions of accommodation units, supplementary local services at the destination, as well as photographs and images. Although it is mainly utilized for brochure and web publication, it is also an essential input for marketing and customer support activities. Given that every tour operator already has their own, historically evolved, content management processes and systems in place, standardization and centralization in this area, carries the potential of considerable cost reductions at a group level (e.g. elimination of effort duplication regarding data collection and system maintenance).

The exploitation of the identified synergy levels was translated to a number of corresponding systems development projects. This case study evolves around the background and challenges associated with the Destination Database project and subsequent system (abbr. DDB), which is intended as an enabler of the COPE synergy level.

Decentralised Content Management: Evolved Portfolio of Processes and Systems

Under closer examination of the content-related activities of the merging parties, one would encounter difficulties locating and classifying them under a particular process or functional area. A variety of departments, ranging from purchasing and publishing to destination services, were all collecting, updating and verifying partially overlapping information from the same source; namely, from the hotel and the corresponding resort. Often, this process was paper-based, while in some cases information and communication technology was (under-) utilized.

TUI Germany, for example, aside from circulating and confirming the contents of brochure pages with the hoteliers, was also sending out and collecting the following paper-based forms:

- *Object questionnaire*: Primarily aimed at collecting fact-based information on a particular accommodation unit. Distributed as an appendix to the hotel contract, it was usually handed out by the contractor, completed by the local tour operator staff and signed-off by the hotelier. The completed forms were sent via company mail to the corresponding business units in TUI Germany's head quarters.
- *Environmental questionnaire*: A questionnaire intended for the examination and evaluation of a hotel's adherence to environmental standards.

Thomson (UK) and Fritidresor (Sweden), besides the standard paper-forms, had also implemented small-scale, custom-built databases. Their population involved manual input and the use of pre-formatted emails. Added to the process and system diversity evident in content-related activities, was the dispersion of corresponding responsibilities amongst a variety of roles and departments. Along with others, contractors, tour representatives, incoming agents and head-office staff, were dealing with different pieces of the same content puzzle.

Enterprise-Wide Content Management (ECM): Destination Database

Bearing in mind the existing situation, the creation of a group-wide depository for factual information and images indicates a clear opportunity. Such a solution mainly consists of a relational database backed by a workflow-engine (to support the population process). Once centrally stored, factual information and images ('un-branded content') would be electronically made available to the various systems and departments in the different source markets; which in turn would be responsible for 'branding it' before releasing it to the end-customers (see Figure 16.1).

Apart from reinforcing TUI's e-commerce foundations, this initiative also offers the following potential benefits:

- *Process efficiency* (COPE): Elimination of effort duplication with regard to data/image collection, updating and verification (i.e. correctness confirmation).
- *Process effectiveness*: Apart from reduced administration complexity, automated workflow support also suggests improved content-process transparency and control. To sum up, the entire process becomes more manageable.
- *Content quality*: Up-to-date, consistent information across the various distribution channels and source markets. This is not to mention the reduction of manual input errors, which can be attributed to the increased degree of digitalization and information-flow automation (from the resort-suppliers to the tour operators).
- *Integration-catalyst*: The successful implementation of a common content-management process at the resort level could be considered as a first step to consolidating destination processes and organizations.

Summarizing, the construction and introduction of DDB is a fairly simple idea, supported by straightforward business reasoning (i.e. COPE). Nevertheless, simplicity can often be an elusive and challenging target; and indeed, simplifying can become quite complicated (De Bono, 1999).

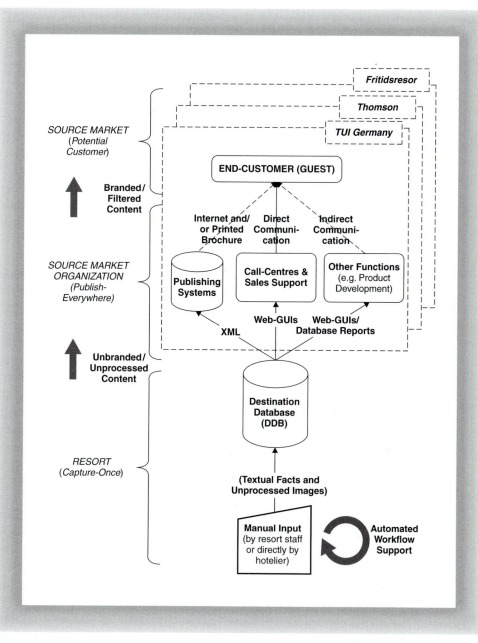

Figure 16.1 Destination database blueprint

Challenges Encountered and Lessons Learned

The first fully functional version of DDB was delivered approximately 9 months after project's initiation, which took place at the end of January 2001. The development phase progressed relatively smoothly, the only complication being the design of a group-wide data-model and its approval by the stakeholders. In particular, the main challenge during this phase concerned the scope of the factual data to be collected, their definition and the semantics around them.

This is best illustrated with an example. Establishing the 'total number of beds' of a hotel represents a fairly simple task, provided that there is clear definition of what a 'bed' actually is! Is a sofa-bed considered a 'bed'? Does the bed-count also include the possibility of adding an extra camp-bed in the room? In fact, is the total number of beds concerned with the count of permanent beds in every room; or with the maximum number of people that could potentially sleep in a hotel? Essentially, this is a matter of definition or preference. Despite the apparent triviality of such semantics, they do, nevertheless, have an effect on the entirety of the core production processes of a tour operator (i.e. from planning to calculation and brochure production). In this light, achieving a common set of data definitions (facts) for all the tour operators involved is more than an intellectual exercise. It can be characterized as a major internal negotiation challenge.

The remaining issues worth mentioning surfaced during the implementation and roll-out phase of the system. Incidentally, implementation and roll-out were the aspects least addressed during the project definition stages. More specifically, since 2001 and up to 2005, integrating DDB into the existing destination processes and structures has proven to be a strenuous and lengthy undertaking. This situation can be attributed to the existence of proprietary semi-automated processes and the historical division of responsibility with regard to content-handling:

- *Why-Reinvent-The-Wheel*: Each involved tour operator had been producing and publishing holiday content well before DDB came into the discussion. At the source-market level, having workable processes in place, reduces the attractiveness of an alternative approach and hence the willingness for granting the required investment.
- *Who-Finances-The-Extra-Cost*: The diffusion of content-related responsibilities across different roles, departments and organizations results to a lack of transparency concerning the as-is situation. The absence of a consolidated cost-view of the pre-existing and decentralized setup blurs the efficiency potential offered by content-process centralization and automation at a group-level. Under such conditions, rolling out DDB is perceived as an additional cost/effort, as opposed to a cost reduction opportunity for the DMCs.

In turn, the above-mentioned perceptions at both source-market and destination organizations could be held accountable for the internal friction regarding the responsibilities for financing the DDB implementation and corresponding re-organization. The resulting impediment in establishing the new DDB-setup throughout the entirety of the group's destinations, ultimately acts as a barrier to its adoption by the source-markets. For such a depository to be beneficial in any way, a critical mass of data is vital. In other words, if a tour operator is to justify the adoption of a content-delivery system, it needs to contain data representing significantly more than a fraction of the contracted hotels and must cover more than a handful of destinations. On the other hand, if a destination organization is to justify the implementation of DDB processes and responsibilities and the corresponding data maintenance effort, an explicit requirement needs to be expressed from the side of the source-markets. The interesting question here is: 'How can one overcome this type of supply-chain dilemma?'

Unfortunately, the promise of a quick and simple solution to this matter is somewhat unrealistic. A reasonable approach, such as the one successfully applied by TUI's DDB team, needs to be twofold and staged in its nature:

- Step 1: 'Destination Push': Focusing all available resources and efforts on the selective rollout of DDB starting by the high-volume TUI countries (e.g. Spain), as to demonstrate the system's feasibility and benefits.
- Step 2: 'Source-Market Pull': Once real, live content is available in the system for a particular destination country, the team's (internal) communication efforts are re-directed to the source-market organizations in order to facilitate the integration of DDB-content in their daily operations.

This procedure is repeated for each destination entering the DDB-schema, conferring the approach's incremental character. Concurrently, the implementation team is also actively pursuing the phased discontinuation of redundant content processes and systems. This type of change tactic requires time and stamina, but is perhaps the only way forward given the situation described.

Conclusion and Future

Effectively responding to the ever-increasing importance of the Internet for the production and distribution of tourism services requires more than web-presence. It necessitates existence of solid and operational content management processes and systems in the background, as to enable the full-exploitation of the web as a distribution medium, while ensuring harmony with the other 'traditional' channels. A website may well be more than an electronic brochure, but still needs to coexist with the conventional printed catalogue available in the travel agency. This requirement is equally applicable to the established, as well as to the aspiring, eTourism players. As illustrated by the DDB case, there are a number of potential difficulties and pitfalls associated with meeting it:

- Content-standardization and data-modelling.
- Process re-engineering and restructuring.
- Business case clarification and syndication.

Furthermore, expanding the ECM model in terms of directly incorporating external parties in the content process (e.g. providing independent hoteliers with direct DDB access), accentuates the importance and challenges associated with the above points. After all, an attempt of this kind would signal a trend towards sector-wide content management, evolving from the existing ECM.

It is worth mentioning that TUI is by no means the only tourism group aspiring towards an ECM model. The situation, challenges and lessons-learned portrayed by this case study are relevant for other tourism companies. Similar initiatives are, and have been, taking place elsewhere (Thomas, 2002). For the larger tourism groups (i.e. the 'big-five'), mastering ECM can be classified as a prerequisite for turning their size into a competitive advantage in the eTourism domain. Indeed, for the 'holiday giants', the 'dancing floor' provided by the Internet does not guarantee an elegant performance.

Key Conclusions

- Maintaining a high volume tour operating business is a logistical and financing challenge, thus rendering aligned processes and systems an absolute necessity.
- The conception and implementation of TUI's platform strategy aimed at consolidating its destination-, carrier- and infrastructure-related operations to achieve synergies.
- An ECM allowed the creation of a group-wide depository for factual information and images.

Review and Discussion Questions

- How can large tour operators take advantage of ICTs?
- Can large tour operators use technology to communicate with the market?
- What platforms are required to perform the entire range of operations?
- What is ECM and what are the key advantages?

References and Further Reading

Blohm, C., & Schneidewind, T. (2002). Strategy & management: A big step. *TUI Profile*, 2, 16–21.

De Bono, E. (1999). *Simplicity*. London: Penguin Books.

Krane, M. (2005). Maerkte im Takt. *FVW International (Dokumentation: Europaeische Veranstalter 2004)*, 4–5.

Liedtke, R. (2002). *Das Urlaubs-Kartell: Der Reisemarkt im Griff der Konzerne*. Frankfurt: Eichborn.

Moss-Kanter, R. (1989). *When giants learn to dance: Master the challenge of strategy, management, and careers in the 1990s*. London: Simon & Schuster.

Papathanassis, A. (2004). *Post-merger integration and the management of information and communication systems: An analytical framework and its application in tourism*. Wiesbaden: Deutsche Universitaetsverlag.

Thomas, D. (2002). *Thomas Cook uses XML to stay ahead*. Retrieved 28 March 2006 from http://www.computerweekly.com.

Weiland, H. (2003). Eine fuer alle: Neue Datenbank fuer Hotel- & Zeilgebietsinformationen. *TUI Times*, 6.

TUI AG Homepage: http://www.tui-group.com.

DDB Page: http://www.tui-ddb.com.

TUI Infotec: http://www.tui-infotec.de.

17

Cultuzz: managing eBay as a distribution channel

Michael Fux

Learning Objectives

- Illustrate how online auctions can be used in tourism.
- Demonstrate how eBay can be used by travel companies as a distribution channel.
- Explain how hotel managers gain access to comprehensive statistics about planned, running and completed auctions.

Introduction and Company Development

The business of Cultuzz Digital Media GmbH – henceforth referred to as Cultuzz – started in 2000 by developing software for the tourism industry. One of its first products was a content management system for websites; offered as an ASP solution. Today Cultuzz specializes in web-based software development for the travel, tourism and hospitality industries. Part of the product portfolio it is also a solution for improving and automating online auctions of hotel offers on eBay (Table 17.1).

Among numerous product categories, a travel section has been available for eBay users since 2002. Nowadays over 2000 offers are sold every day in this category on eBay Germany, the most developed eBay travel market worldwide. More than half of the products of several thousand vendors are sold in auction-style and the rest are purchased directly as 'Buy It Now'. Bestsellers are city short breaks or wellness arrangements.

And though eBay has a massive traffic of visitors neither sellers nor buyers consider it as a travel distribution channel. For hotels, online auctions are a relatively new way to sell offers, thus they have limited knowledge of how to set up auctions on eBay professionally. As a result, they cannot use eBay as an efficient sales channel.

Table 17.1 Cultuzz product portfolio

Product	Product description
CultBay	Service to sell products on eBay
CultBooking	Online reservation system
CultSwitch	Application for standardized data exchange between product providers, distributors and marketing executives
CultMail	Tool for e mail-marketing
CultCMS	Content management system for websites

Main Products/Offerings and Value Added

Knowing the opportunities and challenges hoteliers face by using eBay as a distribution channel, Cultuzz launched a web-based application to support a state-of-the-art presentation and management of offers on eBay in 2002. In the early stage of this new service, hotels were responsible for setting up new auctions, shipping the vouchers and process clearing. In response to hotel complaints about costs in the process of managing this new sales channel, Cultuzz had to advance its service to a full-service solution. They faced the challenge to automate the back office processes to offer auctions on eBay at low costs. Today 90% of the auctions are processed in a full-service license. The full-service solution comprises the following services in the auction process:

- Planning of annual turnover and required actions.
- Design of a standard or customized template.
- Establishment of an own eBay account to appear with personal member name.
- Creation of auctions based on previous designed template.
- Notification of auction winner and information about further steps by email.
- Notification to the hotel about the auction process and the buyer.
- Clearing with an automated process, including processing of eBay provision (Figure 17.1).

In a personal service interface on the Internet, hotel managers gain access to comprehensive statistics about planned, running and completed auctions. Each processed auction is listed with detailed information about selling price, buyer and auction course. This data provides useful insights to optimize future auctions and can be used for market research purposes. Furthermore a monthly account statement containing a list of conducted auctions, payment ledger and outstanding items is available (Figure 17.2).

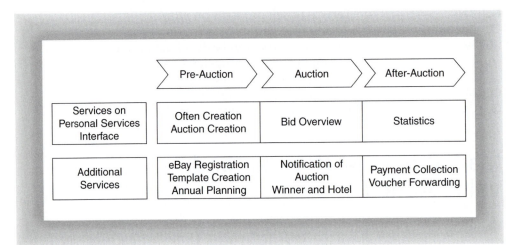

Figure 17.1 Customer service interface

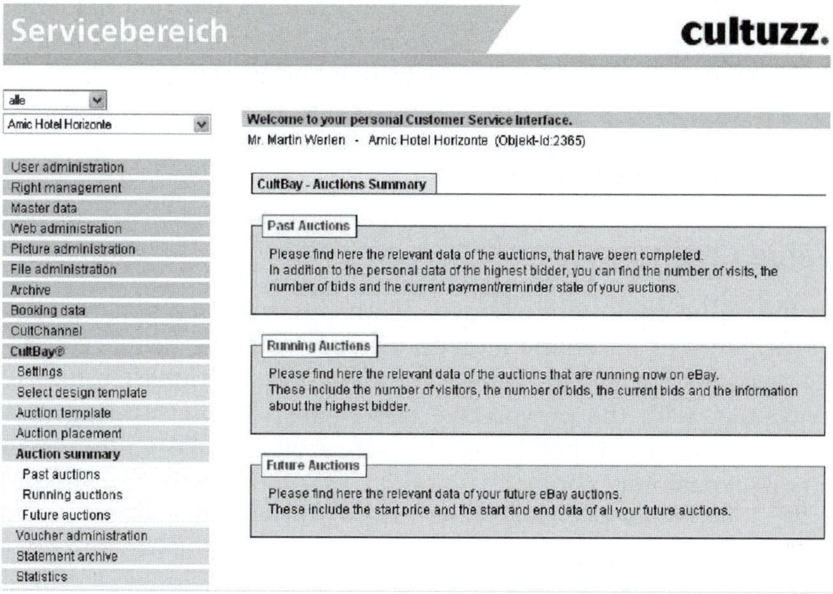

Servicebereich

cultuzz.

| alle ▾ |
| Amic Hotel Horizonte ▾ |

User administration
Right management
Master data
Web administration
Picture administration
File administration
Archive
Booking data
CultChannel
CultBay®
 Settings
 Select design template
 Auction template
 Auction placement
 Auction summary
  Past auctions
  Running auctions
  Future auctions
Voucher administration
Statement archive
Statistics

Welcome to your personal Customer Service Interface.
Mr. Martin Werlen - Amic Hotel Horizonte (Objekt-Id:2365)

CultBay - Auctions Summary

Past Auctions

Please find here the relevant data of the auctions, that have been completed.
In addition to the personal data of the highest bidder, you can find the number of visits, the number of bids and the current payment/reminder state of your auctions.

Running Auctions

Please find here the relevant data of the auctions that are running now on eBay.
These include the number of visitors, the number of bids, the current bids and the information about the highest bidder.

Future Auctions

Please find here the relevant data of your future eBay auctions.
These include the start price and the start and end data of all your future auctions.

Figure 17.2 Cultuzz services along the auction process
Source: http://www.cultuzz.com

Having auctioned a voucher on eBay, customers receive an invitation by email to log into a customer service centre called 'myCultuzz'. In 'myCultuzz' customers have to choose from the following proceeding options: download a printable voucher, receive the voucher attached to an email or obtain the voucher by postal mail. In addition, with an increasing number of hotels, customers can place a room reservation after having checked the availability. Having the payment settled, booking becomes definitive and customer data is directly transmitted to the property management system (PMS) of the hotel.

Offering hotel vouchers on eBay has an enormous advertising effect, as between 200 and 600 people on average viewing each travel offering. Travel customers may see a hotel on eBay and purchase it offline or through other distribution channels. Positioning offers on different marketplaces around the world is very conducive to reaching new customers. On eBay, hotels may also address a customer segment which is not present in other Internet travel markets.

There are some competitors with a similar service portfolio. In contrast to Cultuzz, the European market leader, these service providers act as (power) seller – sometimes with their own shop – and the hotels do not have an own eBay account with a review profile. Thus, customers cannot review a hotel's service. A further USP of Cultuzz is the connection of auctions on eBay to the PMS or CRS of the hotel. This back-end integration allows a one-stop shopping experience for the customer and eliminates the manual processing of availability administration and bookings.

Business Model

Value Chain

In the value chain Cultuzz acts as an intermediary between the participants of an online auction on eBay and the primary service provider, for instance hotels. In full-service auctions, Cultuzz is in contact with the prospective hotel guest during clearing and possible booking. If hotels use the self-service model, Cultuzz has no direct customer contact.

Product Providers

Product providers deploying Cultuzz services include international hotel chains like Marriott, Best Western and Ramada and privately managed hotels. Participating hotels are located in 16 countries around Europe as well as in North America and Australia. The acquisition of hotels is carried out and supervised by subsidiaries or partners in the respective countries. Offers are usually vouchers for an arrangement consisting of a 2–3 night stay in a hotel with some additional services such as spa treatments. In total over 2000 hotels are conducting more than 10,000 auctions each month.

Stakeholder

Main stakeholders are eBay and providers of PMSs. eBay takes a strong interest in the services of Cultuzz, because these services are a crucial element shaping eBay's popularity as a new selling channel in the tourism industry. Providers of PMSs cooperate with Cultuzz to connect their systems to offers on eBay and provide data about room availabilities. Another partner of Cultuzz is the ICE Portal which provides rich media content, such as virtual tours of hotels or destinations. This content is integrated into online auctions to visualize the travel experience.

Profitability

Fees for self-service hotels depend on sales level and range from €10 to €50 per month. Full-service hotels pay €10 monthly per enterprise and additional commission of 7% of the auction proceeds. Additional to these dues hotels have to pay an insertion and final value fee of about 5% to eBay. It comes down to a total commission of 12% for each successful auction.

In this context the profitability of vouchers auctioned on eBay may be interesting as well. Research has shown that prices of auctioned hotel vouchers reach about 50–70% of regular prices. However, a comparison between auction prices and regular prices is complex because offers on eBay are often packages including different services.

Technological and Business Innovation

Cultuzz uses the eBay application programming interface (API) to communicate in XML format with the eBay database. Thereby the tourist service provider or Cultuzz itself are interacting with a third party application which provides a custom interface, functionality and specialized operations not otherwise afforded by the eBay online interface. A switch connects the application with the hotel PMS and enables real-time two-way data exchange between the offer on eBay and the PMS, which allows availability searches during the auction and bookings after having purchased a voucher by auction.

From a hotel's point of view the key business innovation is the outsourcing of the administration of online auctions. After an annual turnover planning is done by a Cultuzz key account manager, the hotel is removed from all other tasks and may observe running auctions in the web-based service centre. By means of the web-based service centre and the integration of different applications, Cultuzz has automated several steps of the auction process. Thus, Cultuzz has not only played a major part in establishing a new distribution channel, but has also turned it into an efficient one.

Key Challenges for the Future

Figure 17.3 demonstrates the key elements of Cultuzz's technological infrastructure facilitating online auctions: a web-based service centre, a switch and a content management system (CMS). The CMS stores information about the hotel as text or images, which is used for several purposes like website maintaining, email

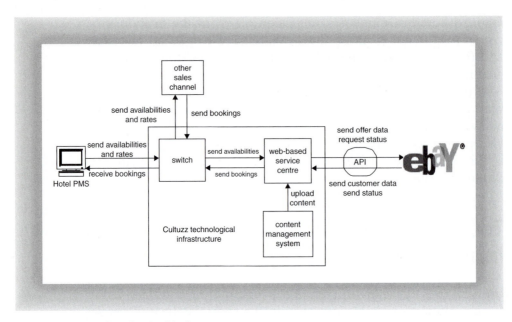

Figure 17.3 Technological infrastructure

marketing or print brochures. Content is also loaded to the web-based service centre into templates to dynamically create eBay offers. The switch sends currently availabilities from the PMS to other sales channels and to the web-based service centre. The entire offer is transmitted by the API to eBay. After an auction finishes, the hotel's PMS receives data of a possible booking, handled in the web-based service centre by the switch.

Both on the buyer side and seller side it is an important issue to position eBay as a booking or as a distribution channel. With travellers eBay has not yet gained much popularity and at the beginning hotels were quite sceptical of auctions with a starting price of €1. Speaking of technology issues, the connection of eBay to various types of hotel PMS and the implementation of booking technology on eBay are two key concepts. In the future Cultuzz will also act as a technology provider for eBay and facilitate the further development of eBay's travel section to a fully fledged online travel agency.

The Future of the Company

In future Cultuzz and eBay will cooperate closely to turn the eBay travel section into an online travel agency with the focus on short breaks and vouchers. With a new 'look and feel' as well as sophisticated search and booking functionalities eBay strives to become a popular place for travellers and suppliers. Cultuzz dynamic packaging is the first step in this direction. In auctions powered by Cultuzz, auction winners can buy additional nights and other services directly after a finished auction on the web.

The auction site is already well-established in the travel sector in Germany. Now eBay is aspiring to an international expansion of the travel sector and will launch several features tested in Germany on other eBay marketplaces worldwide. With the massive consumer pool of 181 million eBay members globally, eBay has the chance to become a dominant player in the online travel industry under condition that they continue to offer a USP, enrich the options of travel online and outperform other market players in terms of customer experience.

Key Conclusions

- Online auctions is a new distribution mechanism in the marketplace and can have wide implications for the tourism industry.
- Streamlining the process of auction, reservation and booking is critical for the operational efficiency of the system.
- eBay is an effective marketplace for the distribution of tourism inventory.

Review and Discussion Questions

- What are the advantages of online auctions for tourism?
- Discuss how an ASP hotel booking system can take advantage of multi-distribution strategies.
- Why would hotels like to outsource the administration of online auctions?

References and Further Reading

Bajari, P., & Hortacsu, A. (2003). The winner's curse, reserve prices and endogenous entry: Empirical insights from eBay auctions. *The Rand Journal of Economics*, 34 (2), 329–335.

Burger, B., & Fuchs, M. (2005). Dynamic pricing – A future business model. *Journal of Revenue and Pricing Management*, 4 (1), 39–53.

Melnik, M., & Alm, J. (2002). Does a seller's e-commerce reputation matter? Evidence from eBay auctions. *The Journal of Industrial Economics*, 50 (3), 337–350.

Ottaway, T., Bruneau, C., & Evans, G. (2003). The impact of auctions item image and buyer/seller feedback rating on electronic auctions. *Journal of Computer Information Systems*, 43 (3), 56–60.

http://www.reise.ebay.de.

http://www.pages.ebay.com/travel.

Company's website: http://www.cultuzz.com.

Conclusion of Intermediaries Section

Travel intermediation has changed dramatically as a result of information technologies and especially the Internet. It is increasingly evident that the intermediaries of the future will need to use a wide range of ICTs to aggregate content and to serve a wide range of markets. The case study clearly show how important the use of ICTs is for intermediaries to anticipate the customers' and suppliers' concerns and demands, enhance customer service, add value to their proposition and interact dynamically with all stakeholders. On the demand side, socio-demographic and psychographic changes are leading to a continuous change in consumer behaviour. In our postmodern society, suppliers and intermediaries both need to focus on the new customer standards and values. The objective is to offer customer-orientated services in a new and convenient manner and to inspire and provide personal advice to the client in his or her purchase decision. This also requires a dynamic and individual interaction with the customers. Solutions, such as dynamic packaging, allow them to plan and design a service individually.

The ICTs support intermediaries, however, not only in their contact with the customers but also by providing a valuable contribution at an inter-business and business-internal level. Since intermediaries trade with information about third-party services, they are dependent on up-to-date and correct data from their partners. ICTs support the effective and efficient dissemination and processing of information, encourage partnerships and extend the value system. In order to ensure the dynamic flow of data between enterprises, both interconnectivity and interoperability must be ensured. Within the business, ICTs mainly act on the operational, structural and strategic level by reducing costs or differentiating. This is reflected both in the reduction of communication and process costs and in the increase in flexibility, interactivity, efficiency, productivity and competitiveness (Buhalis & Egger, 2005). Alongside the e-mediaries, infomediaries and metamediaries have also been increasingly successful over the last few years with new business models in the tourism industry. The professional search for information represents the core competence of these enterprises instead of the marketing of tourism services.

The dynamism of the market, characterized by ever-changing customer behaviour and the prevalent tendencies towards cooperation and concentration, require a high degree of flexibility and a comprehensive differentiation strategy which is based on value added in order to remain competitive against rivals. The emerging transparency in the marketplace demonstrates that only intermediaries that clearly add value will be able to survive in the future.

Reference and Further Reading

Buhalis, D., & Egger, R. (2005). Informations- und Kommunikationstechnologien als Mittel zur Prozess- und Produktinnovation für den Unternehmer. In B. Pikkemaat, & M. Peters (Eds.), *Innovationen im Tourismus*. ESV-Verlag.

Part Three

Destinations
Dimitrios Buhalis
Roman Egger

Introduction

Destinations have a special position within the tourism industry. Destination Management Organisation (DMOs) perform both the role of the producer and that of an intermediary. Although they do not have a clearly defined place of business or a uniform product they coordinate the local product and bring together all resources. Basically, destinations can be seen as bundles of services within a specific geographical area. Management, planning and coordination of a destination are usually handled by the public sector (at national, regional or local level) or through strategic partnerships of stakeholders of the local tourism industry (Buhalis, 2003). Tourism organizations, known as destination management organizations (DMOs), assume the functions of building the tourism product, presenting the offer, lobbying and marketing in order to secure long-term competitiveness as a strategic objective. Some of the most important functions are:

- Profile – appropriate offer planning and development;
- Demand – appropriate coordination of offers;
- Implementation of quality standards for the part – services;
- Saleable preparation of the range of tourism products;
- Image care and brand creation;
- Marketing that is as cooperative as possible;
- Development and implementation of strategies;
- Positioning of the destination;
- Sensitization of the population for tourism (Bieger, 2000).

Destination management organizations interact with a wide variety of stakeholders in an already information-intensive environment. Socio-demographic changes and the individualization and pluralization of lifestyles are leading to a change in travel behaviour. Short holidays are increasing in importance, with the result that their planning requires the provision of destination and travel information as quickly as possible in order to permit impulsive booking decisions. In the meantime, the Internet has become the most important source of information for travel preparations. The potential tourist contacts the destination directly for information via the web and expects up-to-date, correct and relevant information about possible accommodation, activities and services (Case 21: The Province of Rimini). The low-cost airlines trend in particular is permitting inexpensive travel to remote destinations, which requires global dissemination of information in order to provide potential tourists with the information they need for travel decisions. The need for information, up-to-date and quality data are of relevance in particular when a large number of providers are involved in the creation of a total service. In this respect, the concept of tourism network has always been more a necessity than an innovation (Egger *et al.*, 2007). In order to market a destination appropriately and to promote sales, there is a need for a systematic networking between the service providers and all the persons involved in the 'destination' system (Case 19: Spain.info). This requires an effective and efficient distribution of information. Pollock (1995) comments:

> [...] *the internet will have a fundamental impact on the way the destinations are marketed because the real business behind travel is information.*

In recent years, destinations have increasingly recognized the importance of ICTs at strategic, operational and structural level (Case 22: Tanzania). ICTs have become a vital tool for DMOs and their stakeholders for the promotion of tourism networks within a geographical area, the efficient design of processes, the opening up of new markets and trade sectors (such as meeting, incentives, conferences and exhibitions (MICE) Case 25: Destimation.com) and above all the satisfaction of tourists' needs. The Internet enables DMOs to develop and maintain interactive relationships with all stakeholders. This has realigned and revolutionized the entire field of destination management over the last few years (Buhalis and Spada, 2000). Alongside the driving forces on the provider side, a strong pressure has developed towards online marketing of destinations. As tourists' expectations include not only the provision of information but also the theming of destinations as well as the possibility of booking of individual services, DMOs have to work hard to address this demand. Since SMTEs (small and medium-sized tourism enterprises) are largely not represented in the GDS systems, destinations are facing the challenge of filling this gap in the field of electronic distribution.

The first destination-focused computer reservation system (CRS) was created as early as 1968, but there was no apparent further spread of destination management systems (DMS) until the late 1980s. The reasons for this were to be found in the lack of an adequate technology; a lack of understanding of ICTs on the part of the tourism decision-makers working within a destination management that was frequently reduced to local level; the dominance of SMTEs; and the conflict of interests that arose through a large number of stakeholders (Buhalis, 2003; Egger, 2005). Destination management systems (DMS) in the past were characterized by non-homogeneous technical structures with location-specific interfaces, reflecting the decentralized structure of services. These systems were replaced by the centralized web-based systems. Today, increasing use is made of ASP-based destination-wide service systems (Noti & Fux, 2005).

From the point of view of the customer, a destination must develop and operate a destination-wide and integrated search, advice, reservation and handling system. This system should be coherent with the entire marketing proposition and should address the range of markets targeted. Since destinations must satisfy the interests and needs of numerous stakeholders, a major challenge is to keep pace with the dynamism of the online market (Case 18: VisitBritain.com). The decisive factors for the success of a DMS are in particular the high quality of content, value-creating technological functions and services, simple and efficient maintenance and a low level of complexity combined with high performance (Buhalis and Spada 2000). In addition, DMSs coordinate the needs of all stakeholders. Successful DMS solutions present the information structure of a destination and encourage both internal and external coordination and communication with partners and customers. They also target information processing and distribution, and the possibility of inquiry management through an online booking function. In addition, they support strategic management decisions and marketing processes (Case 23: Tiscover, Case 24: Feratel). Thus, information can be provided and coordinated by a variety of channels. Whether by the Internet, kiosks, mobile phones or call centres, multi-channel management permits the centralized distribution of all destination information. The entire inventory of a destination must be available centrally in the DMS in order to provide the customer with access to the complete range of services in a simple and transparent manner and to ensure a comprehensive destination management. This includes information about attractions, accessibility (entire transportation system comprising routes, terminals and vehicles), amenities (accommodation and catering facilities, retailing and other tourist services), available packages, activities and ancillary services (services used by tourists such as banks, hospitals, post offices) (Buhalis, 2003). The maintenance and updating of the contents of a DMS constitutes a technical challenge for the system as a whole. One of the possibilities for offering high-quality content is decentralized maintenance of the data by means of a content management system (CMS). An extranet provides authorized partners with access to the CMS for the updating of their data. Inter alia, the description of services, prices, opening hours and vacancies can be kept up-to-date. It is necessary in particular for small- and medium-sized accommodation enterprises that are represented internationally via a DMS. It requires the individual service providers to have both network access and sufficient resources together with the necessary know-how for handling the extranet. The lack of awareness of the importance of active stakeholder participation also represents a major challenge for numerous destinations.

A public-private partnership (PPP) is appropriate for the development and the management of a DMS (Case 20: BonjourQuebec.com). First, considerable financial funds are necessary in order to establish a high-performance system, and secondly it is necessary to have independent partners who support management and marketing at micro and macro level (Buhalis, 2003). Similarly to the Internet and the extranet, intranet solutions are also necessary at the destination level. Intranets have a coordination function between the individual operational units. Different departments of a DMO or diverse DMOs within a country or a region should have access to a common pool of information that is always up to date and should be able to design their processes more effectively and efficiently, to represent their offers transparently and to have a uniform presence towards the individual stakeholders. Destinations are increasingly required to use a broad range of the ICTs available in order to satisfy the needs for communication and coordination of the service providers and partners as well as within the organization and above all the potential customers. Both providers and purchasers make demands of the dynamism of the market and its complexity. It is only through the professional use of ICTs that the masses of information, growing in both scope and multi-dimensionality, can be communicated to, and processed for, the right target at the right time. The ability of a DMO to integrate all destination-relevant stakeholders together with their needs for information will determine the long-term competitiveness of a destination.

References and Futher Reading

Buhalis, D., & Spada, A. (2000). Destination management systems: Criteria for success – an exploratory research. *Information Technology and Tourism*, 3 (1), 41–58.

Buhalis, D. (2003). *eTourism: Information technologies for strategic tourism management*. Harlow: Pearson Higher Education.

Egger, R. (2005). *Grundlagen des eTourism; Informations- und Kommunikationstechnologien im Tourismus*. Aachen: Shaker Verlag.

Egger, R., Höri, J., Jellinek, B., Joss, M. (2007). Virtual tourism content network. TANDEM – a prototype for the Austrian tourism industry. In M. Sigala (Ed.), *Information and communication technologies in tourism*. Vienna, New York: Springer Verlag.

Freyer, W. (2001). *Tourismus-Marketing*. München: Oldenbourg.

Noti, M., & Fux, M. (2005). Elektronischer Kundenservice bei Tourismusdestinationen. In Arbeitsbericht 173 des Instituts für Wirtschaftsinformatik der Universität Bern. http://www.im.iwi. unibe.ch/publikationen/pdfs/eCustomerCare_vFinal.pdf.

Pollock, A. (1995). The impact of information technology on destination marketing. *EIU Travel and Tourism Analyst*, 3, 66–83.

Case

18

VisitBritain: satisfying the online market dynamics

Cathy Guthrie

Learning Objectives

- Explain the role of ICTs for the management of destination management organizations.
- Demonstrate the role of VisitBritain.com as the online portal for four national tourism organizations (NTOs) for the United Kingdom (England, Scotland, Wales, Northern Ireland).
- Illustrate the business model of www. visitbritain.com.
- Demonstrate the function of EnglandNet as a national online database and content management system for England which would interoperate with industry and regional partners' existing booking systems.

Introduction and Company Development

VisitBritain is one of four national tourism organizations (NTOs) for the United Kingdom (England, Scotland, Wales, Northern Ireland). It was created in April 2003 from the merger of the British Tourist Authority (BTA) and the English Tourism Council (ETC). As such, it is charged with promoting Britain as a destination to overseas markets and England as a destination to UK residents and to France, Germany, Ireland and the Netherlands. The other NTOs in the UK are VisitScotland, the Wales Tourist Board and the Northern Ireland Tourist Board. VisitBritain receives grant-in-aid from the UK government via a funding agreement with the Department for Media, Culture, Sport (DCMS). In 2005–2006, this totalled £35.5 million to promote Britain and £13.4 million to promote England. In addition, VisitBritain generates £17 million funding for its activities through partnership campaigns and commercial activities.

After a fall in arrivals in 2001, due to the combined effects of foot-and-mouth and the terrorist attack on 9/11, inbound tourism to Britain is on the increase. In 2004, the United Kingdom ranked 6th in the world for tourist arrivals, with 27.8 million arrivals generating £13 billion (€21.9 billion) (World Tourism Organization (WTO), 2005). This represents 3.6% of all tourist arrivals, and an increase in the region of 3 million visitors compared to 2003. Domestic tourism by UK residents generated an estimated £59 billion in 2003 across business and leisure tourism (VisitBritain, 2006).

Main Offerings and Value Added

As an NTO, VisitBritain is a service provider rather than a direct product provider. Its roles are to promote Britain and England as destinations, working with various partners and stakeholders (Table 18.1) to provide potential visitors with access to information and services which will both attract them to Britain/England and encourage them to stay longer and spend more during their visit. Neither is it the only organization with responsibility for tourism promotion within the UK. In addition to the three other NTOs, regional development agencies (RDAs), regional delivery partners (RDPs), sub-regional destination management organizations (DMOs) and local authorities also promote and deliver tourism. Indeed, tourism promotion and policy in the UK has

Table 18.1 Key players

Stakeholders			Suppliers	Customers
Tourism partners	Industry partners	Other partners		
VisitScotland Wales Tourist Board Northern Ireland Tourist Board Regional Development Agencies and Delivery Partners	Tourism Alliance British Hospitality Association British Tourism Development Committee UK Inbound	British Council Other Government Departments (Foreign & Commonwealth Officer, Nationality and Immigration, etc.)	Marketing agencies ICT suppliers National quality assurance contractor	Inbound tourists Domestic residents

been and still is bound up with the UK government's devolution agenda (Jeffries, 2001). This has had its own impact on the development of e-business solutions for promoting and selling Britain as a destination, as regional and national tourist bodies developed their own destination management systems (DMS), as did numerous destinations at the local level. Thompson (2001) argues that an alliance may provide solutions where the total customer service package suggests linkages throughout the added value chain, but individual organizations may wish to specialize in their area of competence. VisitBritain has had to negotiate strategic alliances with tourism partners, industry partners and other stakeholders to deliver its targets of increasing numbers of visitors, spread throughout the year and across the UK.

Business Model

In advance of the formation of VisitBritain, the BTA undertook a strategic review of its operations and target markets. This resulted in the closure of some overseas offices, co-location with the British Council in others, and increased investment in www.visitbritain. com. There is still an imperative to maintain a physical presence in key source markets, so VisitBritain continues to operate 27 offices covering 30 markets to assist, advise and inform potential visitors. Unable to move entirely from bricks to clicks, nevertheless VisitBritain has firmly positioned online services at the heart of its marketing activity, with 43 market and language specific versions of its website providing targeted information and services for 35 countries in 18 languages. Initially, www.visitbritain.com was primarily an information and promotional site intended to generate enquiries for brochures, with some links to sites operated by tourism and/or industry partners. Two relaunches later, the website is being transformed into a one stop portal through which visitors can book accommodation, inbound flights, and events and attraction tickets, as well as save information and 'wish list' items in their own travel plan section. The e-business model is thus moving further down the continuum from an information/communication strategy to an online/transactional one, incorporating elements of brand awareness and image building, info-mediary, brokerage, retail and customization (Wen *et al.*, 2001). Table 18.2 summarizes the range of e-business services offered to VisitBritain partners.

Table 18.2 www.visitbritain.com e-business services

Services	SMTEs	Larger product providers	Product consolidators	DMOs	DMS suppliers	NTOs	Travel trade
Worldwide web online distribution	✓	✓	✓	✓	✓	✓	✓
Virtual High Street	✓	✓	✓	✓		✓	✓
Website creation and management			✓	✓		✓	✓
eTourism platform			✓	✓		✓	✓

Technological and Business Innovation

Key to this has been the ongoing development of EnglandNet. Originally established in 2002 as a national online database and content management system for England which would interoperate with industry and regional partners' existing booking systems, the EnglandNet project has now been incorporated as the heart of the redesigned VisitBritain website. Interoperability via a web platform was chosen as the way forward, despite the technical and strategic challenges involved, because it obviated the necessity for EnglandNet to develop a separate interface for each partner; a considerable saving given the existence of regional tourist board and local destination organizations' DMS, all of which had to be incorporated into EnglandNet. The advantage of EnglandNet to the RDPs and industry partners is that it offers local tourism businesses the opportunity to reach a wider audience through the Internet, regardless of whether the business is e-business enabled. Depending on the nature of the agreement between the RDP and the local tourism business, the visitor is presented with a variety of means of obtaining more detailed information and/or making a booking: telephone, email, the business' own website or the RDP booking system, which could be real-time online booking. This flexibility allows VisitBritain to offer visitors greater choice, and additional business opportunities to RDPs and local tourism businesses.

The restructuring which saw VisitBritain take over responsibility for marketing England was also an opportunity to review the EnglandNet project. Originally, a separate joint venture company had been set up to lead the EnglandNet project, jointly owned by the Regional Tourist Boards (RTBs) and the English Tourism Council (ETC). However, in December 2004, after consultation with stakeholders, Tom Wright, chief executive of VisitBritain, announced that EnglandNet had been repositioned as a public sector project within VisitBritain, thus removing the need for the project to be self-financing. No longer driven by profitability, it could concentrate on developing interoperability as a means of delivering competitive advantage. EnglandNet would not be an agent of sale, consolidator or operator, but would simply act as the platform for delivering comprehensive English tourism product content, thus allowing RDPs to continue as consolidators for regional and local tourism product. For the small to medium-sized tourism enterprises (SMTEs), which make up the majority of the tourism product, this means that their primary relationship is still with their local or regional DMO.

It has also allowed VisitBritain to develop the services to visitors on the website without having to provide transactional capabilities to the industry. The advantage for VisitBritain is that they do not handle financial transactions or visitors' personal and financial details, and they can continue to offer maximum flexibility to their tourist and industry partners. From the tourist and industry partners' perspective, there are no commission charges or fees on bookings made via the appointed partners of the regional development agencies (commission charges and/or fees are charged for other commercial partners, such as hotel chains or accommodation marketing companies). The balance between additional revenue from increased bookings and loss of commission income was an issue raised by the implementation of Scotland's national DMS, www.visitscotland.com (Guthrie, 2004). Concerns about this can raise barriers to project implementation. This is particularly true where achieving interoperability has necessitated additional investment in upgrading partner systems to meet minimum data standards.

The next phase of development for the consumer-facing site, underway since December 2005, has been to increase the online services available to visitors by providing a flights engine, real-time accommodation booking and an online shop. All three services are an extension of the EnglandNet platform model, in that the visitor searches for inbound flights to the UK or accommodation within England on the VisitBritain site and is then passed to a third-party agent to complete the booking or purchase. Similarly, the online shop is run by an external agency which handles the transaction. The flights engine searches some 500 airlines, including low cost carriers such as EasyJet. This inclusion of budget airlines distinguishes the VisitBritain facility from other major flight search sites, such as www.kelkoo.com or www.expedia.com, and contributes to the overall vision that the VisitBritain site should be an one stop shop for potential visitors to the UK; making it easy for them to obtain everything they need not just to find out about the UK but to then proceed to action by booking most, if not all, of their holiday through the one site. Table 18.3 summarizes how this contributes to competitive advantage for VisitBritain.

Key Challenges for the Future

In a sense, VisitBritain are outsourcing their product delivery. As with any outsourcing operation, a potential difficulty lies in maintaining quality standards. This is being overcome by promoting only quality assured products, that is, accommodation establishments which participate in the national quality assurance scheme.

Table 18.3 Benefits leading to competitive advantage

www.visitbritain. com element	Industry benefit	Consumer benefit	VisitBritain benefit leading to competitive advantage
EnglandNet	• Resolves market failure • Provides additional route to market for product owners and consolidators • Visitor can use variety of channels for bookings	• Ability to book an encyclopedic range of accommodation product through a variety of channels	• Increases services offered to both consumer and industry • Can track bookings and referral statistics to demonstrate added value • No need to handle visitors' financial details
Flights engine	• Ability to book flights and accommodation through same site drives more traffic to the tourism industry • Additional route to market for carriers	• One stop shop for all travel arrangements	• Kudos of leading edge technology • Distinguishes from other NTO websites
Online shop	• Additional route to market for tourism and non-tourism partners	• Responds to expressed demand • Multi currency service	• Increases services offered to consumer, industry and other partners

Progressively, this will be applied to other elements of the product as well (VisitBritain, 2005).

The new developments on the consumer site are driven by research into consumer and supplier requirements carried out in 2005 on VisitBritain's behalf by Metrixlabs (2005). Once established, however, the interoperability model can equally be applied to business tourism. VisitBritain's business tourism site offers a venue search facility linked to venuefinder.com and it is intended to integrate the business tourism site with the existing accommodation database as part of future developments.

The Future for VisitBritain

It would appear that VisitBritain has been successful in developing an e-business operation which provides added value for customers, stakeholders and the tourism industry within the UK. To do so, it has had to lead a considerable change management programme, persuading industry and tourism partners to work together to improve Britain's competitive advantage and address market failure which was preventing SMTEs presenting their product on the wider international stage. Challenges for the future include tracking referrals and click through to demonstrate the level of business being generated through the site; developing the platform to deliver the same services to mobile devices as well as computers; maintaining and developing the technology; extending the functionality to other product types; extending EnglandNet to a pan-Britain platform; and working with all stakeholders to ensure that the experience delivered in the UK matches up to the promise of the information and services delivered through the website.

Key Conclusions

- VisitBritain has been successful in developing an e-business operation which provides added value for customers, stakeholders and the tourism industry.
- ICTs and the Internet are integral part of a DMO function and operations.
- EnglandNet has allowed VisitBritain to develop the services to visitors on the website without having to provide transactional capabilities to the industry.
- It is critical for the DMO to persuade industry and tourism partners to work together to improve destination competitiveness.

Review and Discussion Questions

- How can destination management organisations employ technology to improve their competitiveness?
- Should destination management organisations perform reservations?
- Who are the key stakeholders in building the destination online presence?
- What are the success factors for destination management organisations?

References and Further Reading

Guthrie, C. (2004). Tourist information centres and ICT: Opportunity not threat. *Insights*, 15, 23–29.

Jeffries, D. (2001). *Governments and tourism*. Oxford: Butterworth-Heinemann.

Metrixlabs (2005). *Online survey: USA, Australia, India, Denmark.*

Thompson, J.L. (2001). *Strategic management: Awareness and change*, 4th ed. London: Thomson.

VisitBritain (2005). *The strategy 2006–2009: leading the world to Britain*. London: VisitBritain.

VisitBritain (2006). *Key Tourism Facts*. Retrieved 27 February 2006 from www.visitbritain.com/corporate/factsfigures/index.aspx.

Wen, H.J., Chen, H.-G., & Hwang, H.-G. (2001). E-commerce web site design: Strategies and models. *Information Management and Computer Security*, 9 (1), 5–12.

World Tourism Organization (WTO) (2005). *Tourism Indicators: Inbound Tourism*. Retrieved 27 February 2006 from http://www.world-tourism.org/facts/menu.html.

http://www.enjoyengland.com.

Company's website: http://www.visitbritain.com.

Case

19

Spain.info: towards stakeholder network

Oriol Miralbell, Esther Pérez Martell and Marta Viu

Learning Objectives

- Explain the role of ICTs for the management of National Tourism Authorities.
- Demonstrate the emerging business models for National Tourism Authorities as a result of the Internet.
- Illustrate the business model for TURESPAÑA.
- Demonstrate a technological platform for supporting the competitiveness of TURESPAÑA.

Introduction and Company Development: A Success Story Looking to Bring Itself Up to Date

From the 1960s onwards Spain began its climb up the international ranking of tourist destinations until reaching its current position as the second most popular destination in the world with about 59 millions international tourists per year. At first, it structured its growth mainly around sun and beach tourism. This established a particular dynamic image of mass tourism destination, based on seasonal business, the predominance of tour operators and travel agents in the role of intermediaries, and a strong price policy. The rapid growth of tourism along the coast, and dependence on sales by powerful intermediaries, contributed to the creation of a characteristic business framework based on family businesses or SMTEs, and lacking in innovative spirit.

Tourism policy, which had been managed by the State administration, was transferred in its entirety during the 1980s to the governments of the 17 autonomous regions, resulting in changes in marketing strategies.

During the 1990s, these characteristics of the public and private structure of the Spanish tourism sector made it difficult to design a Spanish platform for tourism marketing on the Internet administered by a NTO (National Tourism Organization). Other European countries such as Ireland, Austria, the United Kingdom or France were beginning to develop their portals at that time. A flexible proposal was needed that would respond to the needs of the business sector and the public.

Main Products/Offerings and Value Added: The Path to the New Mode of Tourism Marketing

With the growth of the Internet, experts immediately identified tourism as a key sector for this network. Consequently, the tourism administrations of the Spanish autonomous regions promptly developed tourism portals. However, the majority of the private sector, whether because of the commercial inertia they were subject to, or because of insufficient training, took longer to incorporate marketing tools in their web pages.

The Spanish General Secretariat of Tourism and the NTO – TURESPAÑA, created in 1985, offered two technological solutions to the tourism companies during the second half of the 1990s. One of these was TURINTER, for tourism information and promotion. The other was TURCENTRAL, a booking system (CRS) that was not fully accepted by the tourism service providers, mainly due to a lack of understanding of its usefulness.

A strategy was needed that would unite the sector and maximise the synergies of all the players in the area of tourism, both public and private: a strategy that would permit the government to take advantage of the experience and knowledge garnered through TURINTER and TURCENTRAL, as well as the institutional portal TURESPAÑA and the technological developments of knowledge management carried out by the Tourism Studies Institute.

The initial budget for spain.info was €9 million, thus giving sufficient resources to the project and guaranteeing the support of the Spanish tourism sector, essential for its success. Additionally, promotional campaigns were budgeted, including the 2004 advertising campaign in the media, which received a European award. This major technological commitment was undertaken with three important technological partners: Microsoft, Telefónica and Indra. Microsoft contributed its new software development platform Microsoft.net, and Telefónica its network services as well as a significant part of the new portal's content. Indra developed the entire process under the control of SEGITUR.

The setting in moti on of spain.info involved various stages for the incorporation of diverse solutions oriented toward the promotion of tourism. After the first stage, SEGITUR started the creation of an extranet for businesses providing services followed by one for intermediaries, as well as for the implementation of the reservations system. This was, therefore, an integrated commitment.

Business Model: Objective – to Lead Spanish e-Marketing

SEGITUR presented an entirely new model by which an NTO would make use of the ICTs. It did not intend to be a DMS (destinations management system), nor a traditional tourism promotion portal. Its objective was to become the reference platform for the Spanish public and private tourism sector where information, promotion and the commercialization of tourism co-exist, under an e-business model. The platform will ensure integration of

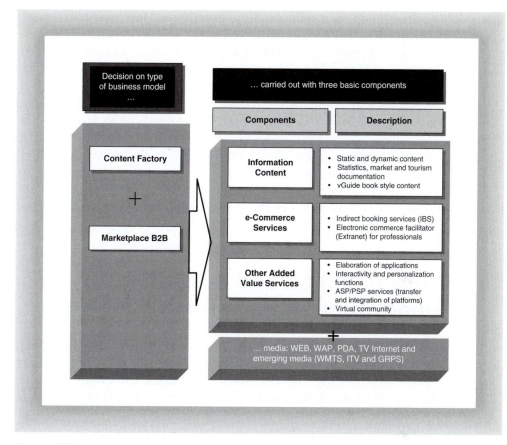

Figure 19.1 Components of the business model
Source: SEGITUR

information and content of regional, local and private sector tourism portals; as well as fostering of a 'marketplace' for businesses and on-line sales, in both the B2B and B2C spheres.

SEGITUR designed a two-directional strategy: the first a product creation using its tool called 'Content Factory' and the second, related to services, through its platform 'Marketplace B2B' (Figure 19.1).

Through the use of this model the intention was:

- To promote the use of the ICTs by the Spanish tourism sector, especially on the Internet.
- To improve the efficiency of the tourism sector by providing adequate tools to encourage access to ICTs.
- *E-commerce*: Support of on-line commercialization of Spanish tourism products and services.
- *On-line promotion*: To facilitate the on-line promotion of Spain as a tourist destination.

This business model made it possible for the different agents involved in the online value chain to be able to offer their services and acquire others. This was meant to be a marketplace where participants would be able to act as suppliers or content aggregators and consumers at the same time.

In this way spain.info is able to offer the tourist comprehensive and personalized service, adapted to the needs of each user, while permitting service providers and travel agents, on the other hand, to make use of a powerful technological platform with which they can do business with the tourist, negotiate with other agents in the sector and take advantage of data mining resources for planning. All of this occurs in a global setting adapted to their own platforms.

Technological and Business Innovation: A Necessary Change

Conscious of the need to advance in a practical sense, which would permit Spain to effectively position itself on the Internet while establishing the necessary conditions for giving impetus to the Spanish tourism sector in e-business, SEGITUR decided to plan their strategy based on three central axes.

First, the decision was made to set up the information and tourism promotion portal, spain.info, with the previously referred to technological partners. In less than one year, in July of 2002, they presented the portal to the sector. This portal offered the possibility to access to a multi-relational database with all the information on tourism resources and services of the 17 Spanish regions. This included 86 different information subsystems covering Spanish services and resources, including more than 14,000 lodging establishments. The information consisted of added value and information services (Table 19.1).

Second, putting the portal into operation helped to obtain agreements with the autonomous governments for the exchange of information and content. This guaranteed the supply of the basic information of the portal, while building loyalty among the principal administrators of Spanish tourist information. SEGITUR created a service known as content factory, whose function was to generate text and multimedia content for use in the portal and for distribution to both public and private Spanish tourism organizations. A part of this content was used to generate digital brochures on demand by the CRM (customer relationship management) designed by SEGITUR

Table 19.1 Information services of spain.info

20	Guided visits
28	Virtual visits
86	Panoramic photographs of Spanish cultural patrimony
36	Animated infographs
35	Videos
86	Sound files
1400	Enriched articles
250	Digitalized brochures
26	Street maps
150	Spoken articles
85	Subsystems

Source: SEGITUR

and other electronic publications. This allowed for the reduction of a good part of the 12 million brochures that the 31 Spanish tourist offices located in foreign countries distribute every year.

Third, e-marketing and e-commerce services were initiated, through putting into operation:

- the EXTRANET, which is the B2B platform for negotiations between providers and agents responsible for commercialization,
- the PISTA actions, as a technological solution for tourist businesses that wish to make use of a reservations system, and
- the electronic billing platform, which allows for simplification and homogenization of billing among tourist businesses.

Fourth, SEGITUR offered different services to various tourism sub-sectors (hotels and other service providers, and travel agents), such as training seminars, advisory services, formation and integration of their systems with spain.info (Figure 19.2). They also launched the PITA plan for technological innovation to the 14,000 Spanish lodging companies, creating their web pages and offering the possibility of using the reservations platform of spain.info. Lastly, SEGITUR has placed at the disposal of both the tourism sector and experts, a platform called Management Scorecard (Cuadro de Mando), through which information can be extracted for analysis, planning and decision-making.

Therefore, a change in the trends of promoting and marketing of the various Spanish tourist services and destinations was initiated. This was accomplished through improved competitiveness, reorientation of intermediation toward more effective channels in keeping with market tendencies and, above all, by promoting

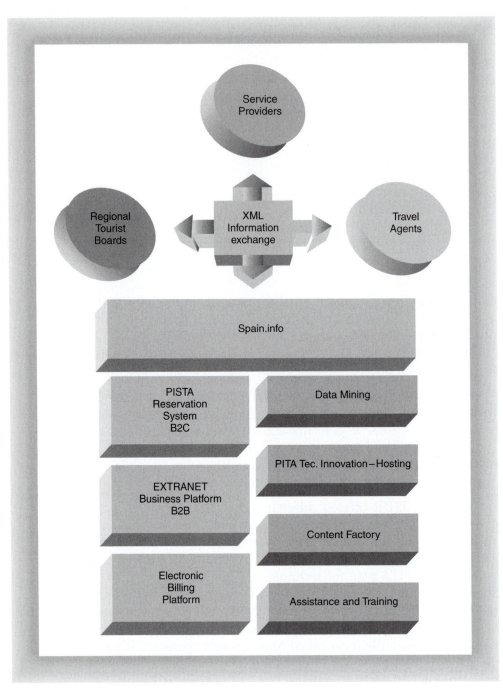

Figure 19.2 The services of Spain.info

a new culture emphasizing marketing and quality tourism. TURESPAÑA was already carrying out these strategies, together with plans for quality services and excellence in the destinations, known as PICTE (Comprehensive Plan for Quality in Spanish Tourism).

Key Challenges for the Future: Consolidating the Role of Facilitator

The strategy of SEGITUR (called SEGITTUR since 2007) continues to aim at achieving the expansion of coverage through collaboration agreements with the various players in the tourism sector that have yet to be incorporated in spain.info, while simultaneously working to improve their components.

SEGITUR has participated, together with some of the portals of the Spanish autonomous regions, in an international R+D project intended to improve the flow of information between members. The HARMONISE project was developed to address the particular needs for information exchange between partners in the tourism domain. The technical R+D was funded by the IST-programme and an e-service has been successfully validated based on an eTEN market validation project, Harmo-TEN, demonstrating that a market exists for this kind of service, even if it is complex and fragmented area. The later project ended with a business and deployment plan and a non-profit association, HarmoNET, to run this service.

Additionally, SEGITUR has developed a real time availability search engine by means of a direct connection via XML-Web Services using OTA standards with the booking engines of the different service providers (hotel chains, airlines, etc.). In this way, SEGITUR aims to incorporate an intelligent information search system.

As services facilitator for the tourism sector, SEGITUR wants to strengthen its model and achieve a return on its activities. Hence it has signed agreements for collaboration and the transfer of technology with Spanish American NTOs, directly participating in the creation of the new tourism portal for Central America.

Furthermore, conscious of the need to take advantage of the appeal of Spain in order to present its content to both transverse and tourism portals, SEGITUR has signed agreements with Yahoo, Terra and with MSN but also with Expedia, Opodo and Lastminute, who will use their European national portals to promote Spain as a destination. In North America, they count on the support of AOL thanks to an agreement with AdLink, while in Spanish America they plan to make use of the network belonging to Terra Networks.

The Future of the Company: The Key to the Future

It would be impossible to imagine the consolidation of SEGITUR without the collaboration of the principal tourism players in Spain, specifically without the tourist services providers, travel agents or the regional and local tourist administrations. A destination as vast as Spain, with so much territory, so many places with enormous tourist appeal, and with such a wide variety of tourism offerings, needs an update of its marketing strategies in an ever-changing and competitive market.

SEGITUR foresees the continuance of its policy of collaboration agreements such as those signed with Spanish business associations, travel agencies and rural hotels; in addition to those signed with local and autonomous tourism administrations. In this way they will increase the usage and exploitation of its platform. At the same time, SEGITUR plans to continue work on technological improvement of its platform spain.info.

Spain.info represents a comprehensive strategy for the promotion of the ICTs in the marketing of Spanish tourism accomplished without having aroused suspicions or objections in the sector, through clearly defining its position as facilitator of services and not as a rival, and in total collaboration with the sector's existing systems.

Key Conclusions

- TURESPAÑA has developed two technological solutions, TURINTER, for tourism information and promotion and TURCENTRAL, a booking system (CRS) which never obtain the hoped-for acceptance from the tourism service providers, mainly due to a lack of understanding of its usefulness.
- spain.info was set as an information and tourism promotion portal.
- The portal offered the possibility to access to a multirelational database with all the information on tourism resources and tourism services of the 17 Spanish regions.
- ICTs and the Internet are integral part of a destination management organization function and operations.

Review and Discussion Questions

- How can spain.info incorporate the various distributors of Spain?
- How can spain.info add value to travellers?
- What are the components of the spain.info portal?
- Should spain.info incorporate user-generated content?

Further Reading

Buhalis, D. (2003). *eTourism: Information technology for strategic tourism management*. Harlow: Prentice Hall.

Getz, D., Carlson, J., & Morrison, A. (2004). *The family business in tourism and hospitality*. Wallingford: CABI Publishing.

Lassnig, M. (2006). The European e-business market watch: ICT adoption and e-business activity in tourism. In M. Hitz, M. Sigala, & J. Murphy (Eds.), *Information and communication technologies in tourism 2006* (pp. 171–181). Vienna: Springer.

Louillet, M.C. (2006). *Proposal for a Success Model for Destination Management Systems*. ENTER 2006 Proceedings. Retrieved from http://www.homes.tiscover.com/sixcms/media.php/3524/louillet.pdf.

Mill, R.C. (2002). *The tourism system*. Dubuque: Kendall/Hunt Publishing Company.

Ministerio de Industria, Turismo Y Comercio. Retrieved from http://www.mityc.es.

Miralbell, O. (2001). *Portales de destinos turísticos en Internet: Una reflexión estratégica. Métodos de Información*. Vol. 8. N. 42–43. (pp. 74–78). Valencia: AVEI.

Ndou, V., Passiante, G., & Carella, R. (2006). Toward e-business models for tourism destination management. *Journal of Travel and Tourism Research*. Turkey. Retrieved from http://www.stad.adu.edu.tr/ing/makaleler/stadguz2005/tammak1.asp.

SEGITUR. Retrieved from http://www.segittur.es.

Sheldon, P.J. (1997). *Tourism information technology*. New York: CAB International.

Sweeney, S. (2000). *Internet marketing for your tourism business: Proven techniques for promoting tourist-based business and economics*. Gulf Breeze: Maximum Press.

WTO (2001). *E-business for tourism – practical guidelines for destinations and businesses*. Madrid: World Tourism Organization.

Company's website: http://www.spain.info.

Case

20

BonjourQuebec.com: a vision, a strategy, a brand

François Bédard and
Marie Claire Louillet

Learning Objectives

- Illustrate how the Quebec tourism industry in Canada takes advantage of the emerging ICTs for the improving their competitiveness.
- Illustrate the advantages of the destination management system 'BonjourQuebec.com'.
- Explain the importance of incorporating SMTEs in the information highway.

Introduction

'BonjourQuebec.com' (BQC) is an innovative destination management system (DMS) from the Province of Quebec-Canada (population of 7.6 million) which enables the Ministry of Tourism (MoT) to accomplish its mandate. The DMS was launched in 2000 in partnership with Bell Canada, the biggest Canadian telecommunications company.

The Quebec tourism industry presently generates some 10 billion Canadian dollars per year in revenue. It constitutes an important source of foreign currency and fiscal revenue for the federal and provincial governments. The economic prosperity of the regions of Quebec depends largely on the 29,000 tourism businesses, in great majority SMTEs, and the 180,000 jobs directly or indirectly linked to that sector.

The main tourism market for Quebec comes from within the province. That market is followed by, in the order of importance, markets from other provinces of Canada, the United States and Europe. Of the 28.3 million tourists in 2004, 75.4% came from Quebec, 12.9% from the rest of Canada, 8.3% from the United States and 3.4% from other countries. The Quebec tourism market is comprised largely of individual tourists who plan their trips themselves. It is thus not a market dominated by tour operators (TOs), although some US-American and international travellers do buy packages from TOs.

The mission of the MoT consists of creating conditions that promote the growth of the tourism industry and its revenues in Quebec. It does so in particular through promotion, information and the improvement of knowledge of the clientele. Faced with the task of updating its digital infrastructures before the Y2K 2000 deadline, and wishing to benefit from the government policy for developing the information highway, the MoT counts the use of new technologies among its strategic orientations since 1997 and has taken the initiative to launch the destination management system 'BonjourQuebec.com'. Its objective is to help the Quebec tourism industry stay competitive by offering global access to information and reservations. In this way it allows tourism SMTEs to participate in the information highway. The strategy took account of the characteristics of the Quebec tourism industry, which is composed mainly of SMTEs that are 'poorly equipped to face the competition on the international markets' (Préfontaine *et al.*, 2002). The MoT also took account of the existence of digital divide within the accommodation and restaurant sectors between the small independent establishments and those average size establishments which are part of a chain (Cefrio, 2004).

Main Products Offerings and Added Value

More than a simple reservation centre, BQC is a tool that allows to promote and market the destination of Quebec. Thanks to its multiple channels, Internet, the call centre (1-800-bonjour), the network of 7 'infotourisme' information centres (kiosks set up with interactive terminals, email, fax), the BQC disseminates information concerning the tourism products and services of the province. The exhaustive information about Quebec takes the form of suggestions for vacations (more than 250 different types are proposed), product descriptions, web photos, interactive maps, tour guide information and downloadable pdf brochures. BQC is a digital B2C market place. Its functionalities allow consumers to reserve or buy tourism products (Figure 20.1).

The MoT performs, for the tourism SMTEs, the update and quality control of all the information disseminated by the BQC. In so doing, the MoT helps certain SMTEs to develop marketing strategies with which they can optimize their use of BQC and formulate their promotional message. The MoT shares its information on the market with the SMTEs of the destination. That information includes consumer profile, fees and types of accommodation searched for and time of reservation.

Finally BQC is a communication and exchange tool for the various tourism actors who use it. These are the hotel operators, the 45 local tourism information offices, the 21 regional tourism associations and the 7 tourist info centres managed by the MoT.

In 1999, before BQC was established, the MoT depended on its information agents to respond to 1,025,000 information requests as well as on a limited website that reached approximately 1 million viewers annually. In 2005, by contrast, 11.1 million clients were served, 92% through the Internet. The scale of BQC is equivalent to that of Visitbritain.com, the official site of the United Kingdom, a country with a population about 8 times bigger than Quebec and slightly smaller than MySwitzerland.com, the official site of Switzerland, which gets 13 million visits per year.

The great majority of French-speaking tourists who made a lodging or package reservation on BQC felt that the process is easy to understand (93%) and that the time required to complete the transaction is short (91%) (Charest, 2005). Client satisfaction varies between 96.3% and 100%. The average delay of processing emails is less than 2 days. The average delay of postal delivery of documents is 3.2 days within Canada and 5.2 days to the United States.

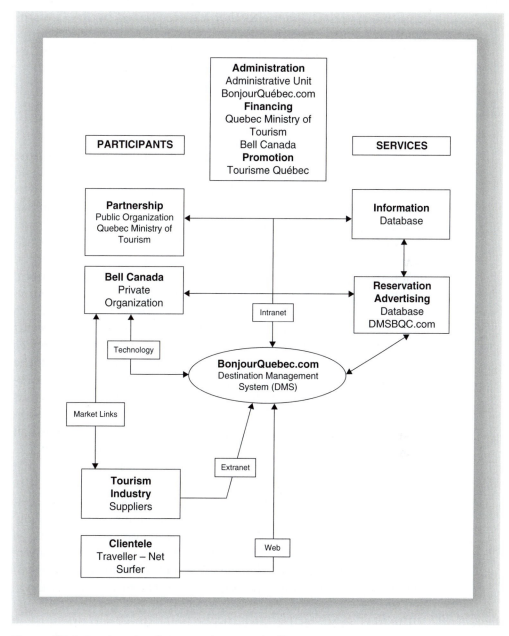

Figure 20.1 BonjourQuebec.com in a nutshell

The average delay of reaching a call centre agent is 43 seconds, and between 84 and 136 seconds at the main tourism information offices. Assistance to consumers is maintained 24/7.

The change management concerning the working methods at the MoT as well as the successful experience of public-private partnership are achievements that are recognized by the Government of Quebec. Since its implementation, BQC received 14 international and national awards for the quality of its website, its ergonomics and its web marketing actions.

Business Model

Having neither the expertise nor the financial means to assume the required investments alone, the MoT sought a public-private partnership (PPP) to realize its DMS. Its invitation to tender was concluded with an agreement with Bell Canada, the Canadian telecommunications giant. The two partners share the financial risk. The MoT covers the costs for the development and the technological processing related to its tourism information services and for the administration of client files of the DMS. It ensures the promotion of Quebec and of BQC on the markets and manages its call centre, its tourist info centres and its reservation website. Bell Canada has the role of technological provider of BQC and assumes the risks and costs of the development and marketing of the reservation services and of the e-commerce component. Other than MoT and Bell, the principal stakeholder of BQC are the tourists visiting Quebec, tourism businesses (mainly hotel operators, rail transport, attractions and some restaurants), non-governmental tourism information offices and regional associations, as well as business partners (all companies susceptible of generating hotel reservations in Quebec).

To date, the BQC has more than 13,000 information files that provide detailed descriptions of attractions and tourism businesses. The MoT assumes the costs of entering and updating those files. Businesses are invited to provide a description and photos to show on the website to the end of marketing and selling their products. Of the 5000 hotels classified by the Quebec Ministry of Tourism, more than 700 are transactional members of the DMS. Transactional members benefit from inventory management and from an online reservation service via a secure extranet hosted by the Bell resource centre.

The MoT provides for the cost-free registration and updating of fact sheets of most Quebec businesses. A team of nine people carry out this work by communicating directly by telephone and email with the managers of the businesses. For the business categories that are most in demand, updates are done once a year. The other categories are re-verified and updated every other year, unless information is supplied in the meantime. Museum events and exhibitions are updated more frequently, depending on the information made available.

Accommodation and camping businesses, as well as hunting and fishing outfitters, are bound by law to be classified. The organizations that classify them, namely the Corporation de l'industrie touristique du Québec (CITQ), the Conseil de développement du camping au Québec (CDCQ) and the Fédération des pourvoyeurs du Québec, verify the information of these establishments through visits of their classifiers. Accommodation establishments and camp grounds are visited every other year and the outfitters every fourth year.

The classification of an accommodation business is charged with a base fee of $190 plus $4 per unit of accommodation. For camping grounds, the classification fee varies between $125 and $245, depending on the number of camp sites. For outfitters, the classification fees are included in the operating permit, which costs between $538 and $1250 per year. No additional fees are charged for the registration or for the modifications in the database disseminated on BQC.

Information gathering by telephone seems to be the best means of validating the information and of ensuring that what appears on the sheets is correct and responds to the standard definitions. Mailed surveys to be filled out by the operators give more random results, which in turn require telephone or on-site verifications. Except for businesses subjected to an obligatory classification, the MoT does not perform on-site verifications as these are too costly.

Through Bell, MoT offers the optional service of an improved and invoiced fact sheet (photos, digital flyer, etc.). The service, which is very affordable, is used by a restricted number of businesses (see fee structure in Table 20.1).

For reservable businesses, the additional necessary information on the available units and the package deals is gathered by Bell Canada and entered into the database. As for the available inventories and the daily prices, the businesses have secure extranets on which this information can be modified at their discretion in real time.

The fee schedule for the reservable businesses is featured in Table 20.1. There is an initial registration fee, an annual subscription fee for the reservation service as well as a transaction fee of 10% of the transaction price if the reservation is done by BonjourQuébec.com and of 5% if the reservation is done by a travel agent. Those fees are payable by the business and not by the tourism client.

The BQC business model is based on:

- a set up fee ranging from $250 to $650;
- an annual membership fee for the transactional service: $150 for hoteliers who are members of a regional tourism association/ association touristique régionale (ATR); $300 for non-ATR's members;

Table 20.1 BQC products and price list 2006

Name	Price	Recipient
Bargains	$150 – 39 units and less/month $225 – 40–199 units/month $300 – 200 units and more/month	Service providers – hotel operators
Bonus	$150 – first sheet/year $75 – additional sheet/year	Attractions
Bonus – Accommodation	$250 – per sheet/year	Service providers – hotel operators
Publicity on the BQC reservation engine	$500 – National Motor/month $450 – Montreal, Quebec/month $300 – Laval, Montérégie/month $200 – other regions/month	Attractions
BQC membership – registration fees *one-time fee, payable only once during the membership	$250 – Youth hostels $250 – Condos and chalets $250 – Tourism lodges $250 – Outfitter (forest inn) $250 – Vacation centre $250 – Student dormitories $250 – less than 39 units $450 – 40–199 units $650 – 200 units and more	Service providers – hotel operators
BQC membership – yearly fees	$300 – non-member ATR[1]/year $150 – member ATR/year	Service providers – hotel operators
Fax option	$55/year	Service providers – hotel operators
Additional package	$100 per package/year	Service providers – hotel operators
Reserve button *must be reservable member of BQC	$300 'Look & Feel' $0 without 'Look & Feel'	Service providers – hotel operators
Internet advertisements – TQ partnerships *must be reservable member of BQC	$450 Bulletin/month $500 Contest/publication	Service providers – hotel operators

[1]ATR: Association touristique régionale – Regional tourism association

- a transaction fee of 10% per reservation, or 5% if the latter is effected by a travel agent.

That fee structure is advantageous for the industry compared with the 25% discount presently negotiated by virtual travel agencies such as Expedia.ca. Currently a maximum of 30 tourism businesses can publish special offers on the BQC site. This also generates an additional form of revenue for BQC while allowing the SMTE tourism participants to offer attractive products online. However, as a government site, BQC guarantees fair access and visibility to each tourism SMTE regardless of its size. BQC also takes care to protect the personal data of the consumers.

The BQC team counts a total of 57 employees among the two partners. Thirty are employed by the MoT and do not include the staff from the tourist info offices. The other 27 are employed by Bell Canada. At the MoT, 12 employees ensure the tourist information services and update and manage the digital databases. A further nine employees work for the web promotion unit and manage a web marketing budget of 1,125,000 Canadian dollars. They implement the following strategies: realization of thematic sections each season, creation of web campaigns, partnership agreements concerning content, indexation and referencing, as well as the realization and sending of newsletters. Finally, the remaining nine MoT employees work at the e-business centre. Bell Canada, for its part, has 12 technicians orr staff who ensure the development of technological solutions, and a further 15 professionals who ensure the marketing development, produce an electronic newsletter for the members and who coordinate the reservation and billing process.

Technological and Business Innovation

The main success of BQC is to have created an information and reservation network that is completely integrated to the scale of the province by deploying a reservation engine in all the regional tourism associations. The network thus allowed the BQC to be one of the most frequently visited DMSs.

Another success factor of BQC is its marketing. BQC contracted specialists to improve the search engine optimization, which had the effect of increasing the number of visitors. BQC has also reached critical mass through partnerships with other service providers (Hertz, Hôtellerie Champêtre, box offices and Billetech), allowing it to present web visitors a comprehensive and competitive offer.

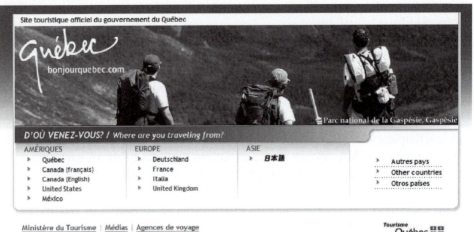

Site touristique officiel du gouvernement du Québec

bonjourquebec.com

Parc national de la Gaspésie, Gaspésie

D'OÙ VENEZ-VOUS? / *Where are you traveling from?*

AMÉRIQUES
- Québec
- Canada (français)
- Canada (English)
- United States
- México

EUROPE
- Deutschland
- France
- Italia
- United Kingdom

ASIE
- 日本語

- Autres pays
- Other countries
- Otros países

Ministère du Tourisme | Médias | Agences de voyage

Tourisme Québec

Figure 20.2 BQC homepage
Source: http://www.bonjourquebec.com

The dynamic of the web promotion team extends beyond Quebec borders, with BQC being cited as an example in one of the training courses of the United Nations Conference on Trade and Development. On the technological level, the site's search engine and dynamic maps make it an interactive tool that allows visitors to plan their trip itinerary and find out which attractions are close to their hotel.

According to the two partners of BQC, the success of PPP in large technological projects is always difficult to achieve and tight deadlines also represent a risk of failure. Transparency and confidence between the partners are necessary. As well, training for change management is essential because without partnerships, BQC would not have seen the day. Knowledge of the market and of the needs of the stakeholders was an asset in the project. BQC continues to evolve thanks to the financial solidity of the two partners and the continual technological developments. The third-generation website launched in March 2006 is more tailored to the profile of the clientele. For example, at the new homepage, the visitor can indicate their place of origin, which then leads him or her to a region/country section (Figure 20.2).

Key Challenges for the Future

Many challenges have already been overcome by the Quebec DMS project (Table 20.2). The marriage of the public and private sectors required that approaches of two partners with different

Table 20.2 Quebec DMS Chronology

January 1996	Adoption of the strategy of the Quebec government to implement the information highway, which includes the plan to realize a tourism destination management system (DMS)
April 1996	The Ministry of Tourisms (MoT) becomes a government agency known as Tourisme Québec. That status as an autonomous service unit gives it the possibility to generate revenue linked to its activities and to reinvest on the basis of its mission (Lachance, 1996)
January 1997	Invitation to tender for a PPP to realize the Quebec DMS
April 1997	Conclusion of an agreement with Bell Canada to realize a study of the administrative and technological development of a DMS
November 1997	Finalization of the development study and beginning of negotiations for a partnership agreement with Bell
March 1999	Conclusion of a 7 year renewable partnership agreement with Bell to realize and operate the DMS BonjourQuebec.com until 2005
December 1999	Putting into operation of the modules for sending documents and for digitalizing the database on the businesses as well as of the new telephone call management system
Spring 2000	Putting into operation of the digitalized database (at call centres and on the website), the electronic magazine as well as the experimental implementation of the reservation module (at call centres and on the web)
June 2000	Official launch of the BQC website
Spring 2001	Set-up of info-reservation services in the seven tourism info centres
2002	Putting into operation of the interactive maps: Reservation modules on private websites and testing of the data module in non-governmental tourism information offices
2003	Consolidation and improvement of functionalities and services; launch of the electronic newsletter for consumers
April 2003	Renewal of the partnership agreement between MoT and Bell Canada until December 2008. The MoT adds to the BonjourQuebec.com initiative an investment of 12.5 million Canadian dollars in technological development in order to link to DMS the 21 regional tourism associations in Quebec
2004	Putting into operation of modules for collecting client profiles and for processing BQC data; launch of an electronic newsletter for businesses
February 2005	The structure of Tourisme Québec, a government agency since April 1996, is changed to MoT
March 2006	Complete revamping of the website to adopt a per-market approach

effectiveness criteria be conciliated: the private partner aims to rapidly generate revenue to benefit from the partnership while the public partner searches for an enhanced visibility and market presence. The retention of human resources of each of the partners is possible if the managers succeed to dispel 'the fear that the private sector is invading the public sector and leads to the loss of jobs' (Cefrio, 2002). The consolidation of work procedures ensures the success of the project and should be maintained in the future. This includes flexible problem-solving procedures, fast decision-making, the sharing of work spaces and the integration of teams.

Two lessons were drawn from the partnership: Confidence and transparency between the partners are very important, and change management requires time and money. The time required is often underestimated.

Among the challenges to meet within the next years are: (i) strengthening of the business model to meet the market competition (e.g. Expedia.ca and mega-search engines such as Yahoo, Google, Kayak, Sidestep and Mobissimo); (ii) growth of revenue to allow continuing with technological developments; (iii) connectivity: direct link to the PMS of the hotels.

The Future of the Company

Even with partners as solid as the MoT and Bell Canada, the stability of the DMS may be in jeopardy by factors such as a change of government, a major reorganization of the private partner or a change of the business environment. Certain measures allow to attenuate the instability such as a good contract, back-ups for key human resources as well as a spokesperson with real decision-making power allowing to make decisions rapidly.

The integration into a shared space of teams from two partners calls for the transfer of indispensable knowledge to ensure the good functioning and improvement of BQC.

In light of the uncertainty of the future, it is important to keep the organization flexible and to review, if need be, the contractual agreements. The business plan should be subject to revision regularly to optimize the longevity of the project and the search of revenues (Cefrio, 2002).

The risks related to the revenue and those related to expenditures should be carefully analysed. It is thus important to invest more in market analysis and to evaluate the technological complexity of the project in order to decrease the costs of the operating budget.

Key Conclusions

- Destinations can opt for the public-private partnership (PPP) model as they rarely have the expertise or the financial means to assume the required investments alone.
- Bell Canada, the Canadian telecommunications giant, was instrumental in the development and the technological processing related to its tourism information services and for the administration of client files of the DMS.
- The main success of BonjourQuebec.com is to have created an information and reservation network that is completely integrated to the scale of the province by deploying a reservation engine in all the regional tourism associations.

Review and Discussion Questions

- How can multi-region DMOs coordinate their regions to improve their competitiveness?
- What are the key advantages and disadvantages of the PPP approach?
- Why should SMTEs be part of the destination digital infrastructure?

References and Further Reading

Buhalis, D. (2003). *ETourism. Information technology for strategic tourism management*. Essex: Pearson Education.

Buhalis, D., & Spada, A. (2000). Destination management systems: Criteria for success – an exploratory research. *Information Technology and Tourism*, 3 (1), 41–58.

Cefrio (2002). Cahier de synthèse des actes du colloque Partenariat public-privé: pour une meilleure performance de l'état; Cefrio. Québec. ISBN 2-921181-85-1; 39-47. www.cefrio. qc.ca/rapports/Actes%20Colloque%202002.pdf.

Cefrio (2004). *NetGouv 2004, business sector*. Unpublished survey.

Charest, F. (2005). *Les pratiques des internautes de la version française du site bonjourquebec.com dans leur recherche d'information et de réservation/achat*. Report presented to Bell Canada in June.

Courville (2005). *Address of Bell Canada at the press conference of the launch of the new BonjourQuebec.com website on March 21 at the Palais des Congrès de Montréal.*

Lachance, L. (1996). *Tourisme Québec prend le virage électronique.* Le Soleil, Tuesday, April 30.

Préfontaine, L., Ricard, L., & Sicotte, H. (2002). *La collaboration pour la prestation des services publics: constats et défis. Nouveaux modèles de collaboration pour la prestation des services publics.* Projet Cefrio, groupe Pivot, January 2002.

UNCTAD (2005). *E-tourism initiative; Taking off E-Tourism opportunities for developing countries, information economy report 2005,* Chap. 4. Retrieved 15 April 2006 from http://www.unctad.org/en/docs/sdteecb20051ch4_en.pdf.

World Tourism Organization – Business Council (2001). *E-Business for Tourism. Practical Guidelines for Destinations and Businesses.*

Company's website: http://www.bonjourquebec.com.

Case

21

The Province of Rimini: communicating with the customer

Rodolfo Baggio

Learning Objectives

- Illustrate how ICTs play a key part in assisting DMOs in their operations, with important functions both in networking of local organizations and in promoting destination brand and products on the global market.
- Demonstrate how the Province of Rimini uses technologies and media for promotion and marketing.
- Illustrate the advantages of the destination management system for Rimini.
- Explain how a thorough analysis of target customers can ensure the development of a useful and usable reference system.

Introduction

The tourism sector has been characterised in the last few years by increasing competition. Destination management has emerged as an effective methodology to help tourism organisations in their effort to intensify marketing activities (Ritchie & Crouch, 2003). Moreover, the wide variety of organisations involved and the complexity of tourism products has rendered the coordination and cooperation among them a critical success factor. The umbrella incorporating all local stakeholders, the destination management organisation (DMO) has thus assumed a crucial role in fostering the development of local tourism systems (Buhalis, 2000).

Information and communication technology (ICT) plays a key part in assisting DMOs in their operations, with important functions both in networking of local organizations and in promoting destination brand and products on the global market. The Internet revolution has, obviously, affected these activities strongly and DMOs have transferred much activity from traditional (mainly printed) media to the Net.

The Destination

The Province of Rimini offers a good example of a coherent and effective planning of the institutional promotion by using in a comprehensive way all the available technologies and media. The province territory is located in the southern part of the Emilia-Romagna coast in central eastern Italy (Figure 21.1).

This area has a long and consolidated tradition in the reception of visitors. In 1843 the first bathing establishment was developed. A few decades later the seafront was sold to private individuals or companies and Rimini turned out to be 'the city of small villas'. In 1908 the Grand Hotel, the first luxury hotel, was built, soon becoming a symbol for the destination. About 6 million tourists were visiting the area in the early 1960s (Conti & Perelli, 2004).

Well renowned for its hospitality, the overall tourist capacity in the province runs to more than 140,000 beds in almost 3000 accommodation units (90% of these are hotels) mainly located on the coastline. In a year the Rimini district receives about 3 million tourists, spending a total of more than 15 million days (Table 21.1).

Italian visitors account for 80% of the total (last five years average); as Rimini is the first summer destination for domestic tourism. Foreign arrivals are mainly (almost 70%) from a few European

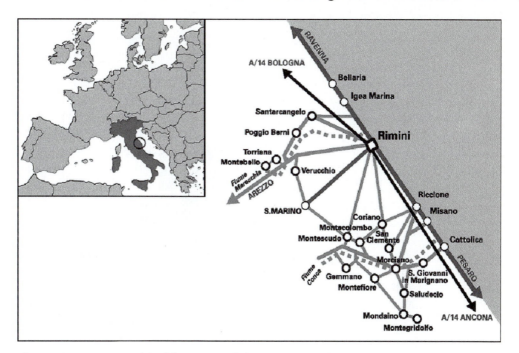

Figure 21.1 Geographical location of the Province of Rimini
Source: http://www.turismo.provincia.rimini.it

Table 21.1 Tourism statistics for the Province of Rimini

Year	Arrivals	Overnight stays
2000	2 661 665	15 823 936
2001	2 704 023	16 044 480
2002	2 674 959	15 695 128
2003	2 677 068	15 349 118
2004	2 680 619	14 988 520
2005	2 728 722	15 013 693

Source: Statistics Bureau of the Province of Rimini, 2006

countries namely: Germany, Switzerland, Russia, France, United Kingdom, Austria, Belgium. Seasonality is very strong. The three summer months (June, July, August) account for 61% of the arrivals (Figure 21.2) and 74% of the overnight stays.

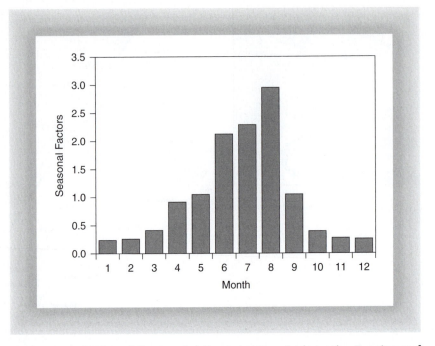

Figure 21.2 Seasonal factors for the tourist arrivals to the Province of Rimini
Source: Statistics Bureau of the Province of Rimini, 2006

The DMO is a public administration: the tourism department of the Province of Rimini. Like in many other countries, its responsibilities are those of planning and coordinating the promotional and informational actions for the destination and managing the collection of statistical data concerning the tourism stakeholders. As for many other countries, such organisations are not allowed any operational or commercial activities.

Business Model

A series of surveys conducted (mainly by Eurisko, a well known Italian social and marketing research company) between 1996 and 1998 identified the typical visitor coming to Rimini as a person not fully mature and not fully conscious in buying tourist products, with limited education and strong dependency from the social signals, but with good spending capabilities.

One of the results of the survey, however, was that this market showed a tendency to evolve towards higher cultural levels, strongly increasing its critical capabilities.

At that time, the local administration started a repositioning program based, mainly, on communication and promotional activities. As a consequence, the overall look of all the promotional materials used on the tourism market was redesigned by using methodologies typical of a private company corporate image project.

Recognising the important role that advanced information and communication technologies were starting to have, a second phase of this project was focused on a revision of the usage of ICTs, with the objective to integrate them fully in the everyday activities. To summarize the efforts, the then councillor responsible for Tourism and Hospitality, Massimo Gottifredi, used the expression 'reshaping and harmonising the physical and virtual access ports to the Province'.

Technological and Business Innovation

The new website (http://www.turismo.provincia.rimini.it) of the Province of Rimini Tourism Department was redeveloped at the beginning of 2002. The Internet presence is considered essential to give a clear sign of a modern and innovative administration, able to satisfy the complex and high expectations of contemporary tourists. Besides that, the website is designed to be the centre of the global tourist documentation and reference system. With these characteristics it proves to be a powerful tool to establish a direct communication channel between tourists (actual or potential) and the destination management organization.

Two main lines have guided the redevelopment:

- a thorough analysis of target customers to ensure a useful and usable reference system, with the consideration that, besides the general public, important users of the system are the local stakeholders and the press;
- a design of an integrated database system able to back the informational needs also for other Internet projects and for add-itional different uses.

The graphical interface, obviously, has been rendered fully coherent with the general image designed for the Rimini district (Figure 21.3). The website (in two languages) contains the following sections:

- news: with the last news on the province and the website;
- identity card: with the basic reference information (maps, addresses, routes to the destination, useful data);

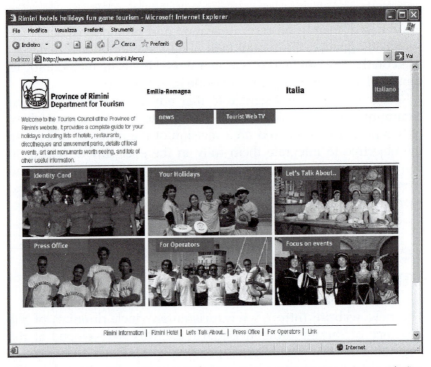

Figure 21.3 The Home Page of the Province of Rimini tourism website
Source: http://www.turismo.provincia.rimini.it

- for operators: section dedicated to the local tourist operators (only in Italian);
- press office: information and documentation for the journalists;
- your holidays: the main area with the information for the visitors (hospitality, sports, recreation, culture, events);
- let's talk about …: articles and commentaries on the territory, the culture, the people;
- focus on events: comments and reports on the main events;
- links: a selection of other websites useful for the tourists;
- help: sitemap and instructions for the main functionalities.

The final architecture of the whole system is depicted in Figure 21.4. Two main databases form the core of the system:

- SITur: collecting all basic tourist information and descriptions for places, infrastructures, environmental and cultural resources;
- Resources and Events: containing the main 'operational' data (schedules, prices, timetables) on accommodation establishments, restaurants, events, etc.

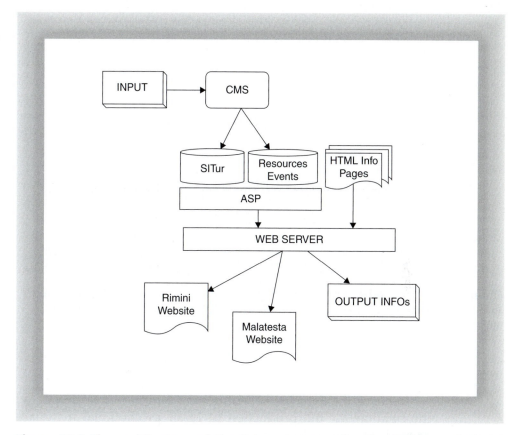

Figure 21.4 The architecture of the Internet system for the Province of Rimini tourism department

All information about the destination and its resources, as well as changes or updates, enter the main databases via a content management system. Microsoft's ASP (Active Server Pages) language was the choice for the scripts responsible to produce (together with some static HTML pages) the website pages published online.

Hotels, restaurants and other establishments are presented online with dedicated webpages containing a link to the specific website (if it exists). Online booking or payment options are provided directly on the single websites. No central reservation system exists.

From the same databases, a second website is published online: the Malatesta Seignory website (http://www.signoriadeimalatesta.it). This is a further destination brand, developed with the objective to reduce the seasonality of the tourist offering and to make the province hinterland autonomous from the seaside area.

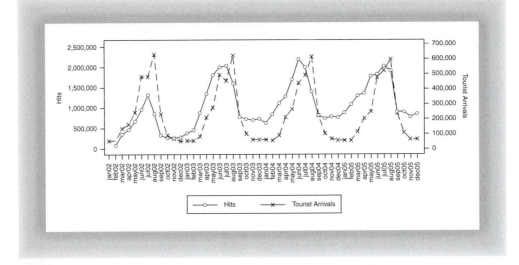

Figure 21.5 Rimini website hits compared to tourist arrivals in the last four years
Source: Data from Statistics Bureau of the Province of Rimini (2006) and Internal statistics from
http://www.turismo.provincia.rimini.it

Moreover, the database constitutes the central source of updated information for the production of other promotional materials: printed catalogues, lists, brochures.

Online since February 2002, the website has reasonably grown in terms of users. The good acceptance of the implementation is also testified by some important recognitions. The Italian Web Award Committee nominated the site among the best 100 in 2002, and awarded the Malatesta Seignory website the first prize in the tourism category in 2003. Hundreds of emails received every week and more than one thousand subscribers to the newsletter are considered to be a good result in terms of popularity among the visitors.

More than that, a possible measure of the effectiveness of the system can be derived by looking at Figure 21.5. It shows the recorded hits statistics (requests to the webserver) along with the arrivals of tourist to the destination in the period 2002–2005.

The general performance is remarkably similar, as almost identical is the seasonality effect. It must be noticed, however, that the website traffic has an almost one month shift with respect to the tourist traffic. This fact may be interpreted as a good appreciation by travellers that consult the website sometime before their trip to the district and gather information and documentation on the resources of the area. This is further confirmed by looking at the ratio pages viewed/visitor which remains rather constant and at a good level throughout the year (the average for the period considered here is 12).

The Future of the Destination and Key Challenges

The good results obtained are, clearly, an incentive to taken good care of the technological infrastructures the Province of Rimini has implemented and to improve them.

The future plans, besides the obvious regular maintenance of the information contents and the basic data handled by the system, include actions regarding:

- a restructuring of the main databases to ease the management of different languages. At present only an Italian and an English version are provided, while a German and a French one would be greatly useful, considering the main target markets;
- development of new possibilities to gather and distribute regular information or updates by using automated messaging systems (via email, sms, fax, etc.);
- establish agreements with the main local Hotels Association to provide users with a central online booking and payment system.

The Province of Rimini is the first public destination management organization in Italy to adopt a clear, coherent and complete communication plan in which both traditional and new technological media are taken into account with equal importance and are given equal consideration.

The outcome of this attitude is twofold. From one side, the efficiency of the 'normal' work activities has considerably improved, allowing limited staff to take care of a large amount of diverse information greatly reducing the possibilities of omissions, mistakes or inaccuracies, which directly translates into a better service to all the 'customers' of the destination. On the other hand, even if is it almost impossible to evaluate the effects of such a system on the 'success' of the Province in terms of visitors, the common belief, among the managers of the destination, is that a good part of these results can be attributed to the efficiency and the effectiveness of the architecture designed and to its implementation.

Key Conclusions

- The Province of Rimini is the first public destination management organization in Italy to adopt a clear, coherent and complete communication plan in which both traditional and new technological media are taken into account with equal importance and are given equal consideration.
- ICTs can increase the efficiency of the DMO activities allowing a limited staff to take care of a large amount of disperse information.
- The Internet presence is essential to give a clear sign of a modern and innovative administration, able to satisfy the complex and high expectations of contemporary tourists.

Review and Discussion Questions

- How can Rimini take advantage of technology to promote their region?
- Explore how different market segments require different information on DMSs.
- How can Rimini work closely with the Italian Tourism Authorities to promote the destination effectively on line?

References and Further Reading

Baggio, R. (2003). A websites analysis of European tourism organizations. *Anatolia*, 14 (2), 93–106.

Buhalis, D. (2000). Marketing the competitive destination of the future. *Tourism Management*, 21, 97–116.

Buhalis, D. (2003). *eTourism: Information technology for strategic tourism management*. Harlow, UK: Pearson/Prentice Hall.

Carter, R., & Bédard, F. (2001). *E-Business for tourism – practical guidelines for tourism destinations and businesses*. Madrid: World Tourism Organization.

Conti, G., & Perelli, C. (2004). Seaside tourism monoculture versus sustainability. The erosion of the social contract in the Rimini model. *The European Journal of Planning*. Retrieved February, 2005 from http://www.planum. net/topics/documents/Conti_02.pdf.

Dall'Ara, G. (2002). *La storia dell'industria turistica riminese vista attraverso cinquanta anni di strategie*. Milan: Franco Angeli.

Eurisko (1998). *Sinottica, report for the Province of Rimini*.

Ritchie, J.R.B., & Crouch, G.I. (2003). *The competitive destination: Sustainable Tourism Perspective*. Oxon, UK: CABI Publishing.

UN World Tourism Organization: http://www.world-tourism.org

European Travel Commission: http://www.etc-corporate.org

Company's website (Province of Rimini Tourism website): http://www.turismo.provincia.rimini.it.

22

Tanzania: extending eTourism tools utilization

Faustin Kamuzora

Learning Objectives

- Illustrate how ICTs can play a key part in even third world countries to promote their products online.
- Demonstrate how ICTs and the Internet can promote cultural heritage destinations.
- Explain the business and technology innovations used by Tanzania tourism.

Introduction

Tanzania is considered as one of the premiere tourism regions and one of the fastest growing destinations in Africa. Due to various endowments, tourism has become one of the main economic activities in Tanzania. Tourism contributes about 15% of the gross domestic product, 12% of which is contributed by wildlife sector alone. Similarly, as a share of total exports, tourism earnings increased from 15% in the 1980s to over 25% after late 1990s. With more than an average of 600,000 international incoming tourists per annum in recent years, Tanzania enjoys a market share in Africa of about 4% of total tourist arrivals and 3.2% of receipts in 2004 (WTO, 2005). Tanzania follows Egypt, Morocco, Tunisia, South Africa and Mauritius in Africa in terms of the receipts from tourism.

Main Products and Value Added

As a destination, Tanzania offers a wide range of natural (particularly wildlife), historical and cultural tourist attractions. With its 14 national parks, 31 game reserves, 38 game controlled areas, Ngorongoro Conservation Area and marine parks, Tanzania's wildlife resources are considered among the best in the world. The leading nature-based resources include the great Serengeti plains, the spectacular Ngorongoro Crater, Lake Manyara and Africa's highest mountain, Kilimanjaro, in the north. In the southern part of the country, the following wildlife areas are located: Mikumi, Udzungwa and Ruaha national parks, and Selous Game Reserve. Selous is the largest game reserve in the world. Elsewhere, additional natural attractions include the sandy beaches in the north and south of Dar es Salaam and Zanzibar and an excellent deep-sea fishing area at Mafia Island which has been designated as a marine park. Also, Tanzania has a rich heritage of archaeological, historical and rock painting sites, a number of which have been designated to World Heritage Sites. Since today's tourists are looking for a variety of travel experiences, different cultures, traditions, heritage and lifestyles, various players in tourism system in Tanzania provide several services to add value to these experiences.

Tourists coming to Tanzania enhance their nature-based experiences thanks to the efforts of conserving the above attractions which were initiated during German colonial era in late 19th century. These efforts were carried over by British colonial government from 1920s and continued by the Tanzanian government after independence in early 1960s. Some of the attractions in Tanzania are equally found in other African countries such as Kenya and South Africa. However, there are some peculiar attractions such as Mountain Kilimanjaro, Ngorongoro Crater, Serengeti National Park, finest beaches of Zanzibar, Stone Town of Zanzibar, Mafia Marine Park, and historical sites such as and Kilwa Kisiwani and Songo Mnara ruins which are only found in Tanzania.

Business Model

As a destination, Tanzania represents the focal point for multiple players in tourism whose interests are interdependent. The industry relies heavily on international tourists since the domestic market is not quite developed. Thus, with exception of incoming travel agents, most of the suppliers who include tour operators, hospitality providers, attractions, airlines, galleries, and museums depend heavily on international tourists. The major source markets for Tanzania tourism industry are European countries led by United Kingdom and United States (URT, 2004).

The business model employed by destination Tanzania combines both old and new business models in promoting itself to the source markets. Various components of Tanzania tourism systems are using multiple channels to distribute information and transaction flows. An example of traditional business model is employed by Tanzania Tourism Board (TTB). In implementing its core function of advertising Tanzanian tourism products, TTB employs several methods such as attending travel and tourist fairs around the world, publication and distribution of brochures, production and distribution of promotion videos on various media such as video cassettes and more recently digital versatile discs (DVD), and conducting on-road shows in various source markets. In addition TTB relies on outgoing tour operators as intermediaries in source markets. In major source markets several outgoing tour operators have been designated as representatives of the TTB to market destination Tanzania. The new business model includes the use of various websites to market the destination.

Technological and Business Innovation

Information is lifeblood of tourism and the Internet is the heart that circulates that lifeblood (Lee *et al.*, 2006). Globally, tourism value chains for distribution of information as well as transactions flows are increasingly converging to the Internet, implying that Tanzania must improve its information and communication technology capacity if it is to benefit optimally from tourism. This is because Internet technologies are increasingly becoming the primary source of travel information to the majority of potential customers of Destination Tanzania. The web offers the opportunity to provide wider, deeper and customized offerings to a greater number of customers, all with a greater level of interactivity, at low costs, and without substantially alter the quality of information delivered (Buhalis, 2003). Thus, appropriate utilization of Internet provides a chance to various businesses in destinations such as Tanzania to diversify and improve their information distribution business model.

In order to determine the extent of electronic tools utilization, a survey was conducted in 2005 among 307 components of the Tanzanian tourism system. The distribution of the components was as follows: 141 tour operators; 19 travel agents; 94 hospitality providing agents; 12 airlines; 4 meeting, incentive, conference, events (MICE) firms; 6 attractions, 6 publishers of tourism related information, 6 destination management organizations (DMOs), 9 galleries, and 1 airport and an air cargo handling company. The descriptive statistical results revealed that on average, about 84% of the surveyed organizations had websites indicating the value the respondents accorded to the new distribution technology. However, only few had dynamic and transactional websites, as demonstrated in Table 22.1. Therefore, most of the components still are at the lower levels of the staged electronic commerce journey (Rao *et al.*, 2003). In addition, the Internet as a source of information for tourists visiting Tanzania had increased from 6% in 2001 to between 15 and 40% in 2005 (Kamuzora, 2006a).

However, the Internet, and particularly the web, has been a source of disruption of tourism earnings to a certain extent in some destinations. For example, some governmental websites of the source markets have been posting travel warnings to specific destinations such as Tanzania without providing the opportunity for authorities in the destinations to respond before the warnings are released on the web. What the above demonstrates is that the web can be a force of disruption to the tourism system if not used responsibly. Therefore, all players in the value chain should be on the vanguard of learning what is being written about their image or brand. As a matter of reaction to misinformation about a destination on the web, the same medium should be used to counter the misinformation.

Table 22.1 Ownership and type of websites by components of Tanzanian tourism system

Category of tourism business	Websites ownership (%)				Type of websites (%)		
	No	Yes	Under construction	Under improvement	Static	Dynamic (database driven)	Transactional
Incoming travel agents	31.6	68.4			84.6		15.4
Tour operator	11.3	85.8	2.8		87.1	11.3	1.6
Hospitality	12.8	83.0	2.1	2.1	67.1	29.3	3.7
Airline	16.7	66.7		16.7	50.0	30.0	20.0
Car rental		100.0			60.0	20.0	20.0
MICE		100.0			100.0		
Attractions		100.0			33.3	66.7	
Publishing		100.0			83.3	16.7	
DMOs		100.0			57.1	42.9	
Curios or galleries	22.2	55.6	22.2		100.0		
Airport		100.0			100.0		
Cargo handling		100.0			100.0		
Average	12.4	83.7	2.6	1.3	76.9	19.0	4.1

Source: Kamuzora (2006b)

Key Challenges for the Future

As much as the Internet has been up taken by the majority of the components of the tourism system in Tanzania, there are still several challenges for the optimum utilization. Most of the challenges are related to digital divide problems. For example, the low levels of knowledge related to harnessing the power of electronic commerce is a major hindrance. Due to this low level of knowledge, most of the websites are still generation one; whereby the websites act more like digital brochures. As shown in Table 22.1, about 77% of the surveyed organizations had static websites with only 19% and 4% of the websites being dynamic and transactional respectively. Even the TTB's website (www.tanzaniatourismboard. com) is only partially dynamic. Low level of web knowledge results into higher designing, building and maintenance costs of the websites. As a result, the majority of websites of small and medium tourism enterprises (SMTEs) remain not-updated. Another constraint facing e-business development in Tanzania is lack of appropriate legal commercial framework which is still paper based. In addition, since Tanzania, as many of its neighbours, still relies on the satellite connection to the global Internet backbone (infrastructure), the bandwidth is another limitation. The cost of bandwidth is relatively high (with an average of US$70 per month for a shared 64 kilobits per second link), making uploading and downloading multimedia tourist related information very difficult.

Another challenge facing tourism business in Tanzania is low acceptance of the credit card as a means of payment. This is because for convenience and safety, the typical international tourist does not carry a lot of cash money. The normal way of paying for services and goods is the use of plastic money in the form of debit and credit cards. During international travel, tourists feel safer if they can get services paid by means of credit cards. Apart from safety against theft, credit cards usually obtain favourable currency exchange rates (despite a premium charge by credit card companies) (Euromonitor, 2003). In addition, credit cards (as their name implies) means that one can spend up front the income that he/she borrows from credit card companies. With these advantages, service providers who were able to accept payment by means of credit card relieved a traveller/tourist from lot of inconveniences. Only 114 (37.2%) of the 307 surveyed business accepted credit cards as a means of payment. However, even among the businesses which accepted the credit cards, some of the local-based businesses considered credit card payment as less convenient due to the time taken to process the payment as well as the commission charged by a monopolist bank that processes the payment.

However, the infrastructural problem of relying on satellite for Internet connection is likely to be solved by a planned East Africa Submarine Cable System (EASSy). The low level of web knowledge and utilization of e-commerce among the majority of players in the tourism system of Tanzania can be resolved by providing more training opportunities (on technological, business and tourism skills) and formulating policies to promote e-commerce in the country. Since the majority of players have already realized the importance of the web in their businesses, it will not be too difficult for some of the players to acquire the necessary web skills to optimize their profits. Using web technologies, several SMTEs in Tanzania have benefited immensely through disintermediation. For example, small indigenous tour operators have been able to increase their market share and profit levels by directly being contacted by tourists from source markets and organize their tours to various attractions without going through some intermediaries (Kamuzora, 2006b). Therefore, another challenge for the stake-holders in the tourism system in Tanzania is to innovatively collaborate (as much as they could be competing in some aspects) in marketing Destination Tanzania in the electronic market place.

The Future of the Destination

Tanzania has a short-term plan of achieving the 1-million tourist mark (from the current 600,000) by 2010. Various players in the tourism system in Tanzania have been mobilized to prepare for the increase in the international arrivals. However, there are no immediate plans to cooperate with the private sector to upgrade the current TTB website into a fully functional destination management system (DMS). Some of the competitors of Destination Tanzania, such as South Africa, are ahead in developing their DMSs. The lack of their own DMS may reduce Tanzanian competitiveness in the electronic marketplace, as more potential tourists from the Western world are turning to the web as an initial source of information for planning their travels. Therefore, the challenge for Tanzania is to advance the eTourism journey from the current low stages to more advanced stages such as operating effective DMSs.

Key Conclusions

- Third world countries in particular have to use the entire range of media to promote the destination.
- The TTB employs several offline and online methods to promote the destination.
- To support the entire range of stakeholders TTB distributes both traditional media such as videotapes and DVDs whilst they use various websites to market the destination.
- Their major challenges reflect digital divide problems.

Review and Discussion Questions

- How can you reduce the digital divide at a destination?
- What is the best way for third world countries to promote themselves online?
- Which international organizations can reduce the digital divide in third world countries and how can they do that?

References and Further Reading

Buhalis, D. (2003). *eTourism: Information technology for strategic tourism management*. London: Financial Times/Pearson Education.

Euromonitor (2003). *US market for tourism*. Euromonitor.

Lee, G., Caib, L.A., & O'Leary, J. T. (2006). WWW. Branding. States. US: An analysis of brand-building the US state tourism websites. *Tourism Management*, 27(5), 815–28.

Kamuzora, F. (2006a). *A Synthesis of Utilisation of Information and Communication Technologies in Tanzanian Tourism System: A Multimethodology Approach*. PhD Thesis. School of Informatics, Bradford University.

Kamuzora, F. (2006b). *E-commerce for development: eTourism as a showcase*. Mzumbe: Mzumbe Book Project.

Rao, S. S., Metts, G., & Monge, C. A. M. (2003). Electronic commerce development in small and medium sized enterprises: A stage model and its implications. *Business Process Management Journal*, 9 (1), 11–32.

URT (2004). *Tanzania Tourism Sector Survey: The International Visitors' Exit Survey Report*. Dar es Salaam: United Republic of Tanzania.

WTO (2005). *Tourism market trends, 2005 Edition*. Madrid: WTO.

Ministry of Natural Resources and Tourism website: http://www.tanzaniatourism.go.tz

Tanzania National Parks website: http://www.tanapa.com

Tanzania Tourism Board website: http://www.tanzaniatourist-board.com

23

Tiscover: destination management system pioneer

Karsten Kärcher and Philip Alford

Learning Objectives

- Illustrate Tiscover as the most successful eTourism solution for destination marketing organizations (DMOs).
- Demonstrate the key and value-added functions of destination management systems.
- Explain the business and technology innovations introduced by Tiscover.

Introduction and Company Development

Tiscover was founded in 1991 through a partnership with the Tirol Tourist Board and has evolved into a leading provider of eTourism solutions to destination marketing organizations (DMOs) and tourism businesses throughout Europe and Southern Africa. The company is headquartered in Innsbruck, Austria, with wholly-owned subsidiaries in Germany, Italy and the United Kingdom.

It provides destination management systems (DMSs), which have been described as the 'ICT infrastructure' of a destination (WTO, 1999). In this field, Tiscover was world-market leader in 2006 with over 2000 DMO customers. Over the years, it has expanded from its base in the German-speaking countries of Austria, Germany and Switzerland, to Italy, South Africa and the UK (Table 23.1).

The company also powers the individual websites of DMOs including the European Travel Commission (VisitEurope.com), the Austrian National Tourist Office (Austria.info), the State of Bavaria in Germany, the East of England region and Italy's Trentino province. As regards tourism businesses, Tiscover supports all types of organizations at a destination, including small independent hotels, guesthouses, B&Bs, restaurants and attractions.

Table 23.1 History of Tiscover

1991	Founding of TIS GmbH and official launch in Tirol
1995	TIS moves onto the Internet with TIS@WEB – one of the first travel websites in the world
2000	Founding of Tiscover AG (i.e. PLC) as successor of TIS GmbH
2001	Launch of http://www.tiscover.com with holiday information on Austria, Germany and Switzerland
2003	Launch of Tiscover Italy
2004	Launch of Tiscover UK and Tiscover South Africa
2005	Winner of contract to power Italy's national tourism portal (http://www.italia.it)

Main Products and Value Added

There are three key elements to the Tiscover service offering:

- *DMS solutions*: Tiscover provides DMS solutions to DMOs at national, regional and local levels. The DMS includes a wide range of modules to support a DMO's internal, partner and consumer communication, including accommodation booking, brochure processing and customer relationship management (CRM).

- *Web solutions*: At the core of the Tiscover proposition is a content management system (CMS), which allows DMOs and tourism suppliers to build websites where they can feature destination content and search facilities for the tourism suppliers in the destination, including accommodation, restaurants, attractions and conference venues. This also enables the DMOs and tourism suppliers to offer site visitors the opportunity to book accommodation online.
- *e-Marketing*: Tiscover has a number of consumer-facing sites including the main Tiscover.com portal, as well as the national portals Tiscover.at, Tiscover.co.uk, Tiscover.de, Tiscover.za and Tiscover.it. Users can register on the sites, and the company undertakes extensive consumer marketing; principally through its online newsletter for which there are in excess of half a million active subscribers.

One of the central value-added propositions of Tiscover is multi-channel distribution; enabling DMOs and accommodation businesses to reach channels they otherwise would not. The principle is based on the data being entered once by the DMO or tourism supplier, and then that information is fed out to a range of channels, including call-centres, websites, kiosks and mobile devices (Figure 23.1).

A multi-channel tourism distribution strategy is essential in order to reach different market segments and visitors who are at different stages of the customer buying experience (Buhalis, 2003). For example, one of the objectives of the East of England Tourist Board's UNITE eTourism project is 'to provide our tourism businesses with many and varied distribution channels'. Tiscover provides the DMS infrastructure for UNITE and enables a host of micro tourism businesses to access channels they otherwise could not. Taking the case of an accommodation provider in the East of England region, the accommodation's information is passed to a range of potential booking channels including the East of England Tourist Board site, the local town and county sites, and the channels which are connected through the EnglandNet system.

Similarly Chelmsford, a mid-sized town located in the county of Essex in the East of England region, for which tourism contributes £120 million per annum, is able as a sub regional DMO to access a range of additional channels. Through UNITE they can input data about Chelmsford just once and it appears on a variety of sites, including visiteastofengland, Tiscover and eventually visitbritain

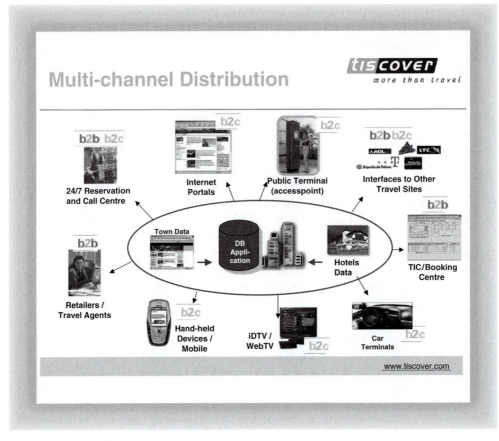

Figure 23.1 Tiscover multi-channel distribution

and visitengland. When Chelmsford signed up to UNITE, the main tourism information centre had just closed and they were considering a variety of ways of filling the information gap. They needed a method to provide up-to-date good quality information to visitors and local residents. A local sub regional economic partnership made a successful bid to the Essex Economic Partnership for three electronic Visitor Information Kiosks. UNITE provided the perfect solution to this in terms of the kiosks' content and a touch screen kiosk was installed in one of the major shopping centres (annual footfall of 10 million customers). Information changed on UNITE is shown instantaneously on the kiosk and all web channels.

Business Model

Tiscover develops and sells technology solutions which facilitate the knowledge broker role of a DMO and which provide

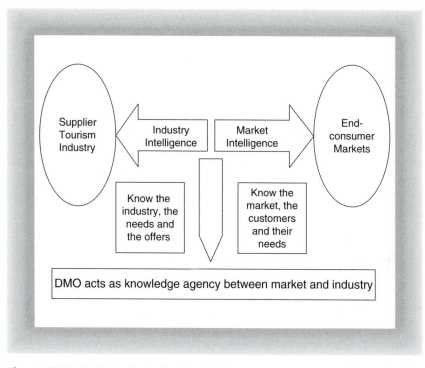

Figure 23.2 DMO as knowledge broker

an e-business platform on which tourism businesses can attain competitive advantage via the Internet (Figure 23.2).

Figure 23.2 shows the vision presented for the Austrian National Tourist Office at the ENTER 2005 conference (Oberascher, 2005). The knowledge broker role was also identified by Fesenmaier (2005) as being significant if DMOs are to retain their position in the Tourism value chain. The Tiscover technology enables a DMO to present its diverse range of tourism businesses and content on an e-business platform which offers a consistent look and feel. It provides a focal point for working closely with destination stakeholders – the diverse range of tourism businesses and sub-regional DMOs. On the demand side, the Tiscover CRM tool enables the DMO to capture intelligence about the market.

Tiscover's core revenue model is based on an application service provider (ASP) solution aimed at two customer groups: DMOs and tourism suppliers (mainly accommodation businesses). Revenue is earned from the former group in the form of annual licenses which are priced according to different DMO levels – town, city, region or country. The license among others allows a DMO to create a destination website which is embedded in the Tiscover family of portals, providing it with access to a range of channels. There are

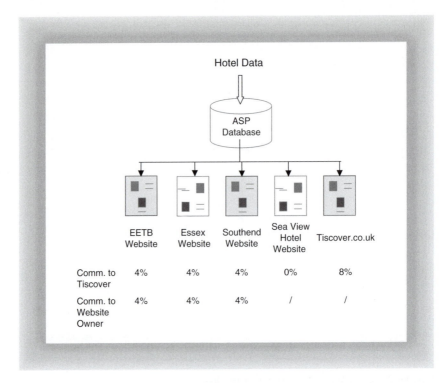

Figure 23.3 Tiscover commission model

optional add-on costs such as tailor-made sites and additional training. Revenue is earned from accommodation businesses in the form of licenses and commission. A hotel, for example, pays Tiscover an annual fee based on the number of bed spaces and also pays a commission on each successful online booking.

The commission model is flexible and follows the principle of wherever value is added to the booking process, a share in commission is attributed, as illustrated in Figure 23.3. For example, if a person books the Sea View hotel on the East of England tourist board's website, then the commission payable by the hotel is shared between Tiscover and the East of England tourist board. If the booking is made directly through the hotel's website which it has built using the Tiscover CMS, no commission is payable. Finally, for any bookings made through the Tiscover UK portal (http://www.tiscover.co.uk), the full commission is payable to Tiscover.

The Tiscover business model is flexible and allows the DMOs to develop a revenue stream. For example, Bournemouth Tourism on the south coast of England contracted Tiscover to provide its

Table 23.2 Visitor figures for Bournemouth Tourism 2003–2004

	April–October 2003	April–October 2004	Diff. +/– (%)
Counter	£239,966	£132,900	−45
Online	£17,784	£91,570	415
Visitor figures	202,655	181,810	−10
Value per booking	£112	£124	11

eTourism platform in 2004, which saw online bookings substantially increase from 2003 to 2004 (Table 23.2).

The flexibility of the business model is due to the Tiscover ASP solution, which offers a number of advantages including:

- DMOs share the hardware costs and support costs with all the other users of the system across all countries.
- DMOs avoid the costly start-up costs associated with developing a bespoke system in-house. These costs can be notoriously difficult to forecast and control.
- Each accommodation provider that purchases a license does so directly from Tiscover. This helps to avoid the problems that arise when DMOs invest in a DMS and then, due to budgetary revisions, can no longer maintain it.

Technological and Business Innovation

As a company offering technology-based ASP solutions, it is essential that Tiscover remains abreast of technical developments. There are three examples of how it is doing this:

- *xHTML*: In 2005, the launch of the Tiscover05 system saw the availability of DMS software in xHTML – the standard for presenting websites on mobile devices.
- *Smart tags*: These allow a DMO or a hotel to assign, through the CMS, special tags for certain keywords. If, for example, the East of England Tourist Board creates an extra webpage featuring a special seasonal promotion in Cambridge, this page can be linked to specific keyword searches. If the user searches for 'Cambridge', then the result is linked directly to the promotional page.

- *Multimedia CMS interfaces*: These allow the DMO or hotel to upload, via the CMS, multimedia files which can be displayed to the user. These are in place for the forthcoming Italia.it portal.

Key Challenges for the Future

Three important elements have been identified for the success of tourism information systems: 'quality of access, quality of content, and ability to customize the whole system' (Proll & Retschitzegger, 2000, p. 182). There are a number of key technical and business challenges which will impact the future of Tiscover:

- The commission model depends on the availability of bookable content online, and this is an ongoing challenge for Tiscover to work with both DMOs and suppliers and to present the advantages of eTourism.
- Competition is intense in the online-tourism space with a range of online intermediaries and technology suppliers vying for content to distribute.
- Consumers increasingly demand sophisticated information online, incorporating rich media, in order to help them choose a destination.
- Continue to develop the CMS to allow DMOs and tourism businesses to customize their websites.

The Future of the Company

As a world leader in DMSs, Tiscover's future lies in gaining an increasing number of DMOs and tourism businesses in different countries as customers. At the same time, the company aims to secure an increasing share in online consumer revenues for its DMO and tourism customers. The speed of new technical and consumer trends will continue to keep the company challenged.

Key Conclusions

- There are three key elements to the Tiscover service offering: DMS solutions that include a wide range of modules to support DMO's internal, partner and consumer communication, including accommodation booking, brochure processing and customer relationship management (CRM); Web solutions which allow DMOs and tourism suppliers to build websites where they can feature destination content and search facilities for the tourism suppliers in the destination, including accommodation, restaurants, attractions and conference venues; and e-Marketing through a number of consumer-facing sites including the main Tiscover.com portal as well as the national portals Tiscover.at, Tiscover.co.uk, Tiscover.de, Tiscover.za and Tiscover.it.
- A multi-channel tourism distribution strategy is essential in order to reach different market segments and visitors who are at different stages of the customer buying experience.
- Tiscover's core revenue model is based on an ASP solution aimed at two customer groups: DMOs and tourism suppliers (mainly accommodation businesses). Revenue is earned from the former group in the form of annual licenses which are priced according to different DMO levels – town, city, region or country. Revenue is also earned from accommodation businesses in the form of licenses and commission.
- Tiscover's future lies in gaining an increasing number of DMOs and tourism businesses in different countries as customers.

Review and Discussion Questions

- Why is it beneficial to use the ASP model for destination management systems?
- What is the unique selling point of Tiscover?
- How can Tiscover increase profitability?

References and Further Reading

Buhalis, D. (2003). *eTourism: Information technology for strategic tourism management*. London: FT Prentice Hall.

Fesenmaier, D. (2005). *Important Challenges Facing Destination Marketing Organizations: An American Perspective*. Retrieved 20 March 2006 from http://www.ifitt.org/enter.

Oberascher, A. (2005). *The DMO in 2010*. Retrieved 20 March 2006 from http://www.ifitt.org/enter.

Proll, B., & Retschitzegger, W. (2000). Discovering next generation tourism information systems: A tour on TIScover. *Journal of Travel Research*, 39, 182–191.

WTO (1999). *Marketing tourism destinations online: Strategies for the information age*. Madrid: World Tourism Organization Business Council.

http://www.etcnewmedia.com/review.

http://www.frontlinecommunication.co.uk/dmoworld.

Company's website: http://www.tiscover.com

24

Feratel Media Technologies: providing DMS technology

Markus Schröcksnadel

Learning Objectives

- Illustrate the preconditions for the use of a DMS.
- Demonstrate Feratel's strategic approach and core competence towards building up a decisive competitive advantage with the help of modern information technology.
- Explain the business and technology innovations used by Feratel.

Introduction

Many European destinations now operate with a Feratel destination management system (DMS). This chapter considers the preconditions for the use of a DMS, Feratel's strategic approach and core competence, and the potential for building up competitive advantage with the help of modern information technology.

The Company

Founded in 1978, Feratel Media Technologies AG is now a leading international provider of tourist information systems. The company became well known at the beginning of the 1990s with the introduction of weather cams as a tourism marketing instrument for transmission on various television channels. In addition to the classic tools of tourism advertising, a buoyant New Economy approach was soon developed with the goal of promoting the European tourism industry through the intelligent use of information technology. Following the implementation of various local, regional and supra-regional DMS, Feratel is now the market leader in Austria, Germany and Switzerland, with prestigious customers such as Sts Moritz, Kitzbühel and Munich. In addition, numerous eTourism projects have been implemented in the last few years in Italy, the Netherlands, Slovenia, Slovakia and the Czech Republic. The company has been quoted on the Vienna Stock Exchange since July 2000. In the financial year 2004/2005, the Information and Reservation Systems Division achieved a sales total of EUR 6.2 million with a staff of 54. Consolidated sales came to EUR 15.4 million in 2004/2005, while the result from ordinary activities was EUR 540 (Table 24.1).

Table 24.1 Consolidated figures for financial 2004/2005 in EUR

Sales	Operating revenues	EBITDA	EBT	Cash flow
15,408,861	16,925,578	2,739,386	539,833	3,280,487

Source: Feratel (2006)

The 21st Century Visitor

Back in 1991 the World Trade Organization spoke about changing behaviour patterns with regard to travel information and holiday bookings: 'The nature of the leisure segment itself is changing. The number of independent leisure travellers is growing' (WTO, 1991). Poon (1993) concluded:

> *This leisure tourist segment is less likely to make use of a travel agent, preferring instead to organise most elements of the trip for themselves.*

According to the Future Institute founded by Matthias Horx, the classic holiday model has become obsolete. Tourists now have complex and individual needs. Time is valuable, especially for people on holiday. 'The more support and service customers receive, the more satisfied they are' (Wenzel & Kirig, 2006).

It can thus be said that, at the beginning of the 1990s, tourism destinations were already moving more and more into the role of information brokers, central administration and reservation facilities; functions that were supported by developments in modern information technologies. Umberto Martini describes the changing role of the public tourist boards as follows:

> *from little involvement in tourism marketing (promotional activities, tourist information and welcome) to mentor and promoter of managerial activities in the resort, with the aim of sustaining its development through the exploitation of the new potential of information and communication technologies. (Martini, 2001)*

Product and Value

Strategic Approach

In its strategic approach, Feratel concentrates fully on the destination as the tourist product (the sum of accommodation, attractions, natural environment, events, etc.), which – according to Faché – plays a special role in the context of holiday decisions.

> *First, the results of recent studies into the customer buying process indicate that in most cases tourists initially decide on the destination they want to visit, then on the mode of transport, and once these decisions have been made, on the tour operator or travel agent who can help them satisfy their requirements, unless they organise their holiday without the use of the services offered by the travel intermediaries. (Faché, 2001)*

With regard to the need for a destination to be noticed in the context of global competition, Buhalis (2003) suggests:

It gradually becomes evident that destinations that provide timely, appropriate and accurate information to consumers and the travel trade have better chances of being selected.

This is where Feratel and its destination management systems come in.

Holistic eTourism Concept

eTourism is often reduced to the use of the Internet as a tourism marketing channel. Within the holistic eTourism concept developed by Feratel, the goal is to provide technological support for as many aspects of destination management as possible and to take advantage of all potential sales channels. Apart from information and reservation services (online and offline) as the core applications, this includes such functions as the creation and administration of electronic registration forms as well as customer relationship management (CRM) for evaluating existing marketing activities and developing new ones. Feratel's holistic eTourism concept also features an electronic enquiry pool and an offers assistant, which enables hoteliers to create professional email offers with a few mouse clicks, statistics and benchmarking tools.

In the context of the holistic solution approach, the Feratel DMSs have three e-core functions (Figure 24.1):

- e-marketing and services: web-based marketing and portal management with a solid information system background.
- e-commerce: online reservations for hotels, cars and other services.
- e-CRM: user profiles and customized solutions.

With regard to e-commerce (use and optimization of various sales channels) and CRM (customized offline and online offers) especially, there is still considerable potential for tourism destinations.

Central Database with Maximum Flexibility

The heart of the DMS is a central database containing all the products and services offered by the destination. The database is located in Feratel's electronic data processing centre, which ensures trouble-free working and avoids the need for the destinations to invest in expensive hardware. The DMS itself is comprised

Figure 24.1 Key applications
Source: Feratel (2006)

of a number of components. The back office modules ensure a professional standard of day-to-day working within the tourism organization. For online information and reservation services, Internet applications are available that are integrated into the existing website in keeping with the destination's own specific style (e.g. www.kitzbuehel.at, www.soelden.com, www.stmoritz.ch, www.muenchen.de). Data updating and availability information are handled via interfaces to the hotels' software or by the businesses themselves with the help of HotelClient, a user-friendly web application.

Flexibility with regard to system architecture and the Internet are among the key technological innovations of the Feratel DMS. In addition to the flexibility needed to respond to today's marketing co-operation models and ongoing mergers among tourism organizations, it is important for the tourist boards to be able to map their own business models in the system. Strategies vary from the classic incoming office with a clear focus on maximizing bookings (online and offline) to a straight information office solution with a policy of equal treatment for all accommodation providers and all enquiries to be forwarded to the hotels.

The technological challenge is to do justice to such wide-ranging profiles. The incoming office needs maximum flexibility for optimum results in terms of online reservations, for example with the offers that are available for direct online booking given priority at the top of the hit list, telephone numbers and other direct contact data suppressed from the details, or yield management tools available to keep track of occupancy rates and propose last-minute offers. The central information office, on the other hand, requires maximum neutrality in sorting the results for the hit list and innovative enquiry management tools.

One System for Maximum Sales Potential

While booking a flight from Salzburg to London is a relatively simple decision-making and purchasing process, booking a family holiday in the Ziller Valley is much more complex with regard to the information involved.

What visitors need in both cases is information that is up to date, complete and above all easily accessible. The main requirement for the system, therefore, is the ability to act as a central clearing house for all relevant data for the destination involved (availability and features of the product, events, attractions, etc.). Then to make the information available to visitors via as many sales channels as possible (Internet, over the counter in the Tourist Office, call centre).

Business Model

With its Deskline®, Eurosoft® and darWIN® products, Feratel now develops and markets three different types of DMS. The system architecture has grown over the years in the framework of an ongoing customer- and market-oriented product development process. For access to the system, tourist boards pay an annual licence fee calculated on the basis of the number of bednights. The system offerings range from economical stand-alone solutions to complete regional or national networks.

The case of the city of Salzburg is a good example of how destinations can make use of the Feratel DMS to maximize their sales potential by doing justice to all customer needs as far as possible. In Salzburg the central database can be accessed by three municipal information offices, and the call centres operated by Tourismus Salzburg GmbH, SalzurgerLand Tourismus GmbH and Salzburg Congress. At the press of a button, visitors can be supplied with information relating to availability, reservations and events. At the online level, the data in the destination management system are imported into a number of Internet platforms. Apart from the city of Salzburg's own website (www.salzburg.info), potential visitors can search for information and make their bookings via the regional website at www.salzburgerland.com or the portal sites run by various partners (www.hlx.com, www.oostenrijkvoordelig.nl). Information kiosks located at Salzburg Airport and at the motorway exits for 'Salzburg Mitte' and 'Salzburg Süd' also access the information and reservation data stored in the central system. Furthermore, hotels can be booked directly via their own websites with the help of a Book button. An availability calendar and room feature information can be imported from the central database. Today a mobile planning tool for visitors travelling to the resort and during their stay there (again by accessing the central database), is also technically feasible as part of the holistic solution approach. This will provide detailed online information on such subjects as the depth of the powder snow in the ski area or the location of the nearest gourmet restaurant. In addition to the Internet, the use of mobile devices (cellular phones, PDAs) will generate additional sales potential for tourism destinations (Figure 24.2).

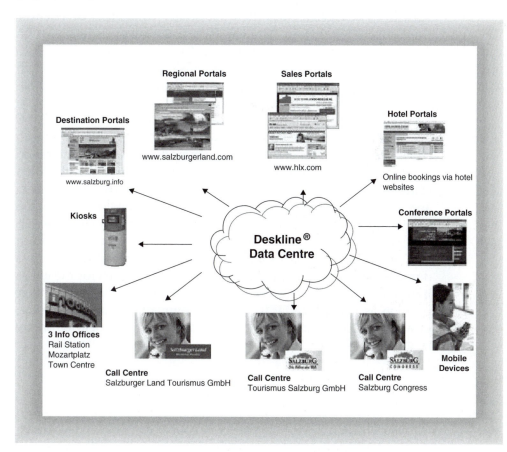

Figure 24.2 Destination management for the city of Salzburg
Source: Feratel (2006)

Summary

Changes in consumer behaviour and progress in information technology were the driving forces behind the development of today's DMSs as the basis for modern and efficient destination management. As the interface between tourism organizations and visitors, they enable destinations to communicate their products to potential visitors via a variety of communications and sales channels, and to handle a variety of related functions – from invoicing to the automated dispatch of brochures.

To that extent, eTourism is more than the use of the Internet as an additional major sales channel. The goal is to provide full support for the European tourism industry in all its activities through the use of modern information technology and thus confer a decisive competitive advantage on tourism destinations.

In March 2008, The German Hotel Reservation Service (HRS) from Cologne/Germany acquired the majority holding in the Austrian Tiscover AG and their subsidiary companies of Tiscover Deutschland GmbH in Munich/Germany, Tiscover Italia Srl in Trento/Italy and Tiscover UK Ltd. in Crawley (West Sussex). HRS was founded in 1972 and has a total of 330 employees, with branch offices in Paris, London, Shanghai and Warsaw providing a world-wide electronic hotel reservation system for private and business travellers. Its database includes comprises more than 225,000 hotels and accommodation worldwide. Customers will be able to choose from more than 300,000 accommodation establishments in Austria, Germany, Europe and through to the whole world. When combined, the two travel portals register about 76 million users and almost 1.5 billion page impressions. In the long term, the significant cooperation between Tiscover and HRS will open up new perspectives and dimensions exceeding by far the current business scopes of both companies. Both companies together have demonstrated outstanding and successful innovations for the entire industry and by joining forces they will further strengthen their position as market leader in different segments. Together they can grow and become the European number one in the field of online reservation systems.

Key Conclusions

- The heart of the DMS is a central database containing all the products and services offered by the destination.
- The Feratel DMSs have three e-core functions: e-marketing and services, e-commerce and e-CRM.
- Feratel employs a holistic eTourism concept that aims to provide technological support for as many aspects of destination management as possible and to take advantage of all potential sales channels.

Review and Discussion Questions

- What is the difference between the Feratel and Tiscover systems?
- What are the advantages of the holistic eTourism concept employed by Feratel?
- How can Feratel increase the profitability and economic impacts of destinations?

References and Further Reading

Faché, W. (2001). New entrants in travel and tourism intermediation and the future of destination management systems. In E. Kreilkamp, H. Pechlaner, & A. Steinecke (Eds.), *Gemachter oder gelebter Tourismus? Destinationsmanagement und Tourismuspolitik* (pp. 41–56). Vienna: Linde Verlag.

Geiger, A. (2002). *Internationale Marketingstrategien im Tourismus durch Informationstechnologie*. Innsbruck (Master Thesis).

Martini, U. (2001). Information and communication technologies as competitive drives for new destination management concepts. In E. Kreilkamp, H. Pechlaner, & A. Steinecke (Eds.), *Gemachter oder gelebter Tourismus? Destinationsmanagement und Tourismuspolitik* (pp. 141–172). Vienna: Linde Verlag.

Morisson, A., & Harrison, A. (1998). From corner shop to electronic shopping mall? *Progress in Tourism and Hospitality Research*, 4, 349–356.

Poon, A. (1993). *Tourism, technology and competitive strategies*. Wallingford: CAB International.

Wenzel, E., & Kirig, A. (2006). *Tourismus 2020 – Die neuen Sehnsuchtsmärkte*. Kelkheim: Zukunftsinstitut.

WTO (1991). *Tourism to the Year 2000. Qualitative aspects affecting global growth*. Madrid: World Tourism Organization.

Company's website: http://www.feratel.at

Case

25

Destimation.com: online solutions for destination management companies

Andrey Glazoy, Ola Kastensson and Jamie Murphy

Learning Objectives

- Illustrate Destimation as an online solution for destination management companies (DMCs) that target lucrative travel markets, such as meetings, incentive conferences and exhibitions (MICE).
- Demonstrate that Destimation manager is a single-inventory scalable back-office system for DMCs that provides a destination and contact database, as well as software modules for registration, program creation and financial management.
- Explain the business and technology innovations used by Destimation for DMCs.

Introduction

Destimation provides online solutions for destination management companies (DMCs) that target lucrative travel markets, such as meetings, incentive conferences and exhibitions (MICE), and leisure groups (Cooper *et al.*, 2005). The leisure group market, for example, is worth 18–24 billion (Travel Research Bureau, 2004). Leveraging an emerging trend, web services (Roy & Ramanujan, 2001; Lim & Wen, 2003), Destimation overcomes communication limitations such as lack of standards and corporate firewalls to offer DMCs a suite of software and database tools for managing and marketing their destination. The web-based product Destimation.com takes advantage of three global business phenomena: workflow software, the power of communities and outsourcing (Friedman, 2006). Since its inception in 2000, Destimation has grown steadily to its present network of 13 DMCs in 17 European countries (Table 25.1). Two additional

Table 25.1 Destimation network

Country	Company	Website Address
Belgium	Brussels International Travel Service	http://www.brussels-international.be
China	DestinationChina	http://www.destinationchina.biz
Czech Republic	Conti Promotor	http://www.contipromotor.cz
Denmark	First United A/S	http://www.firstunited.dk
Estonia	Baltic Travel Group Ltd	http://www.btgroup.lv
Finland	Next Travel Ltd	http://www.nexttravel.fi
Germany	destiMation Germany GmbH	http://www.destimation.de
Iceland	Atlantik Tours	http://www.atlantik.is
Latvia	Baltic Travel Group Ltd	http://www.btgroup.lv
Lithuania	Baltic Travel Group Ltd	http://www.btgroup.lv
Luxembourg	Brussels International Travel Service	http://www.brussels-international.be
Norway	Travel Planners of Scandinavia AS	http://www.travel-planners.no
Poland	Mazurkas Travel	http://www.mazurkas.com.pl
Russia	Russkie Prostori	http://www.russkie-prostori.ru
South Africa	ScanAfrica Incentives	http://www.scanafrica.co.za
Spain	Fasada Incoming S.L.	http://www.fasada.com
Sweden	Risbecker International	http://www.risbecker.se
Switzerland	SM Travel SA	http://www.smtravel.com

members in China and South Africa provide solid bases for future expansion in Africa, Asia and Oceania. These 15 members average about a dozen staff and US$6 million in annual sales. The members use the online tools at destimation.com as well as generating business for network members and suggesting software improvements.

A core team of a half-dozen managers and developers guide Destimation's daily operations from its corporate headquarters in Pully, Switzerland and development centre in St Petersburg, Russia. To complement this staff, Destimation outsources technical aspects of major projects.

Main Products/Offerings and Value Added

Most centrally managed DMC associations and groups rely upon requests for proposals (RFPs) as the main reservation platform. For example, the centrally managed company StarCite resembles a dating agency, letting planners search its supplier directory. The Destimation business plan, however, differs from StarCite and other centrally managed associations. Rather than collect fees and angle for all members, Destimation gives its members a flexible set of online tools and collaborative platform – workflow software and web services (Friedman, 2006; Roy & Ramanujan, 2001; Lim & Wen, 2003). Furthermore, as the members promote their own business, they simultaneously promote Destimation – the power of communities (Friedman, 2006).

Its flagship product – Destimation manager – is a single-inventory scalable back-office system for DMCs ranging in size from a few to hundreds of professionals. Destimation manager provides a destination and contact database, and software modules for registration, program creation and financial management. Drawing on the database and software modules, DMCs can produce myriad customized statistical reports and segmented lists. Unlike software for traditional incoming tourist agencies – standard packages, excursions, hotel bookings, etc. – Destimation software supports client-oriented creativity, quickly delivering unique, tailor-made programs for most everyday DMC tasks including operations, contacts, finances, databases and administration. The software also facilitates networking among members.

DMC management can access an instant picture of their business situation – staff and client activity – without waiting for manually prepared monthly or annual reports. The ability to generate forecasts

Figure 25.1 Access within a DMC environment

with a few mouse clicks makes business planning more deliberate and predictable. The contacts database offers a rich set of tools for personalized mailings and other client communications. Another exemplary benefit, which illustrates the power of communities, is automated leads whereby each DMC registers a lead for other partners. The online system tracks the lead and automatically pays commissions based on confirmed business. Figure 25.1 illustrates the access within a DMC environment.

Business Model

DMCs are Destimation's customers. Every DMC signs an annual contract that gives them country exclusivity, free support, software updates and online presence on Destimation.com. Furthermore, DMCs often suggest improvements and features for routine software development, and custom features specific to that DMC.

Destimation income includes software sales, annual fees and commissions for confirmed business through Destimation.com. Every member pays an annual fee for online presence in Destimation.com, which covers hosting and routine development costs. Custom developments for members cost extra, but no update costs more than 10% of the initial purchase amount. All confirmed business through Destimation.com incurs a commission charge as a percentage of group turnover. An additional income source is advertising for preferred suppliers. Destimation provides banner space for members to sell to their suppliers and if desired, banner design services for the DMCs at an additional charge.

External suppliers include ISPs providing hosting services for Destimation.com and freelance programmers providing outsourced software development. Similar to Boeing Airlines and Hewlett Packard (Friedman, 2006), Destimation outsources some processes to Russian experts. The internal suppliers are the participating DMCs. Destimation takes no liability for services booked through Destimation.com. The DMC selling the particular service takes full responsibility and guarantees services to the client.

A private company, Destimation recouped its initial investment in about 2 years and grows at an average rate of 20–30% annually. This growth rate, however, should increase. Although companies loathe changing their back-office systems, Destimation has three strong selling points for initiating this change. At the global level, recent ISO 9001:2000 accreditation by Destimation's sister company, Russkie Prostori, illustrates trustworthiness. At the country level, years of successful experience with partners in over a dozen countries underscores stability. Finally, the web services model means never having to update software at the company level.

Factors hindering growth include exhibition participation and ongoing investments in development. Other limitations include Destimation targeting only professionals rather than the public, low commission income and some half-hearted member support.

Technological and Business Innovation

Destimation offers a web services model that benefits Destimation and the client (Roy & Ramanujan, 2001; Lim & Wen, 2003). Clients may choose in-house or web-based software; the latter is easier to support. The Destimation server rather than the client houses the software and databases, enabling Destimation to update all client software simultaneously. Thanks to this web services model, DMCs can access their database and software modules from any computer connected to the Internet.

Every DMC partner working with the same software exemplifies the advantages of network externalities (Shapiro & Varian, 1998) and the power of communities (Friedman, 2006). As its user community grows, Destimation's value to those users grows geometrically. A positive feedback loop develops whereby DMC staff gain experience, support other members and vice versa.

Similarly, Destimation reverses the secretive philosophy typical of traditional DMCs keeping prices a commercial secret. The network members provide transparent business options for their clients through Destimation.com, and reflect Destimation's benefits as their businesses grow.

Approaching 6 years on the market and profiting from network externalities, Destimation continues to integrate e-technologies into incentive tourism. The long-range goal is to leverage its growing community in order to establish standard, ISO-certified e-solutions for groups and incentive tourism.

Two important issues for Destimation relate to its market and development. Created by DMCs for DMCs, Destimation reflects the needs of average DMCs. Secondly, the original technological platform serves as the integration base for the DMCs. Its development differs from the common practice of software companies adapting a standard product to a particular market, such as DMCs.

Key Challenges

A US-based Internet service provider – Visual Presence Inc. – hosts Destimation.com, providing quick and reliable access for customers worldwide. The development and support department in St Petersburg, Russia, hosts a secondary site that provides additional services.

Initially management used low fees and preferential terms to grow their network quickly. Yet many DMCs were 'dead' members, participating in few system parts and treating Destimation as just another promotional network. Their information was incomplete and this shortcoming hindered the global Destimation network. Today, only DMCs with full system integration comprise the network. Mandatory full system integration eliminated dead members and leveraged the benefits of the Destimation model, but a growing problem is coverage in large countries.

Destimation envisages revising its country exclusivity. Existing members and the first DMC in new countries will become gateways for other DMCs, as part of country DMC programs and services. Similar to big airlines operating flights through smaller partners, the sub-partners will sell their services through the Destimation country DMC, with agreed commissions automatically calculated for all parties. This system is essential for big countries; the DMCs cannot cover the whole country and already co-operate with other DMCs.

Another problem is a lack of DMC activity in collaborative actions. For example, only a few members join the Destimation stand at international trade shows. The others participate in state- or association-funded stands. This lack of participation increases the exhibition costs for collaborative Destimation partners and helps portray Destimation incorrectly as a software provider rather than as a DMC organization.

Destimation's issues are more organizational than technological. Its philosophy assumes that members will promote themselves and actively participate in internal initiatives. Destimation is working towards a more stable marketing policy and activity program. For now, two annual exhibitions (IMEX and EIBTM) are the sole marketing activities reflecting Destimation as an organization. Destimation needs more promotion of itself as organization, both offline via its members and online via search engine optimization for its website.

The Future of the Company

An ongoing initiative is transforming to web-based solutions. Microsoft .NET web services will help incorporate interfaces such as Microsoft's SQL Server for reliable and scalable data storage. Moving away from Microsoft, open protocols such as XML will help integrate hotel reservations and credit card processing into Destimation services.

A trend towards international purchasing and procurement in corporate travel has Destimation focusing on quality. The recent ISO accreditation should help drive for future growth, particularly with the tagline of using Destimation™ Technology.

A forthcoming initiative, Destimation Mobile, will provide an interface for handheld computers and smart-phones. Instant access for registration, urgent reports, supplier information, etc. as well as sending reminders will enhance business processes for DMC staff and partners. Another future initiative, marketing to leisure and free independent travellers (FIT), has possibilities as both a freestanding product and licensing under the Destimation™ Technology label.

Key Conclusions

- Destimation.com is a web-based product that takes advantage of three global business phenomena: workflow software, the power of communities and outsourcing.
- DMCs are Destimation's customers. Every DMC signs an annual contract that gives them country exclusivity, free support, software updates and online presence on Destimation.com.
- Destimation offers web services as well as and in-house version of the software.

Review and Discussion Questions

- What is the key value added offered by Destimation?
- What is the advantage of a network approach for DMCs?
- How can Destimation increase the profitability of individual DMCs?

References and Further Reading

Cerami, E. (2002). *Web services essentials.* Sebastopol, CA: O'Reilly Media.

Cooper, C., Fletcher, J., Fyall, A., Gilbert, D., & Wanhill, S. (2005). *Tourism principles and practice*, 3rd ed. Essex, England: Pearson Education Ltd.

Curbera, F., Duftler, M., Khalaf, R., Nagy, W., Mukhi, N., & Weerawarana, S. (2002). Unraveling the Web Services Web: An introduction to SOAP, WSDL, and UDDI. *Internet Computing*, 6 (2), 86–93.

Friedman, T. (2006). *The World is flat.* New York, NY: Farrar, Straus and Giroux.

Iverson, W. (2004). *Real World web services.* Sebastopol, CA: O'Reilly Media.

Iyer, B., Freedman, J., Gaynor, M., & Wyner, G. (2003). Web services: Enabling dynamic business networks. *Communications of the Association for Information Systems*, 11, 525–554.

Lim, B., & Wen, H. J. (2003). Web services: An analysis of the technology, its benefits, and implementation difficulties. *Information Systems Management*, 20 (2), 49–57.

Rappa, M. (2004). The utility business model and the future of computing services. *IBM Systems Journal*, 43 (1), 32–42. Retrieved from http://www.research.ibm.com/journal/sj/431/rappa.pdf.

Roy, J., & Ramanujan, A. (2001). Understanding web services. *ICT Professional*, 3 (6), 69–73.

Shapiro, C., & Varian, H. R. (1998). *Information rules: A strategic guide to the network economy*. Boston, MA: Harvard Business School Press.

Travel Research Bureau (2004). *Travel Distribution Report*, 12 (16), 124–125. Retrieved from content.groople.com/PressReleases/tdr-vol12-p124-125.pdf.

EIBTM at: http://www.eibtm.com.

IMEX at: http://www.imex-frankfurt.com/.

Microsoft .NET at: http://www.microsoft.com/net.

StarCite at: http://www.starcite.com.

Company's website: http://destimation.com.

Conclusion of Destination Section

The tourism products of a destination result from the sum of the available experiences and services at the destination region. These are the bundle of services of the individual areas that a tourist compares with each other when selecting his destination. Among the destinations in competition, the customer selects the one that most satisfies his needs. Mostly, he does not differentiate between the individual elements of the service but regards the offer and quality at a macro level and assesses it as a whole. Destinations thus have to regard and support the entire service chain from a process-orientated perspective. Destinations are therefore measured according to how well they align their services to the needs of their stakeholders.

Information and communication technologies (ICTs) make a major contribution by supporting information bundling, coordination and dissemination between all the partners and the customers, making internal processes more efficient and effective. DMOs have a new responsibility to understand and assess the possibilities and effects of ICTs at destination level and to integrate them in the overall destination concept. There is above all a need for action at the following levels:

- Greater networking of the tourism suppliers and stakeholders within the destination.
- Ensuring networking within the organizational units of a destination (intranet) in order to optimize processes and ensure a standard presence as against the individual stakeholders.
- Providing links to the tourism suppliers and the implementation of an extranet in order to permit the decentralized maintenance of the information.
- Optimum presence of the destination information at the level of local and national tourism organizations.
- Linking to domain specific search engines and third-party information and distribution platforms.
- Management and handling of booking inquires and online bookings.

- Designing of web presence in harmony with general brand policy.
- Developing of bookable packages extending as far as dynamic packaging. This demands a radical rethinking in the corporate cultures of the DMOs, which were basically aimed at providing services and not at specific marketing.
- Optimum networking to find and use new and alternative marketing channels.
- Creating ICT awareness among tourism suppliers. The aim is to motivate businesses and employees with respect to the professional handling of ICTs. This requires specific training measures.
- Coordination of information distribution in the sense of strategic multi-channel management.
- Development of a scalable CRM solution within the destination. (Egger, 2005; Posnik, 2006).

References and Further Reading

Egger, R. (2005). *Grundlagen des eTourism; Informations- und Kommunikationstechnologien im Tourismus.* Aachen: Shaker Verlag.

Posnik, F. et al. (Eds.) (2006). eTourism auf Destinationsebene im EUREGIO Raum. In R. Egger, *eTourism – Berichte aus Wissenschaft und Wirtschaft.* Puch Urstein: Eigenverlag.

Part Four

Transportation
Dimitrios Buhalis
Roman Egger

Introduction

The achievements in the field of transportation and the establishment of a new social middle class in the 19th century created the preconditions for a boom in tourism. The international development of transport links, an increase in the professionalism of tourism providers and a rapidly advancing technological development in both transport capacity and management were accompanied by a change in consumer behaviour characterized by an increase yearning for distant places (Egger, 2005, p. 63). The emergence of mass tourism made necessary the development of information and communication technologies (ICTs) in the field of transportation. This was essential in order to be able to manage the transport inventory and planning, to coordinate all the stakeholders involved in the transportation industry and to communicate the corresponding mass of information to the right person at the right time.

> *Airlines were among the first companies creating worldwide electronic networks, not only for the means of selling and distribution, but also for internal management and operations purposes. Also the other types of transport suppliers, car rentals as well as railways or the maritime industry fall into this category: they are all technologically advanced (Werthner & Klein, 1999a, p. 45).*

As a result sophisticated computer reservation systems (CRS) were developed to match the capacity with the customer demand (Sheldon, 1997).

The Airline Industry

The airline industry is characterized by some dominant carriers and a large number of smaller airlines. It is one of the most sophisticated industries, as there are several stakeholders involved in both the strategic and the operational management of the industry. It was deregulated in the USA in 1978 and in Europe between 1987 and 1997. This led to increased competition and an increase in the need to operate cost-efficiently. Specifically, deregulation led to a structural change in the market, increased productivity, improved customer service and lowest prices (Egger, 2005).

The Global Distribution Systems, (GDSs), a development from the computer reservation systems (CRSs), were for a long time the most important distribution channel for the airlines. They were effectively developed as travel supermarkets in the pre-Internet era and their primary objective was to connect travel agencies with airlines (Buhalis, 2004). GDSs are still a vital element in the light of the huge variety of tariffs to be administered. GDSs are the main link between airlines and intermediaries, such as tour operators and travel agents. They are also empowering Internet transactions by providing the background link between electronic travel agencies and airlines. The e-business W@tch 2006 identified a list of broad field of applications of ICTs in the airline industry, as presented in Table PIV.1.

However the cost of distributing through GDSs is one of the major issues in the airline industry. Around 25–30% of the airlines' turnover is estimated to be taken up by distribution costs (Davison, 2002). In order to escape the pressure of GDSs, airlines are making every effort to maximize their direct distribution via the airline's own website. According to the results of the most recent Annual Airline ICT Trends Survey, 90% of the airlines currently use their websites as a distribution channel (SITA, 2007). The British Airways case study (Case 26) shows how the airline's distribution channels have changed dramatically from CRSs, through to GDSs to eAirline solutions and how innovatory ICT solutions and the Internet have helped to advance competitiveness.

In recent years, airlines have increased the direct sale of their tickets by means of e-ticketing in order to save commission and other marketing costs, since the latter amount to up to 30% of the price of a ticket (Buhalis, 2003). While before the turn of the millennium it was practically impossible to buy tickets via the Internet, today, in at least the business models of the low-cost carriers, it is the only way for customers, both B2C and B2B, to obtain tickets. The case study of the South African LCC Kulula.com (Case 27) shows in this connection the importance that the Internet has for the direct marketing of innovatory airlines, how it is used as a tool for customer relationship management (CRM) and how it supports the procurement function of airlines.

Table PIV.1 ICT applications in the airline industry

Strategic issues

- Developing a unified architecture or Internet protocol platform
- Developing an alliance ICT hub (for global alliances)
- How much to outsource

Business to consumer

- Implementing effective distribution strategies
  - online selling
  - use of joint airline portals or online travel agents
  - role of traditional travel agents
- Effective customer relationship management
- Simplifying passenger travel
  - emphasis on self-service
  - electronic ticketing and/or ticketless travel
  - automatic check-in, including baggage
  - common use of self-service check-in kiosks
  - streamlining repetitive checks
  - radio frequency identification baggage tags (RFID)
  - communication through mobile devices
- Use of biometric technology for security
  - pre-screening passengers
  - effective biometric security

Business to business

- Implementing e-business in
  - maintenance planning and control
  - supply chain management
  - procurement and supplier relationship

Source: e-Business W@tch (2006), p. 132

Other electronic applications are easily linkable with e-ticketing. Web e-Check-in allows frequent flyers to check in via the Internet. In addition, passenger notification services via text messages, email or paging increase service quality, as do mobile phone check-in, lost baggage self-services and on board broadband (SITA, 2007). Finnair (Case 28) for instance acts as an innovator in the use of customer-oriented ICT solutions and at the same time it is increasing the efficiency of internal and external processes by means of sophisticated e-business solutions.

Alongside distribution, ICTs in particular assist the efficient arrangement of internal and external processes. The short life of the product also requires highly flexible pricing strategies, the calculation of which is supported by complex yield management systems. The Lufthansa Systems case study (Case 30) examines in detail the challenges faced by revenue management and in this context emphasizes the strategic importance of dynamic pricing solutions.

It is becoming increasingly evident that ICTs will be more critical to the operations and strategy of airlines. It can therefore be predicted that technology will facilitate and support the successful airlines of the future as ICTs will not only formulate all elements of the marketing mix of airlines in the future, but they will also determine their strategic directions, partnerships and ownership (Buhalis, 2003).

Car Hire Industry

In terms of turnover, the second largest trade sector in the field of tourism transport is car hire. The industry is also dominated by a few international players that operate substantial fleets of cars as well as a very large number of smaller players that tend to operate as few as a handful of cars. Similarly to the airlines, larger companies such as Avis and Hertz have long developed and operated comprehensive ICT systems in order to manage their inventory and match demand and supply. Traditionally bookable online via GDS, the car hire industry also uses the possibility of disintermediation as primary service provider. Hence they increasingly push for more electronic sales via direct online marketing.

ICTs support the effectiveness of operational processes. The decentralized marketing systems of rent-a-car branches, which are often located at airports, necessitates high-capacity systems to support internal processes. In particular, a number of functions are critical for the rent-a-car operations. Those include fleet management and the associated logistics processes, central reservation system, claims handling and the module for preparing leasing offers. The Enterprise Rent-A-Car case study (Case 29) shows amongst other things that the internal administration of claims notifications alone would be inconceivable without a high-capacity database structure. It also demonstrates a B2B application where ICTs can streamline the transactions between insurance companies that provide courtesy cars and the Enterprise car hire company to increase the efficiency of both.

In addition, the car hire companies benefit from synergy effects with the airline companies by means of e-collaboration. Thus, for instance, there is the possibility of using the bonus points acquired through the airline customer loyalty programmes (Miles and More) to hire a vehicle from a partner in the car hire sector. Conversely, airlines include a hire car in their packages in order to be able to offer an additional service.

Railways Industry

The railways have always been seen as the backbone of a functioning national economy by providing long-distance and local traffic, passenger and goods traffic across the country. The opening up of the railway networks and the creation of competition between transport enterprises has led to considerable changes in the railway sector over the last few years. Transport enterprises will in future have to work together to establish the continuity of the travel chain, which will require the ICT-assisted networking of existing systems. This is already evident with the formation of the Railteam Alliance that represents most fast trains in Europe. The information intensity of the railway system requires optimum preparation, processing and presentation of information along the entire value added chain. Operational control systems make a major contribution to increasing transport safety, while logistics and fleet management systems lead to a reduction of empty journeys, resulting in cost savings.

However, it is still only a minority of consumers who pre-purchase train tickets, and those are primarily for long distance, overnight or fast trains such as the Eurostar or TGV. As a result there is little research on the ICTs in the railway industry. However this is gradually changing, as a number of online platforms are emerging for railways. For example, bahn.de, the German railways website, is becoming one of the few pan-European sources for train itineraries and often for bookings. Bahn.de is one of the most visited travel portals on the Internet. Information and booking systems are available to the traveller not only via the web but increasingly also via mobile end devices.

References

Buhalis, D. (2003). *eTourism: Information technologies for strategic tourism management*. Harlow: Pearson Higher Education.

Buhalis, D. (2004). eAirlines: Strategic and tactical use of ICTs in the airline industry. *Information and Management*, 41 (7), 805–825.

Davison, R. (2002). Distribution channel analysis for business travel. In D. Buhalis, & L. Eric (Eds.), *Tourism distribution channels. Practices, issues and transformations* (pp. 73–86). New York: Continuum.

e-Business W@tch (2006). *ICT and e-Business in the Tourism Industry*. ICT adoption and e-business activity in 2006. [http://www.ebusiness-watch.org/resources/tourism/SR08-2006_Tourism.pdf].

Egger, R. (2005). *Grundlagen des eTourism; Informations- und Kommunikationstechnologien im Tourismus*. Aachen: Shaker Verlag.

Egger, R. (2006). Online Forschung in der Tourismuswissenschaft. In R. Bachleitner, R. Egger, & T. Herdin (Eds.), *Innovationen in der Tourismusforschung*. Münster: LIT.

Sheldon, P. (1997). *Information technologies for Tourism*. Oxford: CAB.

SITA (2007). *Airline ICT Trends Survey 2007 Executive Summary* [http://www.sita.aero/NR/rdonlyres/2C464901-6574-4AA0-B4E3-17199B9B8D45/0/AirlineIT07Booklet.pdf].

Werthner, H., & Klein, S. (1999). *Information technology and tourism – a challenging relationship*. Wien, New York: Springer Verlag.

26

British Airways: customer enabled interactivity

Marianna Zoge and Dimitrios Buhalis

Learning Objectives

- Illustrate the use of information and communication technologies by the airline industry.
- Demonstrate how airlines have gone through computer reservation system to global distribution systems and eAirline solutions.
- Explain how advanced ICTs and the Internet have helped British Airways (BA) to compete with 'no-frills' or 'low-cost' airlines.
- Illustrate how the Internet provided an innovative platform for airlines to re-engineer their business processes, redesign their distribution and partnership strategies as well as enhance their marketing activities.

Introduction

The airline industry was one of the first to use information communication technologies (ICTs) in order to manage and control its inventory. Back in the 1950s airlines realized the 'need for efficient, quick, inexpensive, and accurate handling of their inventory to communicate with travel agents and other distributors' (Buhalis, 2004, p. 807). In 1962 the first computer reservation system (CRS) was introduced and in the 1990s CRSs were developed into global distribution systems (GDSs) as electronic supermarkets offering a wider range of tourism products, comprised of airline, hotel and car rental products and services. The intention was to centralize inventories to a common database as well as to support the interactivity between travel agents (TAs) and principals (Buhalis, 2004).

With the emergence of the Internet in the mid-1990s there has been a change in the scenery, as this new powerful tool provided its users with a unique opportunity for maximization of performance and minimization of cost (Shona *et al.*, 2003). The Internet has offered an unparalleled opportunity for airlines to use technology to manage their resources efficiently, communicate directly with consumers and collaborate with partners. Innovative air carriers use the Internet as a cost-efficient distribution channel, as a tool for customer relationship management (CRM) and as a procurement mechanism (Jarach, 2002). As a result, the Internet provided an innovative platform for airlines to re-engineer their business processes, redesign their distribution and partnership strategies as well as enhance their marketing activities. This was particularly the case for no-frills airlines that adopted technology as a critical factor for reducing operational costs.

However, Porter (2001) states that the emergence of the Internet led to the standardization and homogenization of products. Although this can often be seen on airlines, as their product is characterized by standardization, many carriers have adopted technologies to differentiate either the product or the purchasing process. Airlines that adopted the Internet early, and particularly no frills airlines such as Ryanair and Easyjet, were able to achieve cost advantage, whilst full service carriers often achieved differentiation by adopting technological innovations. For example Singapore's 'video on demand' or British Airways' (BA) fare calendar allowing passengers to select different fares according to demand have been able to gain those carriers competitive advantage. Hence many airlines are now trying to bypass GDSs, global new entrants and travel agencies by shifting consumers to e-ticketing and to differentiate their product through the personalization of their websites and the implementation of direct sales strategies (Shona *et al.*, 2003).

Main Products and Offerings: British Airways Process Innovation Leading to Differentiation Advantage

British Airways is a full service network carrier, operating about 300 aircraft, flying to over 550 destinations worldwide. The fleet currently includes 57 Boeing 747s, 43 Boeing 777s, 21 Boeing 767s, 13 Boeing 757s, 66 Airbus A319/320/321s, 34 Boeing 737s and 59 smaller aircraft used in the company's regional business. British Airways is the world's second largest international airline, carrying more than 27 million passengers from one country to another. In the financial year to 31 March 2004, it transported more than 36 million people. While BA is the world's second largest international airline, primarily because its US competitors carry so many passengers on domestic flights, it is the tenth biggest in overall passengers carried. During 2003/2004 the group achieved group passenger load factor of 73%. The airline also carried 796,000 tonnes of cargo. An average of 51,939 staff were employed by the Group worldwide in 2003–2004, 85% of them based in the UK (BA Investor Relations, 2005).

The emergence of 'no-frills' or 'low-cost' airlines, that capitalized on advanced ICTs and the Internet for managing their operations and distribution, posed a direct threat to the company's profitability and retention of the existing market share, as well as to the attraction of new potential customers. As a result, BA had to adapt its strategy so as to overcome this threat. In particular, BA had to cut fares to European short haul destinations, while continuing to offer free food and drinks. All non-changeable economy tickets were scrapped with air travellers being able to change their flights, no matter what they have paid for the ticket, up to midnight the day before departure. The carrier reduced one-way prices for UK and European flights by up to 70% compared to a decade ago (BA Press office, 2006). As Rod Eddington (BA's Chief Executive 2003/2004) stated:

> *The new low fares strategy on 180 short-haul routes allowed us to compete more effectively with the no-frills carriers, backed by a simpler business model. (BA Annual Report, 2003/2004, p. 4)*

To achieve this strategy the airline had to improve internal efficiencies, stop paying commissions to travel agencies, reduce GDS and credit card fees and more importantly, to reduce operational costs.

BA's scale of operation and legacy systems effectively meant that it had to undertake a comprehensive ICT review to enhance the interactivity with consumers, improve internal management and streamline collaboration with partners. To reduce cost and make the entire operation leaner, BA adopted an ICT strategy to support the simplification of the airline's business processes through effective use of ICTs. The 2006 Annual report recognizes that:

> High performing ICT and telecommunications systems are vital to the running of the Group's business. Most areas of the Company's business are facilitated by ICT systems, which are closely interconnected. Many of these systems have been developed, and most of them integrated, by the Company's Information Management (IM) department. The majority of systems are operated within the Company's two data centre facilities at Heathrow. Major exceptions to this are Reservations, Departure Control (checkIn), Inventory, Flight Planning and other transaction processing facility (TPF) platform systems, which are operated by Amadeus SA in Germany.

The delivery of the Sabre Airflite solution has provided improved capability to manage the airline's flight schedules and has enabled the retirement of legacy technology. In addition, the delivery of next generation revenue management (NGRM) for BA World Cargo has provided increased capability to make the best use of cargo capacity (BA Annual Report & Accounts, 2005/2006).

Technological and Business Innovation: Customer Enabled British Airways Strategy (ceBA)

British Airways focused on offering a richer experience to customers, resulting into the 'Customer Enabled BA' (ceBA) strategy to support 'a radical self-service for customers across the travel experience' (O'Toole, 2003, p. 47). BA adopted suitable technologies for providing online selling and check-in, the ability to upgrade and manage booking facilities online. As Figure 26.1 demonstrates the aim was to make the entire process so easy to do business with that customers would choose to serve themselves.

Customer Enabled BA was a strategy aiming at simplifying the way of conducting business. It consisted of a cross-functional programme that covered the end-to-end customer experience, while it

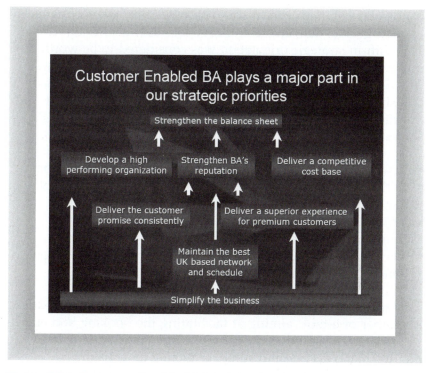

Figure 26.1 Customer Enabled BA: strategic priorities
Source: Parks-Smith (2004)

streamlined the product set. A number of innovations were evident, including the 'Manage My Booking' feature on ba.com that gave customers the ability to be more prepared for their journey before arriving at the airport. They can complete their APIS (Advanced Passenger Information Service) data in advance, check-in online and print their boarding pass, exercise upgrade options and know their baggage allowance.

Eddington (2004) set the transformational targets of the ceBA strategy:

- 100% e-ticket usage.
- 50% self-service check-in (on and off airport).
- 80% core Executive Club interactions self-service.
- 35% visit ba.com before they fly.
- 45% email address capture.
- 60% pre airport APIS data collection.

To achieve those targets more than 1.3 million fares were removed and 3000 fare rules were simplified to three basic types of flexibility. A myriad of variations by route and market has been made globally consistent whilst selling classes were tightly defined within yield bands and common conditions. The new rules were designed to be manageable, deliverable and easy for customers to understand. This shift in strategic orientation was considered to be worth £100 million of annualized benefit to the company (BA Financial Results, 2004/2005; Parks-Smith, 2004). Within the first year of implementing this strategic approach, the company successfully met most of its transformational targets, as BA's Head of eCommerce Simon Parks-Smith (2004) stated:

- 50% of the UK short haul leisure business booked on ba.com.
- 100% of the core Executive Club transactions available on ba.com with 60% usage.
- 50% reduction in the number of fares.
- Doubling in usage of eTicket and email.
- New way for customers to manage their bookings on ba.com.
- Renewal of self-service kiosks at airports.

In addition to the Frequent Flyer Programmes, BA introduced a number of e-tools aiming at facilitating the booking and check-in process. These reduced operational and personnel costs while offering better service and value for money for consumers.

Moreover, BA has effectively externalized its yield management by providing a calendar of fares and enabling consumers to identify their cheaper flights at times that planes were not that busy. This enabled them to compete with no frills airlines that advertised very cheap fares and also to attract consumers to buy directly from them as they now had a much more transparent pricing and hence more choice (Figure 26.2). In the London to Barcelona example, for example fares vary from £23 to £239 depending on the demand for each particular day. These tools included the following:

BA.com and eTicketing

eTicket is an electronic ticketing system that securely stores all ticket details in the BA computer system, issuing to customers an eTicket receipt. eTicket holders may check-in either electronically, at self-service kiosks or at check-in desks at the airports (ba.com). Paperless ticketing saves costs for the carrier and provides better service for consumers through a more flexible, efficient and secure process.

The use of e-tickets continues to grow in particular with regards the short-haul leisure distribution, as demonstrated in Figure 26.3. During the year ended 31 March 2006, 87% of all passenger journeys ticketed by the Company worldwide were issued on e-tickets (2005: 77%).

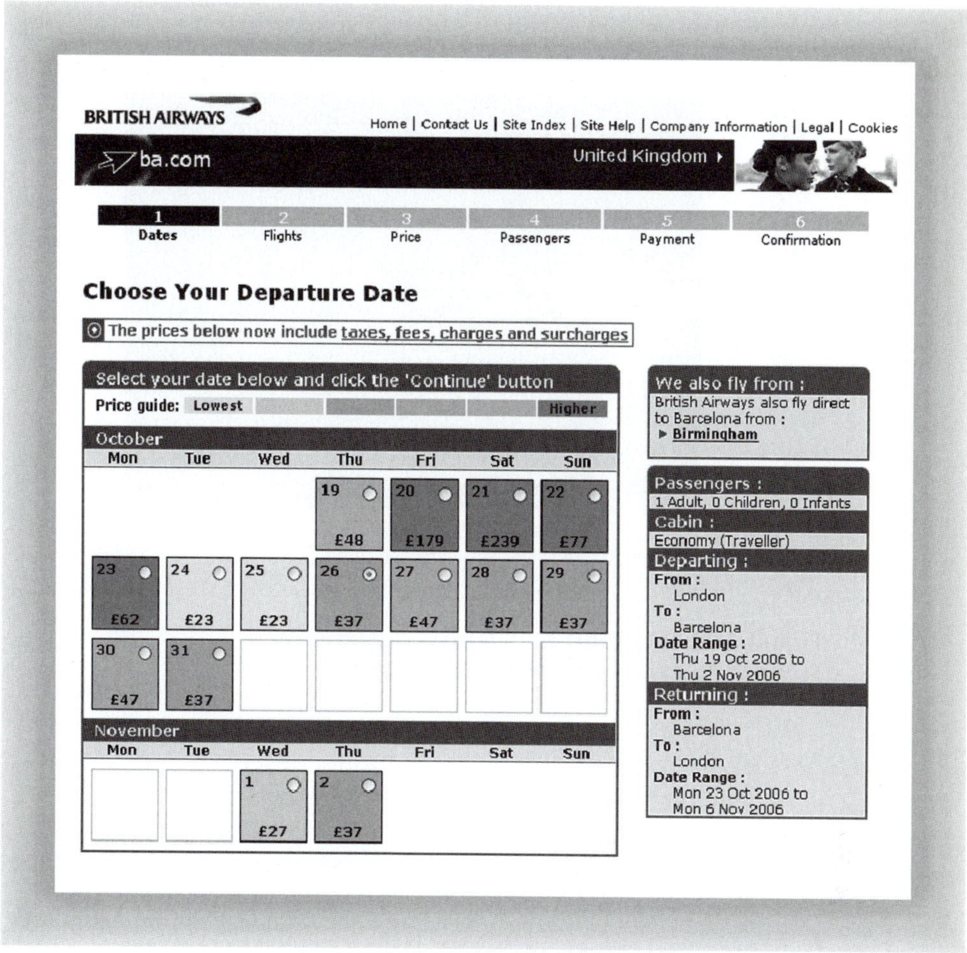

Figure 26.2 BA's calendar of fares
Source: ba.com

eCheck-in and Printing boarding passes

Figure 26.4 demonstrates an electronic boarding card, printed remotely at the time that passengers check in. These boarding passes replace the traditional ones issued at the airport; they are printed on plain A4/letter paper and have a unique barcode that allows customers to proceed directly to security at the airport's departures, without having to stand in the check-in queues. This tool cuts operational costs for the carrier as they require less check in agents and less physical presence at airports. At the same time it saves customers time at the airport as they can check-in online 24 hours before departure at their own convenience (ba.com). In addition

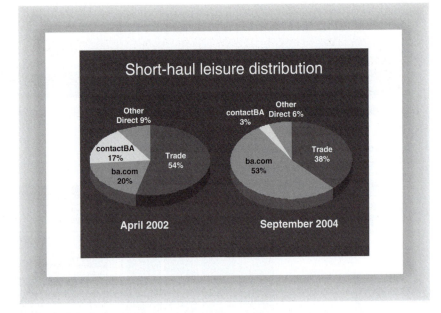

Figure 26.3 BA's short-haul leisure distribution
Source: BA financial results UBS (Q2004/2005)

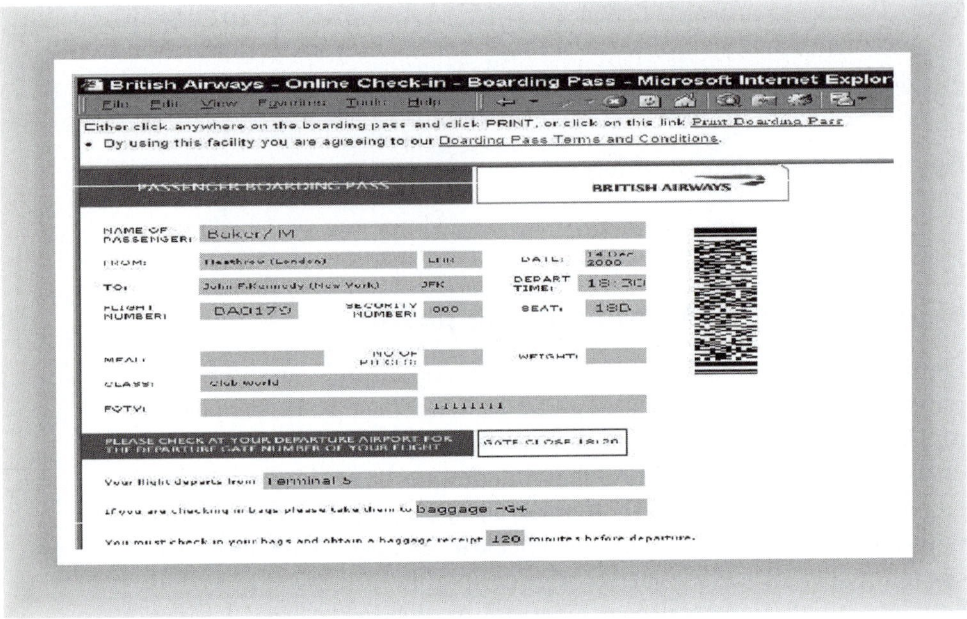

Figure 26.4 Online passenger boarding pass
Source: ba.com

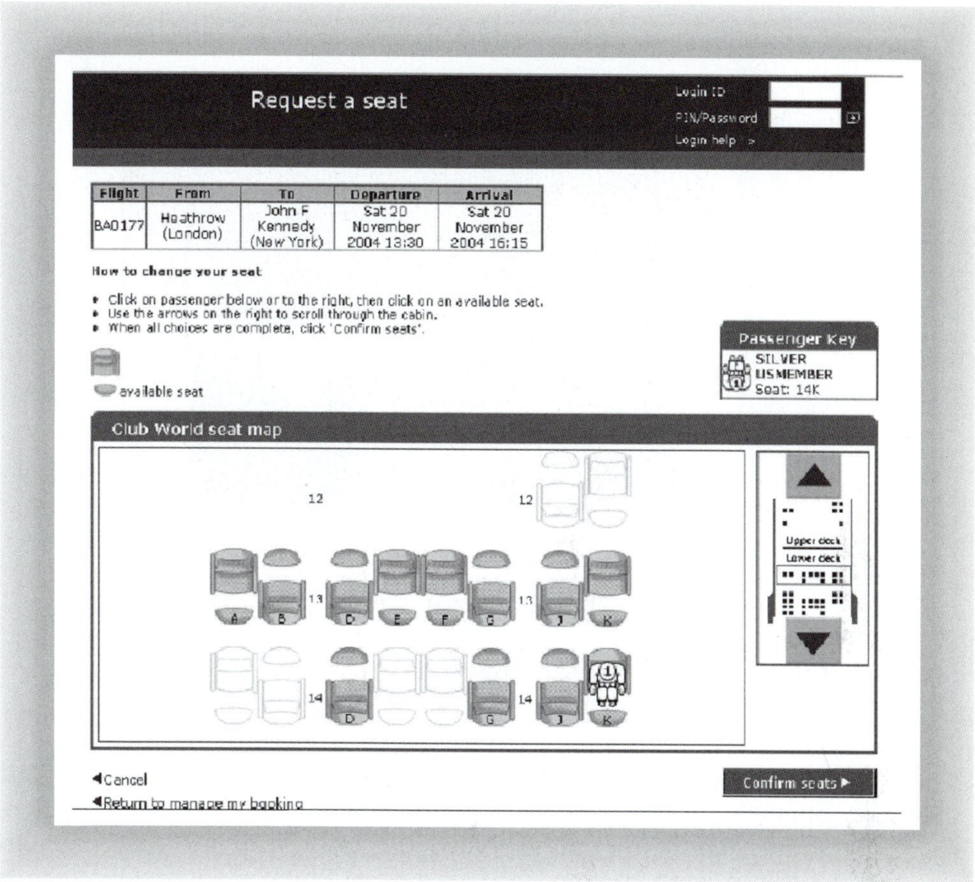

Figure 26.5 Seat allocation on online check-in
Source: ba.com

to the eCheck-in service, BA also enables customers to choose their seat from the interactive seating plan, as demonstrated in Figure 26.5 (ba.com).

Self-service Kiosks and Fast Bag Drop

Another important element is the introduction of self-service kiosks at key airports around the world. They are easy to use, featuring touch-screens that enable checking in within a few minutes. Customers should provide a form of identification (e.g. Credit/ Debit/Executive Club Card), their booking reference and their flight number (should they need to give further details so as to find their booking). Furthermore, customers can also check-in for an onward or return flight, if it is within the next 24 hours. Self-service kiosks also enable the printing of boarding passes and their

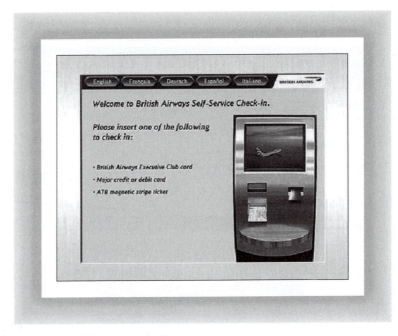

Figure 26.6 Self-service check-in
Source: ba.com

services are presented in English, French, German, Italian and Spanish (ba.com). As of 25 April 2006, all UK domestic travellers should check in online. Now, the only way for customers to check in is on ba.com or at an airport kiosk. Conventional check in desks were converted to 'fast bag drop' desks, for customers with luggage to check in, with dedicated staff available to help customers at the kiosks. British Airways continues to invest in automated check-in systems in expectation that more than 80% of its customers will use self-service check in by the time it moves into Heathrow Terminal 5. The airline is aggressively installing kiosks in airports around the world. As for luggage, customers may go to a dedicated bag drop desk where a customer service agent will tag the luggage and send it to the aircraft (ba.com) (Figure 26.6).

These tools have increased flexibility, convenience and saving of both time and money for consumers, thus leading to increased customer satisfaction and loyalty. Through the introduction of these revolutionary tools, BA managed to launch a new way to manage bookings, allowing more up-selling as well as the facility to change and update bookings on ba.com (BA Annual Report, 2003/2004; Parks-Smith, 2004). At the same time, BA has managed to decrease the required operational and organizational costs throughout its entire value chain. The achievement of these goals has led to important cost savings and to the disintermediation of traditional intermediaries. Furthermore, it has resulted in increased revenues, enhancement of efficiency, effectiveness and performance, as well as in building a strong brand identity.

By accessing its customers directly and by using its own website as the main distribution channel, BA has managed to protect itself from substitutes, increase its bargaining power with its suppliers and maintain a strategic positioning that is difficult for new entrants to imitate. Moreover, BA has accomplished to create and sustain a competitive advantage that differentiates the company from its rivals, by creating an end-to-end self-service experience. BA has enhanced its strategic positioning and increased its market share by adding to its well established offline presence an innovative online representation process. Consumers appreciated those changes and enabled the airline to achieve process strategic competitive advantage.

Key Challenges for the Future

Apart from adopting and successfully integrating to the implementation of its strategy all the afore mentioned e-tools, BA should also aim at taking advantage of emerging technologies, such as interactive digital television (IDTV) and mTourism. According to Buhalis and Licata (2002), IDTV is a richer user-friendly means of interactive communication that provides relevant content at the convenience of the customer whilst mobile applications are also critical, especially for travellers on the road. Recent trials have demonstrated that the market is not ready for these technologies yet, although understanding their capabilities will assist BA to be ready in the future. The Internet and the IDTV are mutually reinforcing thus enabling full exploitation of a firm's potential. As a result, BA will be able to further enhance its strong online presence and to gain an even bigger market share, especially of leisure travellers.

According to Lord Marshall of Knightsbridge, BA's Chairman of the Board, the hallmark of the modern British Airways has been 'business transformation, customer-driven development, brand leadership and operational integrity' (BA Annual Report, 2003/2004). Towards that direction, BA enhanced its positioning by introducing a number of user-friendly e-tools that increased customer satisfaction and loyalty, while at the same time, resulted in important cost savings as well as to direct selling. BA's progress is steady and moving up. The carrier managed to bypass threats, as well as gain and retain an important market share by focusing on differentiation factors and by adapting its strategic orientation to the changing circumstances, which are characterized by the proliferation of ICT and the Internet. Taking advantage of the emerging technologies, such as IDTV and mTourism, will result in the retention of the carrier's leading position within the competitive airline market.

Key Conclusions

- The Internet has offered an unparalleled opportunity for airlines to use technology to manage their resources efficiently, communicate directly with consumers and collaborate with partners.
- Innovative air carriers use the Internet as a cost-efficient distribution channel, as a tool for CRM and as a procurement mechanism.
- BA has used ICTs to adapt its strategy to overcome the challenges and threat that emerged from the external environment.

Review and Discussion Questions

- What are the key initiatives that BA was able to take as a result of the Internet?
- What are the key innovations of BA online?
- How can airlines use the Internet to achieve sustainable competitive advantage?

References and Further Reading

BA Annual Report & Accounts (2003/2004). 1–72. Retrieved from http://www.media.corporate-ir.net/media_files/irol/69/69499/downloads/Report_and_Accounts_2003-2004.pdf.

BA Annual Report & Accounts (2005/2006). 1–114. Retrieved from http://www.media.corporate-ir.net/media_files/irol/69/69499/Report_2006.pdf.

BA Financial Results UBS (Q2004/2005). Retrieved from http://www.media.corporate-ir.net/media_files/irol/69/69499/AnnualReportandAccounts2004-2005.pdf.

BA Investor Relations (2005). Corporate Profile. Retrieved from http://www.bashares.com/phoenix.zhtml?c=69499&p= irol-homeprofile.

BA Press Office. *Radical Shake-Up for European Fares*. Retrieved 20 April 2006 from http://bapress.custhelp.com/cgi-bin/bapress.cfg/php/enduser/std_adp.php?p_sid=&p%20_Iva=&p_faqid=7212.

Buhalis, D. (2004). eAirlines: Strategic and tactical use of ICTs in the airline industry. *Information and Management*, 41, 805–825.

Buhalis, D., & Licata, M. C. (2002). The future eTourism intermediaries. *Tourism Management*, 23, 207–220.

Eddington, R. (2004). *British Airways, 2nd Quarter & Interim Results, 2004/05*, 8 November 2004 presentation to shareholders.

Jarach, O. (2002). The digitalisation of market relationships in the airline industry: The impact and prospects of eBusiness. *Journal of Air Transport Management*, 8 (2), 115–120.

O'Toole, K. (2003). ICT trends survey. *Airline Business*, August, 40–47.

Parks-Smith, S. (2004). *British Airways – Customer Enabled BA*. Presentation Europe Travel Distribution Summit, Eye for Travel, London.

Porter, M. (2001). Strategy and the Internet. *Harvard Business Review*, 103D (March), 63–78.

Shona, Z., Chenc, F., & Chang, Y. (2003). Airline e-commerce: The revolution in ticketing channels. *Journal of Air Transport Management*, 9 (5), 325–331.

Company's website: http://www.ba.com.

27

Kulula.com: low-cost carrier and ICTs

Berendien Lubbe

Learning Objectives

- Illustrate that low-cost airlines have to use advanced technology as they operate in an increasingly competitive market.
- Demonstrate how important it is for the business model of low-cost airlines to use ICTs strategically and operationally.
- Explain the technological innovations that Kulula.com is using to improve its efficiency.

Introduction and Company Development

Kulula.com is a low-cost airline based in South Africa operating domestic and regional scheduled services. The name Kulula is the Zulu word meaning it is easy. The airline started operations in August 2001 as a wholly owned subsidiary of Comair Ltd. (a Johannesburg Stock Exchange listed public company). Comair Ltd. operates two brands: British Airways Domestic and Regional, providing full-service scheduled air services in southern Africa and Kulula.com, South Africa's first low-cost domestic airline. Comair currently operates a fleet of 24 jet aircraft of which, as at March 2006, the Kulula.com fleet had 9.

Since inception Kulula.com has recorded a growth of 45% year on year. Kulula.com currently holds a 20% share of the domestic air travel market. When Kulula.com entered the domestic market in 2001, 4% of the South African population were flying domestically. Kulula.com has grown this market to 7%.

Characteristics of the Environment that the Company Operates in

Low-cost airlines are currently operating in a growth market for budget air travel putting pressure on full-fare airlines. The high volume and reduced cost structure allow low-cost airlines to charge less than full-fare airlines and therefore attract passengers who would generally use other means of transport. Within 2 years of launching, Kulula.com grew the domestic airline market by approximately 10%.

Airline operators in the private sector have struggled for a considerable time to compete against the state-owned South African Airways, leading to several airline failures since deregulation. The conduct of South African Airways has been described as predatory and has led to complaints filed with the Competition Commission regarding abuse of dominance in terms of the Competitions Act. Subsequent findings in a specific case has shown abuse of dominance which should provide for an improved trading environment and the promotion of a level playing field for competing airlines. Despite the restrictive market conditions Comair Ltd. has consistently achieved a growing market share under its British Airways Domestic and Regional, and more recently under its Kulula.com brand.

Main Products/Offerings and Value Added

Kulula.com operates scheduled air services domestically in South Africa and has also started to fly regionally into Namibia, Zimbabwe and from March 2006 is planning, in partnership with Zambia Airways, to fly into Lusaka, Zambia, at about a third of the current fare provided by SAA. Kulula.com has flown from national airports rather than secondary airports but in March 2006 started to fly out of Lanseria Airport, situated just outside Johannesburg. Through the Kulula.com website passengers can also book cars, accommodation or chauffeur-driven cabs to the airport, making them a 'one-stop shop' for the traveller. They describe their product as a travel experience and differentiate themselves through their easy accessibility and affordability. Their mission simply states the following: 'the easiest around, simple, totally honest, great fun, safe and professional, inspirational'.

Kulula's success is attributed to a combination of low prices (initially, approximately 40% lower than traditional airlines), quick access to the Internet and simple booking process. The high frequency of flights, including 12 flights a day between Johannesburg and Cape Town (more than that on offer from other local operators), also gives Kulula.com a competitive advantage.

Business Model

In South Africa there are two low-cost carriers: Kulula.com and 1Time. 1Time entered the market in early 2004 and holds approximately 5% market share. 1Time asserts that it is South Africa's only authentic and sustainable low-fare airline since it was set up from scratch as a low-fare model whereas Kulula.com was established under the Comair Ltd. grouping which has been operating a full-service carrier in South Africa for five decades. Despite the assertion by 1Time, Kulula.com follows a low-cost carrier business model. One of the challenges facing Comair Ltd. in setting up a low-cost airline was the integration of the airline with a traditional carrier which had been in operation for the past five decades. While the basic output in the airline industry is the transportation of passengers between two destinations, the two business models differ in the configuration of the value chain and in the way they create value on the market place.

It would appear that Kulula.com has achieved successful growth despite the incompatibility of operating these business models simultaneously within the same grouping. Graf (2005) developed a set of propositions of how to control the incompatibilities and in applying these to Comair Ltd. the effectiveness achieved in operating the two business models successfully (as shown by the sustained growth of Kulula.com and British Airways) can probably be ascribed to the following:

- *Consistency in the application of the business models*: The low-cost model has been consistently applied within the group which is characterized by Kulula.com's low fares, easy Internet bookings and inexpensive but fuel-efficient aircraft.
- *Differentiation in the product and market approach*: Markets are clearly distinguished with BA primarily serving the corporate market through more traditional distribution channels with a full-service product and Kulula.com aligning its simpler product to the price-sensitive traveller, also expanding the market by stimulating demand from traditional non-flyers and focusing its efforts online.
- *Extensive and clear communication of the products*: Both BA and Kulula.com are clearly defined through their distinct mission statements and reflected in the marketing strategies and use and emphasis on different distribution channels.
- *Separation of branding and resources but sharing of back-office activities*: Branding follows two distinct routes with BA focusing on a business and corporate image and Kulula.com focusing on a youthful and fun-image. Back-office activities such as finance, human resources, service delivery, operations and ICT are shared. One commercial director is responsible for both brands. Cannibalization of the BA brand has been less than actually expected with both brands growing faster than the market over the past 3 years – it would appear gains have been in market share. The BA brand continues to service a particular segment of the market with its more flexible and business travel offering. Further technology innovations for this brand should position it well with business travellers going forward.
- *Leadership characteristics and flexibility of the grouping*: The group is characterized by its flexibility and dynamic management principles.

However, the gap between full service and low-cost airlines is today probably less than that suggested by Graf (2005). The smarter full service airlines are learning very quickly from the low-cost model and adopting elements where suitable. As an example, BA in the UK now offers e-tickets only, are growing web bookings exponentially and offer an online check-in and an online boarding pass. Most of these will be made compulsory in the near future, thereby negating the advantage of low-cost carriers in this particular area.

The convergence is taking place from the low cost side as well with low-cost carriers encroaching on the traditional space of the full service airlines. For example, some low-cost airlines such as Virgin Blue have gone into interlining and code sharing agreements moving away from the simple point-to-point routes to extended networks. The concept of no-frills has also started to erode with low-cost carriers such as JetBlue offering services such as in-seat TVs to enhance their product.

Technological and Business Innovation

Comair Ltd. regards modern technology as the key to the low-cost model and faced the challenge of integrating the low-cost carrier with the traditional carrier where ICT ran on the legacy platform. The current e-business model used by Comair Ltd. is depicted in Figure 27.1.

With the low-cost model flexibility, low price and ease of use are the principal drivers in the travel site. Choice and speed to the market is critical. Changes in the distribution environment in the airline industry and the growth in online distribution made the cost of distribution the most significant of controllable costs. In establishing Kulula.com, the airline realized that serving customers through the web was the primary priority. The initial technology used by Kulula.com was locally developed in six weeks based on the following principles:

- Simplicity
- Efficiency
- Innovation
- Flexibility
- Responsiveness
- Scalability
- Security
- Manageable
- Fault tolerant
- Usable.

Within a year of starting operations Kulula.com moved to the AirKiosk system after finding that the Microsoft SQL-based inventory and reservations system could not cope with the start-up airline's volumes and the need for advanced booking features. The AirKiosk system is an integrated solution for distribution, reservations,

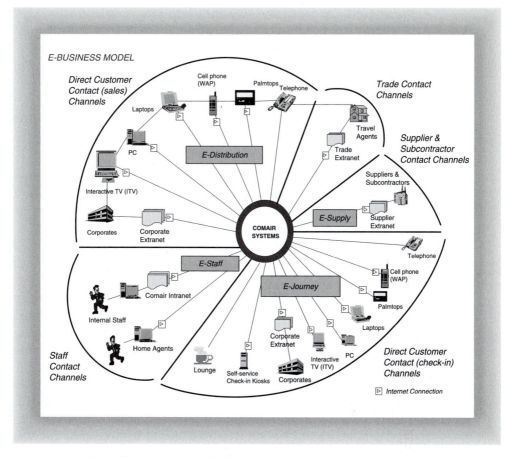

Figure 27.1 The e-business model of Comair Ltd.
Source: Comair Ltd.

inventory management, check-in and revenue management developed by a corporation called Sutra Inc. whose primary business is the AirKiosk system and ASP service, the only travel distribution solution designed for the Internet. The AirKiosk system has functions equal to those of legacy IBM TPF- and Unisys USAS-based mainframe reservations systems, with the added advantages of integrated eCommerce and Revenue Management applications. Using the AirKiosk system, Kulula.com blazed a trail of airline marketing 'firsts', quickly becoming the largest online retailer in South Africa. According to Airkiosk (2006) Kulula.com was the first airline in Africa to offer:

- Online Reservations Change (first airline in the world).
- Low Fare Finder calendar-based search.
- Auxiliary product (hotels, rental cars, taxi services) sales on the web.

- Web-based 'On Hold and Pay Later' option.
- 'Biz Deals' private web access to corporate clients with negotiated fares and reservations change rules.
- Galileo GDS Basic Booking Product for guaranteed sale through travel agencies.
- Galileo Direct Access and Interactive Sell.
- Travel Agent private web access for private fares and the option to incorporate a service fee within a Kulula.com booking.
- XML API for sales through other websites.

Kulula.com was also one of the first airlines to take advantage of the AirKiosk system's full web content management features, which gives an airline real time control over everything on its website, from promotional pages to new routes and fares.

According to Lowman (2005) Kulula.com transaction volumes grew ten-fold since the airline's move to the AirKiosk system, with website bookings during fares promotions exceeding 3000 segments per hour plus sales of auxiliary products. A special offer by airline Kulula.com drew 8 million hits and 111,000 unique visitors to the site in only two days according to Kulula.com commercial director Gidon Novick. During the two-day sale, 55,000 seats were sold. The airline's web server was not affected adversely by the mass influx of visitors, because the site usually accommodates around 5 million page impressions on busy days, during which it can accommodate around 3000 visitors simultaneously. According to Carl Scholtz, the ICT executive manager at Kulula.com, the web server, which usually runs at around 3–4%, was running between 60% and 70% at peak times during the sale. So he says the volumes suggest the South African public now feels secure about online bookings. 'People are not afraid to book online as long as there is value in it', says Scholtz. 'The percentage of people who book our air tickets online is around 60–65% and it has been for years, but the volumes are increasing on a whole', he adds.

Kulula.com has in fact been the single biggest success story of e-commerce in South Africa, and is the first South African consumer website to reach 1.0 billion rand (approximately $150 million) in online sales in a single year. (Goldstuck, 2006)

In January 2006 Kulula.com changed from the Airkiosk system to a locally developed and supported system, running on C#, SQL, .Net. The new system is based on modern technology and architecture principles utilizing the latest thinking in software development. The flexibility offered by this approach has already enabled Kulula.com to react very quickly to the fast changing market and industry dynamics.

Key Challenges for the Future

Technology Challenges

Kulula.com sees its technology future as providing for enhanced platform robustness, flexibility and scalability. The convergence of customer access technology and devices is achieved through convergence of technology standards – with software being used across multiple platforms; deployment and adoption of wireless technology; and increased capability of mobile devices.

Management Challenges

In South Africa the airline industry and low-cost airlines in particular are faced with low average ticket prices, high fuel prices, over capacity in the market and aggressive competition in the domestic market. Airlines such as SAA are offering airfares as low, and in some cases, even lower than the two low-cost airlines operating in the South African market. Kulula.com is facing these challenges by:

- *Expanding its customer base*: Kulula.com was attracting increasing numbers of business people due to its focus on punctuality and target of 90% on time departures, as well as its original target market of students and leisure travellers who did not normally fly.
- *Expanding its fleet of fuel-efficient aircraft to meet growing demand*: With the acquisition of three Boeing 737–400s within the year to cover growing demand.
- *Moving into secondary airports*: Lanseria Airport, midway between Johannesburg and Pretoria for flights to Cape Town.
- Expanding regionally into Namibia, Zimbabwe and Zambia where they believe there is a substantial demand for seats at low prices because thousands of people commute by bus for up to 2 days when air travel would take 2 hours or less.
- *Increasing airline partnerships*: Kulula.com partners with Zambia Airways to offer flights to Lusaka at approximately one third of the price of SAA.
- Launching major community initiatives such as offering the South African Police Service, as well as their families, substantially discounted flights to any Kulula.com destination.

Mindful of the imperative to redress the historical, social and economic inequalities of the past as well as to achieve sustained presence and ownership in business by historically disadvantaged

South Africans, Comair Ltd. has actively participated in the development of the Black Economic Empowerment charter for Transport. Comair Ltd. has made progress towards the targets set in the Draft Aviation Scorecard, including employment equity, training, management, social responsibility and procurement. Comair Ltd. is investigating opportunities for a black shareholding.

The Future of the Company

Comair Ltd. has been successful in operating two business models under the same grouping and this will present an increasing challenge in the future as the low-cost model is proving to be highly successful in the South African and regional markets. However, this may not be sustainable over the longer term as a number of signs pointing to the contrary are evident:

- Increasing customer segments being addressed. A certain amount of cannibalization of passengers has already taken place with Kulula.com gaining some British Airways Domestic and Regional passengers. Kulula.com is also experiencing increasing growth in the business market with research indicating that 50% of travel on Kulula flights is for business purposes, the traditional source of British Airways Domestic and Regional passengers.
- Increasing horizontal co-operations such as partnerships with other airlines for sales activities.
- Multiple distribution channels. In 2003 Kulula.com listed on the main travel agents' bookings system, Galileo. In 2004 Kulula.com launched a corporate extranet called 'Biz Deals' on its website – a step towards accommodating its new expanding business market. 'Biz Deals' is aimed at reducing company travel costs and providing an online business travel product for the increasing number of corporate and business travellers using the Internet. Other channels include third-party booking websites (typically online travel agents accessing the airline inventory through the GDS); flight scanners (they scan the Internet for fares providing the customer with best fares); procurement portals (web-based portals with direct access to airline inventory acting as procurement agents for the corporate market and third-party resellers (they act as agents, selling tickets as commodities, they are integrated with the airline booking system).
- Increasingly comprehensive product. Pre-assigned seating now available, increasing focus on auxiliary products such as cars and accommodation.

In the near future the two models will eventually meet or come very close together and offer an air travel model that relies heavily on technology to support the low-cost benefits. The investment in information and communication technologies to support the management of inventory and the multiple distribution channels that are used will determine the success of both airlines in the Comair group. The answer may not actually be to have both offerings as part of the same airline grouping portfolio (such as currently the case with Comair). We have seen BA International divest from Go as a separate entity only to adopt the same principles into its full service offering. Today BA is increasingly able to compete with the low-cost carriers in the UK and Europe. A similar convergence is anticipated in the Comair environment.

Despite a difficult trading environment Comair Ltd. expects to gain further market share through Kulula.com and British Airways Regional and Domestic. From a technology point of view Kulula.com will probably remain the leading online company in South Africa for a number of years due to continued improvement and innovation in its e-business model.

Key Conclusions

- The high volumes and reduced cost structure allow low-cost airlines to charge less than full-fare airlines and therefore attract passengers who would generally use other means of transport.
- Changes in the distribution environment in the airline industry and the growth in online distribution made the cost of distribution the most significant of controllable costs.
- Innovative air carriers use the Internet as a cost-efficient distribution channel, as a tool for CRM and as a procurement mechanism.

Review and Discussion Questions

- Discuss how Kulula.com can maximize its profitability through technology.
- What are the key challenges faced by Kulula.com?
- How can regional and low-cost airlines reach the mainstream markets?

References and Further Reading

Alamdari, F., & Mason, K. (2006). The future of airline distribution. *Journal of Air Transport Management*, 12 (3), 122–134.

Buhalis, D. (2003). *eTourism: Information technology for strategic tourism management*. Essex: Prentice-Hall.

Buhalis, D. (2004). eAirlines: Strategic and tactical use of ICTs in the airline industry. *Information and Management*, 41 (7), 805–825.

Comair Limited (2005). *Annual Report*. Johannesburg, South Africa.

Graf, L. (2005). Incompatibilities of the low-cost and network carrier business models within the same airline grouping. *Journal of Air Transport Management*, 11 (5), 313–327.

Goldstuck, A. (2005). *Online Retail in South Africa 2006*. Report presented by World Wide Worx. Johannesburg, South Africa. Retrieved 15 January 2006 from http://www.airkiosk.com/news_item_19.php?item=1.

Lowman, S. (2005). *ITWeb*. Johannesburg. Retrieved from http://allafrica.com/stories.

http://www.airkiosk.com.

http://www.itweb.co.za.

http://www.theworx.biz.

Company's website: http://www.kulula.com.

Case

28

Finnair: innovating interactivity

Sanna Andersson

Learning Objectives

- Illustrate how ICT can improve Finnair's value proposal to consumers.
- Demonstrate how technology can support the comprehensive and continually expanding Finnair route network via its OneWorld partners.
- Demonstrate how Finnair applied e-business to interact through streamlined automated end-to-end online process with customers, suppliers, business partners and authorities.
- Explore the technological innovations with regard to wireless services.

Introduction and Company Development

Finnair, one of the world's oldest operating airlines, was established on 1 November 1923. Today it is part of the OneWorld airline alliance and has succeeded to turn its former weakness – geographical situation – to the optimum strength. The Asian network has proven to be the key success indicator for today and tomorrow. Based on geography the airline has sustainable competitive edge as its home hub Helsinki enables the shortest flight times from Europe to Asia. Because of this Finnair is favoured in the various reservation systems as the total travel time defines the order of alternatives which is yet another vital indicator for good availability to consumers. In 2007 Finnair carried nearly 8.7 million passengers. Its turnover was 2,180.5 million euros. The result before taxes was 138.9 million euros (Finnair, 2007). The parent company Finnair Plc was listed 1989 on the Helsinki stock exchange and the major shareholder with a 55.78% holding is the Finnish government. Other shareholders include various companies and private individuals as well. Today the number of personnel of Finnair Group is approximately 9480, and the fleet comprises of 63 aircraft.

Being the market leader in air transportation to and from Finland as well as in gateway traffic through Finland, Finnair's objective is to continue the growth to Asian destinations. Its vision is to become the airline of choice for long-haul travel in the northern hemisphere. Finnair Group operations cover scheduled passenger traffic, leisure traffic, travel services including two travel agency groups, travel information and reservation services and aviation services which comprise technical and ground handling operations, catering and facilities management. The subsidiaries provide air traffic support service or operate in closely related areas. To safeguard profitable business operations and sustainable growth, the Finnair Group began a structural reform process in 2006. With these actions the company expects to gain profit of 80 million euros on a yearly basis in the future.

Main Products/Offerings and Value Added

Finnair's scheduled passenger traffic covers about 60 international destinations in long-haul and European routes as well as 13 domestic trunk routes. The domestic route network is one of the densest in the world in relation to population. In addition to regular scheduled traffic, Finnair operates leisure flights to more than 60 destinations in the Mediterranean, Asia, North and South America.

Finnair's value proposition to consumers is the superiority of the product – direct flights to over 50 international destinations. The morning–evening concept guarantees the best schedules for efficient business travel and yet gives also leisure travellers a choice of flexible travel. Comprehensive and continually expanding its route network via OneWorld partners to cover the rest of world makes it possible to interline globally and mix various price schemes. Punctuality and top class service compose the grounds to develop the service concept to meet tomorrow's air traveller's needs and expectations. According to the flightontime.info website, Finnair was the most punctual scheduled airline in 2005 operating to the world's busiest international airport, London Heathrow. The Survey of Flights in Europe (SoFiE Q2/2006) stated that the airline was the best European airline on customer satisfaction, and the Jacdec (2/2006) survey listed Finnair on second place right after Qantas on air travel security.

Business Model

In 2008 the airline industry is still in shaky financial shape, as air transport is facing a growing demand along with the record high fuel price. Competition remains tough globally. Yet sense is slowly returning within the industry as weaker players are withdrawing from the markets. Finnair's objective is to be a first-class commercial enterprise and for its shareholders a competitive investment in terms of total return. This objective will be reached through strategic solutions that support the return on capital employed. In terms of a profitability target, this means an operating profit of around 6%, given the Group's present capital structure. In other words, an operating profit of around 110–120 million euros is required in the next few years. The ability of business units to add value will guide the development of the group structure in the future. The operations will be enhanced by targeting resources on core processes during the coming years.

According to the strategy the growth is expected to come from the Europe to Asia traffic and neighbouring Scandinavian and Baltic markets. Though being a network carrier Finnair's business model has evolved towards low-cost carrier business model offering a mix of these two. Yet a traveller will be able to enjoy all the best pieces of a network concept as interlining, code share, multi-segment tickets and hub concept but still find competitive prices if that counts for more. Value chain represents the integration of research and development of products, procurement, operations, marketing, distribution and after sales.

As the customer is the key Finnair wants to confront the travellers with open, honest treatment and expert, friendly service. Passenger comfort, together with safety, must be promoted in every situation through out the internal and external processes. The continuing fleet renewal programme overall plays a key role in the service quality experienced by the customer. With modern aircraft and technology, Finnair strives to enhance service efficiency and passenger comfort and meet the demanding needs of Corporate Social Responsibility (CSR) programme. Significant steps forward in this respect have been the acquisition of the Airbus A330 and A340 fleet and investment in Embraer 170 and 190s jet aircraft. A young, most modern European fleet delivers a higher level of safety. Continuously developed service concepts are based on systematically gathered feedback from the customers of all business units. Suppliers of these processes are internal and external partners such as aircraft industry, technical suppliers, facility suppliers, aviation administration, catering, airports, alliance members and other authorities required.

Corporate social responsibility is the company's way of working, including responsibility for the environment, personnel, leisure travel and customers. Being part of the industry that has a huge meaning to the environment globally Finnair has launched a sustainable tourism programme that covers the guidelines of doing things right; not only within the Group but also together with their suppliers and other third parties included. As part of the CSR programme Finnair has also appointed a VP, Sustainable Development to safeguard the realisation of environmental goals and integration of various business areas with CSR.

Technological and Business Innovation

Finnair aims to consolidate its position by being a pioneer as well as a developer and user of the newest technology. This enables the airline to provide an increasingly personal and comprehensive service for its customers. The company has started to safeguard its strong competitive position by making effective use of various distribution channels along with new service concepts. Finnair will improve its competitiveness and cost efficiency particularly by taking advantage of the possibilities e-business offers in its internal and external processes as well as in e-commerce and customer service.

Like its competitors in the early 1990s, Finnair started publishing basic information on the web. Over the years e-commerce developed and gave a real option for online transactions over the Internet. E-business came into the picture years later, making it possible to interact through streamlined automated end-to-end online processes with customers, suppliers, business partners and authorities. Advanced technology enabled internal and external e-business processes (Buhalis, 2004). Above all these lies the e-economy i.e. the utilization of new technologies for different purposes, for example corporate e-network creation, intensified globalization development and structural changes in the economy. Today e-business within the company is business as usual without any extra fuss. E-business consists of supply, internal and customer-related automated and integrated processes while only e-commerce is being the most visual part of the e-business to end consumer. Finnair's e-business development unit has the overall responsibility to support the strategy set by the commercial division and to ensure that the value and objectives for all e-business initiatives will materialize.

There are few new developments to do with automated processes, although the existing technology will need constant updating and enhancing. Automated internal processes contain e-procurement, supply chain management, e-learning, human resources, finance, M&A (mergers and acquisitions) and alliances, legal services, ICT functions, marketing, sales and other e-service solutions. Some of these processes can also be utilized through mobile devices globally.

The Group has centralized all the internal financial services under the economics and finance function. With the help of the main financial system, SAP FICO, the division handles electronically purchase invoice processes and payments, travel invoices, annual statements, authority reports, customer credit control and other related financial information. Other systems used internally involves an invoicing system called Sonet, e-flow (invoice processing system), a banking system, a travel management system WebTraveller and a credit card invoicing system. SAP HR portal was introduced during 2006 to be able to handle all HR-related processes automatically. Various internal e-learning courses have been arranged since 1980s and today e-learning is the major learning method across the organizations within the group.

One of latest internal developments has been the migration to the Altèa DCS (departure control system) that includes customer and flight management as well as the inventory. The product is developed by Amadeus (see Cases 37 and 38) and it enables access to complete travel content and airline internal applications via a single GUI (graphical user interface). Previous departure and load control systems had been developed in early 1970s and due to the complex ICT structure the maintenance and debugging of the system took 70% of the time used. The migration to the Altèa DCS systems means a huge ICT restructure during 2007–2008 globally. Finnair will be the second airline right after Qantas to implement the Altèa DCS. Cost efficiency and the advances of one interface system for different end users are the main reasons behind the implementation.

Finnair air tickets and services can be bought through totally automated processes. The traveller signs up to website www.finnair.com for availability and reservation and pays for the flights with a credit card. Once the flights have been reserved and confirmed the system sends an e-ticket to the email address given or if requested a SMS confirmation to a mobile device. E-tickets can be used to all other routes except for Russia, even for the Arlanda Express train from Stockholm airport to the city center. When using the electronic process the traveller checks into the flights through the Internet at the airline's home page or with a mobile phone or uses self-service check-in counters at the airport prior to the flight. If the traveller belongs to the frequent traveller club, Finnair Plus, the airline proactively checks the traveller into the flights. The traveller receives a SMS message 3 hours prior to a flight suggesting a seat according to the online profile information and all the traveller needs to do is to accept the message by replying 'A'. The seats for the whole journey are confirmed at once. If the traveller only has hand luggage he can go directly to the plane via the security check. Baggage to be carried in the hold of the aircraft can be left at the Baggage Drop desks. The SMS check-in service is available for international journeys starting from Finland, Stockholm or Gothenburg in Sweden at the moment. There are plans to broaden the service in the near future, once the ICT and other authority issues have been resolved.

With a mobile phone a traveller can check flight schedules or their frequent flyer point status. The Best Buy service for Finnair Plus members ensures travellers get the information about valid tax free offers at the applicable airports. Through WAP services on all GSM or GRSP phones a traveller can check the schedules, make a reservation or check-in to the applicable flight. WAP services also allow verification of the frequent traveller programme status together with the location information. The Finnair also has 24-hour service for personal assistance if needed. The Finnair Contact Center utilizes IP-phones (telecommunication based on internet protocol) which broadens the ability to identify the caller and have all the customer-related information at hand when answering the phone. This makes the service process efficient and accurate.

WLAN – wireless local area networks – can be used by Finnair's customer to access a network connection at Helsinki–Vantaa and Stockholm Arlanda airports as well as in other airports in Finland. To be able to use the WLAN network the traveller needs a WLAN adapter and user codes which are given for a charge by the WLAN operator. The Internet connection is offered through the adapter to the wireless access points at the airports. Once a traveller is within the range the WLAN network is automatically identified for further use. The traveller just needs to choose the operator and log in with the ID information received previously from the operator. At the same time the system gives network settings to be used when connecting with other devices through the Internet. The wireless local-area network service enables wireless broadband access to the Internet and also to the company's network, if the company's data and security policy allows it.

A corporate customer will be able to join the Finnair Corporate Solution programme through the airline's website. The solution can be designed according to the specific needs of the corporation. The single sign-in process based on ID information allows the corporation to use the extranet services, such as flight reports, electronic serial tickets, online schedules and bookings. The latest development of the extranet is congress services. This new service concept allows corporations to benefit from organizing or attending international events. Once the event meets the congress criteria, the corporation can enjoy event flight tickets or for delegates Finnair offers special negotiated discount of air tickets.

Digital television will enable more interactive travel services with the larger public once it is available to more people. Finland has migrated to digital television entirely during 2007.

In June 2006, Finnair released a notice that the airline will start improving the efficiency of the ground staff at the home hub Helsinki-Vantaa airport with IBM RFID (radio frequency identification) solutions. During the next three years, IBM will implement and manage an innovative solution for allocation of employee tasks at Northport Ltd, a supplier of ground handling services and a member of Finnair Group. This RFID solution will be implemented to streamline the allocation, workflow and reporting of passenger services, baggage handling, lounge and check-in tasks.

The quality of customer service through increased efficiency and a smoother passenger experiences is expected to improve. Northport has already used RFID technology in the past to track ground staff working hours. The newest solution will cover all the management of ground staff tasks. The staff will be equipped with RFID-enabled mobile phones. The handset will provide information on the sequence of tasks by reading RFID tags located at the working locations. Previously the assignment of the ground duties was very time-consuming as the process was complex. With the new solution ground staff tasks will be transmitted automatically to mobile phones. The technology is based on the Nokia Field Force Solution consisting of mobile phones, work location RFID tags and the Nokia service manager software. The software connects the mobile phones and RFID tags to the IBM WebSphere-based server application and the airport work management system. Through this RFID process information on the location of the phones and the status of each tasks are routed to management.

Key Challenges for the Future

Within the Finnair Group, Balance Score Card has been used for strategic management on group, business unit, department and personal level. This leadership tool relates to e-business by bringing finance, customer, personnel and process view of e-strategy to the management. Knowledge management within the e-business environment will be a challenge as in many cases e-business strategies are filled with technology and process viewpoints and in the end when talking about the industry which lives for high quality service, it is people and their actions that count in the end.

In the future the technological infrastructure of Finnair is likely to remain the same as it is today. Finnair has outsourced the ICT infrastructure to IBM to be able to focus on its core business and develop it further.

The biggest question mark lies over the global network of airports and ground services. Airlines overall have already gone through tough restructuring processes to streamline the business both inside and outside and taken extras away whenever possible. Now there is a real need to unite the ground service, for example check in, cargo, luggage handling and security processes. With a complex mix of various authorities, airlines and other third parties this issue may take a while to be solved if ever. Global security under the ever growing risks is definitely a key issue. The technique required must meet various countries' standards and also requires governments to finance the transition. On a company level, Finnair's short-term goals are to increase online sales and online self-service to lower distribution and other costs of processes involved.

The Future of the Company

The future technological innovations and their effective utilization will have an effect on the whole air travel value chain. As many of these projects are already ongoing, the following topics seem to come up in the air travel development cycle: internet, mobile technology, radio frequency techniques and common ICT infrastructures.

Finnair received good feedback from consumers about their restructured Internet interfaces, once the calendar driven online booking engine was introduced. Nevertheless it will be vital to keep up with developing techniques along with easy, simple to use and instructive interface. Reservations, ticketing, check-in, customer specific meal requests, pre-order duty-free and in flight entertainment have to be available easily through Internet and mobile devices. Further possibilities to lower cost exist outside the company's own boundaries. For example, in procurement, whole value chains were streamlined into B2B marketplaces. Integration of seamless mobile technology into airplanes (telephone, emails, Internet) will force require heavy investment. Smart cards and radio frequency IDs will streamline ticketing and check-in processes along with the sorting and tracking of vehicles, passengers, luggage and cargo in the future. Common ICT platforms at least on an alliance level will finally enable e-ticket interlinking.

Continuous streamlining of internal and external processes and implementation of the newest technology seamlessly, rather than inventing any new e-concepts are vital for the e-future of the company. According to the commerce.net website today's barriers of e-business within the company have become more people-than technique-related issues. For example, organizational culture, management commitment, lack of resources or time, are critical for the airline industry of tomorrow.

External challenges face the barriers of various players wanting to build up the mutual e-infrastructure globally. The integration of the air industry value system between separate companies, will be more of a question of will than technology itself. The low-frequency nature of travel industry transactions and the rather expensive service is a challenge to meet. It's a question whether airlines and authorities want to work together to solve the issue of standardizing the industry across the world. And even so there will always be some third-world countries where the technical infrastructure won't meet the demands addressed by authorities or consumers.

Besides the loyalty by key customers, improved flexibility and cost efficiency will be the corner stones for the future of Finnair. According to the president and CEO of Finnair, the short-term outlook indicates that the strategy chosen continues to show its strength. Finnair aims to be known as a quality, reliable and responsible airline. A further aim of the structural change is to increase transparency and to ensure the competitiveness of all of the Finnair Group operations.

Key Conclusions

- Finnair aims to consolidate its position by being a pioneer as well as a developer and user of the newest technology.
- Finnair improved its competitiveness and cost efficiency by taking advantage of the possibilities e-business offers in its internal and external processes as well as in e-commerce and customer service.
- Finnair's e-business development unit has the overall responsibility to support the strategy set by the commercial division and to secure that the value and objectives for all e-business initiatives will be materialized.
- e-Business consists of supply, internal and customer-related automated and integrated processes while e-commerce is the most visual part of the e-business to end consumer.

Review and Discussion Questions

- Discuss how Finnair can apply advanced technologies for streamlining all its operations.
- Explore the use of mobile phones for airlines.
- How can network carriers improve the operational efficiency of the entire alliance?

References and Further Reading

Buhalis, D. (2004). eAirlines' strategic and tactical use of ICTs in the airline industry, *Information and management*, 41, 805–825.

Finnair, (2007). Finnair Group Financial Statement, 1 Jan 2007–31 Dec 2007. http://www.finnairgroup.com/linked/en/konserni/TP_2007_EN.pdf.

Niskakangas, T. (2006). *The high price of fuel hit the Finnair's result*. Kauppalehti, 9 August 2006, 8–9.

Talouselämä (2006). *The biggest companies in Finland*, 26 May 2006, 44–45.

Survey of Flights in Europe (SoFiE) Q2/2006.

www.flightontime.info.

www.aero.com.

www.flynordic.com.

www.commerce.net.

Company's website: http://www.finnair.com.

29

Enterprise Rent-A-Car: mainstreaming distribution

Florian M. Hummel

Learning Objectives

- Illustrate how rent-a-car companies use ICTs.
- Demonstrate how Enterprise has streamlined the processes between insurance companies and car hire companies, setting up agreements with large national insurance companies.
- Explore the technological innovations employed by Enterprise.

Introduction and Company Development

The US-based car hire company Enterprise Rent-A-Car has been in business since 1957. Enterprise, unlike its main competitors such as Avis and Hertz, currently only operates in the US, Canada, the UK, Ireland and Germany. Although Enterprise operates primarily in the US and from off-airport locations, Enterprise had a revenue of $8.2 billion in 2005 surpassing Hertz as the largest rental car company in the world (Leonard, 2006a; Enterprise, 2006). The company which is family-owned ranks 16th in the largest private companies in the US (Forbes, 2006). Enterprise operates about 6600 branches all of which are company owned, with a workforce of currently more than 61,000 employees (Enterprise, 2006b; Leonard, 2006). The company has opened about 300 new branches each year since 2001 (Leonard, 2006). Europe has been the main focus for expansion, while in the US the company already operates branches within 15 miles of 90% of the population (Enterprise, 2006b).

Main Products/Offerings and Value Added

Enterprise's key product is the provision of rental cars to customers who are in need of a car because their own car was involved in an accident, is in repair or being serviced. Although the company also provides rentals for business and leisure purposes, these activities are not regarded as the main business activities. However, the company offers a strongly publicized weekend product with extremely competitive rates. This is especially marketed in newly entered markets, arguably to establish the brand and to gain brand recognition, but also to compensate for weaker main business at the weekend. The main value of the company's business lies in the provision of mobility whenever and wherever the customer needs a replacement vehicle. Furthermore, the company makes the rental as simple as possible for the customer considering that in this area a fair amount of paper work with insurance companies, car body shops and liable third parties has to be managed. This is taken care of by Enterprise as the rental car provider. This also accounts for requests for payment in case of insurance claims or third-party liability. Overall, Enterprise operates some areas of interchangeable activities with other similar companies. In certain areas however

Enterprise could be regarded as the first mover. While most other car hire companies also operate in the replacement vehicle market, Enterprise has streamlined the processes between insurance companies and car hire companies, setting up agreements with large national insurance companies in the countries of operation. While competitors are generally approached by the individual customer who have an accident, Enterprise in contrast is directly informed by the other party's insurance company as Enterprise is the designated rental provider. This model has clearly been a new approach to the existing car hire business in Europe. In Enterprise's comparably smaller leisure segment however, Enterprise is competing with companies that have more profound leisure locations (e.g. at airports), more streamlined processes (e.g. marketing activities with airlines) and more customized products for the leisure traveller. Nevertheless, Enterprise's customer service plays a key role in adding value to its products. Especially in Europe where customer service is arguably not as emphasized as in the US, free pick-up services and Enterprise's Service Quality Survey add value to the rental experience (Kotler *et al.* 2006). This is in line with the 2005 JD Power and Associates study where Enterprise ranks the highest in customer satisfaction among rental car companies (JD Power and Associates, 2006).

Business Model

Traditionally, Enterprise's business model incorporates a number of stakeholders. Since the replacement vehicle sector is the strongest field of operation, insurance companies and body shops play an important role. While there are set agreements with insurance companies, body shops are also a vital business partner in their function as referral agents who provide customers to the business not only with respect to insurance claims but also when replacement cars are needed because of repair or servicing. In addition, car dealerships have their place in the business model as they fulfil two interrelated functions. On the one hand, they act as suppliers from which Enterprise buys its cars. This is in contrast to competitors who generally buy directly from the car manufacturers. On the other hand, they also act as agents as they also have their own connected body shop businesses. The selection of dealerships from which cars are brought into the fleet can obviously be seen in relation with the possible future business from these entities. Hence, car dealerships are another key stakeholder in the business model.

In more recent years, however, Enterprise has moved into the business travel and leisure market. This can primarily be seen at the growing number of airport locations, especially in the US and Canada. In Europe there are currently only a few examples of airport locations. In 2006 there were 11 airport locations in the UK, 2 in Ireland and 2 in Germany.

Technological and Business Innovation

In the past, the main feature of Enterprise's technological infrastructure was its own network of a satellite-based management information system (MIS) that connected each branch with the headquarters in the US. This technology which was arguably ahead of its time has recently been updated to broadband Internet connections. The MIS manages the data from each branch that is important for management to monitor the performance of the business. Just as with every other international car hire company, these performance figures are number of units on rent, average total rate and average rate by business segment just to name the obvious ones. Nevertheless, there are arguably some shortcomings of this system.

Customer IDs, as they are known by any frequent renter, are produced and available but not automatically stored in the system for worldwide use. While competitors provide their customers with IDs together with a customer or company card, this model is not fully followed by Enterprise in each country of operation. When a company, for example, will have its rates agreed with Enterprise, these are locally stored but not readily available on a national or international basis. Furthermore, each branch can only take reservations for branches in its region. Bookings cannot electronically be transferred outside a business region, which could be the greater catchment area of a city. In both cases the business has to rely on fax or phone communication and on employees at both ends to fulfil what otherwise technology could do automatically. Similar revenue management is not electronically automated but rather lies in the responsibility of each branch manager who relies on the MIS. Although rates are preset in the insurance and business sector, rates for leisure sales are not generated by the system based on the MIS. Again it is the employees' task to follow verbal management guidance as to which rates to sell.

Similar to any other hire car company, the Internet has its place as a sales tool. It is interesting to mention though that in Enterprise's new European markets it has taken quite some years from the start of operations to implementing a website with booking functions. As an example, it was not before 2005 that Enterprise's German website was ready for bookings about 8 years after operations were started in this country in 1997. This sounds astonishing considering the role that the Internet has been playing in the past 10 years in the service industry.

Key Challenges for the Future

By looking at the examples described above, an apparent problem that the company seems to be facing is the way business units are set up where markets are broken down into regional groups. Although this means that local business processes are streamlined, these regional business entities are not completely integrated on a world-wide or even national basis. As the appropriate technology becomes available, this seems to be a key management challenge for the future.

Conclusion

However, considering the huge success of the company, its growth rates (11.2% from 2004 to 2005; Forbes, 2006) and current expansion, one might want to question the often taken-for-granted necessity of ICT and eCommerce innovations. Enterprise seems to be a company that shows how to be highly efficient and successful without relying on the latest technological advancements. Although a missing revenue management system for example would leave most managers in the service industry shaking their heads, it certainly allows for 100% flexibility when it comes to competing on a local level and to satisfy customers as long as there is trust in the communication between management and rental staff.

Key Conclusions

- Enterprise's business model incorporates a number of stakeholders with the replacement vehicle sector is the strongest field of operation insurance companies and body shops play an important role.
- Enterprise seems to be a company that only slowly adopts ICT and e-commerce innovations.
- The MIS manages the data from each branch that is important for management to monitor the performance of the business.
- Similar to any other hire car company the Internet has become a central sales tool.

Review and Discussion Questions

- How can Enterprise achieve competitive advantage in this saturated market?
- Discuss interoperability issues for Enterprise with its stakeholders.
- Can Enterprise become a paperless operation?

References and Further Reading

Enterprise (2006a). Retrieved 3 March 2006 from http://www.aboutus.enterprise.com/file/97/SP_Aminus_rating_Jan06.pdf

Enterprise (2006b). Retrieved 3 March 2006 from http://www.aboutus.enterprise.com/files/rent_a_car_fact_sheet.pdf.

Enterprise (2006c). Retrieved 3 March 2006 from http://www.enterprisealive.com/de/about_us/announcements.html.

Forbes (2006). Retrieved 4 March 2006 from http://www.images.forbes.com/lists/2005/21/9R1I.html.

JD Power and Associates (2006). Retrieved 10 March 2006 from http://www.consumercenter.jdpower.com/cc/rd/cc/travel/ratings/rental_cars/index.asp.

Kotler, P., Bowen, J. T., & Makens, J. C. (2006). *Marketing for hospitality and tourism*. New Jersey: Pearson Prentice Hall.

Leonard, C. (2006). *Enterprise in rental car driver's seat*. Associated Press, 29 January 2006.

Company's website: http://www.enterprise.com.

Case

30

Lufthansa Systems: dynamic pricing

Robert Goecke, Harald Heichele and Dieter Westermann

Learning Objectives

- Illustrate the sophisticated systems for revenue management and global price distribution employed by network airlines.
- Explain how non-GDS but website-mediated ticket sales can support new simplified and adaptive pricing strategies.
- Demonstrate that pricing and revenue management of network airlines remain one of the main challenges.
- Explore techniques for pricing and revenue management.

Introduction

Within the last few decades, network airlines have developed very sophisticated systems for revenue management and global price distribution. With the success of low-cost airlines focused on single-leg-optimization and direct, non-GDS but website-mediated ticket sales, new simplified and adaptive pricing strategies appeared. Lufthansa Systems developed a dynamic pricing solution, which enables network carriers to offer competitive prices based on new adaptive pricing systems without giving up all the benefits of network revenue optimization with classic restriction/rule-based tariff systems.

Pricing and Revenue Management of Network Airlines

The main challenge of price and revenue management for scheduled flights is to maximize the profits of a given network of flight connections with given seat capacities. From a short-term perspective, costs of scheduled flights are semi-fixed and a profit maximum can be achieved by maximizing the ticket sales revenue. The key to classic revenue management is discriminatory pricing. For each flight there are different customers with different demands and a different willingness to pay. Discriminatory pricing segments the seat capacity of a flight into different booking classes matching the demands of different customer-types. For each booking class a different price with restricting rules and the number of available seats (availabilities) is defined before ticket sales starts. The right customer segmentation (varying with the season and perceived purpose of trip), a correct prognosis of demand per customer segment and prices matching the willingness to pay as well as the prices of competitors for any given flight are essential for a successful revenue management process as outlined in Figure 30.1 and explained in the following paragraphs.

A. Customer segmentation and tariff definition
   Based on market research information, marginal costs, historical booking data, negotiations with special customers (tour operators, consolidators, corporate customers, etc.) airline price managers define tariffs/booking classes with prices and restricting rules, which optimally match the expected customer segmentation. Seamless access to the relevant data, a variety of computer-based

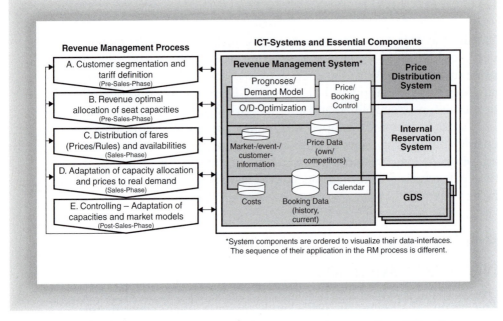

Figure 30.1 Classic revenue management process and supporting ICT systems

statistic analysis methods, cluster algorithms as well as various simulation and decision support tools in a comfortably integrated fare management solution like Lufthansa Systems ProfitLine/ Price (Lufthansa Systems, 2008a) are key requirements for computer supported tariff optimization.

B. Revenue maximizing allocation of available seat capacities
In a next step, (Figure 30.2) the available seats per booking class need to be calculated in a way that a revenue maximum is achieved (Corsten & Stuhlmann 1999; Sterzenbach & Conrady, 2003).

'No shows' need to be compensated by selling 'virtual seats' while overbooking situations need to be avoided at departure. Sophisticated revenue management algorithms based on (EMSR) (expected marginal seat revenue) calculations or stochastic processes deliver revenue maximizing availabilities per booking class from expected customer distributions. Especially for network carriers it is not sufficient to optimize only the revenues of non-stop flights (single-legs). This will lead to sub-optimal profits because in a network most non-stop flights of an airline carry passengers from and to connecting flights of the same airline. The revenue maximum for the whole airline network is different from the single-leg-optimums of the non-stop flights. So-called bid

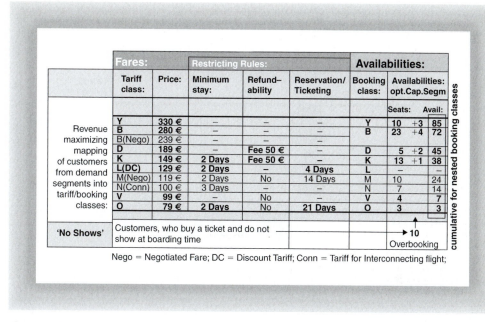

Fares:		Restricting Rules:			Availabilities:		
Tariff class:	Price:	Minimum stay:	Refund–ability	Reservation/ Ticketing	Booking class:	Availabilities: opt.Cap.Segm	
						Seats:	Avail:
Y	330 €	–	–	–	Y	10 +3	85
B	280 €	–	–	–	B	23 +4	72
B(Nego)	239 €	–	–	–			
D	189 €	–	Fee 50 €	–	D	5 +2	45
K	149 €	2 Days	Fee 50 €	–	K	13 +1	38
L(DC)	129 €	2 Days	–	4 Days	L	–	–
M(Nego)	119 €	2 Days	No	14 Days	M	10	24
N(Conn)	100 €	3 Days	–	–	N	7	14
V	99 €	–	No	–	V	4	7
O	79 €	2 Days	No	21 Days	O	3	3

Revenue maximizing mapping of customers from demand segments into tariff/booking classes:

cumulative for nested booking classes

'No Shows' Customers, who buy a ticket and do not show at boarding time → 10

Overbooking

Nego = Negotiated Fare; DC = Discount Tariff; Conn = Tariff for Interconnecting flight;

Figure 30.2 Example for classic booking classes and their availabilities for the economy class of a specific flight as result of classic revenue management

pricing algorithms deliver total-network-revenue maximizing seat availabilities based on simulated competitive biddings of different O/D (origin/destination) pairs for the seats on the relevant flights. Modern revenue management solutions like Lufthansa Systems ProfitLine/Yield modules (Lufthansa Systems, 2008b) support such revenue optimizing capacity allocation methods including their automation).

C. Distribution of fares, availabilities and tickets
Global operating network carriers need efficient ways to distribute their tariffs and rules (air fares) consistently and timely to all sales channels. Air fares are distributed via fare databases of global distribution systems GDS and ticket consolidators. They include both published fares for everybody and unpublished (negotiated) fares for special customer groups (key accounts, tour operators, etc.) with privileged access rights. ICT service providers like Lufthansa Systems offer the complex task of consistently encoding the tariffs and rules. The global collection of fares, their conversion into unique dataformats for the GDS and fare databases and their electronic distribution is offered by ATPCO Air Tariff Publishing Company, a non-profit organization owned by a couple of major airlines. Since

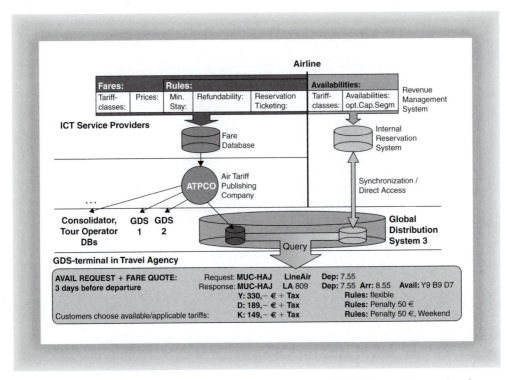

Figure 30.3 Classic distribution paths of fares and availabilities with result of a GDS query

the emergence of the Internet air fares are also distributed directly to the end-customer via the airlines' own websites. To sell tickets globally it is necessary to make seat reservations and to check the availability of unsold seats for specific tariffs of a flight across all distribution channels. It is the historical core functionality of GDSs to provide airlines with different access and synchronization methods to let travel agents globally search airline inventories for available seats, to make reservations and bookings as well as to print the tickets in real time, 24 hours a day. GDSs join the availability information with the tariff information from the fare database (see schematic GDS-terminal view at the bottom of Figure 30.3). The result of a fare quote from a GDS for a special flight is a list of all the offered tariffs together with an indicator of the available seats per booking class. Based on the restricting rules associated with each tariff the customer can choose between all the matching tariffs with available seats. With the information of the PNR (passenger name record) the GDS can enforce the tariff restrictions and triggers the printing of the tickets. OTA (online travel agents) using GDS connections offer the same functionality via direct e-ticket based self-service web-front-ends to end customers.

D. Adaptation to real demand

All price and availability calculations are based on prognoses. With the start of ticket sales (typically 360 days before departure), revenue optimization requires adaptations to real demand. There is a series of checkpoints before departure, where on the basis of sold seats and other market parameters new prognoses are made. Based on these new demand estimations, the booking control system calculates new network-revenue-maximizing allocations of the remaining seats to the booking classes. State of the art revenue management systems provide fully automated forecasting and booking control for all the flights in an airline network: for a specific flight, the closer to the departure date, the smaller are the time intervals between adaptive recalculations. New prognoses and optimal seat allocations are also recalculated, whenever a certain amount of seats is sold.

For flexible demand adaptation special low-price or high-price booking classes exist, which are opened or closed when real demand is lower or higher than expected. As a special feature it is even possible to monitor the booking process with booking corridors: from historical booking data the booking system may calculate lower and upper boundaries for the number of booked seats per booking class for each week or day before departure. If lower or upper boundaries of that booking corridor are exceeded, real demand for a booking class is completely different than predicted and the price management gets an alert.

While the adaptation of availabilities to actual demand is fully automated, price managers still have to monitor the prices of competitors on the market or provide information about special events affecting demand. If price levels or restricting rules of competing connections change, then prices and rules of the own booking classes need to be adapted as far as possible. Because a price correction on one connection has side effects to other connections in the network, price managers should be able to simulate the effects of a price or rule change on the revenues in the whole network, before a tariff change decision is made. It is a special feature of Lufthansa Systems revenue management system to offer integrated simulation tools for this purpose. Tariff change requests from price managers are encoded by service providers like Lufthansa Systems and distributed via the ATPCO price distribution services.

E. Revenue management controlling and capacity adaptation

When the flight departs, it becomes clear how successful the revenue management was. State of the art revenue-management systems provide regular reports with key performance indicators of each flight and the network as well as their development over time. Long lasting under- or over-performance trends indicate either sustainable changes in demand or (seldom) weaknesses of the models. Demand changes can only be addressed by substantial and cost relevant capacity adaptations, for example changes of seat distribution between economy class and business class, exchange of airplanes or changes in the airline network (Echtermeyer, 2000; Sterzenbach & Conrady, 2003). Such capacity adaptations require special impact analysis and simulation methods not only based on revenue maximization but on total profit maximization with different cost scenarios. Analysts play an important role to provide the revenue systems with adequate information to improve the quality of prognoses and optimizations. In this context modern revenue management systems serve as strategic controlling and decision support systems. They also need to be open to modifications of the underlying mathematical models and optimization algorithms as well as their parameters.

Revenue management for network airlines requires a tightly integrated infrastructure of revenue management tools, inventory and fare databases with GDSs. International interlining agreements and IATA regulation led to established tariff encoding standards and tariff distribution procedures.

Pricing and Revenue Management Process of Low-cost Airlines

With the deregulation of the airline industries and the fall of many national airline monopolies the new species of low-cost airlines arose. They focus on highly frequented direct connections and offer economy class flights at very competitive prices. In their efforts to achieve better-cost positions than their competitors some low-cost carriers developed very simplified revenue management and distribution processes (Spann *et al.*, 2005; Becker, 2005) (Figure 30.4).

A. Definition of a great number of unrestricted price levels (step prices)

Instead of a static tariff system with prices and complex restricting rules matching the expected customer segments a fine grained system of many unrestricted price levels or 'step prices' is defined. The term 'unrestricted' in this context does not mean prices without any restrictions but 'undifferentiated' prices. Restrictions like 'advance payment', 'booking change fees', etc. are quite common

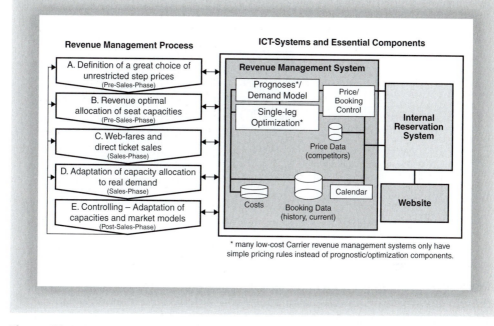

Figure 30.4 Revenue management process and supporting ICT systems of a low-cost airline operating with an adaptive step price system

for low-cost carriers, but in contrast to the old tariff systems here the same restrictions apply to all tickets sold! The price levels start with a very low price and increase in small steps to prices well above the top market price (Figure 30.5). A fine grained system of unrestricted (undifferentiated) step prices allows offering tickets across the whole price spectrum. Ticket sales normally start with the lowest price level. For each price level only a limited number of tickets are available. When all available tickets of a certain price level are sold, the next tickets are offered at the next higher price level. Ticket prices start low and grow with the number of sold seats. The last sold seat is usually the most expensive. Sometimes special sales channels may also offer 'last minute' drop prices as part of special offers or promotions. Depending on the low-cost carriers' company policy, these general rules may be abandoned, when demand is very low or new competition appears. Then prices might fall during adaptation (see section D).

B. Allocation of available seat capacities due to revenue expectations
   Revenue optimization is not based on customer segmentation and discriminatory pricing but on an optimal allocation of

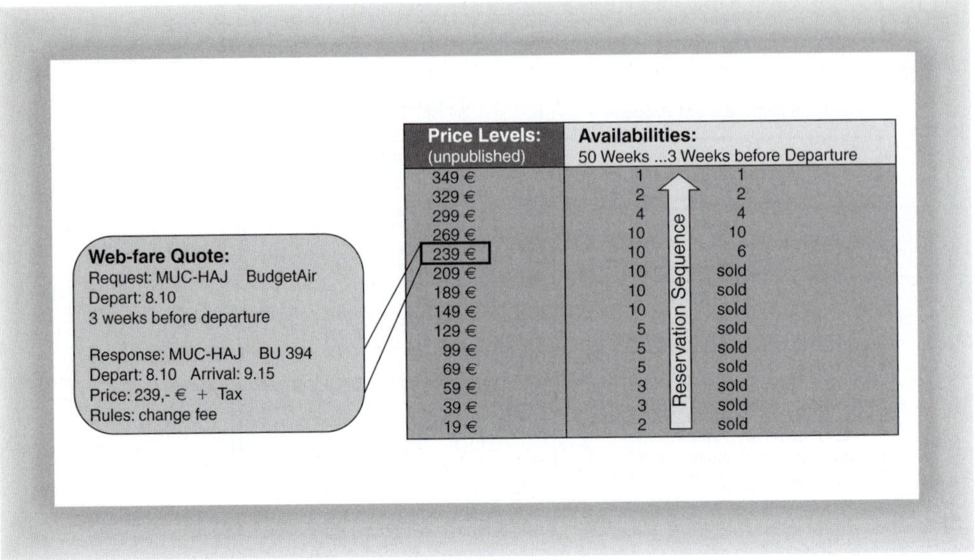

Price Levels: (unpublished)	Availabilities: 50 Weeks ...3 Weeks before Departure	
	1	1
349 €	2	2
329 €	4	4
299 €	10	10
269 €	10	6
239 €	10	sold
209 €	10	sold
189 €	10	sold
149 €	5	sold
129 €	5	sold
99 €	5	sold
69 €	3	sold
59 €	3	sold
39 €	2	sold
19 €		

Web-fare Quote:
Request: MUC-HAJ BudgetAir
Depart: 8.10
3 weeks before departure

Response: MUC-HAJ BU 394
Depart: 8.10 Arrival: 9.15
Price: 239,- € + Tax
Rules: change fee

(Reservation Sequence)

Figure 30.5 Example for a low-cost airline's system of unrestricted step-prices with corresponding availability contingents sold in ascending order. Result of a fare quote

available seats to the price levels. Time series of historic booking data, minimal revenue targets and market research are the inputs to calculate optimal seat availabilities for the different price levels. Because low-cost carriers focus on single-leg connections, no network revenue optimization is necessary. Contrary to the traditional rule-based pricing the price level system has a self-regulating effect without automated booking control. As long as demand is low, the offered prices stay low and vice versa. This represents a real demand and supply market mechanism.

C. Web-fares and direct ticket sales

Most low-cost airlines only use cheap direct sales channels, like their own website and own call centres with e-tickets. When a customer requests a fare quote, only one price level is offered in a 'take it or leave it' way (web-fare). There are no special or negotiated prices. Complex checks of available tariffs, their matching rules and available seats are unnecessary. Data about price levels and availabilities is used only by the own computer reservation system. No price distribution and synchronization of the internal reservation system with GDS or other external fare databases is necessary.

D. Revenue optimization by adaptation of availabilities to real demand

While the price level system has some self-adaptation mechanisms to high or low demands, the maximum revenue of a fully sold flight remains independent from fast or slow ticket sales. Fast ticket sales is an indicator for high demand which could lead to higher revenues if the availabilities are redistributed to higher price levels like it is done by classic automated booking control with booking corridors. This way revenue optimization may also be achieved for the price level system by classic automated booking control adjustments of availabilities to actual demand. But this requires advanced prognostic components to predict 'normal' booking rates, which is uncommon in most low-cost revenue management systems.

The price level system needs no price managers to change the prices according to changes in the market prices. The fine grained price levels spread all possible market prices, and because there are no complex restricting rules, changes in market prices can be adapted solely by the booking control system.

E. Revenue management controlling and capacity adaptation
    The controlling functions and reports are similar to those of classical network carriers. Because network dependencies need not to be analysed and there is no business class, the reporting system and analysis is much simpler. The adaptation of capacities to sustainable demand changes can only be made by a change of the flight schedules, the airplane type, or a change of the connections.

A fine-grained system of price levels with their availabilities filled subsequently with growing ticket sales is less complex and more self-adaptive than the revenue management systems of network carriers. The focus on single-leg optimization and direct ticket sales channels enables low-cost airlines to use much simpler software and system infrastructures with a higher grade of automation. Expensive GDSs and price distribution services are excluded from the value chain. The result is much lower transaction costs of the whole revenue management and distribution system.

Hybrid Revenue Management with Dynamic Pricing

For network airlines, the pricing system of low-cost carriers poses a serious threat. All flights with competing low-cost offerings are priced with procedures that are more complex, more expensive, and less adaptive to demand changes than those of the competition. The first response of some network carriers to this threat was to simplify their tariff systems by eliminating many booking classes and restricting rules for very small customer segments. Most of the available booking classes per flight are now used to offer more fine grained pricing levels with no restricting rules and demand driven dynamically allocated availabilities by the automated booking control system. This approach allows an imitation of the low-cost carrier pricing system for flights with low-cost competition. But the imitation is limited to the standardized 26 price levels (identified by the letters of the alphabet) many of which are still required for business class and negotiated tariffs. While network carriers try to simplify their complex tariff systems, more and more low-cost airlines are faced with growing and more interwoven networks requiring network revenue maximization. To participate with their offerings in the booming market of online travel agencies, low-cost airlines need to distribute their prices and availabilities to OTAs (online travel agencies) via GDS and ticket consolidators. These trends lead to a convergence of the pricing systems of low-cost airlines and network airlines pioneered by Lufthansa Systems with its new dynamic pricing solution ProfitLine/Dynamic Price (Lufthansa Systems, 2008c) (Figure 30.6).

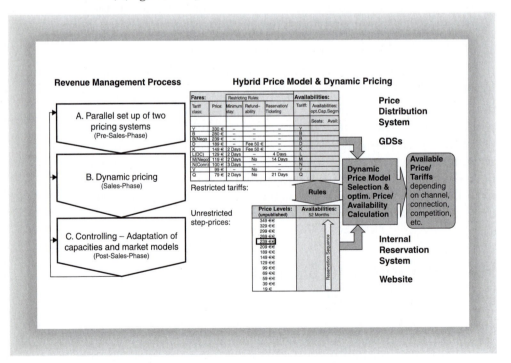

Figure 30.6 Hybrid revenue management based on dynamic pricing of a network airline

A. Parallel setup of two pricing systems

The new Lufthansa Systems dynamic pricing solution enables use of the classic network-oriented price and revenue management system simultaneously with new fine-grained step price systems on the same network of flight connections. For all connections of the airline network the classic tariff system based on customer segmentation and rule restrictions, etc. is used by default. For all connections in the network with competing low-cost offerings additionally to classic tariffs a separate system of fine-grained undifferentiated price levels is initialized. The GDS distribution channel still is limited to 26 (alphabet characters) booking classes. Therefore it is necessary to define how step price systems with more than 26 booking classes are mapped to GDS channels, while at the same time for direct distribution channels the whole fine-grained pricing scheme can be used. Business rules define both the application conditions of each pricing scheme and the channel mappings. Classic tariffs and restrictions are distributed worldwide via GDSs. Low-cost step prices are distributed to the own website or call centre but also via special fare databases of consolidators and GDSs.

B. Dynamic pricing

The key idea of dynamic pricing is that availabilities are not calculated in advance but evaluated in real time for every availability request. It depends on the distribution channel and the specific connection which pricing model is chosen (Becker, 2005).

For each 'availability', 'price', 'sell' or 'cancel' transaction the dynamic pricing system decides whether to use the classic tariff model or the low-cost price levels with respect to the business rules (Figure 30.6).

If the availability request comes from a GDS and asks for a direct flight with no low-cost competition or a non-direct flight with different network segments, then the system will offer rule-matching tariffs with actual availabilities corresponding to the classic pricing model. If the request comes from the website and asks for a direct flight with competing low-cost flights, then the actual price level from the step-pricing model will be offered on a 'take it or leave it' basis.

Many other combinations can be specified. In every case the availability is evaluated in real time, depending on actual revenue expectations, prior bookings and bid prices. For each request the revenue optimal availabilities are calculated individually with respect to the current booking situation. Pre-calculation of availabilities in the pre-sales phase and corrective adaptation of booking or step-price availabilities to real demand are no longer necessary.

C. Revenue management controlling and capacity adaptation
Hybrid pricing offers many new options for price managers to adapt capacities and prices to changing demand patterns in different sales channels. Even the monitoring and comparison of competitor prices could be automated in the future and used to correct the own tariffs or price levels 'in real time' without manual intervention by a price manager. Dynamic pricing therefore requires the most comprehensive reporting and controlling mechanisms because of the high complexity of the hybrid approach. Differentiated analytical tools are needed to identify optimization potentials and weaknesses as well as to understand the effects of the hybrid pricing model on revenues and profits. Of course price managers still need to simulate the effects of price changes and have the possibility to change prices manually. The price changes are distributed to all channels by multi-channel price distribution services.

While dynamic pricing is not reducing the complexity of revenue management, it enables network carriers to compete with the new pricing strategies of low-cost airlines. For low-cost carriers, dynamic pricing offers a migration path to network-based revenue optimization and gives them access to classic GDS-based distribution channels.

The possibility to design channel-specific pricing models and to combine them with network revenue maximizing capacity allocation opens new horizons for airline revenue management.

Synopsis and Future Perspectives

The evolution from classic tariff systems based on discriminatory pricing with restricting rules via self-adapting step-price systems to new hybrid dynamic pricing is also an evolution from static pricing over flexible pricing to dynamic pricing.

Besides the discussed strategic reasons for this evolution it is also enabled by technological innovations; the GDSs were enablers for the global distribution of static tariff systems and the adaptation of booking class availabilities to actual demand by automated booking control. The Internet and the WWW were enablers for direct e-ticket sales over the website and allowed flexible pricing with demand driven changes from one price level to another in real time. Dynamic pricing additionally allows automated real time decisions about the relevant pricing model on each individual customer request and a revenue maximizing allocation of seat capacities across different sales channels. It is the key technology for more advanced channel-specific and customer-individual pricing strategies of the future.

Key Conclusions

- The key to classic revenue management is discriminatory pricing. For each flight there are different customers with different demands and different willingness to pay. Discriminatory pricing segments the seat capacity of a flight into different booking classes matching the demands of different customer types.
- For each booking class a different price with restricting rules and the number of available seats (availabilities) is defined before ticket sales starts.
- A correct prognosis of demand per customer segment and prices matching the willingness to pay as well as the prices of competitors for any given flight are essential.
- Lufthansa Systems developed a dynamic pricing solution that enables network carriers to offer competitive prices based on new adaptive pricing systems without giving up all the benefits of network revenue optimization with classic restriction/rule-based tariff systems.

Review and Discussion Questions

- How can Lufthansa integrate its systems towards achieving competitive advantage?
- What is the principle of revenue management for airlines?
- What is the difference between no-frills and scheduled airlines as far as pricing methods are concerned?

References and Further Reading

Becker, S. (2005). Rechnen als Waffe. *Touristik Report*, 4, 8–11.

Corsten, H., & Stuhlmann, H. (1999). Yield Management als Ansatzpunkt für die kapazitätsgestaltung von Dienstleistungs unternehmungen. In: Corsten, H., & Schneider, H. (Eds.); Wettbewerbsfaktor Dienstleistung. Munich: Vahlen Verlag, 79–107.

Echtermeyer, K. (2000). *Daten für die Netzplanung im Luftverkehr*. Presentation for the IVT Seminar 'Optimierung von Netzen und Angeboten'. ETH Zürich.

Lufthansa Systems (2008a). *ProfitLine/Price – The Fare Management Solution*. (Web-)Brochure, Keisterbach.

Lufthansa Systems (2008b). *ProfitLine/Yield – The Revenue Management Solution*. (Web-)Brochure, Keisterbach.

Lufthansa Systems (2008c). *ProfitLine/Dynamic Pricing – The Smart Way to Real-Time Optimization*. (Web-)Brochure, Keisterbach. Yield – Dynamic Price Engine.

Spann, M., Klein, J., Makhlouf, K., & Bernhard, M. (2005). Interaktive Preismaßnahmen bei Low-Cost-Fluglinien. *ZfB Zeitschrift für Betriebswirtschaft*, 75, 53–77.

Sterzenbach, R., & Conrady, R. 2003). *Luftverkehr. Betriebswirtschaftliches Lehr- und Handbuch*. 3rd revised and extended edition. Munich, Vienna: Oldenbourg Verlag.

Company's website: http://www.lufthansa-systems.com.

Conclusion of Transportation Section

Transportation is a core element of the tourist value-added chain, since the change of location is a defining feature of tourism. Consequently transportation is a 'conditio sine qua non' for a journey. As early as in the 1960s, when the transportation industry started to increase in size and capacity it was recognized mainly in the airline industry that there was a need to restructure internal processes. The use of technology from back then could support the efficiency, operational and strategic management as well as revenue management and cost control.

The proliferation of sophisticated computerized systems and the Internet in particular has revolutionized internal operations of transportation, collaboration with stakeholders and interfaces with consumers. Airlines in particular have profited from the rapid spread of the Internet, since the direct distribution via the Internet is less expensive than via GDSs. It is increasingly evident that transportation organizations aim to develop direct relationships with their clientele to increase interactivity and manage distribution costs. They also use ICTs strategically to manage relationships with collaborators and other players in the marketplace.

Part Five

Information communication technology systems
Roman Egger
Dimitrios Buhalis

Introduction

The Internet economy, also known as the New Economy or Network Economy, is increasingly changing the post-industrial economic structures of our society, leading to new interconnections with impacts on the social, political, economic and business management levels. The new economic rules can be derived from three main characteristics of the Internet, namely: digitization, networking and globalization (Wirtz, 2001). The theses of the Internet economy described below by Zerdick (2001) have also had a lasting effect on tourism:

- Digitization of value creation covers all fields of the economy.
- Mass customization is becoming the key factor of the networked economy.
- Traditional value creation chains are eroding and leave their space to dynamic networks.
- The battle for attention is becoming the decisive competitive arena.
- New complex value creation networks require simultaneous competition and cooperation.
- Mass markets can be individualized by simultaneous cost reduction and differentiation strategies.
- Electronic commerce becomes the norm and displaces physical distribution.
- Digitization facilitates product and price differentiation.
- Previous regulation models are becoming obsolete.

The increase in capacity, nanotechnologies and standardization, combined with the reduction of ICT costs led to a rapid market penetration by the new media. In particular, the proliferation of the Internet has enabled global network connections. Hence individuals and organizations have access to information otherwise not available. However, the Internet does not create any completely new economic rules. Instead, it leads to a new combinations and possibly to an accentuation of individual rules (Zerdick, 2001).

The tourism product is characterized by a high degree of complexity and is mostly created by a large number of actors. In order to be able to adopt a targeted approach to the timely communication and processing of the masses of information involved in tourism, the use of ICTs between the transaction participants is indispensible. However, the term ICT covers not only the corres-ponding hardware and software, but also groupware, netware and the intellectual capacity (humanware) necessary for the development, programming and maintenance of the corresponding systems (Buhalis, 2003). These new technologies have a far-reachingeffect on the tourism industry as a whole, and for enterprises constitute an innovation in the field of strategic management, optimized process design and the development of competitive products (Buhalis & Egger, 2006).

In general, tourism can look back on a long tradition in terms of information technology. The 1970s saw the introduction of CRS (computer reservation systems) the 1980s brought the GDS global distribution systems and the 1990s the Internet. Hardly any other trade sector can look back on such a long and successful history in connection with the information and communication technologies. Although in comparison with other trade sectors tourism has a relatively low innovation, this is counterbalanced by ICTs, in particular. Information technologies are fundamentally enablers of the entire range of business functions and processes in tourism. Thus they themselves are not the solution but rather the necessary tool to solve a problem, realize opportunities as well as the enablersfor operational and strategic management. The drastic increase in the mass of information to be processed over the last decades required the development of appropriate solutions in the tourism sector long before the triumph of the Internet. The objective was to manage the inventory and to ensure the exchange of data between suppliers and intermediaries. In this respect, GDSs are amongst the ICT pioneers in the tourism sector (Case 37: Amadeus – Evolution of GDS). The GDSs that were the byproduct of the airlines' CRSs today constitute the information infrastructure for the global marketing of a wide range of tourism services. Nowadays the world market is shared between three major GDSs namely: Amadeus, Sabre, and Travelport (Worldspan and Galileo). The changes in the distribution of tourism services caused by the Internet, and in particular the trend towards direct marketing and the increase of the low-cost sector, require an ongoing reorientation and positioning together with the development of sustainable business models (Case 38: Amadeus – Global Distribution System's new paradigm). Switch companies emerged in order to ensure interconnectivity between the CRSs of the hotel chains and the GDSs. These companies constitute a reservation interface and allow a certain degree of interoperability between systems. For hotel operations, the link to a switch system involves a solution that is technically simple and inexpensive, compared to the link to the variety of different GDS systems that would otherwise be necessary. The appearance of the switch companies has also enabled hotel CRSs to market their services simply by means of GDSs (Case 39: Pegasus Solutions).

In particular the breakthrough by the Internet has led to a fundamental change in the entire travel sector over the last few years, in turn resulting in far-reaching restructuring along the entire value creation chain. The causes of the changes are however not clearly identifiable. While ICTs generate new processes in the tourism industry and facilitate existing processes, the tourism industry's rapid growth increases the demands made of ICT, which in turn boosts the dynamism of the trade to a decisive extent (Buhalis & Egger, 2006). Intranets and extranets are mainly used for company-internal communication and communication with authorized partners, whilst technology-empowered information exchange with customers takes place primarily via the Internet. Users acquire access to an unbelievable amount of information and offers. Direct access to the product databases of the providers allows the customer to carry out professional information searches and processing, which according to Regele and Schmücker (1998) can be regarded as a democratization of what were once proprietary services. In addition, new technologies such as recommender systems are coming onto the market to support consumers in their decision-making processes (Case 31: Trip@dvice Technology). The increase in direct marketing makes it necessary for businesses to monitor the ever-changing needs of their customers and subsequently to be able to meet the challenges made (Case 32: The Green Card). At the same time, customer loyalty measures must be developed in order to establish a longer-term relationship between the business and the guest.

Information and communication technologies support tourism suppliers and intermediaries at the structural, operational and strategic levels, and if used correctly, can lead to an increased competitiveness that has huge effects on the existence of an enterprise. Table PV.1 sets out an overview of the most important strategic and operative key functions of ICTs.

Table PV.1 Tourism key functions of ICT

Strategic functions

- Increasing organizational efficiency and effectiveness
- Improving quality and service performance
- Strategic market and product research
- Increased competitiveness
- Penetration of, and expansion in, existing and new markets
- Differentiation in the product and market segments
- Creation of new tourist product combinations
- Personalization and mass customization of the services, combined with value increase at all product levels
- Cost reduction and obtaining competitive advantages (financial advantages)
- Achieving time-related competitive advantages by increasing capacity
- Restructuring the business processes and rationalization of operational activities
- Application of new and innovative business practices
- Long-term competitive out-performance
- Development of new strategic partnerships

Operational functions

- Optimized information distribution and reservation processes
- International tourist management and marketing
- Simplification of relationships between service provider – intermediary – customer
- Production and marketing of tourism products
- Organization, management and monitoring of the tourism business
- Front office: reservations, check-in, invoice, communication
- Back office: bookkeeping, wage settlement, purchasing, administration
- Reduction of reaction times in unforeseeable situations
- Increase of customer service and communication with customers and partners
- Dynamic yield management and adjustment of price and capacities
- Performance monitoring and the integration of feedback mechanisms
- Monitoring and administration

Source: Buhalis and Egger (2006)

The following section also addresses several cases dealing with management support systems. These are process-oriented solutions which achieve or should achieve desired or planned results through active involvement, making use of resources. A benchmarking solution (Case 33: CheckEffect), an enquiry management solution for destinations (Case 36: Digital Tourism Assistant) and a travel wholesale management system (Case 35: Tourism Technology) are presented. In conclusion, ICT systems also support the evaluation and success-assessment of planned activities (Case 34: Day Trip Indicator).

Nowadays, it would be impossible to maintain the tourism system without sophisticated ICT solutions. The dynamism of the market, ever-changing customer needs and new technological developments require and encourage the on-going developments of ICT systems. However, it should not be forgotten that new technologies can only be regarded as enablers that take on a supporting function, while effective and problem-solution-focused action continues to remain dependent on management decisions.

References

Buhalis, D. (2003). *eTourism: Information technologies for strategic tourism management*. Harlow: Pearson Higher Education.

Buhalis, D., & Egger, R. (2006). Informations- und Kommunikationstechnologien als Mittel zur Prozess- und Produktinnovation für den Unternehmer. In B. Pikkemaat, & M. Peters (Eds.), *Innovationen im Tourismus* (pp. 163–176). Berlin: ESV-Verlag.

Regele, U., & Schmücker, D. (1998). Vertriebspolitk im Tourismus. In G. Haedrich (Ed.), *Tourismus-Management: Tourismus-Marketing und Fremdenverkehrsplanung* (pp. 405–445). Berlin: de Gruyter.

Wirtz, B. (2000). *Electronic business*. Wiesbaden: Gablers Verlag.

Zerdick, A., Picot, A., & Schrape, K. (2001). Die *Internet-Ökonomie. Strategien für die digitale Wirtschaft*. Springer Verlag.

31

eCTRL Solutions: Trip@dvice technology

Francesco Ricci and Adriano Venturini

Learning Objectives

- Demonstrate that talking to a customer through the web and offering services and products listed in an electronic catalogue containing thousands of items is not an easy task.
- Explain that it is difficult for the traveller to find the right information related to destinations and tourism services he/she may like.
- Illustrate that recommendation technologies aim to guide more effectively customers in the selection of their preferred tourist products.
- Explain the Trip@dvice as a recommendation technology explicitly designed for the tourism domain.

Introduction and Company Development

The Internet has made it possible for destination management organizations (DMO), travel services suppliers and intermediaries to reach directly their customers, to talk with them and offer their proposals. But talking to a customer through the web and offering services and products listed in an electronic catalogue containing thousands of items is not an easy task. Hence, it is difficult for traveller to find the right information related to destinations and tourism services she may like. Recommendation technologies have been proposed in the last years to guide customers more effectively in the selection of their preferred tourist products. These technologies are being integrated in websites of tour operators, travel agencies and DMOs to support travellers in the selection of travel destinations or travel products (e.g. events, attractions, flights, hotels).

Trip@dvice (Ricci *et al.*, 2006) is a recommendation technology explicitly designed for the tourism domain. It has been developed at the eCommerce and Tourism Research Laboratory of ITC-irst, Trento, Italy, a research centre with more than 300 researchers focusing on artificial intelligence and micro electronic. From 2000 to 2005 Trip@dvice has been designed and developed in a national project (CARITRO project, founded by the CARITRO local bank foundation) and an international project (Dietorecs, IST project of the 5th EU framework programme).

In 2005, after some empirical evaluations, demonstrating that the technology was effective (Zins *et al.*, 2006), and a careful analysis of the market demand, ITC-irst and some of the researchers who developed Trip@dvice started up a new company, eCTRL Solutions, dedicated to further improve, commercialize and support this recommendation technology.

eCTRL Solutions' end customers are tourism organizations that want to develop tourism portals capable of interacting with the portal visitors in a personalized way, helping them to find the tourist products and services most suited for their needs.

Trip@dvice

Trip@dvice is a flexible software tool that can be integrated into existing tourism portals to support the user in her trip definition tasks. The tool allows the portal visitor to put together a tailored travel package, choosing a hotel, places to visit, things to do or activities to attend. The user can choose trip components that make up the package in the order he or she wants. Advanced recommendation technologies explicitly designed for the tourism domain have been implemented to identify and recommend in a personalized way a reasonable number of products and services that meet the user's needs.

Thanks to the Interactive Query Management technology incorporated in Trip@dvice, the system can help the user to formulate travel requests. If the request can't be satisfied because few or too many products can be identified, Trip@dvice, like a real travel agent, guides the user toward the best solution by proposing those minimal changes to the requests which make it satisfiable.

Personalized recommendations are provided based on:

- Travel preferences and limitations that the user enters, such as budget, place of origin, travel period and more (Figure 31.1).
- Previous travels (his own and other people's) that match similar requirements.

Figure 31.1 Specifying travel preferences
Source: http://www.veneto.to

Tourist organizations integrating recommendation and personalization technologies gain several advantages. Portal visitors can more easily find the tourist products and services they are looking for, increasing their satisfaction while interacting with the system. In Trip@dvice, personalized and innovative search tools enable users with different decisional styles to find the products they are looking for (Fesenmaier *et al.*, 2003). The results are web portals which increase their visitors' loyalties, simplify the buying process, and improve the looker to booker conversion rate. In addition, the system records the user choices and preferences to base its recommendations. These data are available to tourist organizations to analyse customers' behaviour for their business and market analysis.

Even if there are several large companies active in the customer relationship management (CRM) sector and web personalization technologies (e.g. BroadVision, E.piphany and Vignette), none are as dedicated to the tourism sector than Trip@dvice.

Personalization technologies in tourism have been implemented by some of the largest online travel agencies. They have developed their own technologies to gain competitive advantages on their direct competitors. Thus, they do not (and are not interested to) commercialize the developed technology.

Trip@dvice fills this gap, allowing tourism organizations, which cannot afford large research investments, to integrate advanced personalization technologies explicitly dedicated to the tourism sector in their tourism portals.

Business Model

eCTRL Solutions is a technology provider. It develops personalization technologies and necessary services to integrate them in tourism websites. eCTRL Solutions' main customers are destination management organizations interested in providing personalized contents and travel planning support to their portal visitors. Trip@dvice has been already chosen by several tourism organizations for their tourism portals. For example, VisitEurope.com is the e-marketing tool of the European Travel Commission to promote Europe as a tourism destination. It provides the travel planner tool, a specific Trip@dvice component that supports their world-wide and heterogeneous tourism visitors in their information search process (Figure 31.2). The Italian Veneto region has also integrated the Trip@dvice travel planning and recommendation component in its official tourism web portal (www.veneto.to). The Austrian National Tourism Board is developing a recommender tool based

Figure 31.2 Personalized recommendations
Source: http://www.visiteurope.com

on Trip@dvice for the austria.info portal. The Italian province of Biella is developing a new web portal providing personalization and recommendation functionally supported by Trip@dvice.

Stakeholders of eCTRL Solutions are, first of all, the partners who first studied and developed the product and then founded the company to commercialize the technology. Then, ITC-irst, the research institute where the technology has been studied and initially developed, and the Trentino local government, which supported research and technological innovation in travel and tourism, encouraged this initiative. eCTRL Solutions is an example of how research investments, when addressing the right sectors and focusing on applied research, can create new business and employment opportunities for the community; one of the primary goal of the Trentino Province research efforts.

Trip@dvice is sold in two ways. As provision of technology, thus on a software licence basis, plus services required to customize and maintain the technology. Alternatively, eCTRL Solutions provides Trip@dvice as ASP (application service provider), on a per-year service licence.

eCTRL also provides the necessary services for analysing the specific personalization issue and adapting the data structure and user interface to customer needs. Additional services are provided to analyse the data acquired by the system while it is used by the portal visitors and provide information to tourism organizations about tourist behaviours, their preferences and related choices.

Research and development resources are invested to simplify the integration of the recommendation component in the overall website, improving the quality of recommendations and reducing the maintenance cost to increase the share of potential customers. Another model suited for Trip@dvice technology which is likely to be adopted in the future (mainly for eTravel agency and tour operators) is the brokerage model (Rabanser & Ricci, 2005), where a fee for each transaction enabled by Trip@dvice is charged to the tourist organization exploiting the service.

Technological and Business Innovation

The main technological innovation of Trip@dvice is the capability to learn, directly from the users, the knowledge required to make reliable recommendations. By exploiting and adapting the case-based reasoning methodology (Ricci *et al.*, 2006), it learns from the same user experiences, the relationships between the user travel preferences and the products to be chosen and identifies the products to be recommended according to the users' needs and sought benefits. This is particularly important for the travel sector, where decision behaviour models, which relate users' preferences and tourist products, are still to be well understood and are still subject of academic research.

From the business side, Trip@dvice is an innovative web technology that can be integrated in existing tourism portals, extending without replacing the existing web infrastructure, thus allowing the preservation of the investment already done for the web presence.

To develop and market this kind of technology, several issues should be faced. From the technological point of view, the complexity of the tourism domain should be addressed. It is well known that supporting travellers in their decision process is challenging. Tourism data modelling is complex and not standardized, people's decisions depend on a large set of variables which cannot easily be matched on tourism data (Ricci, 2002). Research on tourism behaviour and recommendation technologies should continue to enhance the Trip@dvice performance.

From the software development point of view, a tool which can be easily integrated in existing portals requires continuous updates to reflect the new approaches and techniques which are introduced at a very fast pace in the field of software engineering and web architectures.

From the business point of view, often it is difficult to market this kind of technology to people not fully aware of the potential impact of recommendation and personalization technologies and to convince them that these technologies are already available and effective (not just research studies) and that they can really improve their business. The advantages of adopting personalization technologies should be made clear in a simple and comprehensible way also for non-experts. In addition, the integration of this technology in existing websites requires interacting with the technology providers that developed the portal. These relationships are not always easy because they could consider eCTRL a potential competitor.

Key Challenges for the Future

Being a company active in a highly technological innovation field is challenging in general. The type of product we are addressing is even more complex. In fact, innovation is required in two main fields, which are related but require different type of knowledge. From one side, the basic algorithms underlying the Trip@dvice technology should be steadily improved. Hence expertise in Artificial Intelligence is needed. New algorithms and solutions should be studied, developed and evaluated. From the other side, having a tool which can easily cooperate with existing web portals, exchange information, and can be easily plugged into existing systems, requires deep knowledge of the most advanced techniques in software architecture and developments. Technical people in the company should stay updated on both the areas. The cooperation with research laboratories and universities helps us to improve the knowledge in these fields.

eCTRL Solutions is a young and still small company (€200,000 turnover estimated for 2006). But there is an increasing interest in its solutions and competences. The challenge is to be able to grow at a sustainable pace, and this can be done only correctly balancing economical and human resources. New human resources entering in the company (both commercial and technician) should be trained to acquire the required competences. Considering the investment that this represents for the company, the personnel selection and acquisition should be carefully analysed and performed with proper medium term budget availability.

Conclusion and the Future of the Company

The eCTRL goal is to integrate this technology in the major national and regional destination management portals. Trip@dvice was created and studied initially for this kind of portals and its effectiveness has been demonstrated. But it is suited also for other tourism areas, like online booking engines, online travel agencies and major tour operators, where Trip@dvice can be fully exploited.

To sustain the growth, in the short-term future other sectors (culture, eGovernment, eLearning) could benefit from Trip@dvice recommendation technologies as well. In fact, the basic approach (exploiting choices that other users make in similar situations), which is used now to identify tourism products and services suitable for a given trip goal, could be adopted. For example in an eGovernment portal it can be used to help citizens to find the documents and services useful to achieve a given goal or manage a situation (e.g. adopt a child or open a new business).

New technologies should be considered both in the software engineering (user interface design, data integration and harmonization, application integration) and artificial intelligence (user modelling, machine learning, human computer interaction) areas to be able to deliver more updated solutions which meet the desires of tourists and the needs of tourist organizations.

Key Conclusions

- Trip@dvice is a flexible software tool that can be integrated in existing tourism portals to support the user in her trip definition tasks.
- The tool allows the portal visitor to put together a tailored travel package, choosing a hotel, places to visit, things to do or activities to practice. The user can choose trip components that make up the package in the order he or she wants.
- Advanced recommendation technologies explicitly designed for the tourism domain have been implemented to identify and recommend in a personalized way a reasonable number of products and services that meet the user's needs.
- The main technological innovation of Trip@dvice is the capability to learn, directly from the users, the knowledge required to make reliable recommendations.

Review and Discussion Questions

- How can recommender systems be used towards achieving competitive advantage?
- What are the key challenges of recommender systems?
- Which industry players would benefit from the application of Trip@dvice?

References and Further Reading

Fesenmaier, D.R., Ricci, F., Schaumlechner, E., Wöber, K.W., & Zanella, C. (2003). DIETORECS: Travel advisory for multiple decision styles. In A.J. Frew, M. Hitz, & P. O'Connor (Eds.), *Information and communication technologies in tourism. ENTER 2003. Proceedings of the International Conference in Helsinki, Finland* (pp. 232–241). Vienna-New York: Springer.

Rabanser, U., & Ricci, F. (2005). Recommender systems: Do they have a viable business model in e-tourism? In A.J. Frew (Ed.), *Information and communication technologies in tourism. ENTER 2005. Proceedings of the International Conference in Innsbruck, Austria* (pp. 160–171). Vienna-New York: Springer.

Ricci, F. (2002). Travel recommender systems. *IEEE Intelligent Systems*, 17 (6), 55–57.

Ricci, F., Cavada, D., Mirzadeh, N., & Venturini, A. (2006). Case-based travel recommendations. In D.R. Fesenmaier, H. Werthner, & K.W. Wober (Eds.), *Destination recommendation systems: Behavioural foundations and applications* (pp. 67–93). Wallingford: CABI Publishing.

Venturini, A., & Ricci, F. (2006). Applying Trip@dvice recommendation technology to http://www.visiteurope.com. In *Proceedings of the 17th European Conference on Artificial Intelligence* [ECAI 2006]. Italy: Riva del Garda.

Zins, A.H., & Bauernfeind, U. (2006). Evaluating travel recommender systems: A case study of Dietorecs. In D.R. Fesenmaier, H. Werthner, & K. W. Wober (Eds.), *Destination recommendation systems: Behavioural foundations and applications* (pp. 240–256). Wallingford: CABI Publishing.

Company's website: http://tripadvice.itc.it.

32

The Green Card (Targeta Verda): a tourist card for the Balearic Islands

Antonio Guevara and Jose L. Caro

Learning Objectives

- Demonstrate that the Targeta Verda is a system based on the TurisCard® platform which enables both tourists and residents to make use of tourist services.
- Explain that the card enables the platform managers to obtain information about the demand profile of tourists and residents.
- Illustrate the technological infrastructure required for operating the Targeta Verda.
- Explore the operational system for the Targeta Verda and the business modelling.

Introduction and Company Development

The Green Card (Targeta Verda) is an initiative of the Foundation for the Sustainable Development of the Balearic Islands. Its purpose is to promote ecological initiatives benefiting the image of the islands as a sustainable tourist destination, provide incentives for environmental protection and the ongoing improvement of nature parks and public estates. The objective is to obtain resources for new infrastructures to support the environmental, historic and cultural heritage of the islands, and to foster the development of educational programmes.

The use of the Green Card provides a series of advantages and discounts in visits to cultural centres, attractions, points of tourist interest, nature areas and leisure and sports facilities for tourists and residents.

Main Products/Offerings and Value Added

The Targeta Verda is a system based on the TurisCard® platform which enables both tourists and residents to make use of tourist services and enables the platform managers to obtain information about the demand profile of tourists and residents.

The following types of product or service form part of the basic offer:

- *Minutes of voice transmission*: When the tourist buys the card he/she obtains a credit from a national operator for 15 minutes of telephone calls. Since the foundation is a non-profit organization, this is equivalent to the total price of the card, so the tourist does not lose money even if none of the other services are used.
- *Discounts*: The card holder can also obtain a series of different discounts:
  - Discounts on tickets to associated establishments: The card holder obtains a reduction in the price of the entry fee to these establishments, such as museum tickets.
  - Consumer discounts: When shopping or consuming products from associated establishments, such as parking discounts, for instance.

- The main benefits for the associated centres are:
  - The associated centres are included in the tourist circuit.
  - The associated centres are included in an excellence category plan in Balear govern initiative.
  - A reduction of the ecotasa (ecological tax in the islands).

The system starts as soon as someone buys a card distributed along the islands at an official tourist bureau, tourist information points, associated hotels, travel agencies, rent-a-car, airport, etc. The Green Card has to be activated using a call-centre, via the web or automatically in the first use of any associated centre's service (see Figure 32.1), providing some information such as nationality, type of visit, duration of visit, etc. No personal data is required. Subsequently, the card is used for different purposes. The system monitors its use and thus obtains the user's profile and applies statistical techniques to the information in order to study the most visited resources; relate the promotion of resources to the number of visits; identify the types of product consumed by tourists; relate the number of visits to a resource to the visitor's nationality; and much more. This analysis informs the authorities of the types of service to be promoted and the tourist profiles to be addressed.

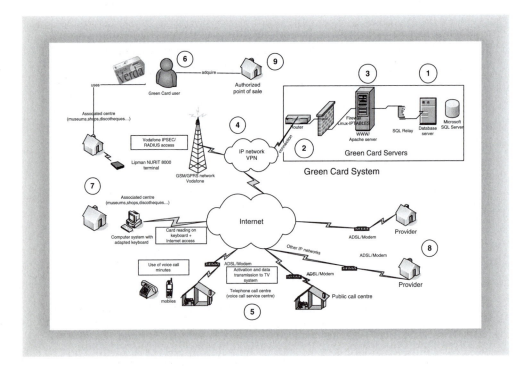

Figure 32.1 Technological model

Business Model

The business model is open and uses ubiquitous computing. It enables card acquisition and activation through different devices: Call centre, Internet or directly in an associated centre upon use. In this respect, there is a difference between a resident card and a tourist card. The former has a duration of 1 year after purchase and three modalities: individual, family or business. It is also compulsory to fill in a form with the resident's personal data. The tourist card lasts for 15 days and does not need this information for activation.

The following agents are involved in the system's business model:

- *Green card system* (Figure 32.1 – 1, 2, 3, 4): The central system is responsible for ensuring that the cards work properly, solving problems, keeping statistical control, formalizing agreements, etc.
- *Green card system providers* (Figure 32.1 – 8): Companies responsible for providing the material and support for the green card system. The most important is the supplier of PET (polyethylene + terephthalate, ecological materials) cards, responsible for their manufacturing and for recording information on their magnetic strips.
- *Centres associated to the green card system* (Figure 32.1 – 7): They provide users with services. These centres have previously signed agreements with the green card system, defining the conditions and the advantages for card holders. They include the telephone operator who controls the use of the card for voice calls.
- *User* (Figure 32.1 – 6): The tourist or resident who buys and benefits from a card.
- *Points of sale* (Figure 32.1 – 9): Associated centres responsible for distributing green cards to users. They include hotels, tour operators, airlines, tourist offices and the associated centres themselves.
- *Call centres* (Figure 32.1 – 5): Responsible for activations and problem-solving. There are two in this model; the operator controlling the minutes of voice calls (telephone operator) and the call centre assistance, which solves problems related to the cards.

The information captured by the system can be classified into the following processes:

- In the activation process some fundamental data like nationality, language, etc. is acquired.

- By using the card, the system acquires information about the preferences of the tourists, because the use services related to associate centres.
- In the last process if the tourist wants to change the points, acquired using the Green Card to gifts the system can obtain the personal data.

The system is configured as a eCRM (electronic customer relationship management) model applied to a destination, managing tourist and resident relations and administering the information generated as they interact with the system.

Technological and Business Innovation

The green card system can be supported by a magnetic strip card or a chip card, especially encoded for use. All the services are structures around the set of green card servers.

Figure 32.2 shows the main components of the service:

- *Database*: Used to store the fundamental data about the system function and Green Card data about the use of the services by the tourist. It is implemented in MS SQL Server, responsible for storing transactions and recording all the cards in the system.
- *Communication systems and firewall*: Responsible for isolating basic data and internally communicating with the database.
- *Green card application*: It is used to manage the Green Card systems and it is capable of administering the system, obtaining the reports required by the associated centres and tourist managers.
- *External communication systems*: Used to connect the associated centres (museums, shops, etc.) to the Green Card system. The systems are based, on the one hand, on RADIUS to control the access of the GPRS (general packet radio service) terminals in each associated centre and access to the IP network via a virtual private network (VPN) to control the access of users, GPRS terminals and system administration.

As for use, the tourist or resident can access the associated centres, who can also activate the card by GPRS connection systems. The centres that do not have a wireless GPRS connection can complete this transaction via the Internet. Each time a card holder benefits from one of their services, it is recorded in the database, so the system managers can obtain information about the tourist's profile and preferences.

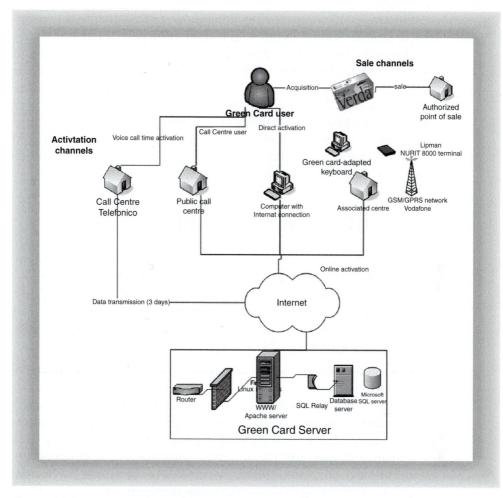

Figure 32.2 Green card use channels

Key Challenges for the Future

The green card system has great future potential. Other regions in Spain have started to use it and one example is the Sustainable Canary Islands Card. The TurisCard® platform is working on increasing the scope of application of the platform.

The most important future project are the customized Green Card project. This version enables the tourist to choose the resources he/she demands. An example for this use would be a congress that can customize both its appearance and the tourist services provided to the card user. Other interesting project is the increasing the scope of the card for citizens: use of public transport, identification, electronic wallet, personal certificate/code storage, tax payment, etc.

Finally, concerning the technological environment, the green card system would improve the data communication system by adapting to the new Universal Mobile Telecommunications Systems (3G) (UTMS) platform. This adaptation considerably increases transmission speed and with the indistinct use of dataphones connected to the GPRS network and mobile devices of any kind. For the card features, it is important to consider increasing the possibilities by using a mixed solution based on a memory chip and magnetic band. This idea is essential for the resident card, which requires greater security and protection.

The Future of the Company

This project has been possible thanks to the collaboration of organizations, companies and public authorities with the foundation for the sustainable development of the Balearic Islands. Although the card has been modestly used in the first few months, the project was designed as a system to obtain results in the medium and long term.

The most desired effects will be:

- A reduction in production costs per card, supporting sustainable development.
- Enable the creation of a tourist observatory issuing recommendations on user demand profiles, so that managers and entrepreneurs can prepare tourist forecasts and plans. This model will instigate the internal competitiveness between the different destination enterprises and will stimulate the tourist product offer in comparison to other destinations.

Key Conclusions

- The Targeta Verda is a system based on the TurisCard® platform which enables both tourists and residents to make use of tourist services as it enables the platform managers to obtain information about the demand profile of tourists and residents.
- The business model is open and uses ubiquitous computing. It enables card acquisition and activation through different devices: call centres, Internet or directly in an associated centre upon use.
- Where the technological environment is concerned, the green card system would be able to improve the data communication system by adapting to the new UTMS (3G) platform.

Review and Discussion Questions

- What are the key benefits of the Targeta Verda?
- How can the card include more value-added services?
- How can mobile technologies make the Targeta Verda more interactive and useful?

Further Reading

Caro, J.L., Carillo, A., Aguayo, A., Gálvez, S., & Guevara, A. (2002). CRM techniques for analyzing client profiles in tourism promotion websites. In K.W. Wöber, A.J. Frew, & M. Hitz (Eds.), *Information and communication technologies in tourism. ENTER 2002. Proceedings of the International Conference in Innsbruck, Austria* (pp. 68–76). Vienna, New York: Springer.

Buhalis, D. (2000). Marketing the competitive destination of the future. *Tourism Management*, 21 (1), 97–116.

Dyché, J. (2001). *The CRM handbook: A business guide to customer relationship management*. Boston: Addison-Wesley.

Fyall, A., Callod, C., & Edwards, B. (2003). Relationship marketing, the challenge for destinations. *Annals of Tourism Research*, 30 (1), 644–659.

Sheth, J., & Parvatiyar, A. (2000). *Handbook of relationship marketing*. Thousand Oaks: Sage Publications.

Amichotels: http://www.amic-hotels-mallorca.com/default. asp? idprod=23336&idcatpad=18708&lang=ES.

Ibizahotelsguide.com: http://www.ibizahotelsguide.com/content/tarjeta-verde/es/ibiza-tarjeta-verde.html.

Company's website (Tarjeta Verde): http://www.tarjetaverda. com.

33

CheckEffect: Benchmarking e-Marketing performance

Roman Egger and Michael Mrazek

Learning Objectives

- Demonstrate how all Austrian service providers were urged to adapt to the age of the Internet.
- Explain that all service providers, including small and medium-sized enterprises, must conduct professional Internet marketing.
- Illustrate how hoteliers can face the challenge of online marketing.

Introduction

The Austrian tourism industry is primarily shaped by its small operators. Tourism managers are faced with the challenge of pointing out upcoming trends and market changes. To this end the appeal was made some years ago to all service providers to adapt to the age of the Internet. The objective was to distinguish the individual web appearances from those of the competition and to create differentiated entities online. More than 90% of the Austria's hotel businesses are now online and many businesses are currently investing in the third or fourth generation of their website in order to meet the quality requirements. With a small budget an Internet appearance can quickly be developed. But how can one stand out in the market if the competition also has an attractive website which meets customer requirements? If in classic economics the rarity of a good was of decisive significance, it is attention in the new economy.

All service providers, including small and medium-sized enterprises (SMTEs), must therefore conduct more professional marketing in order to be found on the Internet and to successfully participate in the online market. Whilst programming a website used to be simple to outsource, marketing now requires a deep understanding of the business. Successful e-marketing is thus a challenge for the management and requires know-how. There are no generally applicable rules for being successful on the Internet for SMTEs. It is in fact the responsibility of every individual business to develop its own online strategy. Until a website has relevant significance amongst the various sales channels, it is a slow process characterized by many experiences. For most businesses it is a novelty to operate with campaigns on Google Adwords or link offers. Hoteliers face the challenge of having to assess the abundance of advertising and sales options, because large budgets can disappear in online marketing. It is therefore important to be better than the competition. To achieve this they have to know their strengths and weaknesses as well as their unique selling points. In addition, successful strategies and measures of the best players on the market must be analysed, adapted and implemented according to one's own business.

Company and Main Products

ncm.at is one of the biggest agencies not only at its location in Salzburg but throughout Austria which have specialized exclusively on the Internet. Since its foundation the company has realized more than 500 Internet projects of all dimensions. The customers are mainly from the tourism industry which has provided the agency with above-average eTourism competence. In order to meet the demands of the market, ncm.at cooperates with its customers in the form of focus groups. Thus new ideas and solution approaches are developed for SMTEs in eTourism.

In the course of these focus groups a hotelier wanted to know the rate of effectiveness of his website. This key figure alone, however, only has a relatively low significance. In order to assess the overall rate of effectiveness of a website of 0.58% accordingly, further statistical data from comparable business is needed. With CheckEffect an analysis tool was developed which has a benchmarking module as its central element. Benchmarking is a methodical comparison of processes and products with compar-ative partners which aims at optimizing the own processes and products by 'learning from the best'.

The Internet-based program presents itself to customers with a user-friendly interface. Statistical data is processed and displayed graphically. Apart from benchmarking, CheckEffect offers the possibility to measure online campaigns and to analyse search terms with regard to their significance for incoming reservation inquiries. With CheckEffect a tool was specially developed for the analysis of tourist websites whose functionality surpasses that of traditional web statistics tools by far.

Business Model

CheckEffect is available in two basic versions: for individual businesses such as hotels and guesthouses, as well as tourism regions and associations. Furthermore, CheckEffect is provided in another version which is compatible with the 'feratel deskline' (see Case 24) booking program which is widespread in Austria. In order to enable as many hoteliers and tourism managers as possible to use CheckEffect, ncm.at offers customers the licence to use the program under the 'using not buying' motto or on an Application Service Provision basis. The usage charge depends on the size of the business. CheckEffect is not only provided by ncm.at but also by numerous other Internet service providers and purchasing associations.

The costs to use CheckEffect depend on the number of beds an establishment has and start from €18.50 (1–10 beds) up to €110 (more than 200 beds). Additionally a set-up fee (€110) is charged.

Technological and Business Innovation

Benchmarking with CheckEffect

Benchmarks are approximate values and target figures which serve as specification for operational services (Zdrowomyslaw & Kasch, 2002).

> *Despite the wide use of benchmarking techniques in quality, marketing, finance and technology innovation in the manufacturing industry, benchmarking is still a vague concept in the service industry, particularly in the tourism field. (Wöber, 2002, p. 2)*

With CheckEffect businesses are provided with a tool to quickly and easily benchmark e-marketing activities. CheckEffect measures all marketing-relevant web data of the participating business on a daily basis and compares them anonymously on request. Businesses can select from the following assessment criteria:

- Number of visitors/PCs
- Page views
- Visitors with only one page view
- Rates of effectiveness of the search engines and linked pages
- Duration of the user session
- Effectiveness of the form
- Overall rate of page effectiveness.

Figure 33.1 shows a graphic illustration of CheckEffect benchmarking. The thin left bar depicts the best, the middle bar the worst comparative business. The thick right bar shows your performance, the dashed crossline illustrates the average value of comparable businesses.

Building up a pool of comparative businesses is the prerequisite for the development of a benchmarking tool. Thanks to the existing customer stock of SMTEs this could soon be realized. Currently some 280 business at 45 destinations use CheckEffect.

All data on the Internet performance of websites are currently checked on a high-performance server by CheckEffect. These enormous data volumes allow anonymous comparison of similar businesses. Thus the evaluation of key values of the Internet performance becomes a specific potential analysis for the management. By assessing the rate of effectiveness of all Internet marketing measures, the website operator is provided with an important control tool. The program's user-friendly interface allows CheckEffect customers to select and change the compared period as well as the number of comparative businesses themselves.

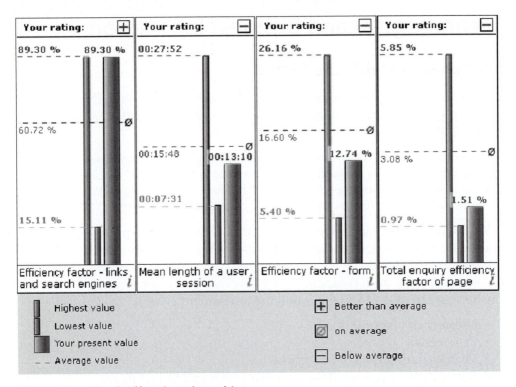

Figure 33.1 CheckEffect benchmarking
Source: ncm.at

To search for comparative businesses the category (3*/4*/5*) and type of business (holiday hotel/city hotel) are used as fixed criteria. Criteria narrowing the groups are the number of beds: (+/− 40%), the main season (summer/winter) as well as the number of seasons (6-month operation/all-year operation).

All businesses in the selection process are searched where all criteria match. Where there are less than three businesses, the number of seasons, main season and the number of beds are gradually dropped and matching businesses are searched. It is also displayed for how many businesses the following criteria match – Optional matches:

- In-house restaurant
- Full board
- Bed and breakfast
- Half board
- Federal state
- Country.

For searches for comparable regions the main season (summer/ winter) is taken as a fixed criteria. Criteria narrowing the group are: the number of seasons (one, two or all year), the number of accommodation establishments, the number of cities and whether there is a travel agent in the city.

For selection the regions are searched first where all comparison criteria match. If less than three regions are found, the number of seasons, accommodation establishments, travel agents in the city and number of cities are gradually dropped and searches for matching regions are searched repeatedly. It also displays how many of the selected regions match the following criteria with your region. Optional matches:

- Country
- Federal state
- Online booking possible?

In order to help new CheckEffect users interpret the data, a CheckEffect coach is available.

Evaluation of Inquiries

The evaluation of inquiries shows the CheckEffect user where the inquiries made really come from. Traditional statistics tools can only display how many references come from a specific link. CheckEffect allows measuring the rate of effectiveness of links (which are, for instance, bought in campaigns) as well as of search engines. Figure 33.2 thus shows, for instance, that Google provides the most references but only achieves a rate of effectiveness

Referring search engines   Time period: Friday, 28.02.2003 - Thursday, 30.11.2006 (1372 Days)

| Search: | | | | |
| Search | Show all | | | |

Search engine	Referrals	Requests	Efficiency factor
1. Google Google	169512	4176	2.46 %
2. MSN Search msn	6631	202	3.05 %
3. Yahoo! YAHOO!	4850	144	2.97 %
4. T-Online Suche	1566	79	5.04 %
5. AOL.de	1327	43	3.24 %
6. AOL Search	658	24	3.65 %
7. AltaVista	661	16	2.42 %
8. WEB.DE	531	14	2.64 %
9. Salzburg Suche	458	11	2.40 %
10. Ask Jeeves	299	9	1.50 %

Figure 33.2 Inquiry assessment with CheckEffect
Source: ncm.at

of 2.46%. Fewer visitors come from T-Online but with a rate of effectiveness of 5%: i.e. twice as many inquiries are generated.

Search Term Analysis

In order to remain competitive in the long term it is necessary to be exactly informed of the behaviour of the website visitors. With CheckEffect one can learn not only under what search terms the company is found on the Internet but also what terms generate inquiries, that is, turnover. The finding that for example 'ski holiday Salzburg' generates lots of inquiries and 'Christkindl market Salzburg' only generates lookers and brochure collectors is the start of any website optimization.

Pathfinder

With the help of pathfinder you can see at one glance, which referring search engines, sites or links generate inquiries at the hotel or the destination. Every inquiry, which was generated online on the website has a path which brought the guest to the hotel. Pathfinder informs the CheckEffect user that, for instance, a Google search with the 'winter holiday' search term by Mr 'John Miller' resulted in a inquiry at the hotel. This information is directly noted in the incoming inquiry email. Sales can thus be assigned and better offers compiled. With the pathfinder data the hotel manager is given important information on the future guest. It is decisive to know what the guest was looking for in order to compile a precise offer. Practice shows that the preparedness to spend one's holidays at a hotel is in close correlation with the suitable offer. At the same time it is known in the case of a booking what search engine, partner site or link produced this sale. Especially on advanced markets, where the competition is also present with a good appearance on the Internet, it is necessary to carry out precise online marketing and to prevent waste coverage. Figure 33.3 shows the details sent by pathfinder in an inquiry email.

Campaigns

Today, hoteliers face the challenge of shifting through an abundance of e-marking activities and finding the ones relevant for the business. Generally a tight budget must be distributed as best as possible. Previously, it was not possible to evaluate the investment made with regard to the bookings made. With the help of benchmark

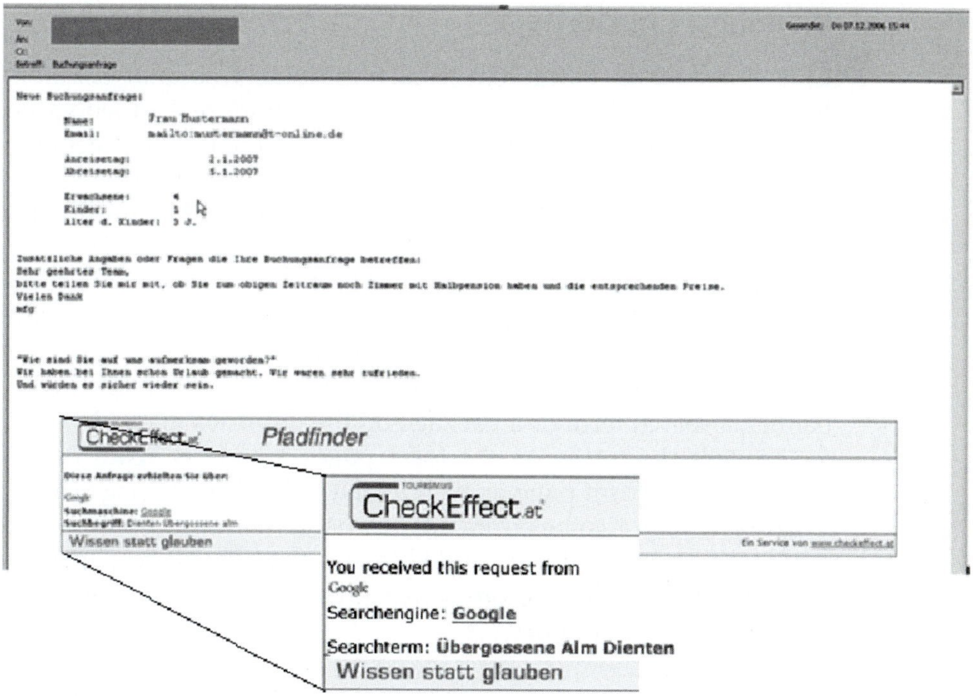

Figure 33.3 Pathfinder
Source: ncm.at

Google Adwords Sommer 05
Costs: € 3432,-
Time period: 05.06.2005 bis 31.07.2005

Total	
Number of visitors (PCs)	1932
Number of enquiries	41
Efficiency factor	2.12%
Costs	
Costs per visitor	1.78
Costs per enquiry	83.71
Daily mean values	
Number of visitors (PCs)	4.0
Number of enquiries per day	0.1
Referrals	

Figure 33.4 Evaluation of campaigns
Source: ncm.at

data and term of the e-marketing activity, CheckEffect evaluates the benefit for the business. How many visitors to the website did the advertising investment generate, and more importantly, how many inquiries did the campaign generate? Figure 33.4 shows a tabular illustration of the campaign analysis.

Installing CheckEffect

CheckEffect is very different from traditional web analysis tools. In order to provide the usual log file values with real added value, a code must be implemented in every site of the CheckEffect user. Only sites with implemented code can be measured. The code is implemented in this page in order just to measure fully loaded pages (Figure 33.5).

After implementing the program into the existing website of the CheckEffect customer, he/she can login to the program from any computer and download the current data.

Especially relevant is information on the contribution of a link, a banner, a search term or a package on the inquiries made. In order to measure the traffic on the form pages a code is again implemented in the form page as well as the "Thank you" page. If, for instance, a visitor comes from an external link this information can be passed on until a form is filled in and the "Thank you" page is then retrieved. It thus becomes clear that a visitor of this link successfully made an inquiry.

```
<!--mymon-->
<script language="JavaScript1.1" src="                    "mymon.js"
type="text/javascript"></script>
<script language="JavaScript1.1"><!-- run_it("xxxxx"); //--></script>
<NOSCRIPT><IMG SRC="                       /index.pl?u=xxxxx&js=0" BORDER=0 width=1
height=1></NOSCRIPT>
<!--mymon-->
```

Figure 33.5 CheckEffect code
Source: ncm.at

Key Challenges for the Future

CheckEffect's future challenges are to enable even more precise benchmarking, to adapt to customer's wishes with regard to user-friendliness and information content and to continue to quickly react to changed demands.

By developing and selling the CheckEffect program, ncm.at aims to unite to dynamic business areas under one roof. In the case of CheckEffect everything is now, having broken even, pointing in the direction of growth – especially abroad. An Italian and English version of the program were recently made.

The management at the ncm.at Internet agency is currently aiming at increasing productivity thanks to more efficient project processing, the exploitation of synergies and success control. This is why every single Internet project is evaluated in detail and verified for its profitability since the start of 2006. As creating or relaunching websites is a rather saturated market, ncm.at is concentrating on special services such as web marketing, search engine management, Internet coaching, web promotion or web text. These business areas are provided as individual services as well as part of support agreements. The CheckEffect program represents an important efficiency control tool for all stated business areas – for the customer and ncm.at project managers.

Key Conclusions

- CheckEffect provides an effective tool for benchmarking processes and products against comparative partners in order to learn from the best.
- CheckEffect offers the possibility to measure online campaigns and to analyse search terms with regard to their significance for incoming reservation inquiries.
- CheckEffect evaluates the benefit of e-marketing activity for the business. How many visitors to the website did the advertising investment generate, and more importantly, how many inquiries did the campaign generate?

Review and Discussion Questions

- How can hotels move their marketing online?
- What are they key success factors for online marketing?
- How can CheckEffect evaluate online marketing and what is the value of benchmarking in this area?

References and Further Reading

Eisenberg, B. (2005). *Call to action: Secret formulas to improve online results*. Austin: Wizard Academy Press.

Kozak, M. (2003). *Destination benchmarking: Concepts, practices and operations*. Wallingford: CABI Publishing.

Michl, P. (2006). *Erhebung des Online-Buchungsvolumens/Online-Anfragevolumens der österreichischen Beherbergungsbranche*. Vienna: ÖW-Eigenverlag.

Sungsoo, P. (2003). *Benchmarks in hospitality and tourism*. New York: Haworth Press.

Wöber, C. (2002). *Benchmarking in tourism and hospitality industries*. Wallingford: CABI Publishing.

Zdrowomyslaw, N., & Kasch, R. (2002). *Betriebsvergleiche und Benchmarking für die Managementpraxis*. Munich, Vienna: Oldenbourg Wissenschaftsverlag.

Company's website: http://www.ncm.at.

Company's website: http://www.checkeffect.at.

34

TAI (Day Trip Indicator): measuring value added in the tourism sector

Klemens Waldhör, Claudia Freidl, Alexander Rind and Kathrin Ecker

Learning Objectives

- Demonstrate the importance for a reliable methodology and software to measure both the attractiveness and the value added of day trips.
- Explain TAI as a software system and service which enables tourism organization to measure the attractiveness and added value for a whole range of tourism offerings.
- Illustrate how the TAI's economic model operates within the input–output analysis framework.

Introduction and Company Development

Tourismus Research Center Krems (TRC or Krems Research) is a research institution located in Krems in Lower Austria focusing its research activities on eTourism and related areas. TRC was founded in 2004 in the framework of ANET, a network of three competence centres for promoting eTourism research in Austria. Besides the product described, the company works in several other areas of eTourism, such as developing online marketing indicators for measuring the success of tourist Internet marketing or improving the quality of tourist websites by means of semi-automated software systems. One main research and consultancy area is the future development and improvement of hotel rooms and researching applications of IP TV in the hotel room environment. Although those activities are mainly research oriented, TRC tries to translate the outcome of the research into real products which are offered to the tourism market.

In the following description TAI (German abbreviation for 'day trip indicator'), one of the main developments of TRC and the business case associated with it, is presented.

Main Products and Value Added

In 2004 Niederösterreich Werbung (NÖW), the official tourism organization of Lower Austria, asked TRC to develop a reliable methodology and software prototype which should allow them to measure both the attractiveness and the value added of day trips in Lower Austria. In addition it should be possible to access the database behind the model on a day-to-day basis and produce reports on demand without having special knowledge in statistics.

For many regions 'day tourism' has become the most important source of revenue in tourism. Its impact is always underestimated compared with overnight tourism. It is therefore one of the key factors for the success in growing tourism income in Lower Austria. Since TAI is not the main focus of public interest valid data of this area is of key importance. It is well known that attention is generally paid to overnight tourism. This can be easily demonstrated if newspapers are checked where one can mainly read the figures about this type of tourism. Especially for a country like Lower Austria (Vienna lies in the heart of Lower Austria) which is traditionally not an 'overnight stay destination' like Vienna, Salzburg or the Tyrol day trip tourism forms an essential touristic income source. But surprisingly no real data is available so far to quantify its economic impact apart from some isolated studies dealing with special events.

A reliable methodology for measuring added value in tourism is not only important for day trips, but it can also be easily extended towards other tourism areas, even to the non-tourism domain. Based on this observation, TRC developed a software system and service which enables tourism organization to measure the attractiveness and added value for a whole range of tourism offerings.

TAI is based on three models which are geared towards a procedural model for a specific project:

1. A data model describing the attractiveness and economic factors of day trips: the data model includes a survey to detect the behaviour of the day trips in Lower Austria, the calculation of the value added and the automatic analysis of interviews taken from different tourist areas (Waldhör *et al.*, 2004a).
2. A computational model for measuring both attractiveness and value added realizing the data model: basically this consists of a database scheme representing the core data. It collects and describes the methods to analyse the necessary data. It also includes methods to control the validity of the data (Waldhör *et al.*, 2004b).
3. A software model implementing 1 and 2: the software mainly executes statistical analysis and graphical display of the results. TRC and NÖW use the software to get on-time information about the behaviour of the day tourists. The tool is developed in such a way that it supports interpreting the data without any statistical background by generating graphs and tables automatically and adding them to reports (Rind & Waldhör, 2005).

Day trip tourism was already researched in some studies both in Germany, in Austria and in other industrialized countries Association Internationale d'Experts Scientifiques Du Tourism (AIEST) (International Association of Scientific Experts in Tourism) www.aiest.org (AIEST, 1988; Department of Industry, Tourism and Resources, 2004; Harrer *et al.*, 1995; Koch *et al.*, 1987; Maschke, 2005; T-MONA, n.d.; Vock, 1992). However, these projects were often one-sided and did not include a continuous measurement of the attractiveness and value added of day tourism. A key difference to existing models is also its ability to compute the value added at a regional level and not only on country level. Moreover it shows both direct and indirect value added effects. This feature especially differentiates it from approaches like T-MONA that just compute the direct effects (T-MONA, n.d.).

Business Model

Day trip tourism was developed to evaluate the gross value added and the attractiveness of day trip tourism in Lower Austria, but the tool is useful in many other cases (e.g. Figure 34.1 shows a set of statistics for value added and average number of trips grouped by motives).

Currently TRC is evaluating the net value of a biotechnology conference held in Krems. For this purpose an adoption of the model in a few steps is required (Waldhör *et al.*, 2006). This also demonstrates the flexibility of the approach as it allows integrating several data sources (e.g. data supplied by the organizer of the conference) in order to gain deep insights into the structural complexities of the economic impacts on a variety of tourism and non-tourism areas.

Another very important project was an evaluation of the exhibition 'Heldenberg' in the region Schmidatal in Lower Austria in 2005. In this case the standard TAI procedure was improved with special questions defined by the organizer. The results helped to justify the expenditures provided by the Province of Lower Austria. It also gave valuable information to the government how well public support turned into local value added.

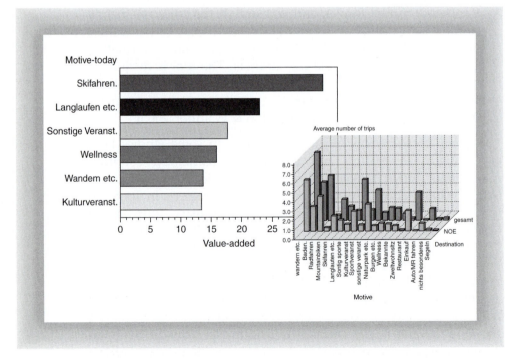

Figure 34.1 Examples results generated by TAI-software

The range of TAI's business cases is wide. Obviously the value-added model can also be used outside the tourism area (e.g. to calculate the value added of certain company subsidiaries in a region or the effects of investing into a new building for a region). Essential questions are:

1. Who are the potential clients?
2. Why could such a service be attractive to those clients?

So far TRC identified the following target groups which should have great interest in this prototype software:

1. Government institutions and politicians.
2. Tourism organizations at various levels.
3. Private (tourism) enterprises (hotels, MICE, etc.).

Given those target groups, question two can be answered as follows:

1. In many cases tourism offerings (such as sport or cultural events, conferences, etc.) ask for funding by some official sources. Until now this was either granted or not but no one could really say how much a specific event turned out to be profitable for a particular region. If checked, it was a costly procedure to determine the figures in detail. In addition, since the methodology changed from event to event, no comparison of data was really possible. TAI can now answer those questions in a fast, reliable and cost effective way.
2. Politicians who are finally responsible for the support and funding can now argue with those figures why funding requests should be supported or not.
3. By comparing and benchmarking the results of different events, one can show the strengths and weaknesses of offerings and help to improve them.
4. Based on this concept changes in tourism can be initiated and tracked. It also gives valuable support even in the pre-implementation of an action as the methodology can also be used to simulate the effects of specific interventions and help to optimize them.

Since there are many opportunities to apply TAI (Figure 34.2), income can be generated with different models based on this analysis:

1. *ASP model*: Clients, for example destinations, have to pay an admission fee and an annual fee for system usage (pricing depending on client needs). TRC provides all the technological services to the client through the Internet.

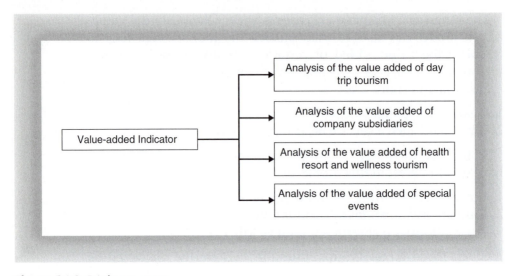

Figure 34.2 Business cases

2. *Offer of the whole product* (€~25,000): The client installs the software on his/her machines and runs the service.
3. *Offer of the methodology* (€~20,000): The client just acquires the (scientific) methodology and implements the services by himself/herself.
4. *Consultancy for specific touristic offerings and events*: TRC estimates that an average analysis will cost something in between €3,000 and €5,000, clearly depending on the size of the event.
5. Specific calculations of the value added for further economic areas where the costs depend on the complexity of the project.

Technological and Business Innovation

The key innovation of this project is of an economic nature, as gross value added is analysed on the scale of a provincial level, not just a federal level. The gross value added is the sum of wages, depreciation and profits. It measures not only economic effects directly induced by a business but also by its suppliers. The TAI's economic model is built on classical input–output analysis which is extended by a multiplier for regionalization (Figure 34.3).

The expenses of day visitors are gathered from the questionnaires in expense categories (e.g. meals in a restaurant, guided tours). This is necessary, because the expenses have to be decreased by the rate of value added tax and then have to be split up among the 57 ÖNACE branches of industry in the Austrian input–output

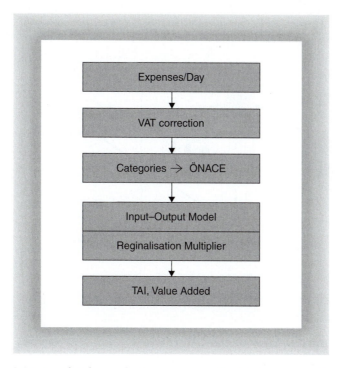

Figure 34.3 Method to calculate value added from expenses

table (Statistik Austria, 2004). Unfortunately, an input–output table for Lower Austria is not available; therefore the result from input–output analysis is refined by a regionalization multiplier, which is in turn derived from statistical data.

From the technological perspective TAI is designed as a web application with the SAS system used for background statistical processing (Rind & Waldhör, 2005). The user can browse through statistical reports in his web browser and can filter the underlying data (e.g. young males interviewed on a ski trip). The reports are specified in the business logic XML files and can be extended by statisticians with SAS experience. It is also possible to produce PDF, RTF or MS Excel output.

The base system is implemented as a Java Servlet (Figure 34.4). At start-up a set of XML files is loaded to provide business logic and configuration parameters for the TAI. Based on a user request and business logic a sequence of SAS commands is composed and then sent to the SAS system via remote procedure call. For easier management the underlying statistical data is also stored as SAS datasets. The resulting charts and tables are converted to HTML by the output delivery system of SAS and sent back to the web application. General user interface elements are added with standard web

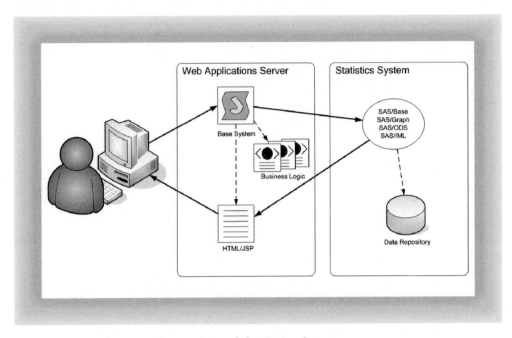

Figure 34.4 Architectural overview of the TAI software

technology such as Java Server Pages. This architecture makes adaptations and extensions of the TAI very easy.

Key Challenges for the Future

Based on the experiences from running a province-wide survey in Lower Austria – until now more than 1500 interviews have been conducted, including areas like hiking, (mountain) biking, winter sports, culture and culinary events (Waldhör *et al.*, 2004a) – the methodology and software of the TAI can be adapted to other provinces, to single attractions or to specific events. This makes it necessary to incorporate additional requirements of the customer. For example to serve the needs of the survey of the 'Heldenberg' exhibition two additional expense categories were added to explicitly monitor consumption at a Heurigen (a typical Austrian tavern, famous for wine and cold cuts).

The same procedure for calculating value added can be used in other federal states simply by substituting the regionalization multiplier. For economic systems smaller than a federal state this is not possible, because statistical data are missing. Thus, it is the most important challenge for the future to research and define different methods to measure value added or a comparable indicator for economic effects below the federal state level.

Accumulating data from several surveys provides interesting opportunities to compare the results. An updated version of the TAI software is currently under development which will provide benchmarking against a second destination or against a group of comparable destinations.

The Future of the Company

On the one hand TRC as a private research organization is based on (mainly public) funded research projects. But on the other hand it also needs to generate revenue from other non-public sources in order to ensure its future. After the research phase TAI is now ready to be rolled out for commercial usage – without having any research aspect lost (Medenbach & Waldhör, 2005). One employee of TRC is now responsible to promote the future sales and marketing of the project. A main goal is to break up the whole process of generating the required studies and reports to make it a very cost- and time-efficient method. The envisaged customers should be provided with short, consistent and easy to interpret information which helps them to facilitate their decision processes.

For TRC this is a very important aspect as decision makers (politicians, etc.) are in most cases not interested in reading lengthy papers where the core information is hidden in a pile of more or less useful statistical data. This will be the key for a future successful operation. Applying this approach consistently to different scenarios TRC estimates that an average study should range in between €3,000 and €5,000, which is considerable lower compared to the prices for such studies today.

Key Conclusions

- The TAI programme evaluates the gross value added and the attractiveness of day trip tourism.
- From the technological perspective TAI is designed as a web application with the SAS system used for background statistical processing.
- The TAI's economic model is using the classical input–output analysis which is extended by a multiplier for regionalization.

Review and Discussion Questions

- Why is it important to evaluate different types of tourism?
- What are the key success factors and prerequisites for the success of the TAI programme?
- How can the TAI programme and methodology be further enhanced by comparing other regions?

References and Further Reading

AIEST (1988). *Day trips and their impacts*. St Gallen: AIEST.

Department of Industry, Tourism and Resources (2004). *Tourism impact model for Australian local government: A user manual and CD*. Canberra: Department of Industry, Tourism and Resources.

Harrer, B., Zeiner, M., Maschke, J., & Scherr, S. (1995). *Tagesreisen der Deutschen*. Munich: DWIF.

Koch, A., Zeiner, M., & Feige, M. (1987). *Die ökonomische Bedeutung des Ausflugs- und Geschäftsreiseverkehrs (ohne Übernachtung) in der Bundesrepublik Deutschland*. Munich: DWIF.

Laimer, P., & Öhlböck, P. (2004). *Indicators Measuring the Sustainability of Tourism*. Retrieved 15 September 2006 from http://www.tourismforum.scb.se/papers/PapersSelected/SD/Paper21AUSTRIA/sustainability_indicators_Austria.doc.

Maschke, J. (2005). *Tagesreisen der Deutschen*. Munich: DWIF.

Medenbach, S., & Waldhör, K. (2005). *Die ökonomische Bedeutung des Tagestourismus in Niederösterreich. Entwicklung eines Geschäftsmodells zum operativen Einsatz der TAI-Software*. Krems: TRC (internal report).

Michigan Tourism Economic Impact Model (n.d.). Retrieved 15 September 2006 from http://www.msu.edu/course/prr/840/econimpact/michigan/MITEIM.htm.

Rind, A., & Waldhör, K. (2005). *Die ökonomische Bedeutung des Tagestourismus in Niederösterreich. Entwicklung eines Softwaremodells im Tagesausflugstourismus*. Krems: TRC (internal report).

Seshadri, G. (1999). *Understanding JavaServer Pages Model 2 architecture. Java World*. Retrieved December 1999 from http://www.javaworld.com/javaworld/jw-12-1999/jw-12-ssj-jsp-mvc.html.

Statistik Austria (n.d.). *Bruttowertschöpfung zu Herstellerpreisen nach Wirtschaftsbereichen und Bundesländern (NUTS 2).* Retrieved 15 September 2006 from http://www.statistik.at/fachbereich_02/regkonten_tab1_neu.pdf.

Statistik Austria (2004). *Input-Output-Tabelle 2000.* Vienna: Verlag Österreich.

Statistik Austria (2006). *Volkswirtschaftliche Gesamtrechnung.* Retrieved 15 September 2006 from http://www.statistik.at/fachbereich_02/vgr_txt.shtml.

Statistik Austria (2005). *Leistungs- und Strukturerhebung im Produzierenden und Dienstleistungsbereich.* Retrieved 15 September 2006 from http://www.statistik.at/_downloads/lse/start.shtml.

SUN Microsystems, Inc. (n.d.). *JavaTM Web Services Tutorial.* Retrieved 19 November 2004 from http://java.sun.com/blueprints/patterns/MVC-detailed.html.

T-MONA (n.d.). Retrieved 15 August 2004 from http://www.manova.at/produkte/webmark/t-mona.

Vock, C. (1992). *Der Tages- und Ausflugstourismus in der Stadt Luzern.* Basel: BAK Basel Economics.

Waldhör, K., Medenbach, S., Fürst, E., & Edlmair, R. (2004a). *Die ökonomische Bedeutung des Tagestourismus in Niederösterreich. Entwicklung eines Datenmodells zur statistischen Erfassung relevanter Kennzahlen im Tagestourismus.* Krems: TRC (internal report).

Waldhör, K., Medenbach, S., Fürst, E., & Edlmair, R. (2004b). *Die ökonomische Bedeutung des Tagestourismus in Niederösterreich. Entwicklung eines Berechnungsmodells zur statistischen Analyse relevanter Kennzahlen im Tagestourismus.* Krems: TRC (internal report).

Waldhör, K., Ecker, K., Freidl, C., & Rind, A. (2006). *Die regionalisierte Wertschöpfung der 6th International Conference on the Scientific and Clinical Applications of Magnetic Carriers in Krems.* Krems: TRC.

Case

35

Tourism Technology: travel wholesale management system

Ian McDonnell

Learning Objectives

- Analyse and describe the strategies Tourism Technology Pty employed to achieve its objective to develop and market the world's leading wholesale travel management system.
- Explain the radical change of the ways that tour wholesalers can promote and distribute their products globally.
- Illustrate that Calypso is designed to minimize the cost of managing the system while maximizing the flexibility for the user. Demonstrate that data need to be loaded once, but is available in various formats and environments.

Introduction

In 1991 Graeme Hunter left the Information Technology department of Qantas Airways. He had identified a need for a flexible tour wholesale management system and with Stephen Garrett purchased a reservation system developed by Viva!, a large Australian tour wholesaler, which was then owned by Qantas. The travel and tourism ICT supplier company Tourism Technology Pty Ltd (TT) http://www.tt.com.au was consequently established to develop Calypso, a wholesale travel management system for mid to large size travel wholesalers and tour operators. The company remains wholly owned by the two founders and now executive directors.

This case study analyses and describes the strategies the company employed to achieve its sole objective: to develop and market the world's leading wholesale travel management system. A consequence of this is to radically change the ways that tour wholesalers can now promote and distribute their products.

Company Development

Once Tourism Technology established key software and hardware partners including IBM and Sun Microsystems, Calypso embarked on a strategic software development path on a robust and reliable UNIX database platform. In 1992, Tasmania's Temptation Holidays were the first customer to implement Calypso. In 1993, connectivity with the GDSs was enabled and in 1994 the system was sold to Qantas Holidays, the company's first airline wholesaler client. In the same year a direct access booking function was introduced that enabled travel agents to book and manage wholesale bookings. Other airline wholesalers who have subsequently become TT clients are British Airways, Singapore Airlines, Tradewinds Holidays, Garuda Orient Holidays and the now sadly defunct Ansett Holidays.

A data warehouse system that enables Qantas Holidays to data mine and consequently refine their marketing efforts was created in 1998, along with an FDRA credit card link that enables credit card payments for travel packages. The onset of the 21st Century saw TT becoming the tour wholesale management system supplier to the Travel Corporation's brands: Creative Holidays; Contiki Travel; AAT Kings; and Aussie Adventure Holidays, and in 2002 the Travel Spirit brands of Venture Holidays, Explore Holidays and African Traveller. To service their UK client base a London office was opened in 2002. A full list of Tourism Technology clients can be found at http://www.tt.com.au/ourClients.html.

In 2003 a product development called Calypso WebBook that enables direct customer bookings was first implemented by Qantas Holidays. This product was chosen in 2004 by www.zuji. co.nz to process all its Australia and New Zealand land bookings as did the State NTO of Tasmania – Tasmania's Temptation Holidays – for its direct online bookings. This year had a flurry of new product launches with CalypsoNet and SupplierNet released to the market to provide an online channel for both retail travel agents and suppliers to access wholesalers' Calypso reservation systems, with obvious increases in efficiencies for both these entities.

New product development continued apace in 2005 with the launch of a new breed of web services products called the Link Series. HotelLink provided wholesalers and their travel agents with instant access to hotel room availability and price. FlightLink saw the biggest new product packaging opportunity for travel wholesalers with the integration of low-cost airfares into Calypso and subsequently into holiday packages. CarLink facilitated hire car bookings and TT's first strategic web services partnership was with Hertz car rental.

In 2006 another product enhancement to CalypsoNet occurred. My CalypsoNet was launched to provide travel agents with a personalized agent central login to multiple wholesaler websites (Figure 35.1).

Along with incumbent travel agent specific sales tools, like single screen multi-wholesaler product search functionality, My CalypsoNet 'sales-tool' style developments are especially welcomed by travel agents.

After 15 years of operations in a competitive environment Tourism Tourism has grown to have a predominate share of the Australian/New Zealand market for its products and a growing market in the United Kingdom. Its competitors are well known international providers such as Tour Plan (http://www.tca.co.nz/), Illusions (http://www.illusions-online.com/) and Anite (http://www.anite.com/content/view/68/368/), based in New Zealand, Dubai and the United Kingdom respectively. Given this intense international competition, it can be seen that TT's strategy of constant product development and enhancement has been the main cause of its success in achieving its objective.

The company employs around 45 staff split between programmers, systems analysts, customer support and management staff. TT's large client list is evidence of its market leading status, particularly in the Australian/New Zealand market.

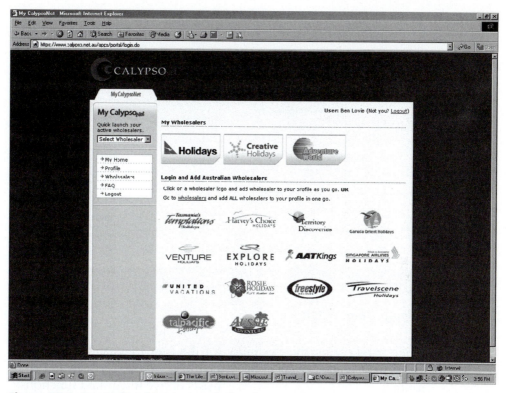

Figure 35.1 Centralized login to wholesalers
Source: http://www.calypso.net.au/apps/portal/

The Calypso Product Line

Figure 35.2 is a representation of how the various components the Calypso Travel System link together to form an integrated travel management system for tour wholesalers/operators.

The Links Series (HotelLink, FlightLink and Carlink) was the technology solution to new travel supplier online distribution methods and an industry desire to improve booking process productivity via automation. TT hosted XML Web Services enabled Calypso system – Travel Supplier system live connectivity. All Calypso users can now access and integrate into a standard Calypso booking, live availability and price from subscribing airline, hotels and car hire suppliers.

Calypso provides travel wholesalers and tour operators with a range of options for establishing and maintaining a travel database, reservations and management system for local or global operations. Calypso is designed to minimize the cost of managing the system

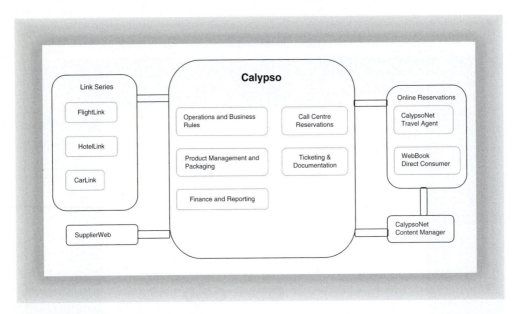

Figure 35.2 Calypso travel system

while maximizing the flexibility for the user by ensuring that data needs to be loaded once, but is available in various formats and environments. The Calypso system consists of five integrated functions:

1. *Operations and business rules*: Provides wholesalers with the ability to load, store and distribute details of all types of travel product, with integrated invoicing of agents via email. Flexible and extensive range of security, selling channel, task and workflow activity scheduling functions.
2. *Product management and packaging*: Enables wholesalers to create modular itineraries and develop holiday templates for FIT (free independent travellers) and fixed package options, with a flexible pricing in multiple currencies capability. This function offers flexibility in loading complex supplier contracts into the system, the opportunity to market a product using different brand names in different regions, automated workflow process, and guaranteed inventory integrity for all types of supplier allocations such as allocated inventory, sell-and-report and free-sale or on request.
3. *Call centre reservations*: This function gives wholesalers the ability to take bookings for their products via either a central internal telephone sales facility, or externally whereby travel agents and direct customers can make an online booking of all elements of a travel package using the Calypso Internet browserbased booking interface. The booking process for

telesales staff is designed to be intuitive, fast and with maximum productivity achieved with minimal training. It has multiple online GDS and airline specific CRS connections so customer PNRs can be managed easily, without CRS training.

4. *Ticketing and documentation*: This allows the wholesaler's system to produce bulk documentation of travel vouchers, comprehensive itineraries and airline tickets. It also enables email delivery of e-documents of all types, which significantly reduces documentation production and distribution costs, while improving service to the customer and/or travel agent.

5. *Finance and reporting*: Gives the wholesaler the ability to have complete control over revenue, creditor payments and profit reports, which can be easily linked with their financial accounts. Calypso is built upon an ODBC (open data-base connectivity) compliant database that enables flexible and detailed data extraction capabilities in a customized or standard format such as budget forecast against actual; profitability reports at booking, destination or package component levels, plus a range of data-warehousing options.

The online reservations function allows Calypso customers to pursue either B2B or B2C or both B2B and B2C distribution strategies, using the Internet as the distribution channel, rather than a phone line.

CalypsoNet provides a B2B (wholesaler to agent) online booking facility for Calypso customers, which seamlessly integrates with all Calypso's back-end processes, accessible via a standard Internet browser. CalypsoNet enables agents to process all aspects of a booking, in a self-service style environment, and consequently decreases the dependency on a wholesaler's manual involvement, which results in a significant productivity gain for the whole-saler a lower transaction cost per booking. Many wholesalers run incentives to encourage travel agents to utilize CalypsoNet and often offer greater commission incentives for CalypsoNet online bookings.

WebBook is an online consumer-friendly booking engine that enables wholesalers to sell direct to consumers (B2C). Although direct-sales was not a traditional sales channel strategy for travel wholesalers, increased travel market competition and a need to improve profit margins has increased the number of Calypso customers implementing WebBook. Tour wholesalers have the option to use a 'white-label' (another brand name to the one sold via retail travel agents) version of WebBook to avoid distribution channel disharmony.

The Calypso Content Manager (CCM) is a single online repository of sales-related content that supports the entire online buying process from a visitor researching a holiday, right through to the online booking process. CCM is an application that delivers rich content in the form of web pages that include detailed product text descriptions and product photos (i.e. hotel rooms) into the Calypso booking process for both travel agents and direct consumers.

As can be seen from this description, Calypso Travel System provides the business critical functionality and connectivity to drive a modern travel wholesaler and tour operators' business.

Business Model

Tourism Technology's business model can be described using Porter's (1980) generic strategies model as one of market focus. That is, they focus on one market segment – medium to large travel wholesaler and tour operators – and then differentiate their product by development and enhancement to better satisfy their market's needs.

Tourism Technology's value chain, using Porter's (1985) model, can be described thus:

- *Inbound logistics*: Only people: a strategy of employing skilled tertiary qualified ICT staff from differing backgrounds, recruited on a continuous intake programme. Support staff from a wide variety of backgrounds in the travel industry and in ICT with the skills to provide competent support to users.
- *Operations*: Transform technological innovations into superior products.
- *Outbound logistics*: Done effortlessly using the WWW and to deliver the system to customers.
- *Marketing and sales*: Undertake new product and user-interface testing, incorporate emerging industry changes into new product development, provide extensive product trials and lead regular customer user group forums.
- *Service*: Training provided in all aspects of the system; customer focused product support team.

Tour wholesalers/operators have a similar value chain. Tourism Technology's products can facilitate their value chain thus:

- *Inbound logistics*: The HotelLink, CarLink, and FlightLink product enable wholesalers to directly access principals' CRSs thereby avoiding GDS fees;

- *Operations*: As access to suppliers' products is done electronically, the packaging of tour products is made simpler, and allows for dynamic packaging by the consumer;
- *Outbound logistics* (distribution): As Calypso provides B2B and B2C capability, distribution made more efficient by the consumer or the retail travel agent completing data entry, saving telephone sales and reservations staffing costs;
- *Marketing and sales*: Allows for instant eDistribution of specials and packages.
- *Service*: Provides tour wholesalers/operators with a platform to provide optimum service to its agents and to its end users.

Technological and Business Innovation

It is probable that TT's most significant innovation has been the introduction of CalypsoNet, which facilitates B2B between wholesaler and agent; as well as WebBook, which facilitates B2C between wholesaler and consumer, with the significant efficiency gains for the wholesaler. This aspect of their system is being enhanced by CalypsoNet content manager. The wholesalers' decision to commence B2B or B2C or both is a strategic one, and depends on the competitive environment in which the wholesaler operates. What is useful to them is the knowledge that Tourism Technology has on the products, to efficiently and effectively facilitate their chosen strategy.

The company offers a suite of complementary products to its wholesaler clients: Website design and development; regular updates of the software, usually every 3 or 4 months; a technology platform operating under Sun's Solaris™ UNIX system and utilizing Informix™ relational database for storing and managing data; the system supports a number of supplier and distribution interfaces (mainly XML) for obtaining and selling travel product; all external (to the wholesaler, i.e. B2B and B2C) applications are Internet browser based; multi-tiered application security, and configurable by the wholesaler client.

Key Challenges for the Future

The ongoing development of Calypso as a Travel Enterprise Application Integration Platform (TEAIP) will aid cross business application interoperability and ICT economies of scale. It will also improve information quality to aid initiatives such as refined and accurate data mining and customer relationship efforts. Calypso has shown strategic efforts to enhance the connectivity of the system and will continue to do so into the future.

Other issues are:

- Increase the number of travel agent online bookings via CalypsoNet to drive down cost of sale to wholesaler;
- Develop online booking solutions congruent with travel buyers' research and booking habits;
- Support and implementation of international Web Services standards, proposed by http://www.opentravel.org;
- Support for industry research and industry association membership such as http://www.cato.asn.au.

Conclusion

In 15 years Tourism Technology has gone from two men with an idea to grow and develop a product, to a market-leading travel technology company with many high profile clients who rely on Calypso for their critical business needs. TT combines unique travel and technology industry staff and a culture of ongoing product development in order to remain relevant to the industry and ahead of its competitors. TT's experience is certainly an example of Werthner and Ricci's (2004) claim that e-commerce can change the structure of the travel business and in the process create new opportunities. TT has provided the technology and insight for travel wholesaler and tour operators to grow their business, thereby benefiting all participants in the package holiday distribution chain.

Key Conclusions

- In 2003, a product development called Calypso WebBook that enables direct customer bookings was first implemented by Qantas Holidays. This product was chosen in 2004 by www.zuji.co.nz to process all its Australia and New Zealand land bookings as did the State NTO of Tasmania – Tasmania's Temptation Holidays – for its direct online bookings.
- Calypso is a wholesale travel management system developed by the Tourism Technology Pty Ltd (TT) for mid to large size travel wholesalers and tour operators.
- Calypso provides travel wholesalers and tour operators with a range of options for establishing and maintaining a travel database, reservations and management system for local or global operations.

Review and Discussion Questions

- Discuss the utility of a wholesale travel management system.
- How does Calypso provide interlinks in its travel database, reservations and management systems?
- What is the unique selling point of Calypso and what are the key markets for its use?

References and Further Reading

Porter, M. (1980). *Competitive strategy: Techniques for analysing industries and competitors*. New York: Free Press.

Porter, M. (1985). *Competitive advantage: Creating and sustaining superior performance*. New York: Free Press.

Werthner, H., & Ricci, F. (2004). e-Commerce and tourism. *Communications of the ACM*, 47 (12), 101–115.

http://www.calypso.net.au/

Company's website: http://www.tt.com.au

Case

36

Digital Tourism Assistant: enquiry management solution for destinations

Roland Dessovic and Roman Egger

Learning Objectives

- Demonstrate how small and micro organizations can distribute their inventory either directly or indirectly using cybermediaries.
- Illustrate the trend towards direct distribution through a full online booking solution.
- Explain the benefits of enquiry forms versus online bookings.

Introduction

Almost every accommodation facility in the small and micro sized Austrian tourism industry has its own website. This allows them to distribute their inventory either directly or indirectly using cyber-mediaries. Depending on the season there are many possibilities to bypass intermediaries, thus saving costs. Although a clear trend towards direct distribution can be seen, just few hoteliers have implemented a full online booking solution.

For many years there has been discussion about how one defines online booking. Is it necessary to complete the entire transaction online or can an email, sent via an enquiry form, also be considered as an online booking? In fact, none of the two possibilities is superior to the other one, because ultimately the only thing that counts is to meet the guests' demands. The necessity to explain a complex product and the wish for personal interaction, as well as security concerns, often lead tourists' desire for a simple enquiry without obligation. To benefit from the full online potential it is necessary to provide both kinds of bookings – the direct online booking and a powerful enquiry management. Practice proves that full online booking solutions work quite well in city and MICE-tourism, but lack acceptance in family and holiday-tourism. The reason for this can be found in old established operational processes, often not facilitating newer innovative solutions. However, the enterprise's size might not justify an implementation, which is not just a question of financial affordance but also of opportunity costs. Furthermore, some hoteliers argue they would like to know the guests before renting a room to them. Therefore, they prefer the enquiry which allows them to select their guests instead of the online booking that binds them by contract prior to knowing anything about them.

Main Products

The digital tourism assistant (dTA) is a powerful enquiry management solution for destinations developed by 'elements. at New Media Solutions GmbH', a full-service Internet agency in Salzburg, Austria. The market share of elements.at as an advertising agency is rather small in Austria, whereas, in the specialized area of eTourism, the company is one of the key-players on the market.

Whilst online bookings have been implemented with the assistance of national and international software products and online booking platforms, enquiry and offer management solutions

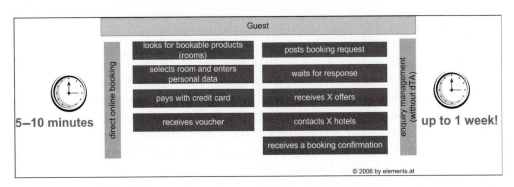

Figure 36.1 Differences between direct online booking and enquiry management

lack consideration. Usually, online booking enquiries reach the hotel via two different channels. There is the direct contact via email or the hotel's website. Alternatively enquiries are incoming via the local tourism bureau or the incoming centre. There is no central control about the time-to-offer or the quality of the offer. Usually, all enquiries received by the DMO are put on a fax-list and sent daily to the accommodation businesses. Consequently, the offers are sent uncoordinatedly to the guest. The guest receives anywhere between no and too many offers, any time with no uniform system for response from the destination and is often not personalized. The problem DMOs face is, that from the moment they sent the enquiries to accommodation businesses, they are no longer involved in the process; nor do they have influence over the communications between guest and accommodation.

Figure 36.1 visualizes that this process results in a suffering guest satisfaction rate and a booking quota which is below all expectancies.

The digital Tourism Assistant (dTA) solves these problems by offering centralized enquiry pools which enables the guests, the DMO, and the hotels to have an overview of the entire enquiry process. This allows each party to interact with each other throughout the process.

Business Model

The dTA is a software application developed for, and exclusively distributed to, destinations and specialized markets (or specialized suppliers or specialized service providers). Until now, there was no direct distribution to individual enterprises due to the dTA's modular configuration. Elements.at can, therefore, be seen as a technology provider, taking into consideration the need for effective enquiry management. The pricing model is designed to be very flexible and orients itself towards the basic conditions of destinations and specialized markets. Various dTA modules are currently being used by approximately 20 destinations and groups, servicing nearly 6000 active establishments. Some regions use the dTA in addition to a pre-existing software, such as Tiscover (Case 23) or Feratel Deskline (Case 24). Others use it with its full range of modules as their exclusive DMS.

Technological and Business Innovation

Tourist destinations are very different regarding size, complexity of their product, their stakeholders and seasonal focus. To make the dTA suitable for all these requirements it has been designed in modules – the assistants. Each module may work independently or in combination with others.

dAA: Enquiry Management

The enquiry management (dAA) is the central module of the digital Tourism Assistant (dTA). It helps tourist regions manage their enquiries. The dTA is responsible for dispatching holiday enquiries and forwarding them to the appropriate establishments. An enquiry can either be received via a web portal (e.g. www.skia-made.com) or it is entered by a tourism office employee on behalf of the guest. Every booking request, no matter if it arrives via web, email, phone, fax or face-to-face, gets channelled into the system. The guest defines their requirements by providing data about their holiday, such as time of arrival/departure, accommodation category, etc., and chooses how many offers they finally want to receive. The system therefore creates a number of 'tickets'. Those tickets can be seen as copies of the enquiry. If the guest for example wants to receive five offers, the system than creates five tickets, which five hotels (matching the guest's requirements, e.g. category, price, etc.) can pull from the enquiry-pool within 48 hours. After this time, unanswered enquiries are marked urgent and sent back to the tourist office. Those accommodation establishments matching the enquiry regarding geographical criteria and category can pull one of these tickets from the system, the faster the better. The system ensures, and this is the big advantage, that the guest does not get more than the ordered offers and drives the competition among the hotels. In average the system is used 16 times a day by hoteliers. In almost all regions using the dTA, 10 enquiry tickets (the average number requested) are taken within 1 hour.

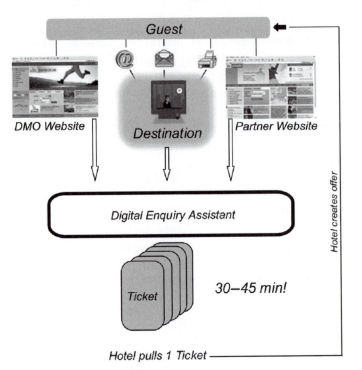

Figure 36.2 Digital enquiry assistant

A deciding factor in using the dTA system is the value of a booking request. A few important features, like the transparency of the system that informs every participant of an enquiry process about relevant events, increases the value. Even the guest has his/her own 'CCC' (Customer Care Centre) where he/she can manage the enquiry (edit, cancel or stop it, where stop means delete all remaining tickets) or post a feedback about the process (Figure 36.2).

The whole workflow of enquiries arriving in the pool, tickets being taken out, feedbacks and booking statistics are being monitored in a statistic module available for the region-administrators. Hence the availability of a system database and instant feedback allows the DMO to place responsibility back with the hotel.

Figure 36.3 shows the interface of the system's enquiry list. This shows all relevant information for the hotelier to select which tickets they want to pull.

dOA: Offer Management

For a successful acquisition, the whole booking-circle has to work on a high-quality level. Therefore the offer management module (dOA) has been implemented. It plugs itself seamlessly into the enquiry-management process after a hotel pulls an enquiry-ticket.

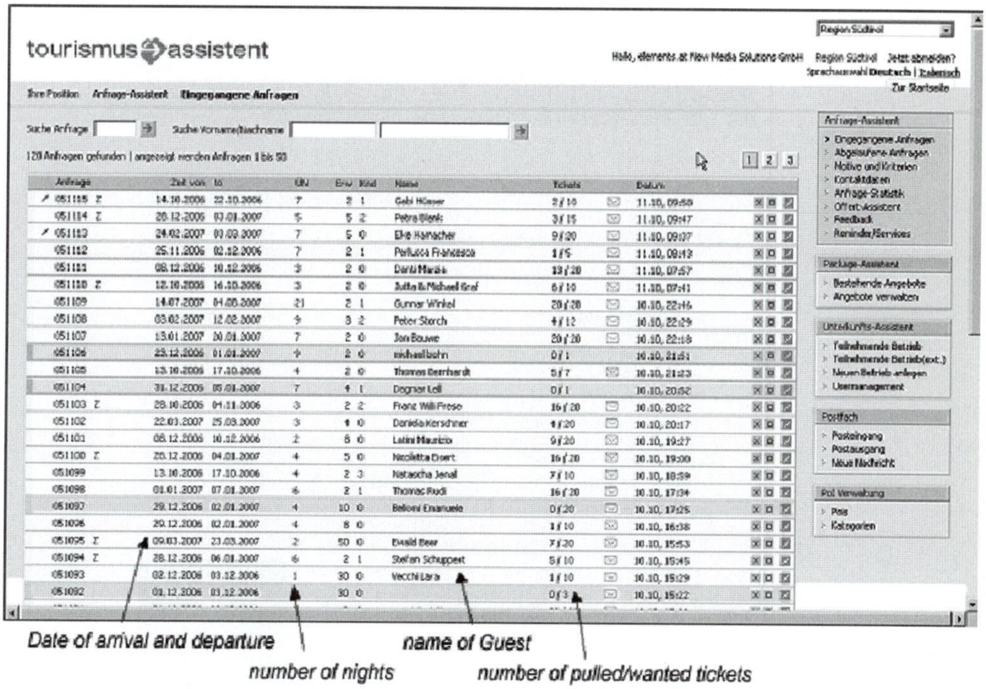

Figure 36.3 Enquiry list

With a few clicks, the hotelier can create a professional-looking offer and send it to the guest. One just has to enter the price, choose a text template (also available in different languages) and compose some individual/personalized lines. After three or four clicks the result is a well-designed one-page-offer in PDF-format. All participants gain with this solution – the destination because its corporate design is widespread, the hotelier because he/she can create an offer within three clicks, and finally the guest because he/she can easily compare the offers receive and has access to all of them through a personal CCC (Figure 36.4).

dPA: Package Management

Another available module of the dTA is the package management module which allows hotels to sell their holiday packages on their regions' web-platforms. Basically, a package consists of a description text, pictures, a category and a price, where the price can be a flat-rate or a price per person. Additionally, there is information such as possible arrival restrictions, a timeframe where the package can be used, a maximum number of persons and, of course, a range of available packages. Instead of waiting for a credit card to clear alternative online payment may be utilized.

Figure 36.4 Screenshot of a sample offer created with the dTA

dUA: The Hotel Search and List Module

Combined with search-masks and filters this module allows the guests to find their appropriate hotel in partner websites. The hotel display consists of a list-entry on partner sites. For further information one can click and be taken to a detailed page which combines all the other modules such as dPA, dAA, dVA on different tabs.

Key Challenges for the Future

Almost every Internet customer attempts to obtain price comparisons and to use the most favourable source for their reservation. The Internet presents a profitable market for expanding distribution channels and achieving sales (O'Connor, 2003).

Nevertheless, the future development of the dTA faces several problems. First, there is the big chance of including hotels' websites as channels for collecting enquiries and using the dTA as the exclusive tool for processing enquiries. The second thread is the emergence of full online booking solutions.

The challenge will always be to keep the status of a niche product developed as close to the market as possible, avoid failures and to break into new grounds in eTourism. The key USP of this software is the fact that it has been designed and developed very close to the market, together with a group of tourism specialists and process designers. Even the experiences and desires of back-office staff had great influence over the development of the software and this ensures its success and future development.

Key Conclusions

- Whilst online booking has been implemented within national and international software products and online booking platforms, enquiry and offer management solutions lack consideration.
- Online booking enquiries reach the hotel via two different channels, namely: direct contact via email or the hotel's website or through enquiries via the local tourism bureau or the incoming centre.
- The digital tourism assistant (dTA) facilitates this process by offering centralized enquiry pools which enables the guests, the DMO and the hotels to have an overview of the entire enquiry process.

Review and Discussion Questions

- Discuss the benefits of enquiries versus online bookings.
- How does the digital tourism assistant (dTA) improve the efficiency of the entire reservation system?
- Explore the business model of dTA and demonstrate how each stakeholder benefits.

References and Further Reading

Buhalis, D. (2003). *eTourism: Information technologies for strategic tourism management*. Harlow: Pearson Higher Education.

Buhalis, D., & Egger, R. (2006). Informations- und Kommunikationstechnologien als Mittel zur Prozess- und Produktinnovation für den Unternehmer. In M. Peters, & B. Pikkemaat (Eds.), *Innovationen im Tourismus* (pp. 163–176). Berlin: ESV Verlag.

O'Connor, P. (2003). Online pricing: An analysis of hotel company practices. *Cornell Hotel and Restaurant Administration Quarterly*, February, 88–96.

A list of clients using the digital tourism assistant can be found at http://www.tourismusAssistant.com/kunden

http://www.woerthersee.com.

http://www.tourismusassistent.com.

Company's website: http://www.elements.at.

37

Amadeus: Evolution of GDS

Patrick S. Merten and Irene Püntener

Learning Objectives

- Demonstrate that Amadeus ICT Group SA is one of the leading providers of ICT solutions for the tourism industry.
- Illustrate the role of GDSs in the tourism industry.
- Explain the business model of Amadeus with its three groups of customers, namely: travel providers, travel sellers, and travel buyers.

Introduction and Company Development

Amadeus IT Group SA is one of the leading providers of ICT solutions for the tourism industry. Air France, Iberia, Lufthansa, and SAS founded Amadeus in 1987 in order to develop a European global distribution system (GDS) as the answer to existing American GDS' Sabre and Apollo. Until today, the GDS represents the major link between airlines and travel intermediaries by holding all relevant flight and passenger information (inventories, schedules, availability, fares, fare rules, bookings and passenger name records), and by providing sophisticated searching, communication, and booking printing facilities.

In 2005, the majority of Amadeus was acquired by WAM Acquisition SA (founded by Air France, Lufthansa, Iberia, and two investment partners). A minority stake belongs to Amadeus' management itself. Amadeus currently has a global market share of 29.2%, being the absolute leader in Europe. National marketing companies (NMCs), and regional offices help to market Amadeus' products, and provide customer services. At the same time, they secure and expand Amadeus' worldwide presence.

Main Business Areas

Originally developed for the airline business, GDS soon became the most important interface and database in the field of tourism. The majority of the main travel providers distribute their products through the Amadeus systems. These are more than 500 airlines, 42 rental companies, and 56,000 hotel properties as well as special providers like ferries, railways, cruise companies, tour operators and insurance companies. Furthermore, around 75,000 travel agencies have access to the Amadeus GDS.

Airlines have a choice of different participation levels that vary in cost and functionalities. As an answer to the increasing importance of low-cost carriers, Amadeus also offers a distribution solution for these airlines. So far 30 low-cost carriers have signed contracts with Amadeus. A range of tools and services helping to optimize the distribution of the travel providers complete the travel distribution business model. Travel distribution still accounts for the biggest share of revenue of Amadeus, but as Holger Taubmann, CEO of Amadeus Germany, admitted in 2005, due to growing online bookings the whole classical GDS market will stagnate or even decrease in the long run as increasing cost pressure and declining margins are foreseeable.

Online sales in the travel industry are constantly growing and an increasing need for e-commerce products and services can be observed for travel providers, as well as travel sellers and travel buyers. Consequently, the e-commerce division of Amadeus, ('Amadeus e-travel'), develops and sells technology and solutions, trying to fulfil these needs. The products and services include online travel booking solutions for corporations, and an Internet booking engine for airlines. Amadeus' Internet booking engine is the back-end of more than 120 websites of over 60 airlines. The 'Amadeus e-travel' business unit is one of the two fastest growing business areas of Amadeus and has been awarded twice as 'World's Leading Internet Booking Engine Technology Provider'.

The second growth area, 'Amadeus Airline IT Services' business area offers a new generation IT platform: Amadeus Altéa customer management solution (CMS). It is built on open system technology and consists of three different modules that provide solutions for reservation, inventory and departure control. The independent Altéa modules can be flexibly combined, as this CMS platform has been designed to be scalable and to fit the needs of airlines, low-cost carriers, as well as airline networks or alliances.

Examining the competing GDS/IT providers, namely Amadeus, Sabre, Galileo and Worldspan, their offerings have become quite similar. Therefore an enforced competition can be observed, leading towards different business models and diverse strategies.

Business Model

Looking at the Amadeus business model, three groups of customers can be distinguished: travel providers, travel sellers, and travel buyers. In this value chain, business relations of the respective groups are fundamentally based on the systems and their functionalities offered by Amadeus, the content provided, and the available connections, as shown in Figure 37.1.

In this value chain, travel providers distribute their products through the Amadeus' electronic reservation and distribution systems. In turn, Amadeus receives usage and booking fees for offering their services. Airline seats still represent the biggest share of these travel bookings. The fees received for travel bookings account for approximately 70% of Amadeus' revenue. The providers' participation level defines the amount of the booking fee paid.

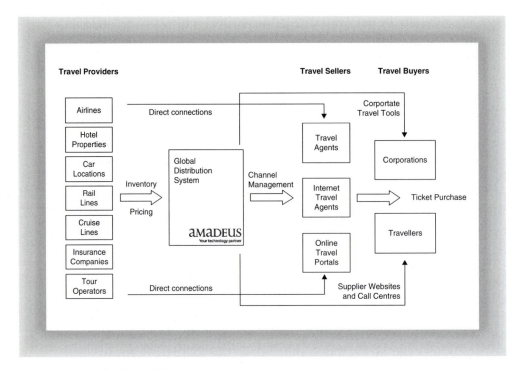

Figure 37.1 Amadeus value chain
Source: Adapted from Vialle (1994) and IBM Software Group (2004)

Furthermore, Amadeus receives subscriber fees from travel sellers for providing them with tools to increase their revenues, integrate and optimize their processes and booking transactions and to make their customer relationships more efficient. Amadeus pays incentives to gain and retain travel sellers. These incentive payments partially offset the revenues from this customer segment.

Through the acquisition of Opodo, a European travel portal, Amadeus also acts as a travel seller and has direct contact with travel buyers. As an independent business unit within the Amadeus Group, Opodo acquired different online travel players itself in the past.

Amadeus has not only acquired Opodo but also other companies. Among them are suppliers of hosted technology products for corporate travel or technology solutions to the hospitality industry. Besides acquisitions, Amadeus also formed partnerships with ICT providers such as IBM, Microsoft, SAP, Unisys, Siemens and software experts such as InterRes or Results Reservation Technologies Ltd. Amadeus calls their ability to enter long lasting, advantageous partnerships as one of their greatest strengths. Besides their partnerships, Amadeus names two other core strengths: their technology and 'global presence, local expertize'.

Technological and Business Innovation

In 2004 the International Air Transport Association (IATA) set a target of 100% market penetration for e-ticketing by 2007. Amadeus was chosen as one of the top global industry providers to support the adoption of e-ticketing. It facilitates electronic ticket distribution for 117 airlines worldwide. Amadeus helped the One World Alliance to become the first global alliance to adapt interline e-ticketing connections between all partner carriers.

Alliances are in fact a very essential issue in the airline ICT business. In 2005, Amadeus was chosen to build a common ICT platform for Star Alliance. This technology platform is based on the Amadeus Altéa Suite of ICT solutions for airlines. The technical infrastructure and software will be the same for all airlines. Prior to this new platform, all airlines had ICT systems with different technology. The new common ICT platform is said to facilitate processes and operations and to help airlines cut costs. An industry report sponsored by Amadeus suggests that other airlines also develop shared ICT systems, in order to deal better with the challenges of the airline industry. The increasing development of low-cost carrier ICT solutions shows the intention of Amadeus to offer products for all types of airlines. Similar to the Amadeus Altéa CMS, they launched a solution for low-cost carriers. In order to be successful as an airline ICT provider, the solutions of Amadeus have to reflect the business models of airlines – network carrier, regional airline or lowcost carrier – and their needs.

Key Challenges for the Future

Events such as terrorist attacks, wars and epidemics, but also high oil prices, financial crisis and severe competition, have caused a downturn in the travel industry and specifically in the airline businesses. Airlines desperately need to cut costs and make their business more efficient. It is therefore not surprising that they look for distribution alternatives which bypass the GDS, and therefore save costs. These bypasses are also reflected in Figure 37.1. In addition, there is a growing trend towards multi-channel distribution as content from airlines and other travel suppliers becomes more fragmented. That means different content is distributed over various channels. Direct online channels led to an increased transparency and ticket prices decreased. The multi-channel environment also increased the complexity for the travel agencies to find the best offer for their customers, since they cannot find them in one single source – the GDS – anymore. Amadeus and the other GDS providers have to find ways to compensate the lost earnings from bookings not performed through their systems, and to convince suppliers – especially airlines – to continue to still distribute all their products and fares through the GDS. In fact, 'content' is one of the greatest challenges for the GDS at the moment.

In order to reduce the dependency from travel distribution, Amadeus has decided to shift the strategic focus from being a classic GDS to a technology service provider of solutions to the travel and tourism industry that go beyond distribution. To emphasize this focus Amadeus changed its company name from Global Amadeus Travel Distribution SA to Amadeus IT Group SA. The tagline 'your technology partner', which completes the Amadeus brand name, is another indicator of this strategic approach. Amadeus aims to become the world's top ICT service provider for the travel industry as a whole, not only to the airline industry, by 2010.

One of the biggest changes in the business model of Amadeus has been the introduction of a new value-based pricing model in 2004. This reflects the fact that an airline has diverse commercial and channel strategies, and that the value of a sold flight differs for an airline depending on the distance of the flight (short or long), or the market that it is sold in (home market or foreign). This new pricing model is an answer to the airlines' complaints about excessive booking fees, and a strategy of Amadeus to retain the airlines' content. Other GDS have started to adopt similar strategies.

The Future of the Company

Legal, technological and economical changes have put pressure on Amadeus to adapt its strategy and product offerings to the changed business environment. In order to maintain a leading position as provider of ICT solutions to the travel industry, Amadeus announced it would invest €1 billion between 2004 and 2007 in the development of new technology solutions. Based on open-source technology and graphical user interfaces, the new systems enable value-based pricing and other features that match the challenges and needs of airlines. For example, self-service technology could become a dominant channel for transacting business in many markets. This is just one example of new technologies that will influence the development of ICT solutions to the travel industry. Amadeus' success depends on their ability to recognize new developments and to transform them into products that meet their customers' needs.

Key Conclusions

- The GDS represent the major link between airlines and travel intermediaries by holding all relevant flight and passenger information (inventories, schedules, availability, fares, fare rules, bookings, and passenger name records).
- GDSs also provide sophisticated search, communication, booking and printing facilities.
- Amadeus was chosen to build a common ICT platform for Star Alliance. This technology platform is based on the Amadeus Altéa Suite of ICT solutions for airlines.
- Amadeus has decided to shift the strategic focus from being a classic GDS to a technology service provider of solutions to the travel and tourism industry that goes beyond distribution.

Review and Discussion Questions

- What are the key challenges of GDS?
- How can Amadeus differentiate itself from the other GDS?
- Explore the business model of Amadeus and demonstrate how each stakeholder benefits.

References and Further Reading

FareLogix (2006). *The new multi-source environment*. Retrieved 31 March 2006 from http://www.farelogix.com.

G2SwitchWorks (2006). *The next generation of travel distribution services*. Retrieved 31 March 2006 from http://www.g2switch-works.com.

Global Aviation Associates (2001). *The history and outlook for travel distribution in the pc-based Internet environment*. Washington: Orbitz. Retrieved 31 March 2006 from http://www.intervistas.com/4/presentations/orbitzfinalbook1.pdf.

IBM Software Group (2004). *GDS solutions*. Retrieved 6 October 2005 from http://www-900.ibm.com/cn/industry/distribu-tion/news/pdf/caac/gds_solutions.pdf.

Lewitton, D. (2005). *Emerging changes in travel distribution economics and technologies: Letting the GNE out of the bottle, Travel Technology Congress*. Berlin: ITB.

Liew, R., & Powers, S. (2006). *Point/counterpoint: GNE versus GDS, TRAVDEX@ITB*. Berlin.

Marcussen, C.H. (2005). *Trends in European Internet distribution of travel and tourism services*. Denmark: Center of Tourism and Regional Research.

Mcdonald, M. (2005). Bypass ahead. *Air Transport World*, 42 (4), 48–50.

O'Connor, P. (1999). *Electronic distribution technology in the tourism and hospitality industries*. New York: CABI Publishing.

Prideaux, B. (2001). Airline distribution systems: The challenge and opportunity of the Internet. In D. Buhalis & E. Laws (Eds.), *Tourism Distribution Channels: Practices, Issues and Transformations* (pp. 213–227). London, New York: Continuum.

Sabre (2006). *Sabre holdings corporation*. Retrieved 31 March 2006 from http://www.sabre.com.

Sattel, J. (2005). *New opportunities in travel it and sales, Travel Technology Congress*. Berlin: ITB.

Vialle, O. (1994). *Global Distribution Systems (GDSs) in the tourism industry – A study prepared for WTO*. Madrid.

Company's website: http://www.amadeus.com.

38

Amadeus: global distribution system's new paradigm

Joan Miquel Gomis and
Francesc González-Reverté

Learning Objectives

- Demonstrate how Amadeus promotes use of its distribution system beyond travel agencies by serving airlines.
- Illustrate how the Altéa Reservation system involves the subcontracting of Amadeus' sales and booking system, whereby an airline can use it internally in all its sales offices, call centres and Internet portals.
- Explain how Amadeus is changing its business model to address the market challenges.

Air Travel Products at the Origin of the Business

Amadeus (www.amadeus.com) was created in 1987 by the European airlines Air France, Lufthansa, Iberia and SAS as a global distribution system (GDS), a centralized database and processing centre through which travel agents could contact travel service providers of all kinds and all sizes from around the world to be able to distribute these services to their customers.

The four GDSs that have dominated the market in recent years (Amadeus, Sabre, Galileo and Worldspan) were created by airlines, who used these systems to control the sale, fundamentally, of flight tickets via travel agencies. This means that the GDS business model has been sustained, traditionally, by the technological platform that linked the airline companies and travel agencies. The advance of Internet has affected the flight business, which has traditionally been the most automated. The web has brought with it online agencies, strengthened direct sales from the provider and boosted low-cost airlines, leading to changes at the core of the GDS business model. Amadeus has chosen to diversify, looking to offer technological services to all kinds of tourism companies and organizations and to own online agencies like Opodo (74%).

Amadeus promotes the use of its distribution system beyond travel agencies. In the past, Amadeus saw that airlines, which had traditionally used their own sales and booking systems, could gain important cost and functionality benefits in terms of their sales strategies by using a distribution platform that supported all sales channels and which could be shared both with other airlines and travel agencies. This system is known as Altéa Reservation and involves the subcontracting of Amadeus's sales and bookings system, whereby an airline can use it internally in all its sales offices, call centres and Internet portals (Table 38.1).

Towards a More Competitive and Flexible Scenario

The GDSs are undergoing a process of profound transformation brought on by the changes in the market and surroundings. The advance of Information Technology, especially the Internet, and the growth of low-cost carriers have led to a new scenario that requires that they revise their structure whereby, in the future, flight

Table 38.1 Worldwide market share in 2006 (net bookings)

Company	Market share (%)
Amadeus	29.2
Sabre	26.8
Galileo	22.5
Worldspan	15.8
Abacus	5.6

Source: Amadeus

distribution no longer represents a substantial part of their business. Amadeus has identified that, over the last 4 years, the total number of bookings around the world on GDSs has not increased at the same rate as have passenger numbers.

The traditional business of the GDSs as bookings systems may well be affected in the future by the development of the so-called GDS new entrants (GNEs), which look to take over leadership by offering technological solutions that help reduce costs. In 2005, the group of airlines members Star Alliance had their first contact with companies like G2 SwitchWorks (www.g2switchworks.com) and ITA Software (www.itasoftware.com) to build a new alternative technological platform to GDSs, that enabled them to reduce distribution costs. This initiative was implemented in the following two years, first in the United States and later in Asia and Europe.

In this light, the GDSs, apart from making efforts to adapt their costs to the market reality, have also opted for diversification strategies to face, among others, the threats that can affect their positioning in the market. All the leading companies (Amadeus, Sabre, Galileo and Worldspan) are opening parallel lines of business alongside the core GDS business. Galileo is part of Cendant and is built as a technological platform for the vertically integrated organizations in which it participates, including virtual agencies like Orbitz. In 2007, Cendant sold Galileo to Travelport, who has acquired Worldspan as well. Sabre has established a similar strategic line of business based on companies like Travelocity, which focus sales online for end customers, complementing their distribution, marketing and promotion strategies. Worldspan took part in the creation and development of Expedia. Amadeus has also opted to position itself strategically among the leading online agencies by acquiring Opodo.

The process of diversification of GDSs' activities, to counteract the expansion of low-cost carriers and GNEs, has led to important changes in the shareholders in each case. Investment groups have come in to take the place of the airlines. Faced with the likely growth of the low-cost business model (in terms of companies and operations) and increased competition, Amadeus has positioned itself as a distribution system that allows for the establishment of comparisons of offers, products and services. Likewise, in order to stand up to the GNEs, Amadeus has based its strategy on a new fees model for airlines, on the flexibility of its technological solutions in adapting to different companies and specific markets, on its worldwide scope and on the high level of content available over the system.

An Offer Based on Technology

Based on the creation of this pioneering distribution model and on the concept of a community made up of a large number of airlines, sharing the services, Amadeus has extended the range of sale and booking services to areas involving more complex inventory management and control of flight departures: branches now known as Altéa Inventory and Altéa Departure Control. In terms of this context, the following stand out from the range of products offered (Table 38.2).

From a Closed System to a Dynamic Technology Provider

Whilst the Internet advances, Amadeus continues to operate as a highly efficient, fundamentally flight-focused, distribution system for travel agencies. However, the system's customers, both providers (for the most part, airlines, who pay for the distribution of their products over this channel) and travel agencies, are both identifying alternative channels to the GDSs for selling their products and pressuring for drastic reductions in the tariffs they have to pay. Amadeus has reacted to this situation by refocusing its business model as a dynamic distribution and management technology provider for any company in the sector (activities which already represent 25% of its business). This has even led to its changing the company name from Amadeus Global Travel Distribution to the current Amadeus IT Group.

Table 38.2 Amadeus portfolio by type of customer

Customer	Solution
Travel agencies	Amadeus sales management: an integrated solution that combines the back- and front-office functions for travel agency points of sale. It includes the Amadeus selling platform (a platform for travel agencies used at more than 150,000 points of sale around the world) and Amadeus agency manager (back-office application) solutions
Airlines	Altéa customer management solution (CMS): a new-generation technological platform for bookings management, inventory management and flight departure control. It includes pioneering CMSs that allow airlines to identify the value of each passenger
Corporations	Amadeus e-Travel management: an Internet travel booking solution that helps companies manage travel policies more efficiently. It offers business travellers the ability to manage, book, purchase and plan travel itineraries that meet company policies and directives. Another solution designed for companies is SAP travel management with Amadeus: an integrated self-booking solution for the management of business travel in SAP environments

Source: Amadeus

This change in the business model has had its effects on the company's shareholders. As has been the case with the other GDSs, the airlines left the business when they saw that it was no longer useful in terms of their strategic positioning in a market that Internet had transformed by introducing open systems for sales and communication (Table 38.3).

In 2004, Amadeus exceeded €2 billion of revenue for the first time, culminating the advances seen over previous years, since 1998, when turnover was €1.2 billon. Net profits reached €208 million.

Table 38.3 Amadeus shareholders in 2006

Shareholders	%
BC Partners Cinven	52.2
Air France	22.9
Lufthansa	11.4
Iberia	11.4
Amadeus Management	2.1

Source: Amadeus

Innovation, a Strategic Option

Amadeus is the leading European travel and tourism sector company when it comes to investment in R&D, according to the European Commission. In 2004, Amadeus invested €153 million in this area. The decision to be innovative is thus a strategic option that is clearly supported by the organization, as a differentiating trait in an increasingly competitive market. In order to reinforce this decision, the product development team at Amadeus has spread the use of an advanced and efficient methodology to develop software that is innovative, quality and quick to market in order to respond to the technological needs of the sector companies.

In this context, one of the key technological elements at Amadeus has been the introduction of an open architecture that allows for solutions to be offered that are based on an open-standard platform. This replaces the mainframes used in the past with their proprietary operating systems. The platform brings together the key elements that allow the integration of different services and advances in terms of portability, scalability and continuous availability. Likewise, the e-commerce business unit, e-Travel, continues to invest in the latest generation technology.

Future Strategies: Tailor-Made Products and Geographical Expansion

All of Amadeus' strategies have a common denominator in the continued support for technological innovation as an element to ensure competitiveness in each of its lines of business. Thus, the

Information Communication Technology (ICT) product range for airlines (Altéa CMS) plays a vital role in its strategy, given that it is pioneering in the development of these services, which are increasingly in demand in the flight industry.

A factor which may influence future strategy in its main market (Europe) is the possible deregulation of the GDSs as proposed by the European Commission. Some groups in the sector believe that the neutrality required by the Code of Conduct would disappear, which would give Amadeus a competitive advantage in certain markets (Germany, Spain and France), thanks to the synergies with its airline partners.

In terms of its international expansion, Amadeus has identified the Asia-Pacific market as an important area for growth, not only in its core GDS activities but also as a dynamic technology provider, an area which the company has identified as the basis for the consolidation of its position in the industry in the long term.

The GDSs and their technology were created to respond to the needs of the traditional airlines. One of the current challenges set by Amadeus is based on providing value-added technological solutions for low-cost carriers that adapt to the needs and flexibility of a very simple business model. Indeed, this sums up its future strategy.

Key Conclusions

- Amadeus IT Group SA is one of the leading providers of ICT solutions for the tourism industry.
- The web has brought with it online agencies, strengthened direct sales from the provider and boosted low-cost airlines leading to changes at the core of the GDS business model.
- The traditional business of the GDSs as bookings systems may well be affected in the future by the development of the so-called GDS new entrants (GNEs), which look to take over leadership by offering technological solutions that help reduce costs.

Review and Discussion Questions

- Who are the key stakeholders of Amadeus?
- How can Amadeus re-emerge as an ICT provider?
- Explore how the business model of Amadeus changes to address market requirements.

References and Further Reading

Accenture (2006). *Alternatives to the Global Distribution Systems (GDS) Model. The Global New Entrants (GNE) Bypass Proposition Uncovered.* Retrieved from www.accenture.com/Global/About_Accenture/Business_Events/By_Industry/Travel/AlternativesUncovered.htm.

Alamdari, F., & Mason, K. (2006). The future of airline distribution. *Journal of Air Transport Management,* 12 (3), 122–134.

American Society of Travel Agents (2001). *ASTA Agency Automation.* Retrieved from www.astanet.com/about/2001automation.pdf?SUBMIT.X=13\&SUBMIT.Y=8#Page=60.

Appelman, J., & Go, F. (2001). Transforming relationships between airlines and travel agencies: Challenges for distribution and the regulatory framework. In D. Buhalis, & E. Laws (Eds.), *Tourism distribution channel. Practices, issues and transformation* (pp. 202–212). London/New York: Continuum.

Buhalis, D. (2003). *E-Tourism: Information technology for strategic tourism management.* Harlow, England: Financial Times Prentice Hall.

Buhalis, D., & Licata, C. (2002). The future eTourism intermediaries. *Tourism Management,* 23 (3), 207–220.

Gomis, J.M. (2005). *Tourism, Distribution and IT. Strategic Approach to the Effects of a New Paradigm on Intermediation.* Doctoral Thesis. Economy and Business Administration Department. Universitat Barcelona (in catalan).

O'Connor, P., Buhalis, D., & Frew, A. (2001). The transformation of tourism distribution channels through information technology. In D. Buhalis, & E. Laws (Eds.), *Tourism distribution channel. Practices, issues and transformation* (pp. 213–227). London/New York: Continuum.

Prideaux, B. (2001). Airline distribution systems: The challenge and opportunity of the Internet. In D. Buhalis, & E. Laws (Eds.), *Tourism distribution channel. Practices, issues and transformation* (pp. 213–227). London/New York: Continuum.

Travel and Tourism Analyst (2006). *Global Distribution Systems,* (7). Company's website: www.amadeus.com.

39

Pegasus Solutions: providing interconnectivity

Rainer Gruber

Learning Objectives

- Demonstrate the wide range of intermediary services between hotels and distribution channels offered by Pegasus.
- Illustrate how Pegasus is acting as an application service provider (ASP) – so that customers do not have to invest significantly in hardware, software and personnel.
- Explain the continuous innovation circle applied by Pegasus.

Introduction

Pegasus Solutions, Inc. is recognized as a leading global provider of technology and services to hotels and travel distributors. Its services are used by the largest hotel chains, smaller hotel groups, individual properties, travel agencies, websites, consumers, and travel wholesalers and tour operators.

Founded in 1989, Pegasus offers a unique mix of services:

- Electronic distribution to GDSs and websites;
- Central reservation systems;
- Marketing representation services;
- Consumer website www.hotelbook.com;
- Call centre voice reservation services;
- Web services;
- Tour operator automated booking service;
- Commission processing and payment services.

Based in Dallas, the company has 16 offices in 11 countries, including regional hubs in London, Singapore and Scottsdale, Arizona. Pegasus has now 1000 employees.

Products

Pegasus offers a wide range of intermediary services between hotels and distribution channels. Pegasus' electronic distribution services connect hotel reservation systems to the GDSs used by travel agents around the world: Amadeus, Galileo, Sabre and Worldspan. Today, this service also includes distribution to more than 1000 websites. Pegasus distributes rates, inventory, property information and images for more than 78,000 hotels.

Figure 39.1 shows the flow of queries from the GDSs, through Pegasus' switch to hotel central reservation systems (CRSs).

The company's CRSs are used by major hotel chains as well as small groups and individual properties. These CRSs are housed by Pegasus and provided on an outsourced, subscription basis – with Pegasus acting as an application service provider (ASP) – so that customers do not have to invest significantly in hardware, software and personnel.

Pegasus' marketing representation services are used by more than 9300 hotels in more than 130 countries. The services enable independent hotels to have a virtual presence and some of the marketing and distribution benefits available to large chains, while retaining their individual branding and identities. Many of

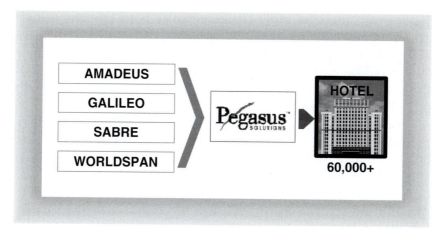

Figure 39.1 Pegasus switch provides hotel information to the GDSs

these hotels are promoted on the consumer site www.hotelbook.com, which offers the largest selection of distinct, independent and boutique hotels.

Hotels can add to these services by using Pegasus' network of call centres. Trained agents help both travel agents and consumers make reservations at participating hotels. Other offerings for hotels include Web services – from site design and marketing to booking engines that power reservations.

Hotels also increasingly choose the PegsTour® service, which helps them with their relationships with participating tour operators and travel wholesalers. The system automates bookings, accommodating the allocations that these companies use.

A final group of services is among Pegasus' most widely valued. The company's commission processing and payment services are used by the majority of the world's travel agencies. Pegasus acts as a clearinghouse – consolidating the payments from all participating hotels and sending agencies a single payment. Payments are made by cheque, bank transfer and direct deposit – always to each agency's desired location and in their chosen currency. Additionally for many travel websites, Pegasus also processes payments to hotels for bookings that the sites receive from consumers. All of these services keep payments flowing smoothly around the world for the hotel industry.

Business Model

Pegasus has a pivotal position in the travel industry – providing a wide range of critical services. As mentioned previously, Pegasus' services are used by hotel chains, smaller hotel groups, individual properties, travel agencies, websites, consumers, and travel wholesalers and tour operators. In fact, many of the company's long-standing customers are also competitors – they use some of Pegasus' services, yet offer their own services that compete with other Pegasus offerings.

Pegasus' services are very important in giving consumers around the world a broad choice of hotels whenever they are booking online, working with a travel agent or purchasing a package from a wholesaler. Other Pegasus stakeholders include the GDSs, which use Pegasus' hotel distribution services to supplement the air, car hire, cruise and other travel products they offer.

Many of Pegasus' technology services are provided on an ASP basis, that is, the systems are operated from Pegasus' data centre, and customers use them remotely. Through this business model, Pegasus is paid by the transaction or booking for many of its services. Throughout its history, Pegasus has generated very good cash flows. Figure 39.2 shows the allocation in 2005 of Pegasus' four service lines.

In August 1997, Pegasus became listed on the Nasdaq exchange through an initial public offering. In May 2006, the company

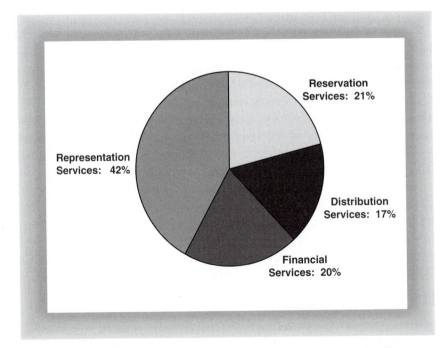

Figure 39.2 2005 revenue allocation among Pegasus' service lines

finalized a transaction to become a private company again, through an acquisition by a group of investors.

Innovation

Innovation has been integral to Pegasus' success. The company was founded on an innovation that revolutionized the hotel industry, then continued on that path. As a technology company, Pegasus must continue to stay current, introducing innovative products, new methods and creative approaches. Its philosophy recognizes that innovation is key to its role as a technology leader.

In 1989, Pegasus introduced the industry's first switch connecting hotels and travel agents through GDSs. Then in 1991, Pegasus was first to introduce travel agent commission processing, and in 1994, the first to connect hotels and the Internet.

In 2003, Pegasus developed an innovative rate and availability engine, known as RAVE, a technology that protects the company's RezView® central reservation system from the crushing volume of queries from websites around the world. As consumers shop for the best rates, these inquiries to hotel reservation systems keep rising – all for just one booking in the end. In 2006, Pegasus announced that it would offer RAVE to hotel chains for their own reservation systems.

In 2004, Pegasus introduced the PegsTour service, which automates booking processes for wholesale operators and connects them to multiple hotel CRSs.

Also in 2004, Pegasus re-introduced a new NetBooker Internet booking engine, which enables hotel and travel websites to connect directly to hotel systems for online reservations. Chief operating officer, John Davis, said at the time:

> [NetBooker]...represents a leap forward in our online booking technology and offers our customers an abundance of new features at truly cost-effective pricing. Moreover, the state-of-the-art design has the features that travel consumers demand from an online experience.

The year 2005 Pegasus was marked by internal innovations, including the adoption of agile management methodologies. The company organized its product development personnel into 'scrum' teams. These teams comprise employees from different departments who have been able to define, develop, test and launch product enhancements more quickly than before.

Technology Infrastructure and Challenges

Pegasus runs a data centre at its office in Scottsdale, Arizona. The data centre encompasses more than 1300 square metres, and the office also has a 180-seat reservations call centre. From this state-of-the-art facility, Pegasus delivers its technology applications to customers around the world. More than 1 billion transactions are handled by Pegasus systems each month.

In past years, Pegasus experienced challenges when it launched commission processing for hotels and travel agencies. The service started slowly while hotel chains waited for travel agencies to join, and travel agencies waited until enough hotels had agreed to this new service. Eventually, Pegasus reached a critical mass of customers from both sides, and the service flourished.

This challenge was repeated recently when Pegasus introduced the PegsTour service. Both tour operators and hotel chains waited until participants from the other side signed on. The other challenge for PegsTour is that the system represents a new way of doing business. Today, quite a few customers have agreed to use the PegsTour service and a number of them have started processing transactions. Management at Pegasus feel that, as with commission processing more than a decade earlier, the success of PegsTour will have a 'snowball effect'.

The Future

What does the future hold for Pegasus? As chief executive officer John Davis stated in the announcement in December 2004, 'Our focus will continue to be on delivering technology and business process solutions that help hotels and travel distributors come together to maximize revenue and profitability'. In the same announcement, COO John Davis added 'We will maintain the same service lines and products and will continue to focus on improving those products and the speed with which we bring them to market'.

Another project critical to Pegasus' future is the work to reach additional geographic regions. To do this, the company must add new language capabilities, including the double-byte characters of Asian languages. The online travel market in Asia-Pacific is expected to reach US$25.7 billion in 2007.

Pegasus is also working to help hotels use the right technology to differentiate themselves. Today, consumers are using on average four or more sites to research a trip. This means hotel websites need more robust content, and the features to close the sale online.

Teams at Pegasus are also working on another issue for the industry, the replacement of legacy reservation and property management systems that for many companies are more than 20 years old. To develop these projects, Pegasus is creating new services and delivering enhancements to existing services. The company is producing them in-house as well as aligning strategically with other companies.

For the challenge described above with the 20-year-old legacy systems, Pegasus' plan is to move these hotel companies to a more modular system, meaning that the parts can be updated without having to rewrite the whole system. Pegasus is essentially developing tomorrow's environment today – how would you build these systems from scratch, knowing what we know today and planning for the future as well? Pegasus is in the process of building a new Central Reservation System and calls the next-generation system, RezView NG, which was developed by Pegasus designers, as well as through work with the best technology companies.

Key Conclusions

- Pegasus Solutions, Inc. is recognized as a leading global provider of technology and services to hotels and travel distributors. Its services are used by the largest hotel chains, smaller hotel groups, individual properties, travel agencies, websites, consumers, and travel wholesalers and tour operators.
- Pegasus distributes rates, inventory, property information and images for more than 60,000 hotels. Today, this service also includes distribution to more than 1000 websites.
- Innovation has been integral to Pegasus' success and Pegasus continues to stay current, introducing innovative products, new methods and creative approaches.

Review and Discussion Questions

- Who are the key stakeholders of Pegasus?
- How can Pegasus benefit from the Internet and expand its value chain?
- Explore how the business model of Pegasus changes to address market requirements.

References and Further Reading

Buhalis, D., & Laws, E. (2001). *Tourism distribution channels: Practices, issues and transformations.* London: Thomson.

O'Connor, P. (1999). *Electronic distribution technology in the tourism and hospitality industries.* New York: CABI Publishing.

O'Connor, P., & Frew, A.J. (2002). The future of hotel electronic distribution: Expert and industry perspectives. *Cornell Hotel and Restaurant Administration Quarterly,* 43 (3), 33–45.

History of Pegasus: http://www.pegs.com/about_us/history.asp.

Links to bios for executive team: http://www.pegs.com/about_us/team.asp.

Company's website: http://www.pegs.com.

Conclusions of ICT Systems

It is not surprising that the rapid growth of a medium such as the Internet has had a significant influence on all commercial and private sectors and that the new generally accepted infrastructure is changing existing rules and structures. The rapid growth of the travel industry requires optimum communication between the participants in transactions in order to be able to communicate and process the masses of information arising in the tourism sector.

On the suppliers' side, the ICTs constitute a major tool for matters of production, distribution, marketing and coordination (Buhalis, 2000). Thus, for instance, customer wishes are satisfied more quickly, more flexibly and more individually. Business-internal and -external processes are optimized, new marketing channels opened, and the information exchange between all stakeholders and the enterprise is made more efficient. However, the fact is that in future the demand side will also be found within the structures of the tourism industry. Consumers will be the participants in the production cycle on an equal footing, not only in the function of the 'prosumer' but also as an individual arranger and planner of the product. This demonstrates the influence that ICTs have on tourism as a whole. The necessary restructuring and reorientation of entire business units will be the consequence if the requirements of the future are to be met.

References and Further Reading

Buhalis, D. (2000). Tourism and information technologies: Past, present and future. In *Tourism Recreation Research*, 25 (1), 41–58.

Part Six

Mobile systems
Roman Egger
Dimitrios Buhalis

Introduction

Today's society and economy are undoubtedly dominated by four closely interrelated trends: globalization, communication, mobility and virtuality. These developments have led to the emergence of the so-called information society, which redefines economic and social life, based on modern information and communication technologies (Gora & Röttger-Gerigk, 2001). The development, commercialization and professionalization of the Internet have been accompanied, in the last 15 years, by the establishment of mobile communications. Within a very short period of time, mobile communications became part of everyday life, both in the professional and private spheres. This has inevitably affected the field of tourism. What is more, mobile communications offer hitherto undreamt possibilities, spawning new mobile applications and services both in the area of B2C and B2B.

Mobile technologies gradually revolutionize tourism. In fact, mBusiness solutions are already implemented in many sectors of the tourism industry. In particular, the possibility of contextualizing, localizing and personalizing applications and services play a key role in the breakthrough of mobile solutions. In future, tourism products will be required to proactively take into consideration mobile developments in order to ensure that they to respond to the demands of travellers during each phase of their holidays.

Whether still travelling to the destination or already on location, mobile applications can provide travellers with suitable information and services to improve their travel planning and actual experience. Modern travellers increasingly expect to be provided with location-based, personalized, up-to-date information to improve their experience. The case study of Aladdin (Case 42), for example, introduces a mobile platform for incoming agencies, allowing them to provide tourists with a large number of location-based and customized information and services.

What was once regarded as the privilege of a chosen few has now turned into an information and communication tool for everybody. Higher data transmission speeds, data roaming between countries, new high performance applications, more transparent charging models and reduced roaming charges help mobile data services spread while at the same time increasing their acceptance. Mobile applications also penetrate social groups that are digital excluded, such as the elderly, lower socio-economic classes and people in less developed countries. Both 'technology push' and 'market pull' forces dominate market developments in the field of information and communication technologies. Technology push is the result of new functionalities and the improved performance of systems. Primarily, technological innovations result from digitalization, miniaturization, localization and standardization which make applications more desirable for consumers. Then market pull acts on these possibilities, driving the demand for new products that offer the customer additional benefit (Nachtmann & Trinkel, 2002). The most important demands of the market are interactivity, individualization, mobility, ubiquity and multimedia capability as well as the reduction of the transaction costs.

This is how new technologies are evolving, being the prerequisite for and the drivers of mBusiness. These technologies comprise the network infrastructure, mobile terminals and the available services and applications (Scheer *et al.*, 2002).

Network Infrastructure

In principle, the establishment of the mobile networks is the responsibility of infrastructure suppliers. However – and this reflects the trend towards concentration – transsectoral mergers give some companies the power to control large chunks of the infrastructure that extends across the entire supply chain. The leading companies are Cisco, Motorola, Siemens, Nokia and Sony-Ericsson. Technology leaps as well as the enforcement of different standards are conditional upon time and geography. In principle, in technological matters we recognize different development generations (2G, 3G). The modernization of old and the development of new technologies is the result of the introduction of services that will not work with the limited network capacities of the previous generation.

Connectivity over mobile telephone networks: From wireless application protocol (WAP) to general packet radio service (GPRS) to Universal mobile telecommunication system (UMTS)

Notwithstanding the enthusiastic expectations in the success of the third generation, the wireless application protocol (WAP) experience does evoke negative memories. Insufficient bandwidths, low-level usability, insufficiently developed services and a lack of business concepts shattered the high hopes for WAP. They also discouraged consumers from exploring mobile services further as they felt that technology was failing to deliver what it promised. The general packet radio service (GPRS) technology which offers a mobile data service available to users of global system for mobile communications (GSM) improved the ability to access the Internet on the move. GPRS is both faster and supports data transfer as it is typically charged per megabyte of transferred data. GPRS made access to Internet communication services such as email and the World Wide Web much easier and faster. The emerging telecommunications system (UMTS) offers third-generation (3G) cell phone technologies and services allowing faster data access and video calls.

Although the limited network capacities are largely a problem of the past, and although the transmission rates are now adequate, this does not mean that the door is wide open for the use of mobile tourism services. For instance, the widespread use of complex tourism applications with a high data volume depends on the penetration of UMTS-capable mobile telephones. In addition, the still exorbitant and obscure roaming fees continue to hamper the use of mobile data services for international travel. Nevertheless travellers are predicted to be among the heaviest users of wireless services. It is only a question of time until the technical infrastructure, high-performance data services, affordable pricing, suitable terminals and business models will be geared to satisfy the users' demands.

From the sociological point of view, it is apparent that we are gradually moving towards a lifestyle that requires a high degree of mobility and depends on a rich supply of information. 3G (the third mobile telephony generation) allows information to be supplied constantly without compromising mobility. It also permits positioning and the safe handling of payment transactions. Furthermore, there is a clear trend towards the convergence of the different media. In future, it is anticipated that the Internet and mobile telephony will converge, and the most diverse transmission technologies will be available in one terminal to enable a situation-dependant use. UMTS is expected to spawn three basic applications with relevance for tourism. The simplest variant is mobile Internet access. mCommerce offers the possibility of buying products and services. The third application, and the one that is of highest interest for tourism, will be the so-called location-based services (LBS) which will support profitable industry and customer interaction within particular regions.

Connectivity over data networks: From wireless local area network (WLAN) to WiMax

In addition to mobile telephony, there are many other mobile technologies that differ mainly in terms of transmission technology, data transmission performance and range, and regarding the system provider.

A wireless local area network (WLAN) links two or more computers without using wires. This is a wireless local area network that serves as an infrastructure extension in the sense of a connection to existing networks. In most cases, the terminals to be used are laptops, handhelds and smart phones fitted with a WLAN chipset. Most of WLANs are supported through Wi-Fi as a wireless technology which supports wireless local area networking based on the IEEE 802.11 standards.

Because of the dependence on hotspots (an area supplied by WLAN), services can be referred to as 'presence-based services'. However, with a radius of approximately 100 m, the range of WLAN hotspots is limited. In the field of tourism, wireless network access is most frequently used at airports, in trade fair and exhibition centres, cafés and in the hotel business to offer the guest the possibility of Internet access in seminar rooms, hotel rooms or the lobby. It should be added that merely providing guests with a wireless connection to a network is anything but the only use of WLAN. As the experiments of Starwood show, WLAN can also be used to optimize the operative processes in companies. For example, it was attempted to avoid queues at the front desk by having front desk employees equipped with PDAs to offer the guest the possibility of checking in directly at the hotel entrance. Other application examples include the networking of wireless security cameras in Mandarin Hotels and the provision of Voice over Internet Protocol (VoiP) phone sets.

The emergence of WiMAX (worldwide interoperability for microwave access) as a long-range system, covering many kilometres that typically uses licensed spectrum to deliver a point-to-point connection to the Internet from an ISP to an end user is gradually changing the wireless world. WiMAX provides a wireless alternative to cable and DSL for last mile (last km) broadband access and will support the wireless Internet access in large areas, such as towns, airports and hotel complexes. Even though innovative services usually focus on the customer as the user, in future it will also be worth considering internal uses of mobile and wireless solutions that will support company efficiency and effectiveness.

For completeness' sake, other technologies such as Bluetooth, IR (infrared) and RFID (radio frequency identification) should be mentioned because many of their applications are also relevant to tourism. Now and in the future, specific scenarios will drive the decision for the use of a certain technology.

Positioning and Satellite navigation: Global positioning system (GPS)

Satellite navigation, established quite a number of years ago, is a mobile technology that has already found its way into the field of tourism with undisputed success. A modern and attractive tourism offer has to satisfy demands such as flexibility, minimal environmental impact, site-specific supply of information and maximum security. Fields of application include hiking, horse-riding, mountain biking and ski touring. To complement terminal-based solutions, there are several platforms in the Internet that offer the user the possibility of selecting and downloading GPS tracks by region, difficulty, altitude metres, etc. In addition, to complement the data material, points of interest (POIs) such as information about tourist attractions, tourism service providers or vantage points can be included. Tourism organizations in particular may find themselves competing with content providers and aggregators. They will have to restructure their information and make it usable for mobile devices. Furthermore, it must be ensured that the information provided by external providers fits in with the strategic orientation of the destination.

Mobile Services and Applications

The mobile business takes different forms, ranging from a purely supportive function for the synchronous or asynchronous communication – via the use of the Internet as an information or distribution medium – to a comprehensive mobile business that incorporates the supply chains and processes between businesses and between businesses and their customers (Picot & Neuburger, 2002). Gora and Röttger-Gerigk (2001) point out a series of distinguishing features that are relevant for successful mCommerce solutions.

Localization: Localized information will increasingly be key for mCommerce. If data are combined with personalization and permanent accessibility, they open the door for a totally new service quality where information is specialized, appropriate and contextualized. Especially in the B2B area, positioning data is important because it facilitates better control and monitoring. However, before location-based services can be successful, it is necessary to overcome considerable concerns regarding the issue of surveillance, privacy and data protection. In principle, mobile telephone customers are located as they log into the network, but it is prohibited to pass on the data to third parties.

Personalization: The development of a personalized offer improves the communication basis and creates a closer relationship. At the same time, it has a positive effect on acceptance. Customers can choose an offer tailored to their personal preferences while the provider can respond to the customer's needs in a more targeted manner.

No site dependence: One of the biggest advantages of mCommerce is that the user has access to information and the possibility of concluding transactions irrespective of his or her location at the time. This may apply even to international services.

Security identification: In the short term, security is one of the most important factors, but in the medium term a certain common standard will be taken for granted. As a general rule, security – compared with the traditional Internet access – will be improved, and the terminals can potentially fulfil the role of a pocket book because the SIM card permits a clear identification of the user.

Convenience: The mobile terminals are much less expensive and offer greater ease of use than the PC, reducing the reluctance to use these devices. Mobile devices are cheaper, more transferable and often have better and easier interfaces. As a result they already enjoy a high level of acceptance and are generally widespread.

Cost effectiveness: As the number of users increases, the costs for processes, devices and services will stabilize. To introduce mCommerce successfully, the providers need to provide user-friendly and efficient applications that enable the downloading of data at affordable prices. Roaming is also of great importance for travellers, as the cost of downloading information and accessing services may be prohibiting. The success of mCommerce applications will depend on both the content and the cost of these services.

With mobile terminals, transactions will be freed from restrictions in terms of time and place. Tourism applications such as mobile ticketing, which include bookings and reservations, are attractive business applications that are naturally require mobility. According to Killermann and Vaseghi (2001), there are two complementary business models for mCommerce. Firstly, there is the communication services model, which is dominated by the communication between two or more customers. In this environment, the service provider offers one or several communication media or channels. Typical products in this respect are telephones, e-mail,

SMS or MMS. The service provider ensures that the mobile communication channel is available. Secondly, there is the content services model, in which the interaction of the customer with the provider's contents is dominant. Typical products of this business model from the customer's point of view are messaging and information services. For the customer, this content is accessible via his or her terminal from any location. The provider determines the quality of the content. In the following, two services will be presented whose complexity and performance differs, yet they are both used successfully in tourism applications.

Short message service is a telecommunication service to transmit text messages. Although a number of higher-performance technologies are available in the market, the high rate of use of SMSs has led many enterprises to develop their services on the basis of older but proven technologies, instead of applying the latest technological standard. For instance, the guest receives SMS alerts with local information about news and events, snow reports or weather forecasts provided that he or she has previously subscribed to the service in the web. Equally, bus and rail tickets as well as tickets for the cinema, concerts and museums can be ordered via SMS. However, acceptance and use rates of SMS differ worldwide.

In addition to mobile Internet access and the possibility of buying products and services (e.g. mTicketing), location-based services (LBS) are regarded as a highly promising application with relevance for tourism. This special variant of mBusiness offers the user site-specific information and services. The transmitted information is chosen to suit the geographic location of the terminal. Apart from individual localization, it is also possible to create a customer-specific profile. Acting as a filter, it personalizes information to user requirements. Experts largely agree that LBSs will play a pioneering role with regard to the development of mobile services. Services believed to fare well include interactive city guidebooks and indications of nearby restaurants, Internet cafes, filling stations and cash machines. In this connection, the Rivertale case study (Case 40) presents a location-based guide on cruise ships for the river Danube, which supplies the travellers with information about the environment via a kiosk or a PDA (personal digital assistant). In particular, the demands and the concept of such a system are addressed.

Location-based (LBS) services exploit the possibility of locating the caller through his or her mobile telephone, which must be switched on. The mobile phone dials into to the mobile telephone network through a radio cell, and it is the latter which reveals the approximate whereabouts of the caller. Now the user can get information and services relevant to his or her current location sent to the mobile telephone. Therefore, a person looking for a restaurant or the nearest cash machine away from home has to call up the appropriate services on his or her mobile telephone. LOVO's case study (Case 41) presents such a mobile solution. By means of localizing the user, responding to the personal profile and checking the situation-dependent enquiry of the user, the 'Lifestyle Assistant' provides personalized proposals with detailed information. Searching for a vacant room in the immediate vicinity or booking a table in a restaurant are classic examples of LBS-based mobile offers.

The following case studies show that mobile services have a rightful claim to high potential. This is particularly the case when a link can be drawn between information which is current, personalized and related to a location. They also demonstrate that both technological competence as well as business proposition should be in harmony if there is possibility of success.

References

Buhalis, D. (2003). *eTourism: Information technologies for strategic tourism management*. Harlow: Pearson Higher Education.

Egger, R. (2005). *Grundlagen des eTourism; Informations- und Kommunikationstechnologien im Tourismus*. Aachen: Shaker Verlag.

Egger, R., Hörl, J., & Jooss, M. (2006). *mTourism – mobile Dienste im Tourismus*. Forschung Urstein.

Ghandour, R., & Buhalis, D. (2003). Third-generation mobile services and the needs of the mTravellers. In *Information and communication technologies in tourism 2003* (pp. 222–231). Vienna, New York: Springer.

Gora, W., & Röttger-Gerigk, S. (2001). *Handbuch mobile-commerce*. Berlin, Heidelberg, New York: Springer Verlag.

Killermann, U., & Vaseghi, S. (2001). Wege zwischen Technologie und Wertschöpfung. In W. Gora, & S. Röttger-Gerigk (Eds.), *Handbuch mobile-commerce* (pp. 43–58). Berlin, Heidelberg, New York: Springer Verlag.

Mitchell, K., & Whitmore, M. (2003). Location based services: Locating the money. In B. Mennecke, & T. Strader (Eds.), *Mobile commerce: Technology, theory and applications* (pp. 51–66). Hershey, PA: IRM Press.

Nachtmann, M., & Trinkel, M. (2002). Geschäftsmodelle im MCommerce. In W. Gora, & S. Röttger-Gerigk (Eds.), *Handbuch mobile-commerce* (pp. 7–18). Berlin, Heidelberg, New York: Springer Verlag.

Picot, A., & Neuburger, R. (2002). Mobile business – Chancenpotenziale eines Mobilfunkbetreibers. In R. Reichwald (Ed.), *Mobile Kommunikation – Wertschöpfung, Technologien, neue Dienste* (pp. 55–70). Wiesbaden: Gabler.

Scheer, A., Feld, T., Göbl, M., & Hoffmann, M. (2002). Das mobile Unternehmen. In G. Silberer, J. Wohlfahrt, & T. Wilhelm (Eds.), *Mobile commerce. Grundlagen, Geschäftsmodelle, Erfolgsfaktoren* (pp. 87–106). Wiesbaden: Gabler.

Wirtz, B. (2001). *Electronic Business*. Wiesbaden: Gabler.

Case

40

Rivertale: mobile services for cruise ships

Astrid Ch. Dickinger and
Andreas H. Zins

Learning Objectives

- Demonstrate what information should be provided by river transportation and tour operators (RTO) for their customers.
- Illustrate how a location-based guide on cruise ships can be implemented as an information kiosk or as PDA (personal digital assistant) to provide travellers with information about their surrounding area.
- Explore the strategic questions for the product positioning, the technical conceptualization, and the operation for such an information system.

Introduction and Market Background

Travelling by ship is an increasingly popular way to enjoy one's holidays. Constantly increasing passenger numbers in the cruise industry hint at this prosperous development. It is important for river transportation and tour operators (RTO) to decide what sort of information should be provided for their customers. On-board location sensitive information systems have become increasingly popular. In this case study we present a location-based guide on cruise ships that can be implemented as an information kiosk or as PDA (personal digital assistant) to provide travellers with information about their surrounding area. This case provides a comprehensive dual view of operators and customers with respect to river cruise information systems. The example of Rivertale – a map-based, interactive cultural tourist guide for the river Danube – helps to illustrate the possibilities and degrees of interactivity to be configured to achieve a successful and sustaining information platform. Strategic questions for the product positioning, the technical conceptualization, and the operation for such an information system are raised and discussed at the end.

Travelling by ship is a niche market in tourism which has not yet received much attention. Gradually, market practitioners and scholars recognize the dynamics inherent in this market. On a global scale cruise ship passenger numbers expanded from 500,000 in 1970 to about 10 million in 2000 (Kester, 2003). The most recent report on the Cruise Ship Market published by the German Travel Agencies' Association at the ITB 2006 reports about 600,000 German passengers partaking of 300,000 river cruises. The compound growth rate of about 10% for Germany and Austria promises a prosperous and louring business.

Demand undergoes substantial structural changes. Cruise operators increasingly address demographic cohorts much below the age of 60 including families with children. While the luxury segment is losing market share, middle class cruises gain popularity. Themed cruise packages in particular on rivers allow segmentation, diversification and customer retention. One main question involves the rapid dissemination of travel-related services on the Internet: which role are the web-based services and location-based services for the various stakeholders in the river cruise market? Recent developments suggest that the dissemination of such services is overdue in this niche market.

Rivertale is a map-based, interactive cultural tourist guide for countries and regions along the river Danube and currently in the

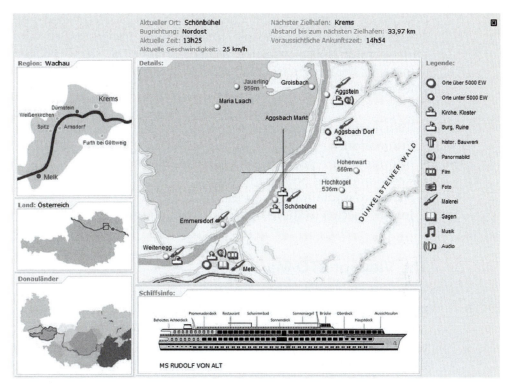

Figure 40.1 User interface of Rivertale with map

stage of a prototype. With reference to the current position of the river cruise vessel the traveller receives multimedia information such as historic paintings or movies of actual places, quotations of famous authors, regional music, actual pictures and texts, and also movie and audio files of the region. Further travel-related information such as the daily programme or an introduction to the next port of call can be displayed. The system can be provided as an information kiosk or on a PDA. A prototype of the interface is shown in Figure 40.1. It depicts a map indicating the ship's current position along the river Danube with varying degree of detail.

Business Model

State of Implementation of Web Information

From European projects such as the ship information and management system (SIAM) and teleshipping (Maglogiannis *et al.*, 2004) some insights into this topic can be gathered. Similar to the practice of accommodation companies a set of web-based and integrated services is feasible for the river transportation and tour operator (RTO) websites. Maglogiannis *et al.* (2004) elicited some core areas of particular interest to ship travellers in their Teleshipping project:

- Information on facilities on-board, at the ports, and at the destination.
- Information on packages, prices, schedules.
- Reservation and booking facilities.
- Access to infotainment services on-board.
- Internet access to shore-based information services.

The View of RTO Managers

For a more comprehensive view, managers of the major European RTOs were asked to report on the facilities already offered and planned to be offered on their websites and the potential of a location-based information system on cruise ships. Taking into account that two RTOs within the sample had no website available, ship descriptions and deck plans can be found on every RTO website. Images of vessels can be found on 56% of the sites. Even the core information on the offered packages, dates and itineraries, is not always available.

For some areas the current availability and the managers' perception of what is available on their websites differs. Ship localization and webcam services are currently wishes or plans at best. Managers agree to show destination information. However, this is often only a teaser for a particular tour. A fully integrated, flexible and interactive offer about the geography, the cultural sights and the leisure infrastructure cannot be found so far. Similarly, direct booking facilities are in their infancy.

What kind of information channels do RTOs offer to cruise passengers? Summarizing both phases, before and during the trip, printed and personal information and communication take the highest frequencies while interactive electronic channels are much less popular.

RTO representatives were asked to rate the importance of various benefits they could expect from implementing Rivertale. Improved company image and competitive advantage ranged among the most important. Regarding concerns involved with such a system, ease-of-use is the most urgent concern, followed by cost aspects.

Passengers' View

The average Danube river cruise passenger is 62.5 years old (Dickinger & Zins, 2006). Most of the Danube river cruise passengers in Austria are pensioners (63%), employees (22%), and self-employed (11%). Two thirds of the travellers in the survey sample are from the United States and Germany, followed by the United Kingdom (7%) and Austria (4%). The usage of mobile phones (83%) by far exceeded the usage of the Internet (54%). In order to balance the future content of an interactive river cruise information system, the travellers were asked to evaluate the usefulness of different types of information on board. Apart from schedule, itinerary, and ship information, river cruise passengers are highly interested in the region they pass by. Thus, together with general destination information it is important to get relevant information to decide and plan various shore visits.

The general attitude of travellers towards an interactive location-based information system is very good. Eight of ten consider it as positive and equally as many as useful. Most of the travellers expect to find relevant information more easily and quickly (60%). Six out of ten are convinced that a kiosk system is valuable.

When it comes to the reputation of the tour operator the implementation may have a positive impact, just as the RTOs assumed. They even think an RTO providing an interactive information service cares more about their customers. More than a third of the cruise ship passengers would like to use such a system via Internet before the trip. The majority of 80% would use an interactive location-based system when available on-board. They consider it as entertaining when a part of the route is not particularly exciting. Half of the travellers think that Rivertale would be a good pastime and fun. This shows that fun and entertainment are very important motivators of technology use. Half of the respondents would like to use a system like Rivertale on their next cruise.

Key Challenges for the Future

Three major issues should be highlighted and discussed: (1) the conceptualization of the information system as lean-forward or lean-back technology, (2) the degree of integration of various services, and (3) the operation of such a system. All three aspects are not completely independent from each other.

First, information about itineraries, cultural background on destinations, ship infrastructure, etc. could be offered in a rather pre-fabricated fashion and fed into a cabin-TV system or, in contrast, into a more individualized and interactive information kiosk (with touch screen) or PDA solution. Adoption rate, implementation and maintenance cost as well as content scope are some but definitely not all aspects contingent on this first decision.

Second, the type of information offered to the passengers is a core question to be solved. Closely related to this is the system architecture: it can be either based on a proprietary database gathering all the necessary information into one basket or integrating information on a platform or portal from various sources and providers. A critical issue in this respect is the geographical coverage since many ships cruise on different rivers and pass several countries even in single trip.

Third, it is essential to include all the stakeholders involved in this kind of business. One key player is the ship owner or charter company. Their primary objective is to promote and position their products and tours. Another party in this value chain are distribution partners or travel agencies. They, sometimes, specialize in the cruise travel business and try to make profit from the detailed knowledge they acquired and exploit for the customers' benefit. From the destination point of view a good deal of tourism information is already available in a digital format. However, on a national or even cross-national level the information offered is not comprehensive, harmonized or centrally available. Hence, destination information systems could share their content to be fed into a cruise information portal, yet these systems are not suited to take the lead part for an integrated solution.

The Future of On-board Information Systems

Current industry examples (see the links in the Reference list) may indicate the direction for the future development in the river cruise market. Commercial products have been developed and implemented by technology companies (either specialist in interactive TV or in the entertainment field). Such products are basically shell solutions which fit into any particular company specific environment. In some cases interfaces to reservation or booking tools and to destination or map-based information systems are part of the service portfolio. For a system like Rivertale, which focuses on interactive cultural multi-media information services enriched by a location-based module, two basic strategies can be followed: either progressing towards a forward and backward integration of additional services which are core to the river cruise business or looking for strategic partners to offer a specialized information service (Rivertale) under the umbrella of a larger industry solution like Cruise Show, Travelnet Cruise or SeaWise.

Acknowledgements

This research was embedded in two studies with financial and organizational support from Wiener Wirtschaftsförderungsfonds, Niederösterreich Werbung, Wanderman OEG and Rainer Krankl. We are grateful for the fruitful cooperation.

Key Conclusions

- Rivertale is a map-based, interactive cultural tourist guide for countries and regions along the river Danube and currently in the stage of a prototype.
- The system takes the current position of the river cruise vessel into account to provide multimedia information such as historic paintings or movies of actual places, quotations of famous authors, regional music, actual pictures and texts and also movie and audio files of the region.
- The system should be integrated with various other systems and services.

Review and Discussion Questions

- What are the key benefits of Rivertale?
- Who are the key stakeholders of Rivertale and how can they benefit from its operation?
- How can Rivertale benefit from the Internet and expand its value chain?

References and Further Reading

Dickinger, A., & Zins, A. (2006). Adoption of innovative river cruise information systems. In: M. Hitz, M. Sigala, & J. Murphy (Eds.), *Information and communication technologies in tourism 2006* (pp. 209–220). Vienna: Springer.

Maglogiannis, I., Kormentzas, G., & Panagiotarakis, N. (2004). Emerging web-based services for ship travellers. *Information Technology & Tourism*, 7, 23–31.

Kester, J. (2003). Cruise tourism. *Tourism Economics*, 9, 337–350.

http://www.teleshipping.net

http://www.moller.de/cs_main.htm

http://www.euronav.co.uk

http://www.idf.de

http://www.allin.com

41

LOVO: the mobile lifestyle assistant

Roland Fleischhacker

Learning Objectives

- Demonstrate that when selecting the appropriate advertising message, the LOVO system is able to reflect the current mood, special preferences and actual geographical location of each individual consumer.
- Illustrate how the ubiquitous-use system enables the display of leisure tips to practically every electronic medium available on the market.
- Explain how each lifestyle group shows typical behaviour patterns and is targeted for specific information.

Introduction and Company Development

LOVO provides an innovative lifestyle-information service which delivers accurate personalized recommendations for leisure time and holidays to individual consumers. LOVO acts as a behaviour-targeting advertising medium: when selecting the appropriate advertising message, the LOVO system is able to reflect the current mood, special preferences and actual geographical location of each individual consumer. These capabilities make LOVO the most precise advertising medium in the world.

The system was developed as a multi-channel application, and consumers use it via mobile devices, web-based devices and set-top-box-based devices. The system is therefore available around the clock and can be used at the consumer's convenience.

LOVO Lifestyle Service GmbH, the company that created the system, was founded in 2003 and is based in Vienna, Austria. The first of 11 research projects for the system development started in 2001, while the service was launched in summer 2006. It took an interdisciplinary team – comprising of mathematicians, statisticians, sociologists, ICT experts and researchers – almost 10,000 person-days to develop the system.

Products/Services and Value Added

The LOVO Lifestyle Assistant is an interactive, digital lifestyle tool offering recommendations for travel and leisure time. The context-sensitive system creates optimized recommendations for the user's leisure-time activities, based on the following criteria:

- Current mood and needs of the user (mood-based)
- Current or planned location of the user (location-based)
- Current weather conditions at the location and a short-term weather prognosis
- Season (at the location)
- Time of day (at the location)
- Basic personal character of the consumer (e.g. adventure-orientated, consumption-orientated)
- Personal interests, preferences and hobbies of the consumer (personal profile)
- Opinions and preferences of the lifestyle group to which the user belongs.

The ubiquitous-use system enables the display of leisure tips to practically every electronic medium available on the market, and it also allows the addition of new devices with little effort. Currently, the system can be used with the following:

- Thin web-clients (Internet Explorer, Firefox, Opera, etc.);
- Rich web-clients (Ajax);
- Mobile messaging (SMS, MMS, WAP Push, email);
- Mobile web-clients (Pocket Browser, WAP, i-mode, Opera, etc.);
- Set-top boxes (interactive television, hotel television);
- Web services (SOAP).

Registration

To use the LOVO Lifestyle Assistant, the consumer has to register, either through the LOVO website or via a mobile phone. This enables LOVO to collect demographic and sociological data as well as preferred system settings. At some stage in the registration process, the consumer completes a brief questionnaire which is used to determine the lifestyle group into which she or he fits (Zellmann & Opaschowski, 2004). Each lifestyle group shows typical behaviour patterns, which can be verified on the basis of statistical studies. Despite the fact that these studies contain only statistical figures, LOVO is nonetheless able to draw from them relevant conclusions about the leisure-time habits of each user. As a result, from the very first time the consumer begins using the system, LOVO delivers leisure-time-use information of high personal relevance.

As soon as a consumer's individual profile – even if it is in only a very basic form – is available to the LOVO system, the consumer can begin using the LOVO Lifestyle Assistant. However, the consumer can specify, with a very high level of precision and detail, several hundred parameters regarding his or her favourite leisure-time activities and areas of interest (Figure 41.1).

Requesting Recommendations

The consumer submits a predefined request by sending an SMS, either by simply choosing an item on the web interface or on a hotel television set. The request is recognized by the system, and this starts a business process, which is defined in business process execution language (BPEL). In the first step, LOVO identifies the consumer either by evaluating the incoming mobile phone

Figure 41.1 Example of a leisure-time tip on a Smartphone (GPRS, UMTS, WLAN)

number (MSISDN) or the session ID in the webcase. The next step is to locate the consumer by calling a web service of the mobile carrier, which returns the geographic co-ordinates in WGS84 format. The accuracy of the locating varies by 10–50 metres in urban areas, and by several kilometres in rural regions. Once the consumer is located, another web service is called to get the present weather information for the given location. Then the system loads the consumer's personal profile into the session:

To determine the most suitable leisure recommendations, LOVO uses input data from four domains:

- The domain 'environment' indicates the time of day, season, location and the weather data at that location.
- The domain 'situation' transmits leads about the consumer's present mood and needs.
- The domain 'user' conveys extensive information concerning the consumer's personality, favourite leisure-time activities and past behaviour patterns.
- The fourth domain, 'lifestyle', provides indications about behaviour patterns of people with similar lifestyles and in similar situations.

The system gives a rating to every objective (recommendation) that is suited to the consumer's needs. According to the channel used, the most accurate recommendations are forwarded to the output system for data-processing.

In addition to the actual data provided by LOVO about a leisure-time recommendation, the business process makes an effort to gain, from web services, relevant supplementary information relating to this recommendation. Such supplementary data

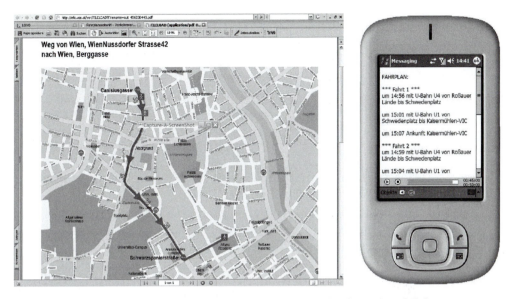

Figure 41.2 Example of included door-to-door guide (web and mobile)

include time-tables of public transportation services or routing information for passenger-car traffic. Using the precise geographic co-ordinates of the consumer together with the recommended objectives, LOVO is able to provide exact door-to-door guides (Figure 41.2).

ICT Architecture

The ICT system is composed of seven layers which communicate with each other through standard interfaces. The first (topmost) layer is the device layer. The requested devices are to be identified either automatically or by the consumer in the process of registration. Layer 2 is the gateway layer. These gateways, which do not usually belong to the LOVO infrastructure, enable the conversion of the data stream into the corresponding output format. Examples of gateways are presented in Table 41.1.

Layer 3 is the presentation layer, which is implemented as a 'multi-channel interaction engine'. This layer makes it possible to conduct user dialogues across different channels. The basis of every data output is an XML structure.

Corresponding to the requirements of a particular device and of its gateway, an XML SAX stream is formatted in such a way that the gateway can accept and forward the data to any end device. Thanks to the generic structure, new device classes can be put into

Table 41.1 Gateways for data presentation

SMSC	Mobile
MMSC	Mobile
WAP	Mobile
SMTP	Mobile, web
HTTP	Mobile, web

service within minutes, and users have the option of optimizing the output for the individual end devices.

Within the fourth layer, all high-level decisions are made. The implementation of the entire business logic takes place in BPEL. This allows maximum flexibility for the planning and adaptation of business processes. New use cases can be activated and ready for use within just a few hours.

Layer 5, the service layer, is a collection of web services available to the business layer. Layer 6 is the data-abstraction layer, which converts relational data into objects by means of object-relational mapping tools. Finally, the seventh layer is the data layer, which represents a relational databank.

Business Model

The content of the LOVO Lifestyle Assistant is not provided by tourism service suppliers but by the consumers themselves. Users can generate content by using a web interface which enables them to maintain descriptions and pictures of tourist hotspots. Thus LOVO-content (LOVOversum) represents the favourable perspectives the community looks for. This process is supported by a professional content organization sponsored by LOVO (Figure 41.3).

The major revenue is realized by advertisers who pay for each commercial message that is sent out together with lifestyle recommendations. For example, the request 'luxury diner' is answered by the recommendation of a gourmet restaurant. The user gets a description of the restaurant, address and telephone number, opening hours, etc. The restaurant tip includes an advertising message of an exclusive credit card or a champagne trademark.

As described in the previous section, the context-sensitive system processes the input parameters and calculates the leisure-time recommendations which are most appropriate for the requesting individual. Another system type (instance), with a different basis of regulation, calculates, based on input parameters, which advertising

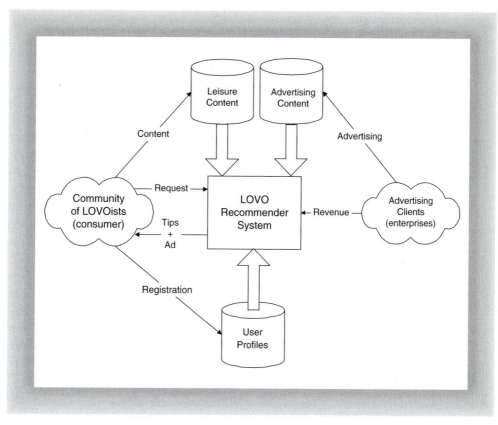

Figure 41.3 The LOVO business model

message is most appropriate for the consumer at the time of request and then selects the best match from a pool of prepared messages. So the advertising message is also highly personalized and takes the environmental conditions into account (e.g. actual weather). Raw data – whether for a leisure-time recommendation or an advertising message – is forwarded in XML to the presentation layer, where it is processed in a device-specific manner.

Advertisers are charged for every transmitted commercial message. This guarantees that advertisers pay only for those ads which definitely accomplish their purpose: the awareness of prospective consumers. As a consequence, scattering losses are effectively ruled out.

Technological and Business Innovation

The LOVO Lifestyle Assistant is one of the first professional Web 2.0 applications in eTourism. Since the system uses context-sensitive information, many consider it a Web 3.0 application. It is entirely based on a service-orientated architecture. This enables the system to use web-based resources, for example, for localization, weather forecasts, mapping and traffic routing.

The system employs social mechanisms to generate and update premium content in rich user-interfaces, and it takes advantage of the community's in-depth knowledge to rank the recommendations. LOVO's ability to cluster the mass of consumers into different lifestyle groups, and the rating of recommendations by these groups, is nothing less than an electronic version of word-of-mouth ('birds of a feather flock together'). Hence, all transmitted recommendations are of heightened significance to the individual consumer, and this also enhances the quality of the extremely individualized recommendations.

Conventional systems ask what one is looking for, for example, restaurants, clubs, attractions or hotels. But to be able to specify a venue or event, the consumer must usually be familiar with the opportunities available in the immediate surroundings, for example, knowing the name of a hotel or restaurant nearby and whether it is currently open. However, people rarely have such information when they are in an unfamiliar place. LOVO solves this problem, as it is mood-orientated. By selecting one of the predefined 'LOVOmoods' (e.g. 'I am bored') the consumer informs LOVO about the present mood, and the recommendation engine then calculates the best concepts by using the semantic-structured content provided by the community.

The recommendation engine uses rule-based (LOVO world model), case-based (user behaviour) and collaborative (peer-group behaviour) mechanisms, together with environmental information, to extract the most advantageous recommendations for the consumer. The weighting of different mechanisms depends on the kind of request. When the consumer needs instant fulfilment (e.g. being short of time, being thirsty or hungry), the points-of-interest in the vicinity are of high importance, and the geographic component (distance from consumer's location to recommendation's location) is weighted more than it would be in other search strategies.

Key Challenges for the Future

LOVO faces one major question: will the lifestyle service be valuable enough to attract a community with a critical mass? Research indicates that the population in German-speaking regions can be

Table 41.2 Affinity for using leisure-time-orientated recommendation systems within the population of Germany, Austria and Switzerland

Type/grade of affinity	Share of population (%)
Pioneers (early consumers)	15
Prospective consumers	35
Sceptics	23
Resistants	27

Source: LOVO market research (2004)

divided into four meta-clusters in terms of affinity for using lei-sure-time-orientated recommendation systems (Table 41.2).

These results are similar to research published in 'One-to-One Webmarketing in der Reisebranche' (Conrady & Schuckert, 2002), which showed that the majority of web users are more willing to maintain personal profiles if they get individualized leisure and travel information.

The Future of the Company

LOVO piloted the project in Austria, because this country offers an excellent tourist infrastructure, more than 100 years of tradition in tourism and a mature mobile market in a relatively small country. Nevertheless, LOVO intends to establish a global, dynamic com-munity of consumers, called LOVOists, who share the experience of their leisure time to achieve 'More Life Now!'

Looking ahead to the future, LOVO's three top priorities are (1) to permanently expand the geographical area for which content is offered, (2) to increase the number of active LOVOists and (3) to permanently extend the functional range. Especially in the field of functionality, LOVO is greatly benefiting from the flexibility gua-ranteed by the IT architecture. For the future, LOVO is planning a shift from leisure-time information to transactional services, which will also provide booking opportunities, both mobile and web-based. In this area, the focus is in particular on collaboration with Internet-based booking platforms for events, hotels, car-rental services and travel.

Key Conclusions

- LOVO provides an innovative lifestyle-information service which delivers accurate personalized recommendations for leisure time and holidays to individual consumers.
- The system was developed as a multi-channel application, and consumers use it via mobile devices, web-based devices and set-top-box-based devices.
- Consumers register to LOVO Lifestyle Assistant providing demographic and sociological data as well as preferred system settings to create a lifestyle profile.

Review and Discussion Questions

- What are the key benefits of LOVO for consumers?
- How can tourism suppliers use LOVO effectively?
- How can LOVO benefit from interconnectivity with other service providers?

References and Further Reading

Conrady, R. & Schuckert, M. (2002). *One-to-One Webmarketing in der Reisebranche*. FH Heildronn, Germany.

Herlocker, J., Konstan, J., Terveen, L., & Riedl, J. (2004). Evaluating collaborative filtering recommender systems. *ACM Transactions on Information Systems (TOIS) archive*, 22 (1). Retrieved from doi.acm.org/10.1145/963770.963772.

Russell, S., & Norvig, P. (2002). *Artificial intelligence: A modern approach*. London: Prentice Hall.

Schulze, G. (1992). *Die Erlebnisgesellschaft. Kultursoziologie der Gegenwart*. Frankfurt/New York: Schulze.

Zellmann, P., & Opaschowski, H. (2004). *LOVO Freizeittypologie* Internal paper.

42

Aladdin: a mobile destination management solution for incoming agencies

Frank Schröder

Learning Objectives

- Demonstrate how a mobile destination system can combine a Mobile Incoming Tour Operator workspace (B2B) and a Mobile Content and Service-Management (B2C) for destinations.
- Illustrate how Aladdin supports tour guides in the destination with a sophisticated mobile work application for different customer care and relationship activities.
- Explain the different usage scenarios for the B2B but mostly for the B2C environment provided by Aladdin.

Introduction

The Aladdin project provides a combined mobile platform to small and medium sized Incoming Agencies in order to enable them to offer tourists a broad array of location-based and customer-tailored information and services during their stay in the destination. Incoming-Tour-Operators, tourist offices, restaurants and museums are typical SMTEs that need to provide different services to tourists in a cost efficient but attractive way. Given the trends of mixed individual/group travelling and highly volatile business-processes that increase the complexity and costs of operations, Incoming Agencies face several challenges, including optimized tour-transfer-set-ups, tailored offerings, the handling of last-minute changes for hotel bookings.

Aladdin supports tour guides in the destination with a sophisticated mobile work application for different customer care and relationship activities. The system allows tour guides to interact electronically with the incoming tour operator system and other information providers and therefore provide an efficient and flexible means of work for optimized processes. Thus the Aladdin system increases the competitiveness of European SMTEs by enhancing their business potential.

Company Development

ISO Software Systeme GmbH delivers optimized software solutions for the tourism industry. ISO was founded in 1979 and today, more than 25 years after its foundation, approximately 220 employees work for the company. The company's turnover reached more than €19 million in 2005. The ISO headquarter is located in Nuremberg, with branch offices in Munich, Frankfurt and Stuttgart and international offices in Canada, Austria and Poland.

As a result of 25 year experience in product development of tour-operator solutions and projects for international clients, ISO was able to build up comprehensive and diversified knowledge for tourism-related software solutions. ISO provides components and entire solutions for outbound and incoming tour operators and for different market segments ranging from specialist tour operators, that organize things like hiking group travel to high volume tour operators (package and modular business).

ISO's main focus is now on the development of high-volume and premium tourism software solutions based on the ISO

Dynamic Travel Components Strategy. The Mobile incoming workspace of Aladdin is based on some of these components.

Main Products/Offerings and Value Added

The EU project Aladdin aimed at developing a mobile destination system that combined a mobile incoming tour operator workspace (B2B) and a mobile content and service-management (B2C) for destinations. Figure 42.1 describes a short process flow through all participating actors.

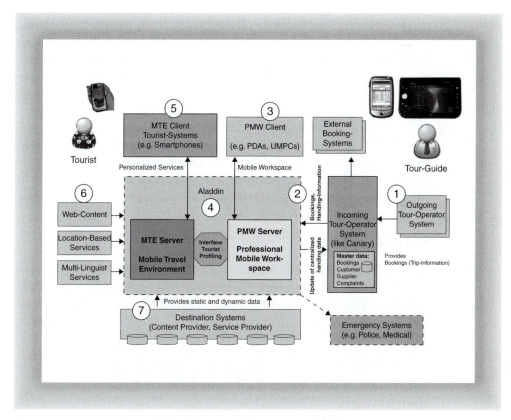

Figure 42.1 Overview of Aladdin ICT Infrastructure

Outgoing Tour Operator System(s)

A tour operator in the source market usually provides booking data with the relevant information about arriving guests to the destination. Usually a list of all booked services, all participants and additional address data will be sent to an incoming tour operator in the destination. The incoming tour operator has a contract with the outgoing tour operator to manage all booked services in the name of the outgoing tour operator for the guests.

Professional Mobile Workspace and Incoming Tour Operator

The incoming tour operators are using standard booking systems (like the solution 'Canary' from ISO) to maintain their daily business but without any mobile capabilities. Aladdin provides the 'Professional Mobile Workspace' (PMW) that enables a tour guide to provide various downstream and upstream services to tour guides. He/she can interact electronically with the back office and has access to context information such as arrivals, allotment status, etc. In order to access this information the PMW consists of two major components: the PMW Server and the PMW Client.

The PMW Server

The PMW Server integrates Standard Incoming Tour-Operator Systems (like Canary) and provides services for the PMW Client (Synchronization, etc.) handles all communication between the MTE and the PMW Environment.

PMW Client

The PMW Client is the mobile application that is working on a specific mobile device that the tour guide is using for the daily business. The PMW Client allows all workflows to be handled on the mobile device (e.g. checking arrivals) and to create, update and synchronize incoming tour operator data with the server.

Interaction between B2B and B2C in the destination

Interaction between B2B and B2C in the destination is one of the most important parts of the solution. The booking data and the preferences of the guests are transferred – with consent of the guest – to another part of the solution (Mobile Travel Environment, MTE) that provides additional services for the mobile phone of the guest (B2C).

MTE Client

The guests will use their own mobile phones to receive various new services. Starting from basic information (guides) about the destination to location-based services that enable the tourist to receive more accurate and valuable services in the destination.

Additional Services from Third-Party Service Provider

The interfaces to the MTE will allow to connect different third-party service provider to the platform. The services and providers may vary from destination to destination. Tourists have the advantage to select a service in a convenient way (using their own mobile phones) from various sources.

Business Model

Aladdin will consider different usage scenarios for the B2B but mostly for the B2C environment, having in mind on one side an ageing society with the growing demand for safety and on the other side a young generation with their well established mobile behaviour. Raising the quality of service and the average revenue per tourist but reducing the process costs for a tour guide organization in the destination is the aim of the B2B part of Aladdin. The combination of B2B and B2C services allows to create several business models. The actors in the market can be identified as follows:

- Technology provider for the Aladdin-Platform (providing the solution);
- Outbound tour operator (providing traveller and booking data);
- Inbound tour operator (managing the traveller and their profiles);
- Content provider;
- Content aggregator;
- Platform operator;
- Service provider (restaurants, POIs, etc.);
- Network provider.

The key success factor of the business model will be the question of who will operate the platform commercially. Hence who will be receiving revenues from the participating travellers and tour operators for using the solution but having substantial costs to maintain the platform. Every destination will have its own – heterogeneous – business relations and as a result Aladdin should be able to support these varying business models with different kind of settlement procedures.

Mobilization of the Tour Guides

The daily life of a tour guide or tour representative is determined by unplanned events and problems and the pressure of time. The functionality and the ergonomics of the application are paramount. A total of 174 use cases were identified in the analysis and specification of the project. All use cases can be associated to a certain use case package (UCP). The following UCP were identified:

- UCP administration of destination information (AD);
- UCP use of destination information (UD);
- UCP payment and ticketing (PT);
- UCP guided tours (GT);
- UCP leisure activities (LA);
- UCP business activities (BA);
- UCP organization of accommodation (OA);
- UCP organization of transportation (OT);
- UCP departure (DE);
- UCP arrival (AR);
- UCP quality assurance (QA);
- UCP organization of meals (OM);
- UCP administrative tools (AT).

As an example for the benefits of the solution for tour guides, some details of the UCPAR will be explained. Figures 42.2 and 42.3 demonstrate that the UCPAR contains all use cases that deal with the arrival of a traveller at a destination. This includes use cases to check the attendance of a traveller group as well as the management of ad-hoc changes during arrival. The capability to have all data up to date on the mobile device (PMW Client) and synchronize data with the centralized server (PMW Server) increases the quality of service and speeds up the business workflows (headquarters are automatically informed as well as all other tour guides). A graphical overview of the UCP is given in Figure 42.3.

UC100AR 'Check confirmation data'
Actors: Tour organizer

The tour organizer checks the confirmation data (received from the tour operator system) before the travellers arrive in the destination and after the travellers have left the home location. The tour organizer needs to initiate an action in case of a deviation from the plan (e.g. one/more traveller(s) is/are not arriving as planned).

UC200AR 'Check attendance of traveller group members'
Actors: Tour representative

The tour representative checks the attendance of all tourist group members, e.g. at airport/train station/etc. and sends them to their busses according to the list he received from the back office.

UC300AR 'Send Welcome Message'
Actors: Tour representative, traveller

Once the tour representative has ticked off the traveller's name (e.g. traveller has arrived as planned and is ready to go with the next form of transport), the traveller receives a welcome message which will include the traveller's transport and accommodation data (which bus number, which hotel) and the booked tour and leisure activities. The message may also include a link to 'upload' the Aladdin client, additional POI information, etc.

UC400AR 'Manage ad hoc changes within UCP Arrival'
Actors: Tour representative, tour organizer, traveller

This Use Case describes eventualities and deviations from the plan during the arrival of a travel group, which require immediate action. Some of these ad hoc changes mean that a tour representative must act, no matter where she/he is at that particular moment (airport, train station, etc.). Some ad hoc changes can be handled by the tour organizer in the back office. Ad hoc change may be:

- Traveller is not on plane (before arrival)
- Traveller missing (after arrival)
- Traveller is ill
- Traveller loses baggage
- Traveller's baggage was damaged
- Traveller needs wheelchair

If a traveller has special request this could also lead to a complaint and this will trigger the **UC300QA 'Manage Complaint'**.

Figure 42.2 Tour guide use cases

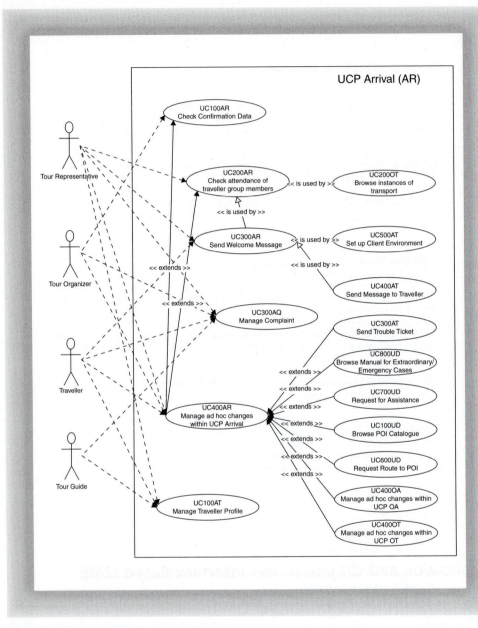

Figure 42.3 Use case diagram of UCP 'Arrival'

Technological Innovation

The platform Aladdin consists of two major solutions: the MTE (mobile travel environment) and the PMW (professional mobile workspace) (Figure 42.4).

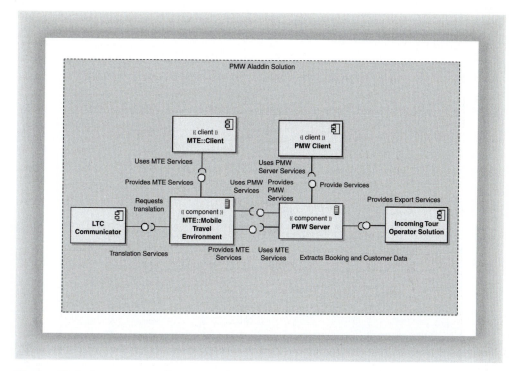

Figure 42.4 Component diagram of PMW and MTE components

Ad hoc Translation Services

The LTC communicator provides language translation services that give the MTE and PMW clients the capability for ad hoc language translation services. This is a tremendous advantage for every traveller having a convenient solution on their mobile hand set that provides fast translation services.

Application and Graphical User Interface-Based J2ME

The MTE client is developed in the J2ME (Java 2 platform micro edition) environment. The main challenges are to provide a homogeneous solution for the very heterogeneous mobile hand sets that are on the market.

Component Model for Mobile Application (PMW Client)

The application for the mobile devices consists of many components that need to be orchestrated and the information output

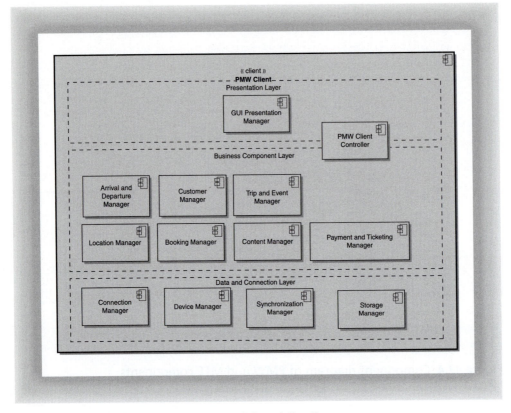

Figure 42.5 Overview component model mobile client

aggregated into an easy to use interface. Figure 42.5 shows the components that are integrated in a Pocket PC or Ultra Mobile PC (UMPC). It is clear that this is a major challenge even with the increasing capabilities of the current existing generation of Pocket PCs and UMPCs.

Easy to Use Mobile User Interface

One of the major requirements is the restriction that the tour guides will use the application with their fingers rather than with any pen-like device. Therefore the standard control set of a usual windows application cannot be used. A complete new set of controls was created for the mobile device handling. Figure 42.6 shows a first design of the user interface that is implemented for the tour guide application.

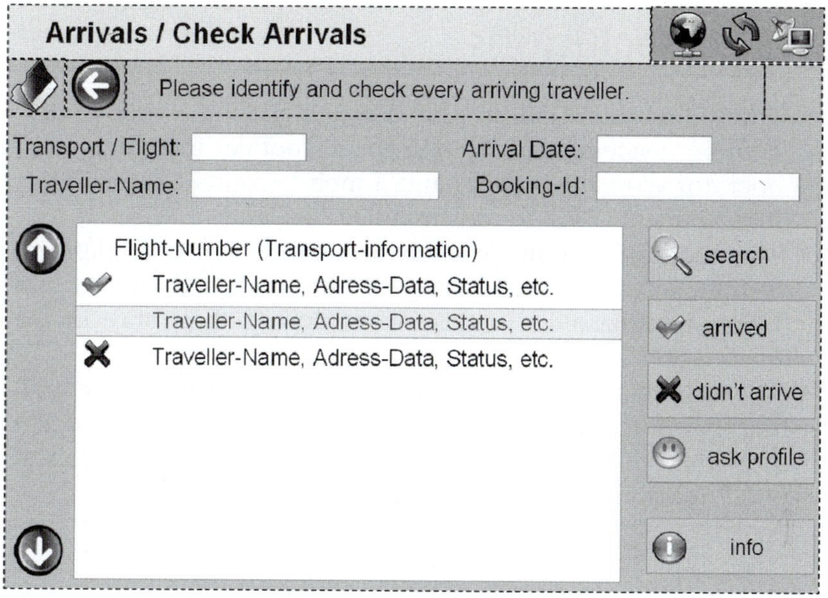

Figure 42.6 Screenshot check arrivals display

Key Challenges for the Future

The selection of the necessary hardware (terminals, smart-phone) for Aladdin is essential for the success of the system. Therefore the partners monitor the market closely to identify when new devices (like devices from the Ultra Mobile PC strategy) become available and decide on alternatives accordingly.

Services are based on the definitions and specifications identified by partners. The definition of the evaluation phase brings up a lot of questions and considerations regarding the testing of the applications. It is the nature of setting up a test environment that in-depth analysis of the product usability is performed. Feedback is integrated into the ongoing evaluation and development process. Naturally, this may result in minor (or even major) change requests for the development of the components.

The tests of the product will determines whether the developments are according to the specifications. The dissemination and exploitation is an ongoing process that was intensified with the more 'visible' results of the project (e.g. prototype or first version of Aladdin). There are several major events (FVW Congress, ITB) that allow collecting additional feedback from users and tour operator companies.

Key Conclusions

- The EU project Aladdin aimed at developing a mobile destination system that combined a mobile incoming tour operator workspace (B2B) and a mobile content and service-management (B2C) for destinations.
- The Aladdin system provides a combined mobile platform to offer tourists a broad array of location-based and custom tailored information and services during their stay in the destination.
- The system allows tour guides to interact electronically with the incoming tour operator system and other information providers and so provide an efficient and flexible mean of work for optimized processes.

Review and Discussion Questions

- Who are the key stakeholders for Aladdin?
- What are the key success factors and prerequisites for Aladdin?
- How can Aladdin improve its profitability as a system?

Further Reading

Clarke, A., Altenhofen, C., & Frings, S. (2007). *At home in the destination – The Aladdin platform*. Stuttgart: Fraunhofer IRB.

www.isogmbh.com/leistungen/touristiksysteme/mobilesolutions.html?L=1.

Company's website: www.aladdin-project.org.

Egger, R. (2005). *mTourism – Spielerei mit Zukunftsmusik*. In Management Handbuch Austria.

Conclusion to Mobile Systems Section

Even though a multitude of tourism operations has already ventured into the new territory of 'eTourism', the development of mobile services seems to be the next battle field in the tourism arena. Thus the question to be posed is how these applications should be developed to meet the needs of both the market and the suppliers, how they can maximize the value-added proposition, and what are the critical success factors for the future.

If a mobile service is to be appraised for the first time, the following questions can be helpful for the assessment:

- Does the service offer a concrete benefit to the user and all its stakeholders?
- Are benefits communicated clearly?
- Is the service logically structured and is its use intuitive?
- Is the interface appropriate and accessible?
- Who offers the service?
- How is location-based information updated, and who is responsible for updating?
- For which special unit is the service available?
- Do the transmission technology and terminal satisfy the situation-specific requirements?
- How does the content provider interact with the network operator and the device manufacturer?
- Is the service optimally supported by the relevant mobile terminals, and does it run on different technology platforms?
- Is it assumed that the user owns the relevant terminal, or is there a possibility of hiring the terminal?
- What is the business model behind the service?
- Who charges for the service and how is charging implemented?
- What is the cost of using the service?
- Are the necessary foreign language versions of the service available so that foreign guests are able to use it also?

(Egger, 2005)

Before a large-scale penetration of mobile terminals in tourism will occur, it is necessary to overcome a series of obstacles. Technical standards will continue to present a key challenge for the creation of network effects and facilitation of a corresponding level of penetration. These problems have to be addressed on an international level and require the dialogue between mobile telephony operators, service providers and tourism experts.

Decision makers in the tourism industry must also develop a basic awareness of the use of possible mobile services in tourism, and they have to be able to evaluate the contribution the service can make for the relevant business. Information specific to a particular site, including geographic referencing, must be prepared and processed on the local, regional and national level in order to develop location-based services. Some of the questions that are still pending are: Which business models are most suited to the purpose? How can content and service providers be coordinated? Which role will destinations and tourism organizations assume? Nevertheless it is evident that mobile applications will play a critical role for the future competitiveness of the entire tourism industry.

Epilogue: The eTourism Future

Roman Egger
Dimitrios Buhalis

ICTs Empower Tourism will Thrive in the Future

In conclusion there are several trends that emerge in the marketplace as demonstrated by the case studies in this book. The tourism industry has been re-engineered globally as a result of the Information Communication Technologies' (ICTs) capabilities emerging in the marketplace. Technology increasingly generates a new paradigm-shift, altering the industry structure and developing a whole range of opportunities and threats. ICTs play a critical role for the competitiveness of tourism organizations and destinations (Egger, 2005; Buhalis, 2003; O'Connor, 1999; Sheldon, 1997; Poon, 1993). ICTs support the globalization of the industry by providing organizations with tools for developing, managing and distributing offerings worldwide. Successful ICT deployment requires innovative management to constantly review developments and adopt the suitable technological solutions in order to maximize organizational competitiveness. Equally ICTs bring utter transparency in the marketplace empowering consumers to identify, customize and purchase tourism products.

Werthner and Klein (1999) have identified the most significant technological developments forcing a new wave of technological evolution. The underlying trend of all developments is the integration of hardware, software and intelligent applications through networking and advanced user interfaces. Technological convergence leads developments and only blurred boundaries between systems exist to illustrate dependencies and relationships. However, all technologies need improvements in order to enhance their speed, interoperability, reliability and adaptation to the industry and consumer needs. Perhaps the next major revolution will emerge in the form of Ambient Intelligence. In the future Ambient Intelligent environments surrounded by intelligent interfaces supported by computing and networking technology that is embedded in everyday objects, such as furniture, clothes, vehicles, roads and smart materials – even particles of decorative substances like paint will support all human activity. Eventually Ambient Intelligence will enable the formation of virtual enterprises, the fluid configuration of business processes, and the seamless interoperation of underlying information systems.

The case studies in this book demonstrate that already several key trends are evident in the marketplace. Tourism organizations use ICTs extensively for a number of purposes but perhaps more importantly for:

- Getting close and interacting dynamically with the customer;
- Managing the extended business value chain;
- Adopt technological innovations as a source of competitive advantage.

Getting Close and Interacting Dynamically with the Customer

The Internet empowers consumers to be more knowledgeable, and encourages them to seek exceptional value for money and time. Experienced, sophisticated, demanding travellers require interaction with suppliers to satisfy their specific needs and wishes.

Many tourism organizations have realized this and increasingly provide tools to dynamically engage with consumers directly. In the case of tourism suppliers, their key aims are to enhance brand integrity, to develop customer loyalty and reduce the need of consumers to search around for suitable products. Two interconnected objectives are evident in many case studies, including British Airways, Intercontinental Hotels and Hotel Sallerhof. Organizations aim to reduce their dependency on intermediaries for delivering to customers, through the development of websites that reinforce their branding and loyalty whilst reassuring consumers that this is the distribution/communication channel of choice. Increasingly ICTs and CRM in particular enable organizations to acknowledge that every tourist is different, carrying a unique blend of experiences, motivations and desires. Personalized interfaces will enable consumers to state their preferences and be directed to suitable products and services efficiently. In addition they outsource company functions and empower consumers to manage almost the entire transaction and relationship through intuitive and integrated platforms. This enables them to reduce operational costs whilst empowering consumers to fulfill their objectives faster and more effectively. Increasingly customer satisfaction will depend highly on the accuracy and comprehensiveness of tourism information and the ability of organizations to provide tools for customization. ICTs therefore place users in the middle of its functionality and product delivery as it is evident in the 'Lovo' and 'Holiday Check' case studies.

Managing the Extended Business Value Chain

Technology needs to be able to contribute to profitability of organizations. Emerging tools can support production increase, improvement of load factor/occupancy levels and enhance scheduling. Equally ICTs can reduce administration and production costs by integrating internal data and processes. It is evident in several case studies, such as 'Enterprise', 'InterContinental Hotel Group' and 'Omena Hotels', that operational and communication costs can be reduced by integrating operational systems, maximizing internal efficiencies, decreasing back office labour costs, reducing number and length of personal communications, and enabling consumers to have direct access to information.

Disintermediation and reduction of commission and fees for intermediaries also reduces costs through direct distribution. By distributing directly organizations can save commission and fees and reinforce their brand throughout the process, engage relationships with consumers, satisfy personalized needs and better understand consumer preference and price elasticity. Selling products directly also increases customer loyalty and reduces leakages to competing organizations. Organizations are also increasingly able to purchase products from global electronic marketplaces supporting their procurement function. Hence, ICTs should contribute to profitability through increase of revenue and reduction of costs.

Where ICTs make a real difference is to the empowerment of partnerships and the extension of the value system. Few other industries depend on partnerships as much as tourism. ICTs empower networking throughout the industry and also improve the interactivity between tourism production and distribution partners, supporting a closer cooperation towards the provision of seamless products. ICTs increasingly transform distribution to a global value system, where access to information and ubiquity is achieved, while interactivity between principle and consumers provides major opportunities. The globalization of the industry intensifies the information required for all tourism transactions and requires instant confirmation and purchasing abilities. Tourism organizations need therefore to use ICTs to ensure a certain degree of interconnectivity and interoperability between organizations that will allow the flow of information and data in this complex value process. By doing that they will be able to enhance their value system and be able to serve their consumers more holistically and profitably. Case studies such as 'Lastminute.com' and 'TUI' demonstrate that they have managed to extend their value chain profitably. Hence, the Internet propels the re-engineering of the entire process of producing and delivering tourism products, as well as it boosts interactivity between partners that can design specialized products and promotion in order to maximize the value-added provided to individual consumers.

Adopt Technological Innovations as a Source of Competitive Advantage

It is evident through several case studies that technological innovation is a never-ending story with a number of technologies emerging in the marketplace on a daily basis. It is therefore critical for the tourism industry to keep a close eye on technological developments that will enable it to maximize its efficiency, enhance its ability to interact with consumers and partners, and improve its profitability.

Emerging innovations are evident in the case studies of 'Trip @vise', 'CheckEffect' and 'Finnair'. Even established technology organization such as GDSs are now moving forward to adopt new technologies and even change their business model to address the new market requirements. Amadeus for example is emerging as an ASP for airlines, as a retailer (through OPODO) and as ICT supplier for travel agencies. Only tourism organizations that appreciate the capabilities of the entire range of these new technologies and implement them in their organizations will be able to keep up with the developments and serve their markets adequately. Equally they should engage with technology providers to ensure that they fully understand their concerns and user requirements and develop suitable technological solutions to achieve their strategic and operational goals. A closer interaction therefore between technology providers and tourism organizations will ensure that appropriate applications will be developed and utilized in the future maximizing the potential benefit for both.

ICT Trends and Implications for Tourism

It is evident that increasingly ICTs will provide the 'info-structure' for the entire industry. ICTs evolve constantly, providing new tools for tourism marketing and management. They support the interactivity between tourism enterprises and consumers and as a result they re-engineer the entire process of developing, managing and marketing tourism products and destinations. Innovative tourism enterprises will have the ability to divert resources and expertise to servicing consumers and provide higher value-added transactions supporting their profitability.

Buhalis and O'Connor (2006) demonstrate that the future of eTourism will be focused on consumer centric technologies that will enable organizations to work on their profitability through a network of partnerships. Agile strategies are required at both strategic and tactical management levels to ensure that the ICT-raised opportunities and challenges are turned to the advantage of tourism organizations to enhance their innovation and competitiveness.

References

Buhalis, D. (2003). *eTourism: Information technology for strategic tourism management*. Pearson: Financial Times/Prentice Hall.

Buhalis, D., & O'Connor, P. (2006). Information communication technologies. In D. Buhalis & C. Costa (Eds.), *Tourism management dynamics: trends, management and tools* (pp. 196–209). Oxford: Butterworth-Heinemann.

Egger, R. (2005). *Grundlagen des eTourism. Informations- und Kommunikationstechnologien im Tourismus*. Aachen: Shaker Verlag.

O'Connor, P. (1999). *Electronic information distribution in tourism & hospitality*. Oxford: CAB International.

Poon, A. (1993). *Tourism, technology and competitive strategies*. Oxford: CAB International.

Sheldon, P. (1997). *Information technologies for Tourism*. Oxford: CAB International.

Werthner, H., & Klein, S. (1999). *ICT and tourism: A challenging relationship*. Vienna: Springer Verlag.

Index

Index

Index

Index

Index